Government and Politics in Tennessee

Government and Politics in Tennessee

WILLIAM LYONS
JOHN M. SCHEB II
BILLY STAIR

The University of Tennessee Press

Knoxville

First Edition.

The paper used in this book meets the minimum requirements of ANSI/NISO Z39.48-1992 (R 1997) (Permanence of Paper). The binding materials have been chosen for strength and durability.

Library of Congress Cataloging in Publication Data

Lyons, William, 1948–
Government and politics in Tennessee / William Lyons,
John M. Scheb II, Billy Stair.— 1st ed.
p. cm.
Includes bibliographical references and index.

ISBN 1-57233-140-2 (cl.: alk. paper)
ISBN 1-57233-141-0 (pbk.: alk. paper)

1. Tennessee—Politics and government—1951–
I. Scheb, John M., 1955–
II. Stair, Billy, 1952– III. Title.
JK5216 .L86 2001
320.4768—dc21 2001001838

Contents

Figures

Tables

Preface

In a society where many institutions—from restaurants and hotels to newspapers and shopping malls—become ever larger and more standardized, state governments remain among the most unique elements of American culture. Each state government provides essentially the same menu of education, health care, transportation, public safety, and public welfare services to its citizens. But each of the fifty states has evolved with a distinct set of cultural values and a political system that reflects those values. These "laboratories of democracy" perhaps constitute the most brilliant and successful aspect of the American political experiment. Tennessee plays an important part in this story. As in all laboratories, some of Tennessee's initiatives have been more successful than others. These successes and failures have reflected Tennessee's unique political system and culture.

Our purpose in writing this book is to explore the structure, processes, and personalities of government and politics in Tennessee. One of the ironies of American politics is that many citizens know less about their state and local governments than they do about the federal government hundreds or even thousands of miles away. Most Tennesseans do not know or care a great deal about state government. In this respect, Tennesseans are not much different from other Americans for whom the pressures of work and family leave little time to study a political system that is often confusing and remote from their daily priorities. When they leave their homes each morning, most fail to register the fact that state government is responsible for the roads on which they drive, the schools where they leave their children, and, in many instances, recruiting the businesses where they work. When these Tennesseans return home, they do not associate state government with either the quality of the water they drink or the safety of the neighborhoods in which they live.

This book examines the responsibilities of state government, with a special look at how a number of major state programs were shaped during the last quarter of the twentieth century. We hope the book can serve as a reference guide for students of government and provide a historical context for those seeking to understand the forces at work in the state's political system. In addition to policies and programs, this volume also acknowledges the extraordinary extent to which Tennessee's political system has been shaped by the personalities of several individuals who served in state government. Among the states, Tennessee's unique blend of legislative and executive powers is far more a product of personality than political ideology. Attempting to explain how Tennessee chose this political path was among our most enjoyable challenges.

The reader must keep in mind that this book is only a snapshot of Tennessee government at the dawn of the twenty-first century. We have focused on how the content of that snapshot evolved as a result of events in Tennessee since World War II. While Tennessee's culture and institutions well may survive for decades, it is just as possible that unforeseen events and personalities will shatter many of the assumptions and conclusions of this book. Such is the nature of any political system. We cannot determine how change will occur and in what direction it will lead. Until that change occurs, we hope this book captures the essence of the forces that shape Tennessee state government.

We would like to thank the University of Tennessee Press, and in particular the press's director, Jennifer Siler, for giving us the opportunity to work on this project, as well as Stan Ivester, managing editor. We also acknowledge debts to many of our UT colleagues from whom we have gained understanding and insight. In particular, we wish to acknowledge the influence of Joe Johnson, president emeritus of the University of Tennessee, Knoxville, and the late Lee Greene, founder and for many years head of the Department of Political Science at UTK.

Finally, we would like to thank our wives for their patience as we completed this project. This book is dedicated to them, and to a special little girl whose courage gave us inspiration.

Any errors of commission or omission contained herein are attributable only to us.

William Lyons
John M. Scheb II
Billy Stair

Knoxville, Tennessee
March 1, 2001

Part I

FOUNDATIONS OF TENNESSEE POLITICS

1

Political Development and Culture

Anyone who drives from Bristol to Memphis cannot help noticing the tremendous geographical differences that characterize the state of Tennessee. Geography has been a major determining force in Tennessee's development, culture, and politics. Tennessee's "grand divisions" are natural, and the corresponding labels are simple: East, Middle, and West. The eastern third of the state is mountainous, with the Great Smoky Mountains to the far east and south and the Cumberland Mountains across the north. The Cumberland Plateau serves as a natural divide between East and Middle regions. Middle Tennessee is centered around the Central Basin and surrounded by the Highland Rim. The Mississippi River and the Tennessee River define the boundaries of the state's flatter western third.

Tennessee's geography has exerted profound influence upon the state's economic development. Due to its hilly terrain, most of East Tennessee is unsuitable for large-scale farming. Historically, East Tennessee agriculture consisted primarily of tobacco and subsistence farming, although in recent years it has become more diverse. West Tennessee, on the other hand, is relatively flat, with rich soil, especially along the bottom land of the Mississippi River. This third of the state is much more conducive to large-scale agriculture, which historically was dominated by cotton and today also features soybeans. Middle Tennessee, which also is relatively fertile, consists of rolling pasture lands ideally suited to raising beef and dairy cattle. Nashville, the state capital, sits at the center of this region.

In some respects, Tennessee has been fortunate in its geographical diversity. Its economy has not depended upon one crop or one industry and thus has avoided the booms and busts that such concentration can cause. But this diversity often has led the state's citizens to view Tennessee in terms of regions rather than as a unified whole. Not as readily apparent are the political variations that are rooted in these geographical differences. In many ways, Tennessee has three political cultures corresponding to the traditional grand divisions of the state. These variations in political culture helped to create the underlying dynamics of contemporary Tennessee politics. To understand Tennessee's political culture, and the contemporary political system of the state, we must examine Tennessee's political development over the last two centuries.

Historical Foundations of Tennessee Politics

Tennessee was not one of the original thirteen states. Since being carved out of North Carolina in 1796, however, Tennessee has been important in American history. Tennessee's political development began long before anyone had thoughts of statehood.

Early Tennesseans

The first Tennesseans were prehistoric tribes who migrated to North America from Asia during the Ice Age some fifteen thousand years ago. By the time the first Europeans set foot in Tennessee, several well-established tribes of Native Americans were living there. The Creeks, the Yuchi, and the Shawnee tribes actually were expelled from Tennessee in the early eighteenth century not by Europeans, but by the Cherokee. The first Europeans to visit Tennessee were Spanish explorers led by Hernando de Soto. In 1540, de Soto led an expedition from Florida into Tennessee, following the Hiwasee River. De Soto was looking for gold, a fruitless quest inspired by tales spun by Native Americans. Subsequent Spanish forays into Tennessee led to the establishment of the first European forts in the area, but the Spanish soon abandoned these forts and never attempted to establish any settlements in Tennessee.

The French and English first came to Tennessee in 1673. The English ventured across the mountains from Virginia; the French came down the Mississippi River. The legacies of the French and English in Tennessee reflected a fundamental difference in the long-term goals of the two national groups. The French established a network of trading posts but did not develop significant settlements. In contrast, the English-speaking people who came over the mountains from Virginia and North Carolina were intent on establishing farms and towns in the valleys and coves of East Tennessee (see fig. 1.1). As these settlers began to spill into the area, they made uneasy alliances with the Native Americans.

Fig. 1.1. John Oliver's cabin, located in Cades Cove in the Great Smoky Mountains National Park, is typical of the homesteads of early settlers. Photo by John M. Scheb II.

In 1756, following the outbreak of the French and Indian War, the English established a fort at the confluence of the Tellico and Tennessee rivers in eastern Tennessee. Fort Loudon was established in part to protect Cherokee women and children during the war, but it soon became a point of conflict between the settlers and the native Cherokee. In August 1760, after English troops left the fort, the Cherokee attacked. Paul Demere, the fort's commander, was tortured to death, setting the stage for vicious English retribution and years of unrest between Anglo-Americans and native peoples.[1] Ultimately, many years later, the conflict between the Cherokee and the settlers would be ended by the brutal expulsion of the Cherokee from the state.

Tennessee during the War of Independence

During the American Revolution (1775–83), Tennessee settlers were mostly preoccupied with their continuing conflict with the Cherokee, who allied with the British. However, in 1780 the British tried to establish firm dominance of the frontier that would become Tennessee. The British were eager to drum up support for the Crown in anticipation of Revolutionary War battles to be fought throughout the Carolinas. Two men, Isaac Shelby and John Sevier, led the settler resistance against the English, culminating in an attack at Kings Mountain in South Carolina. The settlers prevailed in a bloody battle, which some commentators have characterized as the turning point of the revolution in the South.[2]

First Attempts at Self-Government

Prior to the American Revolution, people living in the area that is now Tennessee were governed haphazardly by the colonial governments of Virginia and North Carolina. The Tennessee settlers' first attempt to create their own government came in 1772. Settlers living the in areas surrounding the Watauga and Nolichucky rivers in upper East Tennessee established the Watauga Compact, a primitive constitution of sorts modeled loosely after the Mayflower Compact of 1620.[3] The Watauga Compact established a rudimentary government consisting of a five-member "magistrate's court" that possessed both legislative and judicial powers and employed a sheriff and a clerk. Although the framers of the Watauga Compact did not intend to establish an independent state, Theodore Roosevelt later would observe that the Wataugans "exercised the rights of full statehood for a number of years, establishing in American style a purely democratic government with representative institutions."[4]

In 1776, the state of North Carolina annexed the Tennessee territory extending all the way to the Mississippi River. North Carolina could not effectively govern such a large area. In particular, the mountains constituted a serious barrier to transportation and communication, and hence to governance. As the settlers moved farther west into what is now Middle Tennessee, they made another attempt at self-government. In 1780, a group of pioneers led by John Robertson and Louis Donelson established a settlement along the Cumberland River near present-day Nashville.[5] The Cumberland Compact provided for twelve individuals known as "triars" to make collective decisions. The compact also provided for recall of triars who failed to perform their duties, thus foreshadowing the American constitutional concern for limited government and accountability.[6]

Statehood

While the Cumberland Compact had modest goals, attempts to establish the State of Franklin represented a much grander effort. The leader of the fledgling government was the extremely charismatic John Sevier. In 1784, Tennessee was in a state of limbo. North Carolina had ceded its western territory to the newly created federal government, which had not officially provided a designation for it. On August 24, 1784, delegates from three counties that later would form part of Tennessee met in Jonesborough, with the intention of forming a new state. The delegates drafted and adopted a constitution, elected John Sevier as governor, and petitioned the Congress for admission to the Union as the State of Franklin.[7] The state was short-lived, however. The new settlers soon came to be at odds with the Cherokee, whose land claims had been supported by North Carolina but not by the settlers in Franklin.[8] Following some particularly violent confrontations between the settlers and the Indians, the State of North Carolina reasserted its control over the territory, and the State of Franklin ceased to function. In 1789, North Carolina again ceded its land west of the Appalachian ridge to the United States government. Between 1790 and 1796, this area was called the "Territory of the United States South of the River Ohio."[9] The new territory's governor was William Blount, a wealthy land developer. Blount established the capital at a location that later would become the city of Knoxville.

In the 1790s, American politics were defined largely by the struggles between the Federalists, whose number included George Washington, John Adams, and Alexander Hamilton; and the Republicans, guided by the policies of Thomas Jefferson and James Madison, who envisioned a nation of small farmers. Despite the Washington administration's appointment of William Blount as Territorial Governor, most Tennesseans identified with the Republicans. This tension, combined with the belief that the federal government was not doing enough to solve "the Indian problem," led Blount to mount a campaign for statehood. Delegates convened in Knoxville in January 1796 to forge a state constitution and formally petition the Congress to grant statehood.

Tennessee's first constitution was the product of fifty-five delegates, five from each of the eleven counties in the territory. Not surprisingly, these men created a document that did not differ greatly from the constitution of North Carolina. They assured citizens of continuity throughout the transition to statehood by keeping intact all laws that were in effect at the date of statehood and by pronouncing the common law of North Carolina to be the common law of Tennessee.[10] The common law, derived from England, provided the basis for the legal systems of the new American states.

Statehood for Tennessee was not without controversy, as the Federalists opposed admission of a new state that was likely to support Republican candidates. This opposition destroyed what little support remained for the Federalists in Tennessee. After some political wrangling and an eventual compromise, Congress acted favorably on the proposal. On June 1, 1796, President Washington signed legislation formally admitting Tennessee into the Union as the sixteenth state. John Sevier was elected the first governor of the new state. In the U.S. Senate, Tennessee was represented by William Cocke and William Blount. Andrew Jackson, an ally of Blount, was chosen the first congressional representative. After the War of 1812, Jackson would emerge as the dominant personality not merely in Tennessee politics, but in American politics in the first half of the nineteenth century.

The Jacksonian Era

Andrew Jackson's enormous political influence was built largely on the basis of his military career, highlighted by his famous rout of the British in the Battle of New Orleans at the close of the War of 1812 and a number of successful campaigns against the Indians in Florida. When Tennessee was struck by a banking crisis in 1819, many of General Jackson's friends promoted him as a presidential candidate in hopes of gaining political advantage in the state. Tennesseans reacted warmly to the heroic Jackson, casting their votes for him in overwhelming numbers in the 1824 presidential election. Because no candidate received a majority in the Electoral College, the election was thrown into the House of Representatives, which ultimately chose second-place finisher John Quincy Adams as president.[11]

Although he failed in his bid to become President in 1824, Jackson (see fig. 1.2) became a powerful force in state and national politics. His popularity was broader and more complex than the public adoration often accorded a military hero. Jackson genuinely supported farmers and other less influential groups in their struggle against the political power of urban special interests. Despite considerable personal wealth, Jackson's image was that of an earthy, feisty man of the people with a healthy distaste for the aristocracy and their ways. In the eyes of many Tennesseans, Andrew Jackson's most important accomplishment was his key role in removing the Cherokee Indians from the state, thereby insuring the security of settlers.

By 1818, Native Americans were removed from the western sections of the state, opening this region to settlement.[12] By the late 1820s, the Cherokee living in southeastern Tennessee had made great strides as a society. They were adept at agriculture, had organized towns, were probably more literate in their native language than most white Tennesseans were in English, and had even organized a representative form of government with a charter patterned after the U.S. Constitution. Indeed, the Cherokee leaders hoped that their nation would be admitted into the United States as a separate state. This was not to be. Antipathy toward the Cherokee in Georgia and Tennessee prompted Congress, at the urging of Andrew Jackson, who was elected President in 1828, to enact legislation calling for the

Fig. 1.2. Probably no other American has come to symbolize the virtues, as well as the faults, of the common man as fully as Andrew Jackson. *Source:* University of Tennessee Special Collections.

removal of the Cherokee to the West. The Cherokee resisted. Their eventual removal by federal troops led to the deaths of thousands through disease and starvation. The path the Cherokee followed to their new home in Oklahoma became known as the Trail of Tears.

By contemporary standards, the forcible removal of the Cherokee, and Andrew Jackson's leading role therein, are shameful blots on American history. But in Tennessee in the early nineteenth century, there was little concern for the plight of the Cherokee. Speaking for the Tennessee Supreme Court in an 1835 case, Judge John Catron described the Cherokee as "mere wandering savages" who "deserve to be exterminated as savage and pernicious beasts."[13] There is little doubt that Judge Catron's appalling characterization of the Cherokee expressed the view of many, if not most, Tennesseans of his day. Two years after Catron made these remarks from the bench, President Jackson appointed him to the U.S. Supreme Court.

Hostility toward Native Americans notwithstanding, the Jacksonian era in American politics is associated with the expansion of political democracy. During this period, 1828–40, most states eliminated or lessened property qualifications for voting and holding public office. States also moved away from gubernatorial appointment of judges, which was viewed as a vestige of aristocracy, to partisan judicial elections. Tennessee reflected these trends. The state's Constitution of 1835 eliminated property qualifications for holding public office. Another populist initiative in the new document terminated life tenure for justices of the state supreme court, although they were still chosen by the General Assembly. Land was taxed according to its value—a win for hardscrabble farmers and a loss for wealthy plantation owners. Another important step in the democratization of Tennessee was recognition of the need for public education. On the other hand, the Tennessee Constitution of 1835 contained a regressive step in the development of democracy. Free African Americans, as distinct from slaves, lost the right to vote that they had gained under Tennessee's original state charter. This antidemocratic move reflected Tennessee's cultural drift in the direction of the values of the Deep South and foreshadowed the coming conflict over the rights of persons of African descent.

Probably no other American has come to symbolize the virtues, as well as the faults, of the common man as fully as Andrew Jackson. Jackson had the appetites and the temper of a rough and ready frontiersman, honed through years of frontier living. As Wilma Dykeman points out, "Instinct, more than intellect, shaped Jackson's response to issues."[14] While Jackson displayed little interest in enriching himself through his government service, he valued loyalty and utilized the "spoils system" to reward friends and associates with government jobs. Jackson's values and goals were never in doubt; in every respect they were those of his native Tennessee.

Slavery

Throughout its history, Tennessee has had a significant African American population, although not as large as those of some other southern states. From the time of statehood, at least one in ten Tennesseans has been black. In fact, at the time of statehood, a substantial number of free black citizens resided in Tennessee. Their status was protected to some degree in the earliest state constitution. However, changes in agricultural practices brought about major changes in Tennessee and the other states of the Deep South. Particularly in West Tennessee, slaves became much more numerous in the early 1800s, as labor-intensive cotton production expanded rapidly.

Slavery was a not a particularly divisive issue in the early days of Tennessee statehood. The English had traded in slaves and, as English descendants, most Tennesseans accepted slavery as a legitimate institution. The Tennessee General Assembly reacted to the news of the Nat Turner slave uprising in Virginia by passing legislation forbidding free slaves from coming to Tennessee.[15] In 1836, the General Assembly passed a law banning anyone, "black or white, found printing or speaking doctrines calculated to excite discontent, insurrection, or rebellion amongst slaves or free persons of color."[16] As the Civil War approached, the majority opinion in the state was clearly in favor of slavery, although pockets of abolitionist sentiment existed in East Tennessee.

The level of slave ownership was significantly lower in Tennessee than in most southern states. In 1850, only about one in five Tennessee families owned slaves. With the exception of Arkansas, Tennessee had the lowest proportion of slaveholding families. Most slaveholding farms were in the middle and western sections of the state. Even in East Tennessee, which had far fewer slaves, many whites supported the institution. Largely because slavery was not critical to its economic base, East Tennessee became the center of the state's emancipation movement. In 1819, Elihu Embree created a newspaper later known as *The Emancipator.* Embree used the paper to argue the cause of abolitionism, setting the stage for conflict between those in favor of maintaining slavery and those opposed to "the peculiar institution," a polite term for slavery. This conflict would later be played out in Tennessee and the rest of the country, culminating in the Civil War.

The slavery debate intensified in the late 1840s. In Congress, the controversy centered on the status of states admitted to the Union. Tennesseans, like other southerners, worried with good reason that the expansion of "free" states represented a threat to slavery and to the South's economic future. The Tennessee Democratic Party took a clear stand in favor of slavery, articulating a belief that abolitionists would never succeed in eliminating slavery. Despite some regional ambivalence, political thinking in the state clearly was predominantly pro-slavery. The expected consequences of the looming sectional conflict served to unify the political establishment in Tennessee and throughout the South to adopt a united front against any national movement to eliminate slavery.

Civil War

The Civil War defined Tennessee politics for more than a century. Although its impact lessened in the 1980s and 1990s with a host of changes in Tennessee's population and economy, the imprint of the Civil War is still evident in the state's political structure. The war split the state, with the eastern part remaining staunchly pro-Union. The rest of the state was overwhelmingly committed to the Confederacy. This sharp division led to an unfortunate situation in which "brother fought brother." Tennessee was the last state to leave the Union and the first state to return following the Union victory.

The vote on secession from the Union reflected the differing cultures of the three grand divisions of Tennessee. In Shelby County (Memphis), the vote was overwhelmingly in favor of leaving the Union. But in many counties in East Tennessee, the vote was weighted equally in favor of remaining. There is no doubt that, throughout the state, there was substantial pressure to vote as one's neighbors voted. The total vote (104,913 to 47,238) reflected the dominance of Middle and West Tennessee over East Tennessee.

Tennesseans paid a heavy price during the Civil War. More battles were fought on Tennessee soil than in any other state except Virginia. Well over one hundred thousand Tennesseans, representing both the Confederacy and the Union, died during the conflict. In 1857, prior to the outbreak of the war, a move to call a constitutional convention to consider the state's role in the federal system was defeated (69,387 to 57,798). However, once war broke out, another vote was held to determine whether Tennessee should join the Confederacy or remain in the Union.

Reconstruction

The aftermath of the Civil War was quite difficult for the state. Tennessean Andrew Johnson of Greeneville (fig. 1.3) assumed the presi-

Fig. 1.3. U.S. President Andrew Johnson had served as military governor of Tennessee during the state's occupation by Union troops. *Source:* University of Tennessee Special Collections.

dency of the United States after Abraham Lincoln's assassination in 1865. A Democratic Vice President in Lincoln's Republican administration, Johnson previously had served as military governor of Tennessee during the state's occupation by Union troops. As President, Johnson presided over the Reconstruction period that followed the war. Johnson believed that the South had suffered enough and refused to support the harsh measures that Congress wished to impose. Johnson's refusal to punish the South further almost led to his removal from the presidency; he was impeached in the House, and in the Senate he came within one vote of being forced from office. Johnson's travails reflected the deep hostility remaining between the former Confederate states and the rest of the Union.

In 1865, an oligarchy of Unionists chose William Brownlow as governor. Brownlow was a rabid East Tennessee Unionist with a strong desire to punish those who supported the Confederacy. He declared a state of emergency, suspending the writ of habeas corpus, and permitted arrests and trials without "due process of law." Under Brownlow and a legislature dominated by the "Radical Republicans," Tennessee ratified the Thirteenth Amendment (1865), which abolished slavery; and the Fourteenth Amendment (1868), which expanded the power of the national government over the states in matters of civil rights. By so doing, Tennessee was readmitted promptly to the Union and thus avoided the harsh program of military rule imposed on other southern states during Reconstruction. In 1867, Governor Brownlow was reelected, with the aid of many black voters, who just recently had been granted suffrage in the state. Not surprisingly, as African Americans were enfranchised, they supported the party of Lincoln. The Republican Party received credit not only for abolishing slavery, but also for establishing the Freedmen's Bureau, which distributed aid to blacks and assisted in their education.

Governor Brownlow's reelection, as well as the enfranchisement of African Americans, led to reaction in the form of the Ku Klux Klan, founded in the Middle Tennessee town of Pulaski two years after the end of the Civil War. In 1867, a former Confederate general, Nathan Bedford Forrest, was selected as "Grand Wizard of the Empire." Controversy continues about the purpose and methods of the early Klan. Some historians contend that the early Klan in Tennessee was established with the sole purpose of resisting those—especially northern "carpetbaggers"—who used extortion to benefit from the economic plight of southerners after the war. Doubtless some members of the Klan had darker motives that included terrorizing newly freed slaves with acts of arson, rape, and murder. The pro-Unionist state government responded by outlawing the Klan, just as the federal government did in enacting the Civil Rights Act of 1870. In 1869, after Governor Brownlow resigned to assume a seat in the U.S. Senate, General Forrest formally disbanded the Klan, claiming that its objectives had been largely accomplished. The Klan would reappear in the 1920s, this time on a national scale and in response to a broader platform of religious and ethnic intolerance.

Tennessee Enters the Modern Age

In 1870, Tennessee adopted its third constitution, the charter that remains in effect today, although it has been amended many times (see chapter 2). Although the Constitution of 1870 formally abolished slavery and recognized black suffrage, many blacks were effectively denied the right to vote by the imposition of a controversial poll tax, or fee paid for the privilege of voting. The constitution stipulated that proceeds from the tax had to be used toward public education. Tennessee Republicans opposed ratification of the proposed constitution, but they lost in a referendum that signaled the restoration of Democratic Party dominance in the state.

With the Civil War and Reconstruction behind them, Tennesseans in the late nineteenth century concentrated on rebuilding their society and economy, with very impressive results. During the latter decades of the 1800s, Tennessee saw rapid economic growth, emergence of industrial and commercial sectors, in-migration of workers from the North, and dramatic expansion of the state's urban areas. A working system of public schools finally was achieved, fostering widespread literacy among a population previously largely illiterate. These changes in the socioeconomic structure created tensions between those who favored the traditional agrarian society and those who supported "progress." Members of the landed aristocracy and their supporters found themselves increasingly challenged by proponents of the "New South." Vestiges of this conflict persist today, although the advocates of a New South gained the upper hand long ago.

Memphis and "Boss Crump"

The emergence of large cities in Tennessee gave rise to a new kind of politics and a new kind of political figure—the "boss." One of the most influential and colorful fixtures of Tennessee politics during the mid-twentieth century was Edward H. Crump of Memphis. Crump was known as "Boss Crump," for his control over Memphis politics and his strong statewide influence. Crump was able to deliver large numbers of Shelby County votes to whomever he decided to back for statewide office. Any candidate running for Governor or United States Senator would have to contend with Crump. One prominent politician who came into conflict with Ed Crump was Estes Kefauver. In 1948, Crump claimed that he was like a raccoon who had been caught reaching into a drawer. Kefauver uttered what later would be regarded as a classic rejoinder: "I may be a raccoon, but I am not Mr. Crump's pet coon."

Tennessee Valley Authority

Two of the most significant developments in Tennessee's twentieth-century history were the establishment of the Tennessee Valley

Authority (TVA) in 1933 and the reapportionment of legislative and congressional districts in the 1960s. Both these events helped to propel the modernization of Tennessee's economic, social, and political systems.

Prior to the creation of TVA, the Tennessee River Valley was one of the poorest regions of the country. The difficulty of navigating the flood-prone river always had made the Tennessee valley less accessible than most other major river valleys in the eastern United States. The lack of accessibility hampered economic and social development. As a major component of President Franklin D. Roosevelt's New Deal program, TVA was a broad-gauged effort to control flooding and promote economic development through the generation of cheap

Fig. 1.4. Douglas Dam in Sevier County is one of TVA's hydroelectric dams. *Source:* University of Tennessee Special Collections.

electric power. The centerpiece of TVA's plan was the construction of a series of dams along the river. These dams (fig. 1.4) created deep lakes that facilitated navigation, controlled flooding, and reduced the problem of soil erosion. Moreover, the dams contained hydroelectric generators that produced abundant electricity and thus made possible the electrification of a major area of the South. Today, TVA provides electricity to seven states, not only through its hydroelectric plants but also via a number of nuclear power plants built during an ambitious expansion program in the 1970s and 1980s.

Few question that TVA was instrumental in the development and modernization of Tennessee. Today, however, many critics of TVA believe that the agency has outlived its original mission. TVA is a massive bureaucracy with minimal accountability to the public. Established by the federal government as an independent government corporation, TVA has no state or local government oversight and minimal oversight by Congress. TVA certainly has its defenders, but many critics would like to see its power generation program sold to the private sector and its myriad non-power programs turned over to state or local governments.

Reapportionment

It is difficult to overstate the importance of legislative reapportionment in Tennessee politics. Reapportionment refers to the process of redrawing the lines defining legislative districts of relatively equal populations. Prior to the 1960s, congressional districts, state legislative districts, even local electoral districts (school boards, county commissions, etc.) in Tennessee and many states were—by design—often grossly unequal in terms of population. This inequality came to be known as *malapportionment.* Under malapportionment, the influence of each voter in the more populous districts is diminished; the influence of voters in the less populated districts is enhanced.

Historically, malapportionment in the Tennessee General Assembly favored the less populous rural districts over the more populous urban ones. Constituents from Chattanooga, Memphis, Nashville, and Knoxville attempted unsuccessfully to get the General Assembly to reapportion itself. Before the federal courts intervened and forced the reapportionment of the General Assembly, state legislative districts had not been redrawn since 1901. Between 1900 and 1960, Tennessee experienced substantial growth and redistribution of its population. In 1901, Tennessee's population was 2,020,616, of whom 487,380 were eligible voters. In 1960, the state's population was 3,567,089, of whom 2,092,891 were eligible to vote. A disproportionate share of the population growth occurred in the state's urban counties. The district lines of the state House and Senate had not been redrawn in six decades, so these urban areas were grossly underrepresented. In fact, prior to court-ordered reapportionment, 37 percent of Tennessee voters elected 60 percent of the state senators; 40 percent of the voters elected 64 percent of the members of the state House.

In 1959, Charles Baker and a group of plaintiffs representing voters in Chattanooga, Knoxville, Memphis, and Nashville brought suit in federal district court in Nashville against Joe C. Carr, Tennessee's Secretary of State.[17] The plaintiffs in *Baker v. Carr* claimed that, by failing to reapportion the legislature, the State of Tennessee was denying them equal protection of the laws in violation of the Fourteenth Amendment to the U.S. Constitution. Unfortunately, legal precedent was not on the side of the plaintiffs. The U.S. Supreme Court in 1946 had held that apportionment of legislative districts was a "political question" best left to the state legislatures.[18] State legislators eager to maintain the status quo of political power were not eager to surrender power in the name of fairness.

The federal district court dismissed *Baker v. Carr* on the grounds that it lacked jurisdiction over the subject matter. In a landmark decision, the U.S. Supreme Court reversed the district court, overturned precedent, and reinstated the complaint. Writing for the Court, Justice William Brennan concluded that the "allegations of a denial of equal protection present a justiciable constitutional cause of action upon which appellants are entitled to a trial and a decision."[19]

Two years later, in a similar case originating in Alabama, the Supreme Court held that state legislative districts had to be reapportioned according to the principle of "one person, one vote."[20] Ultimately, this meant that legislative districts in Alabama, Tennessee, and all states had to be redrawn to cover essentially equal populations. Other Supreme Court decisions in the 1960s extended this requirement to U.S. House districts, as well as districts for local governing bodies. In Tennessee, the battle over reapportionment continued into the 1970s and involved both special sessions of the legislature and continuing litigation. Ultimately, the conflict was settled, and the principle of "one person, one vote" prevailed.

Considered revolutionary in the 1960s, reapportionment today is an accepted part of American political life. Every ten years, after the federal government completes its census of population, each state legislature reapportions its own districts and the congressional districts in its state. Failure to do so inevitably means that the legislature will be sued and ordered by a federal court to undertake reapportionment. Indeed, even when the legislature does reapportion itself, certain parties are bound to be displeased. Lawsuits challenging reapportionment plans have become routine in the federal courts. While reapportionment can be very tricky, both legally and politically, the reapportionment revolution unquestionably has rendered the American political system more democratic. In a democracy resting upon the premise that all citizens are equal before the state, there is no justification for allowing one person's vote to count more than another person's.

In Tennessee, reapportionment in the last half of the twentieth century gave the urban centers of Memphis, Knoxville, Chattanooga, and Nashville a measure of influence in state government commensurate with their population. This shift in turn has led to state policies geared more to economic development, education, and transportation—areas in which cities lead the way. It also has led to an increasing professionalization of state politics and decreased reliance on personal relationships and contacts for employment and state business.

A Distinctive Political Culture

Political culture consists of widely held values, attitudes, and beliefs that shape political dialogue and behavior, popular expectations of government, and ultimately public policy.[21] The political culture of Tennessee is linked inextricably to that of the United States, and especially that of the South. However, each state is unique in many ways, and Tennessee certainly is no exception. The state's political culture reflects many of these unique elements, as well as those common to the country and the region.

As a southern state, Tennessee reflects much of southern culture. Southern culture is basically traditionalistic, which means that there is strong societal support for traditional values and institutions.[22] Traditionalistic political culture also is characterized by a popular desire for low taxes, resistance to reform and innovation, ambivalence toward public education, and acceptance of traditional inequalities. These elements certainly have characterized southern political culture over the years and to some extent still do.

However, in many ways Tennessee has been a somewhat reluctant southern state. To put it more accurately, Tennessee has been a solidly two-thirds southern state with an ambivalent eastern third questioning this direction. While West and Middle Tennessee have had much in common with Mississippi and Alabama to the south, East Tennessee has more in common with eastern Kentucky and western North Carolina.

Tennessee, in short, has retained a split personality. The lack of geographical and cultural unity has hampered the development of a statewide identity and caused most Tennesseans to think of themselves as residents of their area of the state rather than the state itself. It is common to hear citizens refer to themselves as residents of East,

Middle, and West Tennessee rather than as "Tennesseans." This regional identity has had a major impact on Tennessee politics. To a great extent, the tale of Tennessee has been the tale of "three geographies, three memories, three regions."[23]

Chapters of that tale have yet to be told, however. The regional hold on Tennessee politics may be weakening, as gaps widen between urban, rural, and suburban interests across the state. By the 1980s and 1990s, the regional basis of party differences showed similar signs of breaking down.

Much of the lore of Tennessee, and many of its symbols, are associated with the mountain yeoman. This image of the independent farmer-hunter does well describe the early settlers. Prior to the Civil War, the vast majority of Tennesseans were employed in agriculture. The farms were small, for the most part, and most farmers worked their own land. They lived off what they produced and traded with their neighbors. This led to a strain of independence that has become an integral part of the Tennessee culture. This independence has given Tennesseans a healthy skepticism of government and a distaste for any government action that would impair their freedom. Tennesseans' commitment to limited government is an expression of the dominant philosophy of early statehood—the republicanism of Thomas Jefferson.[24] This philosophy placed clear restraints on government, ensured equality before the law, and distrusted "aristocrats."[25] The political culture of Tennessee has kept taxes relatively low and government comparatively small.

Ever since Andrew Jackson, Tennesseans have championed the notion of the "common man." While many from among the wealthy have been elected, few have done so without making clear their allegiance to their roots, real or imagined, with the "common people." The most memorable image of successful attorney and actor Fred Thompson's 1996 campaign for the U.S. Senate was a red pickup truck. Tennesseans were interested not so much in whether Thompson drove a pickup truck as in his awareness of the more humble status of those he would represent.

Religion and Politics

One of the basic building blocks of political culture is religion. Religious beliefs inform moral values, which in turn shape political attitudes and behaviors. Although this connection usually goes unstated, at times religious leaders take an active role in the political process by advocating policies based upon religious principles. Examples include opposition by conservative religious groups to abortion, gay rights, and legalized gambling. Another example is civil rights activism by African American clergy and congregations.

Tennessee is overwhelmingly Protestant, with Baptists, Methodists, and Presbyterians being the most numerous (see table 1.1). However, Tennessee is peppered with minor sects and independent congregations. In the Appalachian and Cumberland mountains, a few congregations still practice snake handling as a demonstration of faith, although today Tennesseans generally regard such practices as oddities.

TABLE 1.1

RELIGIOUS AFFILIATIONS OF TENNESSEANS, 1990 (PERCENTAGE)

Baptist	43.0
Methodist	10.7
Protestant—No denomination supplied	9.5
Nonreligious	6.0
Churches of Christ	5.4
Roman Catholic	4.7
Pentecostal	2.6
Episcopalian	1.1
Lutheran	1.0
Seventh Day Adventists	0.7
Jehovah's Witnesses	0.6
Holiness	0.5
Judaism	0.3
Unitarian	0.1
Islam	0.1
Latter-Day Saints	0.4
Other	13.3

SOURCE: Barry A. Kosmin and Seymour P. Lachman, *One Nation Under God: Religion in Contemporary American Society* (New York: Harmony Books, 1993), table 3.1: "Religious Composition of State Populations, 1990," pp. 88–93.

Fundamentalism, a conservative version of Christianity that stresses biblical literalism, always has been strong in Tennessee, especially in rural areas. In 1925, the small town of Dayton, Tennessee, was the setting of a national confrontation between fundamentalism and modernism. The conflict focused, of course, on the teaching of evolution in the public schools. This conflict could have occurred anywhere in the country, but a combination of circumstances, including a statute

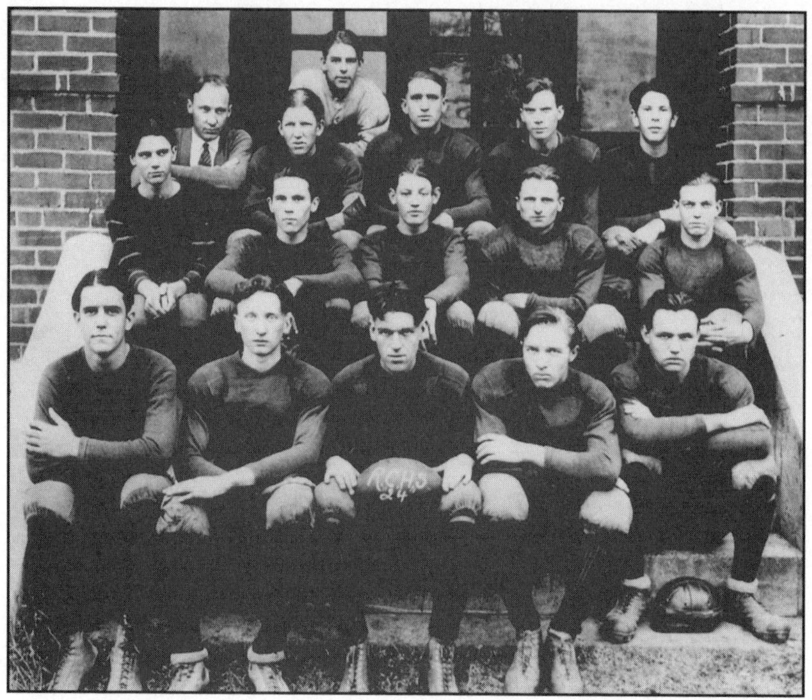

Fig. 1.5. Rhea County High School was runner-up in the 1924 state football championship. Its coach, John T. Scopes, appears in the upper left corner. Photo by Phillips Studio, Dayton, Tennessee. *Source:* Tennessee State Library and Archives.

recently enacted by the General Assembly, cast Tennessee in the spotlight. The new statute made it a crime "to teach any theory that denies the story of the Divine Creation of man as taught in the Bible, and to teach instead that man has descended from a lower order of animals." John Scopes, a high school biology teacher (see fig. 1.5), was prosecuted for violating the statute, and his trial became one of the most famous in American history. William Jennings Bryan, the great populist orator who had carried Tennessee in his three unsuccessful bids for the presidency, was invited to aid in the prosecution. Clarence Darrow, a renowned litigator, libertarian, and agnostic, was enlisted to aid in Scopes's defense. Although most observers in the press believed that Darrow bested Bryan in arguing the case, Scopes was convicted nevertheless. However, the Tennessee Supreme Court reversed the conviction and recommended that Scopes not be retried in the interests of the "peace and dignity of the state." No one else was prosecuted under the anti-evolution law, and it was repealed in 1967.

In the wake of the Scopes Trial, many fundamentalist Christians eschewed the political process altogether. In the 1980s, national politics witnessed the rise of the Christian Right, which followed the emergence of socio-moral issues like school prayer, abortion, and gay rights. The Christian Right advocated direct political involvement by conservative Christians, including running for public office. The Christian Right has not been as strong in Tennessee as in, for example, North Carolina, and it has not emerged as a major force in state politics. However, it is fair to say that Christian conservatism has helped to maintain conservative social policies in Tennessee.

Racial Conflict

Although racial strife has played a large role in the political development of many of Tennessee's communities, the state has not had to overcome a fearful legacy of violence and confrontation, as some of its neighbors have. Until the early 1960s, most communities in Tennessee practiced segregation of blacks and whites. Small towns had a white high school and a black high school. Blacks could not eat at public restaurants or sit downstairs at most movie theaters. Black students could not attend the University of Tennessee. Churches, civic clubs, and neighborhoods had racial boundaries that seldom were crossed. What makes Tennessee's history and culture unique among southern states is that the transition from a segregated to a more integrated society was, for the most part, smoother than in such states as Alabama, Arkansas, Georgia, and Mississippi.

This is not to suggest that integration was accomplished without problems. In Memphis, "white flight" from the schools created an overwhelmingly black city school system and produced lasting racial divisions in the city's political structure. In Nashville and Chattanooga, efforts to integrate the schools encountered emotional resistance. Throughout the 1960s and early 1970s, sporadic episodes of violence and resistance accompanied the collapse of formal segregation and the gradual inclusion of blacks within the economic mainstream. Still, civil disturbance and the resulting legacy of racial overtones in state politics never were as broad or persistent in Tennessee as in most other southern states.

One important explanation for Tennessee's relative racial harmony is the leadership of Gov. Frank Clement in the 1950s and early 1960s. By the standards of his day and in stark contrast to segregationist Governors in Alabama, Arkansas, Georgia, and Mississippi, Clement was a proponent of civil rights who resisted pressure to defy court-ordered integration (table 1.2). Clement's 1956 decision to send the National Guard into Clinton, Tennessee, to protect the black community after segregationists blew up the local high school was a statement that predicted Tennessee's future. One can argue that Tennessee's relatively peaceful path toward integration was blazed by Clement's decision to take a stand on behalf of racial equality.

TABLE 1.2

AFRICAN AMERICAN POPULATION OF TENNESSEE AND CONTIGUOUS STATES, 1990 (IN THOUSANDS)

	African American	*Hispanic*
Alabama	26	1
Arkansas	16	1
Georgia	27	1
Kentucky	07	1
Mississippi	35	1
North Carolina	22	1
Tennessee	15	1
Virginia	19	2

SOURCE: U.S. Census of Population, 1990.

A number of examples, large and small, illustrate Tennessee's approach to racial integration. Unlike several southern states, in Tennessee blacks never were prevented from voting in any significant degree. The integration of public schools never stimulated development of private schools at the rate seen in states such as South Carolina or Mississippi. The first black football player in the Southeastern Conference played at the University of Tennessee. The South's first black legislative committee chairman and the nation's first black head of a university system came from Tennessee. Together these examples point to a social culture that, in at least some important ways, differs from those of many southern states.

Despite the subdued presence of racial politics at the state level, there have been major changes in the politics of Tennessee's urban areas. In particular, the last part of the twentieth century has witnessed the growth of African American politics in Memphis and Shelby County. In 1974, Harold Ford became the first black member of Congress from Tennessee, elected from the majority-black Ninth District. His son succeeded him in 1996. Following years of divisive racial politics, Willie Herenton was elected mayor of Memphis in 1991 and reelected in 1995 and 1999. Herenton and Ford represented different power bases in the African American community. Their electoral successes ushered in a new political era in Tennessee's largest city, as well as another power base in Tennessee state politics.

A Changing Economic Environment

Some states historically have been dominated by one industry, such as oil in Oklahoma and farming in Iowa. In contrast, Tennessee has been more diverse economically since the creation of TVA brought more industry to the state. This diversity has softened the periods of economic boom and bust characteristic of more one-dimensional state economies. Until the 1980s, Tennessee lagged in overall economic development, with some areas still experiencing severe poverty. Despite a substantial surge in the state's average income in the 1980s and 1990s, pockets of poverty remain—in the state's urban centers, in several of the rural counties of West Tennessee, and in a number of mountain communities scattered throughout the Appalachian region of the state.

Tennessee's relative poverty and a comparatively low level of educational attainment go hand in hand. In 1990, in household income and the percent of adults having graduated from high school, Tennessee ranked near the bottom among U.S. states (see table 1.3). Many factors contributed to these deficits. Until the 1980s, the General

TABLE 1.3

SOCIAL AND ECONOMIC INDICATORS: TENNESSEE'S RANKING AMONG THE FIFTY UNITED STATES, 1990 AND 1996

	1990 Ranking	*1996 Ranking*
Population Size	17th	17th
Median Household Income	47th	32nd
Percent of Adults with High School Education	45th	45th

SOURCE: U.S. Census of Population.

Assembly did not provide adequate funds for public education. The pattern was repeated in dozens of local county governments; some of these did not have an adequate tax base, while others simply were more concerned about keeping property taxes low. In some areas, wealth and educational quality reflected long-term problems associated with the demise of the plantation economy or the coal industry.

In other communities, poverty resulted from the closing of textile factories. Prior to the late 1980s, much of the state's manufacturing growth was concentrated in a few areas of the state. Beginning roughly in the late 1970s, initiatives of three Tennessee Governors succeeded in changing the nature of the state's economy. The most significant change came in 1981, when the Nissan Company of Japan announced that Smyrna, Tennessee, would be the site of a new automotive assembly plant. In a period of dramatic growth from 1982 to 1994, Tennessee went from producing no cars and light trucks to ranking third among the states. By the close of the century, more than one hundred thousand Tennesseans worked for automotive assembly plants or their suppliers. In the summer of 2000, Nissan announced a major expansion of its automobile plant in Smyrna. The growth of the state's automotive industry, more than any single factor, caused a parallel growth in the average income of Tennesseans. Between 1990 and 1996, Tennessee's ranking in median household income rose fifteen places, from forty-seventh to thirty-second among fifty states.

The Context of State Politics

Tennessee state government is older than all but a handful of the world's democracies. In its first two centuries, Tennessee evolved a distinctive political culture, partly as a legacy of the Old South and partly due to a mixture of unique personalities and events that shaped the state's future. As the state entered its third century, many traditional challenges remained. These challenges would not be met by a few thousand farmers who never traveled more than fifty miles from their homes, as was the case in 1796. The culture and ideas of these early Tennesseans have been passed on to a society of more than five million persons, connected to the wider nation and world in ways their ancestors never could have imagined. How these modern Tennesseans view their challenges, and how their political institutions respond to them, is the context for the study of state government in Tennessee.

2

The State Constitution

By 1998, the state senator from Memphis had reached the point of absolute frustration. For nearly eight years, he had sought to convince two-thirds of his fellow legislators to adopt a resolution proposing a state lottery. State lotteries had been established recently in Kentucky and Georgia, where the gusher of new revenues had been used to bolster public education. Upstart candidates had defeated incumbent Governors in Alabama and South Carolina on a platform of legalizing lotteries. Polling indicated the number of Tennesseans supporting a lottery had climbed from a minority to more than 70 percent. Despite the regional trend toward state lotteries, the Tennessee senator's obstacle was unique among southern states. In Tennessee, establishing a lottery required changing the state constitution, a daunting prospect.

The United States Constitution guarantees to each state "a republican form of government." This mandates that every state must conduct its governmental processes under a representative democracy, with a chief executive and legislature elected by a popular vote. To establish this political process, every state has its own constitution, not only to specify the form and function of the state government, but also to protect its citizens against abuse of governmental power.

State constitutions must always yield to the federal constitution. The U.S. Constitution is the "supreme law of the land," which means that it prevails over any conflicting provision of state law, including state constitutions. For example, the Tennessee Constitution provides that "no Minister of the Gospel, or priest of any denomination whatever, shall be eligible to a seat in either House of the Legislature."[1] In 1978, the U.S. Supreme Court held that this provision violates the freedom of religion guaranteed by the First Amendment to the U.S. Constitution.[2] Although the provision has not been stricken from the state constitution, it is legally unenforceable.

Despite federal constitutional supremacy, state constitutions retain considerable importance. Much of the work of government—education and criminal justice, for example—is done at the state level, and state constitutions set the structure for getting that work done. Constitutions empower but also limit government. The more specific the provisions of a constitution, the more policy makers are limited in their options. For example, for many years the Tennessee Constitution limited the interest rates that banks could charge on loans. Thus the General Assembly was powerless to raise these limits, despite the pleas of banks that they could not compete with banks in other states. In such a case, it makes no difference that a majority of the popularly elected members of both houses of the legislature might approve such a change. The state constitution is superior to the will of the popular majority, no matter how large the majority or how serious the issue. Of course, given a sufficient consensus, the constitution itself may be changed. In Tennessee, this is not easily accomplished, as we shall see.

In mistrusting government, constitutional limits reflect the wisdom of the founders and popular majorities. Most commentators, however, agree that constitutions ought to be confined to fundamental principles. When constitutions become overly detailed, they veer into territory best left to elected representatives. Most state constitutions, including that of Tennessee, contain a good deal of detail, and thus stand in stark contrast to the U.S. Constitution. This explains why most state constitutions have been revised substantially over the years, while the U.S. Constitution, with a few significant exceptions, remains essentially as it was when it was adopted in the late eighteenth century.

State Constitutions

State constitutions vary greatly. There are two basic types. One type, much like the U.S. Constitution, is quite short, providing the fundamental principles of government and individual rights. Others are much longer, with numerous specific provisions that would—and, many would argue, should—otherwise be left to the legislatures of those states. Alabama's constitution, with 174,000 words, clearly falls within this group. In contrast, the Tennessee Constitution, with 15,300 words, is relatively short.

Establishment of State Constitutions

The thirteen original American colonies grew from small early settlements into viable political communities, each with its own charter issued by the King of England. These charters were brief documents, containing the rights of English subjects and the principles of government. After the American Declaration of Independence was adopted, each of the thirteen colonies became an independent state. In 1777, the states formed a confederation called the United States of America, but it was not until the Constitution of 1787 was ratified that the United States became one nation. During the American Revolution, each of the thirteen states adopted its own constitution. Although there were significant differences among them, all the state constitutions provided for separation of powers between the legislative and executive functions of government. Most states also provided for an independent judiciary.

The early state constitutions were much more elitist than the constitutions we have today. In most states, service in the state legislatures was limited to white "men of property"—that is, landowners. Early constitutions also contained property qualifications for voting. Even among the more enthusiastic advocates of democracy, the prevailing sentiment was that only wealthy white males should be allowed to participate in the affairs of government. In retrospect, the nascent American democracy does not appear to have been very democratic. One must remember, however, that the establishment of the state and federal constitutions was only the first step in a long process of development from monarchy and colonialism to a mature democracy.

The early state constitutions shared a bias against a strong executive. This bias was a reaction against the abuses the colonies suffered at the hands of the King. The state constitutions not only severely limited the authority of their Governors, but also limited governmental powers in other ways by employing the same sorts of checks and balances employed to limit the national government. Resentment toward the British Crown motivated the authors of the original state constitutions to place far more severe limits on their respective Governors than the framers of the U.S. Constitution imposed on the President. Most early Governors were chosen by the state legislatures and were limited to one term in office.[3]

This limiting of the executive produced a predictably ineffectual set of Governors in the early part of the nineteenth century. Many states reacted to a new set of political currents and amended their constitutions to allow popular election of Governors. Reflecting the immense influence of Andrew Jackson in the 1830s, states began placing greater power in the hands of the electorate to choose many statewide officers.

Over the years, state constitutions evolved to address a number of pressures and concerns in their respective states. As the notion of a more egalitarian democracy took root in the young nation, property qualifications for voting and serving in the legislature were eliminated. One byproduct of the Civil War was the extension of suffrage to black males. The Fifteenth Amendment, ratified in 1870, prohibited racial discrimination in voting. But it would take a century of struggle before African Americans would enjoy unfettered voting rights in all states. By the 1960s, "grandfather clauses," poll taxes, literacy tests, "white primaries," and other devices to keep blacks from voting had been done away with, either by federal judicial decree or congressional legislation.

By the late nineteenth century, states were beginning to recognize the right of women to participate in elections and hold government office as well. The ratification of the Nineteenth Amendment to the U.S. Constitution in 1920 cemented the right of women to vote in both federal and state elections.

As state constitutions evolved, Governors became more powerful, and state judiciaries became more independent. With the passage of time, state governments came to resemble the federal government, with its three independent, more or less equal branches of government.

In the American federal system, states have responsibility for their local governments—cities, counties, and towns. Thus state constitutions also deal with a variety of issues involving the operation of local governments. By the 1950s, numerous state constitutions had become clogged with provisions detailing the operations and financing of local government. Moreover, these constitutions often contained sections dealing with issues (for example, steamboat racing or "prisons for Negroes") that were legally and practically antiquated. In the latter half of the twentieth century, most states have updated their charters, eliminating many of the more anachronistic and irrelevant provisions.

Developing the State Constitution

Tennessee government currently operates under a constitution approved in 1870, although this constitution has been amended frequently since its adoption. The 1870 version was the third constitution in the state's history. The first constitution took effect at the time statehood was achieved in 1796. That document was modeled closely after North Carolina's constitution, although it borrowed from the constitutions of Virginia and Pennsylvania as well.[4] Because Tennessee had been a part of North Carolina, and because so many early Tennesseans migrated from that state, it is not surprising that the first Tennessee Constitution was modeled largely after North Carolina's fundamental law.

Constitution of 1796

The first constitutional convention was held in Knoxville in 1796. The delegates constructed a document fairly typical for their day. Tennessee's basic law, like that of other states, provided for a separation of powers into legislative, executive, and judicial branches. It also contained a basic declaration of rights. Legislative powers were placed in a bicameral (two-chamber) General Assembly, consisting of a House of Representatives and a Senate. The House had twenty-six members. However, more members would be added after the state's taxable population reached forty thousand. The Senate was smaller, being limited to between one-third and one-half the size of the House. Senate districts could not cross county lines and could not divide counties. Thus the county was the unit of representation.

State representatives and state senators served two-year terms. The General Assembly chose judges, various state executive officers, and state's attorneys. In the words of one commentator, the General Assembly "was to be the most powerful branch of government, possessing the lawmaking power, control of all appropriations of state funds, and also the right to appoint all officers 'not otherwise directed'" by the state constitution.[5]

Voters chose the Governor, who held a relatively weak position. The Governor was granted no power to veto legislation, nor was his signature required for legislation to take effect. Tennessee's early Governors essentially served as chief administrators. They could recommend legislation and had the power to call special sessions of the General Assembly. In an era when the threat of Indian unrest was real and the judicial system was crude, among the most important powers granted to the Tennessee Governor were to raise and direct a state militia and to grant pardons to persons convicted of crimes. The Governor's term of office was limited to two years.

Suffrage was fairly democratic for the day, allowing for participation as broad as any state constitution at the time granted.[6] All free males over the age of twenty-one could vote, along with free slaves, although the latter were exempted in 1835.[7] However, the Governor and members of the General Assembly had to be property owners.

Like the North Carolina charter after which it was modeled, the Tennessee Constitution of 1796 failed to provide for an independent judiciary. Rather, the judicial power was "vested in such superior and inferior courts of law and equity as the legislature shall, from time to time, direct and establish."[8] Appointment of judges, too, was vested in the General Assembly. Although judges served for life during "good behavior," the legislature could overturn judicial decisions through private acts.[9] In short, the judiciary was subordinate to the General Assembly.[10]

The General Assembly appointed county judicial officials. Two justices of the peace had to be appointed in each county. The county courts appointed local officers: sheriff, coroner, trustee, register of deeds, and a ranger. The county court heard lawsuits and ran the local government. This practice lasted until 1817, when the courts were split into administrative and judicial components.

A notable provision of the Constitution of 1796 required that land be taxed in a uniform manner, based on acreage. The most productive farm could be taxed at no higher a rate than the rockiest wasteland. This was a fairly common approach to property taxation in the 1790s; but as Tennessee became more populous, more developed, and more urbanized, great disparities in real estate values arose. Controversy over this provision led to the creation of a new state constitution in 1834.[11]

Constitution of 1835

The political climate in Tennessee changed significantly over the thirty years following 1796, especially with regard to the life appointment of judicial officers. Public outrage concerning incompetent judges, as well as resentment over the uniform taxation of land, led to the calling of a constitutional convention in 1834. Moreover, it had become clear that the legislature was hopelessly involved in the politics of the judiciary.

The convention had wide-ranging authority to revise the state constitution. As would be the case with subsequent constitutional conventions, the delegates exceeded their call to create a more responsive judiciary. They went so far, in fact, that they created Tennessee's second constitution. The document they drafted contained several provisions that merely revised similar items in the first constitution. Nonetheless, there were some notable changes.

The second Tennessee constitution, which took effect in 1835, reflected the spirit and ideology of Jacksonian democracy. Land would be taxed according to its market value instead of its acreage. Property qualifications were removed from the list of qualifications for all offices. County officials would be elected locally. For the first time, the state formally recognized the need for public education and a "common school

Constitutional Convention of 1796

When Congress approved statehood for Tennessee, territorial governor William Blount issued a proclamation asking each of the eleven counties to choose five persons to meet to create the first Tennessee Constitution. This group convened in Knoxville in January 1796. Fifty-five members met for twenty-seven days. Each received $1.50 a day for their trouble, along with a travel stipend of $1 for each thirty miles they traveled to Knoxville. The convention employed two clerks and one doorkeeper, at a combined salary of $7 a day. Other expenses included $22.50 for firewood, $10 for seats, $2.62 for oilcloth, and $166.66 for printing expenses. The total expense for the entire convention was $3,007.08. The convention did not submit its work to the people for a vote. After the work of the convention was approved by the delegates, it was delivered to the United States Secretary of State Thomas Jefferson. It met with high praise. Jefferson noted that it was "the least imperfect and the most republican in form of any state constitution adopted by any of the American states."

SOURCES: Robert White, "Remarks Made to the Constitutional Convention of 1953," in *Journal and Debates of the Constitutional Convention, 1953* (Limited Constitutional Convention, State of Tennessee, 1953), 518. Fig. 2.1. William Blount. Tennessee State Library and Archives.

fund" was established for "the equal benefit of all the people" of Tennessee. In the view of the Tennessee Supreme Court nearly sixteen decades later, this language "established a legal right to public education in Tennessee."[12]

One of the major changes in the Constitution of 1835 dealt with the court system. The new proposal called for a Supreme Court comprised of three judges, one from each of the state's grand divisions. The justices would serve twelve-year terms after being chosen by a joint vote of the General Assembly. Inferior court judges were appointed for eight-year terms. Thus life tenure of judges was ended.

Another fundamental change in the Constitution of 1835 affected the right to vote. The suffrage that had been granted to free African Americans by the Constitution of 1796 was removed. This denial of basic rights powerfully demonstrated the cultural drift in the state toward the values of the Deep South.

The authors of the Constitution of 1835 wanted a document that would be difficult to change. By design, they put in place a process that made it extremely hard to amend the Tennessee Constitution. Proposed constitutional amendments were required to pass with a majority vote of all members elected to the legislature. Following passage, the proposed amendment was held until the next meeting of the General Assembly, at which time two-thirds of the members had to ratify the proposal, written exactly as before. (This technicality would surface as a major issue 160 years later, when the General Assembly considered a constitutional amendment to allow lotteries.) Any proposed amendment that survived these two votes then was submitted to the electorate, where an amendment needed to gain a number of votes greater than half the votes cast for state representatives. This process could occur only once in a six-year period. Not surprisingly, the Constitution of 1835 was rarely amended. In fact, over the next thirty-five years, only two amendments were adopted.

Constitution of 1870

As noted in chapter 1, Tennessee suffered greatly during the Civil War. The conflict divided the state, with East Tennessee favoring the Union and Middle and West Tennessee supporting the Confederacy. Tennesseans voted to join the Confederacy, and numerous battles took place on Tennessee soil. However, in 1866, Tennessee amended the Constitution of 1835 to abolish slavery and ratified the Fourteenth Amendment. By these actions, the state managed to avoid the harshest

Tennessee Ratifies the Fourteenth Amendment to the United States Constitution

A visitor to the Tennessee Capitol who climbs the grand staircase is likely to notice that the marble handrail is damaged. This occurred during the General Assembly's session in 1866 to consider ratification of the Fourteenth Amendment to the United States Constitution. Feelings on this issue ran strong on both sides, as this amendment basically ratified the Union victory in the Civil War and extended citizenship to the newly freed former slaves. Knowing that they would lose the vote, opponents of ratification attempted to leave the Capitol to deprive supporters of a quorum. They were confronted by armed guards and forced to remain. It was during this confrontation that a shot was fired, damaging the banister. Opponents reentered their chambers, and the General Assembly voted to ratify the Fourteenth Amendment.

of the Reconstruction measures imposed upon other southern states. Even so, bitterness and conflict continued to characterize Tennessee politics. Gov. William Brownlow declared emergency conditions, suspending the writ of habeas corpus and allowing arrests without due process of law. Brownlow also had kept the General Assembly meeting almost all the time over a four-year period, causing more than a little hardship for the lawmakers. These and other concerns culminated in the General Assembly's issuing a call for a constitutional convention, which met in January 1870. The voters approved the constitution it produced by a vote of 98,128 to 33,872.[13]

The 1870 convention adopted a number of key constitutional changes, though it was by no means a total revision of the 1835 document. The net effect of these changes was to rein in both the governor and the legislature. The new constitution gave the General Assembly the power to declare an emergency, at which time the Governor could call out the militia if necessary. It also provided for a limited number of days for the lawmakers to receive pay. Members of the General Assembly could collect pay for no more than seventy-five days in each biennial session. The Governor had the ability to call the legislature into special session. The specific purpose for a special session had to be included in the Governor's call. Pay for a special session ceased after twenty-five days. These changes put effective limits on the length of time the assembly could meet.

The Constitution of 1870 imposed other changes on the General Assembly. Growth in the state's population had created a need for more representatives. The size of the House of Representatives was limited at 99; the Senate could not exceed one-third the size of the House. Lawmakers were required to redraw district lines every ten years, following a required count of citizens in the state, although there was no requirement that districts had to be equal in size. The 1870 document also sought to regulate the assembly's way of operating. It required that each bill deal with only one subject. Moreover, the title of the bill must identify that one subject. This provision later was the basis of a 1997 Tennessee Supreme Court ruling that a very controversial bill was unconstitutional. Earlier in 1997, the General Assembly had passed what was known as the "Tiny Towns" law, which allowed a few hundred people to form a town on the border of another city or town. However, the title of the bill legislators had voted on referred only to methods of assignment of tax collections.

The delegates to the 1870 convention added a provision to allow the General Assembly to send a call for a convention to the citizens. Once a convention call was placed on the ballot, approval by a majority of those voting on the call was required.

Still difficult to amend, the Constitution of 1870 went until 1953 without major modification. It consists of eleven articles, many of which are complex. The arcane language and complexity of the Tennessee Constitution stand in contrast to the elegance of the U.S. Constitution. This is understandable, given the complexity of counties, cities, and other local units that fall under the jurisdiction of the state. This third constitution has served as the basis of Tennessee government ever since 1870. However, beginning in 1953, Tennessee embarked upon a process of convening limited conventions to make alterations to this document. Many of these changes have had enormous political significance.

Constitutional Convention of 1953

In November 1952, following a call from the General Assembly, elections were held in the ninety-nine House districts to select delegates to a constitutional convention.[14] The delegates came from a variety of backgrounds. Some were legislators, but many came from backgrounds other than politics. In April 1953, following the inauguration of thirty-two-year-old Gov. Frank Clement, the delegates gathered in Nashville to consider issues that reflected changes taking place in Tennessee after the end of World War II. The delegates met for two months to examine legislative compensation, whether the Governor's two-year term of office should be lengthened, whether the Governor should be granted a stronger legislative veto, questions of voter eligibility, how cities could govern themselves, and how cities and counties might combine governments.

The convention approved a variety of changes to the Constitution of 1870. Legislative pay was increased, and the poll tax was eliminated. The Governor's term was a major consideration. The two-year term presented great difficulty, as Governors had to worry about campaigning for election soon after being elected. The delegates to the convention proposed changing the governor's term to four years, with a one-term limit. This later led to "leapfrogging" between Frank Clement and Buford Ellington, before being changed in 1977 to allow for two consecutive gubernatorial terms.

The 1953 convention also addressed the process of amending the Tennessee Constitution. Delegates clarified the legislature's right to limit the work of the convention to the issues specified in the call. They reduced from six to four the number of years that had to elapse before new amendments could be considered by the electorate. The convention also proposed a change in the way amendments would be ratified. While previously an amendment needed to gain approval by more than half the votes cast for state representatives, the new proposal required an amendment to exceed half the votes cast for governor. This certainly did not make it easier to secure ratification of amendments.

Delegates to the 1953 convention also dealt with a number of issues important to local government. The General Assembly had found itself devoting an increasing amount of time to local issues by considering so-called "special acts" that affected a particular city or county. The delegates proposed a measure requiring a two-thirds vote of the city or county before state legislation aimed at that governmental entity could take effect. Under home rule, local municipalities could hold referenda to change their charters. The change represented a landmark shift in authority from Nashville to local communities. Significantly, the new authority for local governments did not include a repeal of the prohibition against city income taxes.

Other important changes in local government were considered in the 1953 convention. Among the most innovative were provisions authorizing cities to consolidate their governments with the counties that surrounded them. This proposal, which later was the framework under which Nashville and Davidson County consolidated their governments, required that a charter be prepared and presented to the electorate in the affected county. In order for the proposed consolidation to take effect, the measure required separate and concurrent approval from the voters in the central city and from those in the portion of the county outside the city.

Conventions of 1959, 1965, and 1972

Having gone more than eighty years between constitutional conventions, Tennessee legislators sent three calls for conventions to the public between 1953 and 1972. Each was approved by the electorate. Tennesseans were becoming more comfortable with making changes in their fundamental law, although they limited these changes to narrowly defined issues. In 1959, the convention delegates placed on the ballot increasing the term of county sheriffs and trustees to four years and lowering the voting age to eighteen. The voters approved only one suggested change: lengthening the county trustee's term.

In 1962, the U.S. Supreme Court ruled on a Tennessee case with major national implications. As discussed in chapter 1, *Baker v. Carr*[15] dealt with malapportionment in state legislatures, a situation in which districts' state representatives were chosen by grossly unequal populations of voters. In 1964, the Court held that states must regularly redraw state House and Senate lines so that districts would be of roughly equal populations.[16] In Tennessee, the ruling necessitated a call for a constitutional convention to consider this issue.

In 1965, the convention approved staggered terms for state senators, who then would serve four-year terms, with half elected every two years. State representatives and state senators would represent districts based purely on population. This change necessitated dividing counties into districts when the county had enough population to justify more than one representative. (This was the first of several times when the guidelines of the state constitution, which discourages legislative districts from crossing county lines, collided with guidelines of the federal constitution, which places a greater emphasis on districts of equal population.) The convention also approved the concept of special sessions of the General Assembly, which could be called either by the Governor or by two-thirds of both legislative chambers. Finally, the convention allowed sessions of the General Assembly to be split over two terms. The voters approved all these changes in 1966.

In 1972, delegates considered a number of issues: changes in the complex and confusing court system, sessions of the General Assembly, local government, lowering the voting age, and, most important, changes in the classification of property for purposes of taxation. The electorate only approved the part of the call that allowed the convention to consider property tax classification. According to Greene, Grubbs, and Hobday, state voters simply were not ready for such sweeping changes.[17]

The voters approved another call for a convention in 1977. Some of the proposed changes were substantial, including one to allow the Governor to run for consecutive four-year terms, another to extend the terms of elected county officials from two years to four, and a third to remove the outdated 10 percent ceiling on interest rates. Other proposals sought to eliminate from the state constitution antiquated prohibitions against interracial marriage and integrated schools that were similar to legal provisions that had been struck down by the U.S. Supreme Court.[18]

The voters ratified these changes, although in some cases by narrow margins. However, the most controversial proposal, reforming the judicial system, once more failed to garner enough votes. The proposal had been for a complete overhaul of the judicial system—consolidating specialized courts and professionalizing judicial selection and administration. Most informed observers supported the idea of reform. However, the proposed changes included giving the General Assembly final approval of court rules and the ability to change the salaries of sitting judges. One Supreme Court justice, Joe Henry, was bothered by these last two proposals and actively campaigned against the court reform proposal. Again, court reform was defeated, and the judiciary remained confusing and chaotic.

The Constitution Today

The Tennessee Constitution serves as a blueprint for government in the state. It begins with a rather lengthy preamble, followed by eleven articles.

- Article I contains a declaration of the rights of Tennesseans.
- Article II defines the distribution of governmental powers and addresses the structure and powers of the legislative branch.
- Article III deals with the executive department of the state government.
- Article IV addresses voting and elections.
- Article V pertains to impeachment.
- Article VI constitutes the state judiciary.

- Article VII deals with state and county officers.
- Article VIII concerns the militia.
- Article IX sets forth disqualifications for holding public office.
- Article X discusses oaths, bribery of electors, and new counties.
- Article XI contains a set of miscellaneous provisions.

Article I: Declaration of Rights

The original federal Constitution did not contain what is today known as the Bill of Rights. What later came to be recognized as the core principles of American personal freedom were added as amendments only after it became clear that they were necessary to obtain ratification of the Constitution by the various state legislatures. Significantly, the Tennessee Constitution places its Declaration of Rights in Article I. The fact that the enumeration of rights is placed first in the state constitution is no accident. The framers of the Tennessee Constitution wanted to leave no doubt that the Declaration of Rights would be considered "an integral part of the constitution rather than an appendage."[19] Indeed, Article XI, Section 16, states: "The declaration of rights hereto prefixed is declared to be a part of the Constitution of this State, and shall never be violated on any pretence whatever."

The Tennessee Declaration of Rights is quite extensive, consisting of thirty-four sections.[20] The enumeration of rights includes a number of provisions that are identical or similar to those found in the Bill of Rights, including guarantees of freedom of speech, press, assembly, and religion; the right to keep and bear arms; and the right to a jury trial; as well as protections against unreasonable searches and seizures, double jeopardy, excessive bail, and cruel and unusual punishments. Tennessee's Declaration of Rights also contains a number of interesting provisions not found in the federal Constitution, including prohibition of state-granted monopolies, protection against being imprisoned for the failure to pay one's debts, and protection against being compelled to bear arms.

Each citizen in Tennessee is thus protected by both the national and the state enumeration of rights. One's rights under the U.S. Supreme Court's interpretation of the federal Constitution take precedence over the Tennessee Constitution as interpreted by Tennessee courts. The federal Constitution thus serves as a floor beneath which the states are not permitted to sink, while it allows states to grant additional rights to their citizens under the applicable terms of state constitutions.

Freedoms of Speech and the Press

Arguably, the freedoms of speech and the press are the most fundamental in any democratic society. The Tennessee Constitution contains more elaborate language respecting these two freedoms than does the First Amendment to the U.S. Constitution. Article I, Section 19, provides:

> That the printing presses shall be free to every person to examine the proceedings of the legislature; or of any branch or officer of the government, and no law shall ever be made to restrain the right thereof. The free communication of thoughts and opinions, is one of the invaluable rights of man, and every citizen may freely speak, write, and print on any subject, being responsible for the abuse of that liberty. But in prosecutions for the publication of papers investigating the official conduct of officers, or men in public capacity, the truth thereof may be given in evidence; and in all indictments for libel, the jury shall have a right to determine the law and the facts, under the direction of the court, as in other criminal cases.

Although the Tennessee courts on occasion have held that these protections are stronger than those contained in the First Amendment, as a practical matter the Tennessee courts "have made no significant deviation from the federal decisions."[21]

Freedom of Religion

The Tennessee Constitution contains the following guarantees of religious freedom:

> That all men have a natural and indefeasible right to worship Almighty God according to the dictates of their own conscience; that no man can of right be compelled to attend, erect, or support any place of worship, or to maintain any minister against his consent; that no human authority can, in any case whatever, control or interfere with the rights of conscience; and that no preference shall ever be given, by law, to any religious establishment or mode of worship.[22]

For the most part, these guarantees have been interpreted as being "practically synonymous" with the Religion Clauses of the First Amendment to the U.S. Constitution.[23]

One of the more interesting cases the Tennessee courts have addressed in this area involved a challenge to the Tennessee statute that prohibits "handling snakes so as to endanger life."[24] Members of the Holiness Church, who sometimes handle poisonous snakes to

Fig. 2.2. Snake-handling service at Habersham Chapel in Campbell County, 1940. *Source:* Tennessee State Library and Archives.

demonstrate their faith (fig. 2.2), challenged the constitutionality of the law. In 1975, the Tennessee Supreme Court said that, despite the state constitutional protection of religion, such actions "may be limited, curtailed or restrained to the point of outright prohibition, where it involves a clear and present danger to the interests of society."[25] This ruling is consistent with U.S. Supreme Court decisions holding that freedom of religion does not include an exemption to a generally applicable criminal prohibition.[26]

Right to Keep and Bear Arms

The Tennessee Constitution assures a number of other basic rights, including freedom of assembly and a right to bear arms. Section 26 provides "that the citizens of this state have a right to keep and to bear arms for their common defense; but the Legislature shall have power, by law, to regulate the wearing of arms with a view to prevent crime." Because the U.S. Supreme Court never has applied the Second Amendment of the U.S. Constitution to the states,[27] Tennessee gun laws can be challenged only on the basis of Section 26 of the state constitution. However, the language of Section 26 permits broad regulation of firearms; and Tennessee, like most states, has enacted statutes that address the use and sale of firearms.[28]

Protection against Unreasonable Searches and Seizures

Although the language of the Tennessee Constitution differs somewhat from the language of the Fourth Amendment to the U.S. Constitution, the protections conferred are essentially the same. The touchstone of the protection is reasonableness. Absent exigent circumstances, warrants are required before searches and seizures can be conducted. Warrants may not be issued unless a judge has determined that there is "probable cause" to think that a search is justified. However, there are two ways in which Article I, Section 7, of the Tennessee Constitution is more protective than the Fourth Amendment. The Fourth Amendment provides little protection to "open fields,"[29] but the Tennessee Constitution protects fields that are cultivated from unreasonable searches.[30] Another deviation involves a judge's decision whether to issue a search warrant based on a tip from a confidential police informant. Under prevailing Fourth Amendment standards, magistrates consider the "totality of circumstances" in making "probable cause" determinations in such circumstances.[31] The Tennessee Supreme Court has rejected this approach, requiring instead that magistrates determine that informants' tips are both credible and reliable before issuing search warrants.[32]

Excessive Bail, Cruel and Unusual Punishments, and Rights of Prisoners

Article I, Section 16, provides that "excessive bail shall not be required, nor excessive fines imposed, nor cruel and unusual punishments inflicted." This language is identical to that found in the Eighth Amendment to the U.S. Constitution. The U.S. Supreme Court has held that the Cruel and Unusual Punishments Clause of the Eighth Amendment applies to the states under the Fourteenth Amendment.[33] However, the Court has never applied the Excessive Bail Clause to the states. Tennessee courts therefore are free to interpret the corresponding provision of the state constitution without regard to what the federal courts have said on the question of excessive bail. The Tennessee Constitution contains an additional provision on the subject of bail. Article I, Section 15, states that "all prisoners shall be bailable by sufficient sureties, unless for capital offenses, when the proof is evident, or the presumption great." This language means that defendants have the right to pretrial release on bail except in capital cases where there is strong evidence of guilt. This provision of the Tennessee Constitution goes hand in hand with the traditional presumption of innocence (an individual is presumed innocent until proven guilty). Even if a defendant in the past had failed to appear in court after posting bond, that person cannot be denied bail. The fact that the defendant jumped bail in the past has been interpreted by the Tennessee Supreme Court to be a legitimate factor in setting bail in a future case.[34] The term "sufficient sureties" refers to the dollar amount of the bonds that defendants must post to get out of jail prior to their trial. A "sufficient surety" is one that seeks to insure that the accused will appear in court when required to do so. The provision's intent is to prevent judges from setting bond at levels so high that it becomes a practical impossibility for the defendant to secure pretrial release.[35] Despite the intent, judges regularly set bonds of several hundred thousand dollars in cases involving violent felonies, aware that the defendant has no chance of raising the money and will be forced to stay in jail until trial.

Tennessee courts are free to interpret the Cruel and Unusual Punishments Clause of the state constitution according to the state's values and traditions, so long as they observe the minimum requirements of the corresponding language of the federal Constitution. The Tennessee Supreme Court basically has followed the lead of the U.S. Supreme Court in this area of law, having upheld the death penalty[36] as well as "habitual offender" statutes.[37]

Article I, Section 32, of the state constitution used to require "the erection of safe and comfortable prisons, the inspection of prisons, and the humane treatment of prisoners." The phrase "safe and comfortable prisons" was included in the Constitution of 1870 to prohibit the brutal prison conditions that many prisoners of war suffered during the Civil War. In 1998, state voters approved an amendment to the Tennessee Constitution removing the words "and comfortable." One of the Senate sponsors of the amendment argued that the term "comfortable" was "vague language that . . . could be used to attack the constitutionality of the whole system."[38] Like much in political life, the amendment was a largely symbolic attempt to respond to a public misperception that the constitutional language was responsible for rising prison cost or "country club" prisons. There was little prospect that the Tennessee courts would use the long-standing language of Section 32 to impose stricter standards on the Tennessee prisons than were already in effect. Inasmuch as prison conditions in Tennessee are subject to federal court review under the Eighth Amendment to the U.S. Constitution, the effect of the amendment on actual prison conditions is apt to be negligible.

Protection Against Retrospective Legislation and Impairment of Contracts

Article I, section 20, of the Tennessee Constitution provides that "no retrospective law, or law impairing the obligations of contracts, shall be made." The Tennessee Supreme Court has interpreted this language to proscribe laws that "take away or impair vested rights acquired under existing laws or create a new obligation, impose a new duty, or attach a new disability in respect of transactions or considerations already passed."[39] In determining whether a retrospective law impairs "vested rights," the courts are apt to consider whether the provision in question advances the public interest, how it affects the people concerned, and whether the provision is merely remedial or purely procedural.[40]

Due Process of Law

The Tennessee Constitution states that "no man shall be taken or imprisoned, or disseized of his freehold, liberties or privileges, or outlawed, or exiled, or in any manner destroyed or deprived of his life, liberty or property, but by the judgment of his peers, or the law of the land."[41] This language is identical to that found in the Magna Carta (1215 A.D.), which is one of the fundamental texts in the Anglo-American legal tradition. This provision is virtually synonymous with the provisions of the Fifth and Fourteenth amendments to the U.S. Constitution that prohibit the federal and state governments, respectively, from depriving persons within their jurisdiction of life, liberty, or property without due process of law. Due process, or "the law of the land," requires government to treat citizens fairly and reasonably and to follow the applicable procedures of law when dealing with citizens. In short, due process encapsulates the fundamental American ideal of the rule of law.

Sovereign Immunity

Under English common law, the sovereign, or government, could be sued only with the sovereign's consent. This doctrine of sovereign immunity, while somewhat questionable in light of the American commitment to the rule of law, became a part of American law when the common law was received by the states. The Tennessee Constitution of 1796 did permit Tennesseans to sue their state government. The Constitution of 1835 extended that right to all persons, although conditions under which citizens could sue the state were regulated by the state legislature. Even today, Article I, Section 17, of the state constitution provides that "suits may be brought against the State in such manner and in such courts as the Legislature may direct." In 1873, the General Assembly enacted a law prohibiting the courts from entering monetary judgments against the state, thus effectively reinstating sovereign immunity. This statute is still in effect today. Thus, a person injured as the result of the negligence of state employees is effectively barred from suing the state in court. Rather, a claim must be filed with a state administrative agency called the Claims Commission.[42] Rewards from the Claims Commission are capped at $300,000 per case. The Tennessee courts have interpreted sovereign immunity quite broadly, going so far as to extend legal immunity to athletic departments of state universities.[43]

Equal Protection of the Law

Unlike the federal Constitution, the Tennessee Constitution does not contain an explicit requirement that the state provide equal protection of the law to persons under its jurisdiction. Article XI, Section 8, requires that the General Assembly pass only "general laws"—that is, laws that apply equally to all members of the political community. This requirement, when read in tandem with the "law of the land" provision of Article I, Section 8, can be viewed as effectively imposing an equal protection obligation on the state.[44] In the landmark "Small Schools" decision of 1993, the Tennessee Supreme Court relied in part on the equal protection requirement of the state constitution in striking down the funding system for the public schools.[45]

Right of Privacy

The federal Constitution does not mention "privacy," but the U.S. Supreme Court has said that there is an implicit right to privacy that applies to the states via the Fourteenth Amendment.[46] Likewise, the Tennessee Constitution makes no mention of privacy, but the Tennessee Supreme Court has held that there is such a right under the state charter. In *Davis v. Davis* (1992), better known as the "frozen embryos case," the Tennessee Supreme Court observed that "the notion of individual liberty is . . . deeply embedded in the Tennessee Constitution" and concluded "that there is a right of individual privacy guaranteed under and protected by the liberty clauses of the Tennessee Declaration of Rights."[47] In *Davis,* the court ruled that the right of privacy under the state constitution includes the right to procreate and the right to prevent procreation. Thus Junior Davis was able to prevent his ex-wife from utilizing frozen embryos that had been created with his sperm.

In 1996, the Tennessee Court of Appeals relied on the right of privacy under the state constitution in striking down an act of the General Assembly that prohibited consensual, private homosexual acts.[48] The court noted that, although the U.S. Supreme Court previously had held that such conduct is not protected by the federal constitution,[49] the right of privacy under the Tennessee Constitution is more extensive than the corresponding right to privacy under the U.S. Constitution. Moreover, the court found the state's reliance on traditional morality to be unpersuasive:

> We recognize that many of the laws of this State reflect "moral choices" regarding the standard of conduct by which the citizens of this State must conduct themselves. However, we also recognize that when these "moral choices" are transformed into law, they have constitutional limits. In this case, since the law in question infringes upon the plaintiffs' right to privacy, a fundamental right, the law must be justified by a compelling state interest and must be narrowly drawn to advance that interest. Even if we assume that the Homosexual Practices Act represents a moral choice of the people of this State, we are unconvinced that the advancement of this moral choice is so compelling as to justify the regulation of private, noncommercial, sexual choices between consenting adults simply because those adults happen to be of the same gender.[50]

The Tennessee Supreme Court also has said that the right of privacy includes "the right of parents to care for their children without unwarranted state intervention."[51] In *Doe v. Sundquist* (1999), a group of plaintiffs challenged a new state law requiring disclosure of adoption records to adoptive children who have reached the age of legal majority. Plaintiffs argued that the new law infringed their right to procreational and familial privacy. The Supreme Court disagreed, saying that "although the prospect of having the records of the adoption released to the child 21 years later may have some bearing on the decision, it is far too speculative to conclude that it interferes with the right to procreational privacy."[52]

Article II: Distribution of Powers and the Legislative Branch

The second article establishes the basic structure of Tennessee government—the legislative, executive, and judicial branches. Thirty-one of the thirty-three sections deal with the structure, function, and limitations upon the legislative branch, known in Tennessee as the General

Assembly (fig. 2.3). The basic structure of the General Assembly is presented in section 3. Terms are set at two years for each member of the state's House of Representatives and four years for state senators. The speakers of the House and Senate also are mentioned, thus being accorded the status of "Constitutional Officers." Respective Senate and House districts usually vary in population by less than 10 percent. The assembly is instructed to redraw the lines after each U.S. Census (once each decade). The Tennessee Constitution encourages that county lines be used as district boundaries. Since the 1981 reapportionment plan, the state constitution's guideline not to split counties has been overruled, primarily in the House, by the requirement of the federal Constitution that districts be of approximately equal population.

Section 5 instructs those redrawing districts as to the geographical and political criteria to be used in reapportionment, to the degree that the federal courts will allow. While representatives and senators do not formally represent counties, where possible county boundaries are the preferred lines between districts. If a county is entitled to more than one representative, each must represent a distinct district within the county. This type of district is a "single-member district," as distinct from the "multimember districts" used in Tennessee until the

Fig. 2.3. The Tennessee Capitol in Nashville as it appeared in the nineteenth century. *Source:* Tennessee State Library and Archives.

1960s. In this latter system, a county might be entitled to three representatives, each running countywide and representing the whole county rather than a portion of that county. In Tennessee, any House district that extends across more than one county must consist of adjoining counties. Section 6 outlines a similar set of rules for drawing district lines. These provisions express a strong preference for preserving the county as a unit underlying representation when possible.

The Tennessee Constitution is quite specific about legislative sessions, specifying that in January of odd-numbered years a newly elected General Assembly will meet to organize itself. This session will last no longer than fifteen calendar days. It is in this organizational session that the speakers of the House and Senate are chosen and committee appointments made. However, no legislation can be considered for final passage during this organizational session. The regular session begins on the first Tuesday following the organizational session unless majorities of both houses wish to begin earlier. The legislative article also specifies the eligibility criteria for service as a representative or senator and the procedure for filling vacant seats.

The Tennessee Constitution is also quite specific in regard to the legislative process. Unlike the U.S. Congress, the state legislature each year must enact a balanced budget, with debt allowed only for the construction of state buildings and roads.

Article II, Section 17, provides that "no bill shall become a law which embraces more than one subject, that subject to be expressed in the title." For the most part, this requirement has been interpreted liberally. However, in 1997, the Tennessee Supreme Court struck down a controversial state law that dramatically reduced the requirements for municipal incorporation. The court relied on Article II, Section 17, holding that the content of the act was broader than its restrictive caption.[53]

Taxation

Article II, Section 28, goes into great detail concerning taxation. The intent is obvious—to limit the General Assembly's options. The state constitution allows the General Assembly to collect sales taxes and to set their rates. No provision is made for a general income tax, although the legislature is permitted to tax dividends paid from stocks and bonds. In 1932, the Tennessee Supreme Court held that the state constitution prohibits the imposition of a state income tax.[54] However, the Tennessee Attorney General since has opined that only a graduated, as opposed to a flat-rate, income tax is prohibited.[55]

Although there is no property tax at the state level, the state constitution regulates property taxation by local governments. All property in the state is classified into three categories—real property, tangible personal property, and intangible personal property. The categories form the guidelines for collecting a property tax. Rates for such taxes are set by cities and counties, with the amount of the property subject to taxation depending upon its classification. Real property classifications have proven controversial over the years. For instance, property of public utilities such as phone companies and railroads is assessed, for tax purposes, at 55 percent of its actual value, while industrial and business property is assessed at only 40 percent. Such limits adversely affect cities and counties, who rely heavily on the property tax.

Article III: The Governor

The Tennessee Constitution has somewhat less to say about the Governor than about the General Assembly. The authors of state constitutions typically saw the need to limit the powers of future legislative bodies, as they are responsible for the passage of laws. It is not necessary to so limit the Governor, who can sign only what the General Assembly passes. Rather, it is necessary to provide checks on the chief executive's vast appointment powers.

The Governor must be thirty years old and have lived in Tennessee for seven years prior to election. He or she is elected for a term of four years and can serve only two consecutive terms. The state constitution lists the powers of the Governor. These include the role of commander-in-chief of the militia (today, the National Guard), which can be called out only in the case of "rebellion or invasion" after a determination by the General Assembly that public safety requires it. The Governor also is given the power to pardon and reprieve those convicted of any crime other than impeachment.

Sections 9 through 12 go to the powers of the Governor relative to the General Assembly. The Governor has the power to call the General Assembly into a special session. However, if the Governor makes such a call, he must specify the subject matter the assembly can consider, and the House and Senate are limited to the subject of the call. In 1997, there was some speculation that Gov. Don Sundquist would call the legislature into session to consider the privatization of prisons, but he made no such call. However, in the fall of 1999 and the spring of 2000, Sundquist called the legislature into special sessions to consider reform of the state's tax structure (see chapter 14).

The Governor also is required periodically to inform the General Assembly about the state of government and his recommendations for legislation. Most Governors meet this obligation by delivering a "State of the State" address prior to the opening of the legislative session each February. This speech has become the Tennessee equivalent of the United States President's annual "State of the Union" speech.

Tennessee's constitution provides for transition of power in case the Governor is removed from office, resigns, or dies. While many states elect a Lieutenant Governor to serve this function, Tennessee places the Speaker of the Senate next in line. For this reason, the Speaker of the Senate often is referred to as "Governor." Long-time Speaker John Wilder is popularly known as "Governor Wilder." The Speaker of the House is next in the line of succession.

There are other members of the executive branch who are not appointed by the Governor. Section 17 authorizes the position of Secretary of State, who is chosen by the General Assembly for a four-year term. The person holding this office is required to keep a record of all the official acts of the state.

Section 18 outlines the governor's veto power. Once the General Assembly passes a bill, it is presented to the governor for signing. If he signs the bill, it becomes law. However, the Governor can return it to the House where the bill was first introduced with specific objections. At this point, the House or Senate can begin reconsidering the vetoed bill. If a majority of the membership of both houses votes again for the bill, it shall become law. This system limits the Tennessee governor's veto power; in the federal system, two-thirds of the members of the House and Senate are required to override a presidential veto. No "supermajority" is required to override a Tennessee governor's veto.

The governor does have the option of neither signing nor returning the bill. If the Governor chooses to ignore the bill, it becomes law within ten days. This holds even if the legislature has adjourned. However, if the governor vetoes a bill after the legislature adjourns, the bill does not become law.

Using what is referred to as the "line-item" veto, the Governor can reduce or eliminate any spending item in a larger bill while letting the rest of the bill become law. The General Assembly has the opportunity to override a line-item veto by simple majorities in both houses.

Article IV: Elections and Voting

The Tennessee Constitution sets the voting age at eighteen years. Most other requirements for voting are left to the General Assembly, with the provision that they must be uniform across the state. The General Assembly is given leeway to exclude those having committed "infamous crimes" from voting. Accordingly, it has enacted the following provision:

> Upon conviction for any felony, it shall be the judgment of the court that the defendant be infamous and be immediately disqualified from exercising the right of suffrage. No person so convicted shall be disqualified to testify in any action, civil or criminal, by reason of having been convicted of any felony, and the fact of conviction for any felony may only be used as a reflection upon the person's credibility as a witness.[56]

Article V: Impeachments

Impeachment is the term used to describe the formal process for removing an elected or appointed official from office, usually for a serious breach of ethical conduct. Because impeachment can involve overturning the results of a public election, the process includes checks and balances among the three branches of government to insure that impeachment will be initiated only in the most serious circumstances. Impeachment in Tennessee parallels the federal model. Those liable for impeachment include the Governor, Supreme Court judges, other state judges (including chancellors), the Treasurer, the Comptroller, and the Secretary of State. Impeachment extends to any crimes or serious breaches of conduct committed while acting in an official capacity.

The House of Representatives, by majority vote, must adopt an article of impeachment. Such a vote does not mean a person is guilty, only that enough evidence exists to warrant a trial. The House chooses three members from among its ranks to prosecute the impeachment. The trial is then held in the Tennessee Senate and is presided over by the Chief Justice of the Tennessee Supreme Court, unless the Chief Justice is the individual under impeachment. In such a case, the senior associate justice presides. Two-thirds of the senators must vote to remove an official from office. If removed by impeachment, an individual is barred permanently from holding state office. The impeachment process has been used rarely in this state.[57] The most recent instance was in 1958, when Raulston Schoolfield, a criminal court judge, was impeached and removed from office for bribery and other misconduct.[58]

Article VI: The Judiciary

Unlike the legislative and executive branches, the Tennessee Constitution does not provide for a unified or even particularly logical judicial branch. In 1970 and 1978, proposed constitutional amendments to modernize the judiciary failed to gather the necessary electoral support. The result is one of the most complex and confusing court systems in the nation.

The state constitution establishes one Supreme Court and authorizes the General Assembly to establish Circuit, Chancery, and other "inferior courts."[59] The Supreme Court consists of five justices, but no more than two can live in any one of the state's three grand divisions. Here the state constitution explicitly recognizes the state's political regionalism. The justices choose the Chief Justice from among themselves.

To reach a legal decision, the constitution mandates agreement among three judges. The Supreme Court hears only appeals of lower court decisions. The manner of choosing Supreme Court judges is left up to the General Assembly, with the provision that they indeed must stand for election. A recurring debate among legislators, Governors, and judges is whether this "election" should mean statewide election between candidates or a simple "yes or no" referendum by the public on their performance. Tennessee has used both methods, with the latter currently in effect. Supreme Court and appellate judges, who must be thirty-five years old and have been a resident of the state for five years before appointment, serve for eight years. Judges for Circuit, Chancery, and other lower courts also must be elected in the districts they serve. They too serve for eight years.

State Attorney General and District Attorneys General

The Attorney General (AG) represents the State of Tennessee in civil litigation and criminal appeals. The AG also provides formal opinions interpreting state statutes and provisions of the state constitution. The consequences of these rulings range from insignificant to far-reaching, such as whether the state constitution prohibits the legislature from enacting a tax on income. The AG also is designated as the official reporter of judicial decisions in the state.

Most American states elect an attorney general. Tennessee does not. Article VI, Section 5, describes Tennessee's unique method of choosing its chief lawyer. The justices of the Supreme Court appoint the Attorney General for a period of eight years. Some critics charge that this violates the separation of powers, in that an attorney general is normally thought of as an executive officer. Yet there is little prospect that this unusual method of selection will be changed.

District Attorneys General prosecute criminal cases at the trial level. According to Article VI, Section 5, they are elected to eight-year terms by the voters in their respective judicial districts. If a District AG refuses or fails to prosecute a case, an Attorney Pro Tempore can be appointed by the state's Supreme Court. Unlike the United States Congress, the Tennessee General Assembly has no power to appoint a special prosecutor.[60]

Article VII: State and County Officers

Much of the conflict in the General Assembly involves counties, cities, and towns. These units are creatures of the state and enjoy no sovereignty other than that which the state provides. This feature is unlike the role of the states in the American federal system, where the states are guaranteed certain rights relative to the national government. The State of Tennessee controls its local governments, to the extent that the state constitution even specifies the structure of local government and identifies a number of officials that county voters must elect. Article VII, Section 1, refers to the county "legislative body" and six executive officers: the county executive, the sheriff, the trustee, the register, the county clerk, and the property assessor.

- The county executive is the chief executive official for the county. Prior to 1977, the executive and legislative power of the county were vested in a county court. In 1977, the county court was abolished and a new form of county government instituted, one that vests executive power in the county executive and legislative power in the county commission.
- The sheriff is the chief law enforcement officer and jailer for the county.
- The trustee is the treasurer for the county.
- The register is the custodian of deeds, mortgages, and other documents relating to land ownership.

- The county clerk issues marriage, hunting, and fishing licenses; handles automobile titles and registrations; and collects taxes for automobile sales and business taxes, among other things.
- The property assessor determines the value of land and other real property for the purpose of collecting property taxes.

The qualifications for each of these offices and their associated duties are left to the General Assembly. All of these officers are elected by the voters and hold office for four years. County commissions must be chosen from districts whose boundaries are redrawn every ten years to reflect population changes. No more than three members may be assigned to each district, with a maximum commission size of twenty-five members. The General Assembly may provide for other ways of organizing county government and may allow a county to vote on a new charter. When a vacancy occurs, the commission chooses a successor to serve until the next county election.

State Constitutional Officers

Article VII, Section 3, turns abruptly to state-level constitutional officers—Treasurer, Comptroller, and Secretary of State.

- The Treasurer oversees the receipt and expenditure of all state funds.
- The Comptroller is the principal auditor and general financial manager of the state.
- The Secretary of State is the official repository for official state records.

Each of these officers is independent of the Governor, as they are elected to four-year terms by the House and Senate in joint session. All serve functions as staff and advisors to the legislative leadership and, depending on relationships, to the Governor.

Article VIII: The Militia

Article VIII sets forth requirements for election of militia officers and appointment of the Adjutant General and other staff officers. The section also exempts citizens belonging to religious sects opposing the bearing of arms from attending "musters." When the Tennessee Constitution was adopted in 1796, the militia was an essential component of state government. The authors of the constitution expected that the militia would be called into service in case of war, rebellion, or Indian uprising. Today, the state militia has been superseded by the National Guard. The Governor is responsible for appointing an Adjutant General, a cabinet-level position, to manage the National Guard.

Article IX: Disqualifications

As noted earlier, the original language of Article IX, Section 1, prohibited priests and ministers from serving in the state legislature, a provision that the U.S. Supreme Court declared unconstitutional in 1978. Section 2 provides that "no atheist shall hold a civil office" in the state. While the U.S. Supreme Court has not ruled on this Tennessee provision, it has struck down a provision of the Maryland Constitution requiring officeholders to declare their belief in God.[61] Presumably, if enforced, the Tennessee constitutional prohibition on atheists holding public office would be declared invalid as well.

Article X: Oaths of Office, Electoral Bribery, and New Counties

Article X, Section 1, requires all public officials, whether elected or appointed, to take an oath supporting the state and federal constitutions. Section 2 specifies a particular oath for members of the General Assembly, in which members swear (or affirm) that they will "vote without favor, affection, partiality, or prejudice" and that they will not propose or support legislation that is "injurious to the people" or abridges citizens' constitutional rights.

Article X, Section 3, prohibits electoral bribery—i.e., giving or receiving things of value in exchange for votes. The language requires the legislature to criminalize electoral bribery and bars persons who commit this offense from holding public office for a period of six years.

Creation of New Counties

Article X, Section 4, authorizes the General Assembly to establish new counties. The provision was important in the early years of statehood; however, it is less important today. New counties must encompass at least 275 square miles. No other county can be reduced to less than 500 square miles to form a new county. When a new county is proposed, at least two-thirds of voters in the area to constitute the new county must approve. At present, Tennessee has ninety-five counties, and there is little likelihood that any new counties will be created. Indeed, since the development of a modern system of roads and communication, a strong argument could be made for the consolidation of many existing counties, although such an argument is unlikely to engender much political support. A more likely form of consolidation is the merger of city and county governments within a county, as has occurred with Nashville and Davidson County.

Article XI: Miscellaneous Provisions

Article XI contains a number of provisions, some of which are fairly unimportant today. Provisions prohibiting the legislature from granting divorces[62] or changing the names of persons[63] are apt to generate furrowed brows or even chuckles. But Article XI contains several provisions that continue to have great importance in Tennessee politics. One of these is found in Section 3, "Amendments to the Constitution."

Amending the Constitution

The manner of changing the Tennessee Constitution always has been controversial. The document does not allow for an "initiative and referendum" process in which a specified number of registered voters can petition to place a certain question on the ballot of a scheduled election. California is particularly well known for the ease with which it is possible to place constitutional changes on the ballot there.

Tennessee's constitution is particularly difficult to change. Any move to change the constitution must originate in the General Assembly. The legislature can initiate the process in either of two ways. The first is by voting to place a particular amendment to the Tennessee Constitution on the state ballot. This is not a simple process. To begin with, a majority of all elected members of the House and Senate must vote in favor of the proposed amendment. That done, the amendment is held in abeyance until a new General Assembly is elected. The new legislature then must reconsider the proposed amendment and adopt it, with precisely the same language, with a two-thirds majority of those elected to both houses. If the amendment clears both these hurdles, it is placed on the ballot at the time of the next Governor's election, at which time it must receive a number of popular votes greater than half the votes cast in the election for Governor. In practical terms, that means that a person going to the polls and voting for Governor while skipping the amendment vote counts as a "No" on the amendment.

The second method of amending the Tennessee Constitution involves calling a constitutional convention to propose amendments later to be submitted to the public. The General Assembly, by majority vote, may choose to place a "call" for a convention on the ballot of any general election. The call can be either general, allowing for a total rewrite of the state constitution; or specific, with the proposed convention limited to considering only a part of the constitution. The question of whether to have a constitutional convention is then placed on the ballot of a statewide election. If a simple majority of those voting in that election approve, the process moves to the next step.

Once the Tennessee electorate has approved, another election must take place, this time to choose delegates to the convention. The state constitution entrusts to the General Assembly the authority to establish the delegate selection process. In the 1953 convention, one delegate was chosen from each of the thirty-three state Senate districts. If the delegates approve a change to the constitution, the proposed amendment is submitted to the voters in an election designated by the General Assembly. A proposed amendment receiving a majority vote becomes part of the constitution. Historically, it has been common practice for Tennessee voters in a given election to approve some proposed amendments and reject others. Conventions can be held only once in a six-year period.

Prohibition of Lotteries

Because nearby states, such as Georgia and Kentucky, use state-sponsored lotteries to raise revenue, there has been considerable interest in establishing a lottery in Tennessee. In fact, since the early 1980s, public opinion has become increasingly supportive of establishing a state lottery. Article XI, Section 5, of the Tennessee Constitution states: "The Legislature shall have no power to authorize lotteries for any purpose, and shall pass laws to prohibit the sale of lotteries for any purpose, and shall pass laws to prohibit the sale of lottery tickets in this state." The language is a legacy of the turmoil caused in the nineteenth century when dozens of Tennessee counties established poorly managed and often corrupt lotteries. In the 1990s, there were a number of attempts to remove the lottery prohibition from the state constitution. The proposed amendments received the needed two-thirds approval in the House, but failed to gain the required two-thirds vote in the Senate. In February 2001, the General Assembly approved a resolution to hold a statewide referendum on the question of a state lottery. If approved by the voters in November 2002, the measure would change the state's constitution to allow the establishment of a state lottery, the proceeds of which would be earmarked for education.

Provisions Governing Cities and Counties

Article XI, Section 9, contains four distinctive parts relating to local government. The first paragraph of the section authorizes the General Assembly to delegate powers to cities and counties. The second paragraph protects local governments by prohibiting the General Assembly from passing special acts removing local officials or reducing their salaries or terms of office. The section also requires that any special act affecting a particular local government be approved by a two-thirds majority of the local legislative body. The third part of Section 9, which includes paragraphs 3 through 8, authorizes municipalities to establish "home rule," which further insulates a municipality from state legislative control. Home rule permits cities to amend or replace their charters without the approval of the General Assembly.

The final paragraph of Section 9 allows for consolidation of city and county governments, as long as the merger is approved by concurrent majorities of city voters and county voters outside the city. This happened in 1961, when voters approved the merger of Nashville and Davidson County governments. In Knoxville, however, voters have rejected unification of city and county government four times, most recently in 1996.[64]

Public Education

Article XI, Section 12, "recognizes the inherent value of education and encourages its support." The General Assembly is charged with maintaining a public school system and authorized to support a higher education system. Does this language confer upon Tennesseans a fundamental right to an adequate and free public education? In 1988, an association of smaller school districts brought suit in Chancery Court in Nashville to challenge the constitutionality of the existing system for funding public education in the state. Plaintiffs argued that the existing system, in which there were large funding discrepancies among the state's 139 school districts, violated students' fundamental right to a public education as well as the equal protection requirements of the state constitution. In 1991, Chancellor C. Allen High ruled in favor of the plaintiffs and ordered the General Assembly to reformulate its plan for funding public schools. In 1993, the Tennessee Supreme Court upheld the Chancellor's decision, noting that the state constitution "contemplates that the power granted to the General Assembly will be exercised to accomplish the mandated result, a public school system that provides substantially equal educational opportunities to the school children of Tennessee."[65] Reformers applauded the state judiciary for "kick-starting" the process of educational reform. Others characterized the court's unprecedented decision as "judicial activism." In any event, the court's ruling prompted educational reform by the governor and the legislature. The result was higher levels of expenditures for the state's public schools, accompanied by higher expectations regarding their performance (for additional discussion, see chapter 11).

Assessing the Constitution

The Tennessee Constitution has provided the basis of the state's government since 1796, with only two substantial revisions. The state's three constitutions have worked reasonably well, even though the relative influence and power of the executive and legislative branches have shifted considerably during the state's history. Tennessee's constitution differs from those in several other states in that the document is quite difficult to amend. The authors of the document provided no initiative or referendum procedure. Moreover, they insured that the legislative action necessary to allow a popular vote to change the Tennessee Constitution is prolonged and difficult.

How one evaluates Tennessee's constitution depends to some extent on one's priorities. That there have been relatively few attempts to amend the constitution is evidence that the document is, on the whole, well conceived and flexible enough to adapt to economic and social change. The constitution has not been an impediment to economic growth since the method of taxing property was changed in the 1830s. Personal freedoms generally are equal to or greater than in other states. The constitution's requirement of a balanced budget long has been an asset to sound management of state government.

Despite these positive attributes, the Tennessee Constitution is not without flaws. The state's judicial system remains an outdated hodgepodge of courts that is confusing to most Tennesseans. The Attorney General's lack of constitutional authority to prosecute most crimes has made it difficult on occasion to address the problem of modern organized crime. The constitution's lack of emphasis on public education has contributed to poor educational quality in many areas of the state. Finally, the constitution's vague language regarding whether the General Assembly can enact a tax on personal income has left in serious doubt one of the issues most important for the future of state government.

In the end, one must weigh the state constitution's strengths and weaknesses in the context of two centuries that witnessed civil war, economic turmoil, and the transformation of Tennessee from a rural frontier to a modern industrial society. In this context, Tennessee must be viewed as one of the world's two dozen oldest democracies, with a constitution that has weathered the test of time quite well.

Part II

INSTITUTIONS OF TENNESSEE GOVERNMENT

3

The General Assembly

The darkness of the room surprises a visitor upon entering the private office of John Wilder, Speaker of the Tennessee Senate. The eyes are immediately drawn to the single recessed light shining down on the Speaker's chair. In the dim light, two art pieces dominate the walls. Opposite the Speaker's desk is a traditional painting of Thomas Jefferson. Immediately to the Speaker's right, a second painting shows what appears to be a well-dressed business executive listening intently to Jesus Christ, who is seated in a leather chair by his desk.

The Traditionalist Senate

John Wilder personifies one of the two political currents that together define the culture of the Tennessee General Assembly. A genuinely kind person, Wilder is an attorney and the owner of a cotton plantation and cotton gin on the Mississippi border. John Wilder has been Speaker of the Senate for thirty years, longer than any Senate or House speaker in the United States. First elected to the Senate in the early 1960s by a coalition of blacks and progressive whites, Wilder was a central figure in the turmoil that accompanied integration efforts in Fayette County,

Tennessee's only county with a majority-black population. Wilder's willingness to stand up on behalf of universal voting rights ensured lasting support from the region's black political activists, among them A. C. Wharton, a young Memphis attorney who three decades years later would become Shelby County Public Defender and the first black chairman of the Tennessee Higher Education Commission.

Wilder's political career and philosophical evolution in many ways mirror that of the Tennessee Senate. Staunchly pro-business, he fashioned a working coalition among Democrat and Republican senators who shared his notion that the legislature has an obligation to fiscal and moral conservatism, a close working relationship with the Governor, and the avoidance of partisan confrontation whenever possible. For twenty-four of his thirty years as Speaker, Wilder's Finance Chairman has been Douglas Henry. A patrician Democrat from Nashville who speaks French and classical Greek, Henry's wealth, Vanderbilt education, and genteel courtesy on the Senate floor would have made him as at home in the nineteenth century as today. Although an adamant foe of efforts to adopt a tax on income and lower the state's regressive sales tax, Henry has long been the Senate's most consistent champion of social services for the poor.

Wilder's closest legislative ally is Ben Atchley of Knoxville, leader of the Senate Republicans. The unusual relationship between the Democratic Speaker and the Republican leader resulted from efforts by a majority of Senate Democrats in 1987 to oust Wilder, whose leadership skills had been called into question by younger and more partisan members of the Democratic Caucus. After the caucus refused to renominate him for Speaker, Wilder persuaded six of his fellow Democratic senators to bolt the caucus and form an alliance with the Senate's ten Republicans. Wilder was reelected Speaker by one vote, whereupon he appointed the six loyal Democrats and three Republicans as committee chairs. Although some three years of bitter feelings followed, Wilder's position and power as Speaker have since never been challenged. Republicans have held a majority in the Senate for only two of Wilder's thirty years, yet the Senate has rarely posed a serious problem for the legislative initiatives of three Republican governors.

A More Diverse and More Activist House

The one hundred feet from Wilder's office to the House Speaker's office belie the gulf that often exists between the Tennessee House and Senate. More activist, more diverse, and less concerned with the protocol

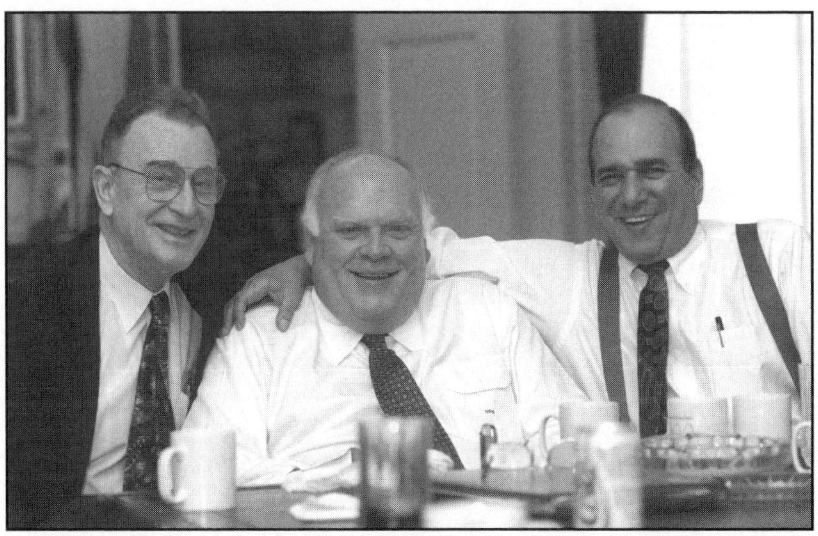

Fig. 3.1. John Wilder, Ned Ray McWherter, and Jimmy Naifeh, three of the most influential personalities in Tennessee politics in recent years. *Source:* State of Tennessee Photographic Services.

of decorum, the House in many ways represents the alternate political current in the Tennessee General Assembly. The House Speaker is West Tennessee Democrat Jimmy Naifeh, son of a Lebanese immigrant. Twenty years younger than Wilder, Naifeh perfected his legislative skills as Majority Leader under two former speakers. Naifeh's Speaker Pro Tempore is Lois DeBerry, a black woman first elected from inner-city Memphis in 1972. DeBerry is a dynamic speaker, moving easily from the House podium on Thursday to the pulpit on Sunday. Naifeh's Finance Chairman is Matt Kisber, a young Jewish businessman from Jackson educated at Vanderbilt University and born six years after his Senate counterpart was first elected to the legislature. The diversity evident in a man of Arab descent, a Jew, and a black female being at the center of the House leadership reflects a markedly different Tennessee that has emerged in the last two decades of the twentieth century.

Relative Legislative Harmony

The convergence of two political cultures—the largely traditionalist Senate and a less ideological, more aggressive House—has produced a legislature with a unique and somewhat inconsistent blend of fiscal conservatism, bipartisan cooperation, and innovative social policy rarely duplicated in other southern legislatures. In some states, political decisions are most often played out in the context of the legislature versus the Governor. Other states find legislative decisions motivated by more partisan concerns. In either instance, the politics of race can sometimes override less emotional factors. For two primary reasons, policy decisions in the Tennessee legislature are less often motivated by partisan, racial, or constitutional jealousies.

One explanation for Tennessee's relative legislative harmony is the influence of demographic features. Among the most important is the size and location of Tennessee's black population. At 16 percent, Tennessee's black population is the smallest of the eleven states in the Old Confederacy. Even more important in the political context, one-half of all black Tennesseans live in Memphis and surrounding Shelby County. While tensions associated with school integration in the 1970s surfaced in several communities, particularly Memphis, Nashville, Chattanooga, and Jackson, the presence of a relatively small black population statewide has meant that contemporary legislative issues are less often accompanied by racial overtones. Even Tennessee's white population is largely homogenous. Compared to most American cities their size, Tennessee's four metropolitan centers have comparably few Hispanics, Asians, or other ethnic groups. A quick glance through the directory of state legislators underscores what Tennessee is: overwhelmingly Western European and Protestant. While the House leadership demonstrates that each decade brings a gradual change to this face, the commonality of background and values among Tennessee legislators has played an important role in their ability to reach consensus on a variety of controversial issues.

Molded by Two Personalities

A second reason for Tennessee's unique nonpartisan brand of legislative politics can be traced to the legacy of two leaders whose personality and philosophy had an extraordinary influence on the legislature's political identity. John Wilder's election in 1971 as Speaker of the Senate was followed in 1973 by the election of another rural West Tennessee Democrat, Ned McWherter, as Speaker of the House. Many states, such as Florida, find it common for the Speaker's position to rotate every one or two terms. Indeed, Tennessee had the same pattern until Wilder and McWherter, who from 1973 served together as unchallenged leaders of the House and Senate for fourteen unbroken years.

Although McWherter on occasion took notable exception with Republican governors on such issues as the location of a new medical school or the priorities of a road construction program, the overview of those fourteen years provides an unmistakable pattern of fiscal conservatism and bipartisan cooperation with the executive branch on substantive budgetary and policy matters. Throughout this period, both Wilder and McWherter deemed off limits any attempts to play partisan games with the state's fiscal policies. Equally important, humiliation of legislative opponents was not tolerated. Neither of the two Democrats would allow projects of helpful Republican legislators to be rejected on partisan grounds. Both speakers protected incumbent Republicans as well as Democrats during the emotional process of legislative reapportionment. For these reasons, each was able to construct an effective and enduring bipartisan coalition. A lasting benefit of the Wilder-McWherter legacy is the culture of civility that in most years sets Tennessee apart from other, more acrimonious, state legislatures.

Like Wilder, McWherter (fig. 3.1) had a knowledgeable and conservative ally, John Bragg, a printer from Murfreesboro who served as House Finance Chairman from 1973 to 1996. Balanced budgets were passed on time without accounting gimmicks or the need for special sessions. To discourage debt generated by the excessive use of bonds for construction projects, a statute enacted at the initiative of McWherter and Bragg required that all bonded projects be accompanied by the appropriation of the first year's debt service. Putting a halt to special interest retirement legislation strengthened the state's pension fund to the point that Tennessee's retirement system became one of only a handful among the states to be fully funded. Such fiscal policies were unnoticed by most of the public. They were, however, well received on Wall Street, where a low debt and strong pension system placed Tennessee among fewer than a dozen states with a AAA bond rating. By the early 1980s, Tennessee had established a deserved reputation for fiscal discipline.[1] The reputation was unchallenged until the emergence of consistent revenue shortfalls at the turn of the century.

A Strategy of Nonpartisan Conservatism

While the development of Tennessee's nonpartisan fiscal conservatism in the 1970s and 1980s was a philosophical product of two speakers and two finance chairmen, fiscal policy was also part of a conscious strategy to stimulate economic growth. Both Wilder and McWherter believed that as a poor state, Tennessee's chances of attracting new industry and personal income growth were enhanced by providing a conservative climate for foreign and domestic investment. After fourteen years of emphasis on this strategy by the two speakers, a majority of the legislature came to address most major policy decisions against the backdrop of this philosophy. Thus, from the early 1970s until the late 1990s, the bitter budgetary debates that divide many state legislatures became a secondary aspect of the political process in Tennessee. With the exception of a minor rebellion in the House by the party's right wing in 1991, Republican legislators voted overwhelmingly for the budgets of Democratic governors. Until 1999, their Democratic counterparts consistently voted for the budgetary initiatives of Republican governors. The annual appropriations bills recommended by the respective governors were rarely modified by more than 1 or 2 percent, most often in the form of a small additional raise for teachers and state employees or minor pork-barrel projects.[2] Gov. Don Sundquist's proposal of a state tax on income in 1999 and 2000 led to a mutiny of both House and Senate Republicans against their Governor. Because revenues for the budget were linked to the unpopular income tax, the debate generated a degree of animosity unfamiliar to most legislators and threatened a generation of partisan cooperation.

The legislature's customary deference to the Governor on budgetary matters has produced a similar willingness on the part of most governors to defer to the legislature on a surprising number of other issues. The pattern of both Democratic and Republican governors has been to refrain from taking sides in a broad range of legislative affairs so long as the consequences do not affect the state's fiscal integrity. Of the three thousand or so bills filed each legislative session, it is common for the administration to take an active position on no more than fifty to one hundred of the bills unless they require state expenditures not contained in the Governor's proposed budget.

The Unspoken Contract

The legacy of John Wilder and Ned McWherter was an unspoken contract between the Governor and the General Assembly that defined the Tennessee legislative process for the last quarter of the twentieth century. Put simply, if the legislature offered its cooperation on budgetary matters and major policy initiatives, the Governor in turn provided the legislature enormous latitude to address remaining legislative issues. In particular, McWherter believed that a strong legislative branch could enhance, rather than threaten, a Governor's power. This fourteen-year working relationship was institutionalized when, after retiring as House Speaker in 1986, McWherter was elected Governor for two four-year terms.

Perhaps no other state in America has seen its legislative process shaped as fully by two individuals, one a Speaker for thirty years, the other a Speaker fourteen years and a Governor for eight years. Neither the Senate, with its bipartisan governing coalition, nor the House, with its substantial Democratic majority, has sought to challenge the assumptions of a process that most observers would contend has served them well. This is not to say that Tennessee's legislative process is better than that of other states, or even that the process in place at the end of the 1990s will survive far into the twenty-first century. It does suggest, however, that one must take care when examining why, despite a leadership that appears to represent all that is conservative and traditionalist, Tennessee in the 1980s and 1990s has been in the forefront of some of the nation's most ambitious and creative policies. In this chapter, we examine the peculiar culture of the Tennessee legislature, including an analysis of its powers, its customs and its gradual movement toward a more pluralistic and professional institution.

Constitutional Framework

Since achieving statehood in 1796, the Tennessee General Assembly has been composed of two chambers, the House and Senate. The post–Civil War Constitution of 1870 established the House with ninety-nine members. Oddly, the Constitution did not specify the number of senators, only that the number of senators would not exceed one-third the number of representatives. The Senate has thirty-three members.[3]

Qualifications for the General Assembly

Constitutional qualifications for the General Assembly are few. A legislator must be a citizen of the United States and a citizen of Tennessee for at least three years. Senators must be thirty years of age and representatives at least twenty-one. In recent years the most significant and controversial qualification has been the requirement that a legislator reside in the county or district which "he represents (for) one year immediately preceding the election." This restriction was not a problem for more than a century, when legislative districts did not cross county lines and legislators rarely changed their residence. As urban districts experienced demographic changes in the 1970s, some legislators sought reelection after moving their residence outside the district but continuing to reside in the same county. Although a candidate's actual residence is sometimes an issue in a campaign, a legislator must only be a qualified "voter" of a district, meaning in effect that owning property in a district satisfies the Constitution's residency requirement.[4]

Legislators may not hold any office appointed by the Governor or elected by the General Assembly. Most significant, this provision prohibits legislators from serving on state boards and commissions and requires them to resign if appointed to the Governor's cabinet. The Constitution does not prohibit legislators from serving in local government positions such as the city council or school board.

Terms of office are four years for senators and two years for representatives. All ninety-nine House seats are up for election every two years, the primary election coinciding with county elections in August and the general election held on the same day in November as elections for federal officials. Elections for Senate seats are staggered, with seventeen seats up during the year of presidential elections and the remaining sixteen seats two years later. Except in the case of the respective speakers, if a legislator is defeated or is not on the ballot in the November election, the seat is vacated to the successor immediately after the election. Tennessee legislators do not face term limits.

Legislative Sessions

The General Assembly was a biennial legislature until 1968, when it began convening on the second Tuesday in January of each year. Following an election, the legislature convenes for not longer than fifteen days in Organizational Session. Most Organizational Sessions are conducted in three days. The first order of business on Tuesday is the election of the respective speakers and, on rare occasions, a determination of the qualifications of a person involved in a contested election. Wednesday is devoted to the election of three constitutional officers, the Treasurer, the Secretary of State, and the Comptroller of the Treasury. The constitutional officers are elected in joint session of the House and Senate, with each legislator receiving one vote. Because Democrats have held a majority of the combined House and Senate, Republicans in the last quarter of the century have not mounted a serious effort to promote candidates for these offices. The Organizational Session's final day is customarily dedicated to the naming by the speakers of committee chairs and the assignment of members to the respective "standing," or permanent, committees. No legislation can be enacted during an Organizational Session.

The Tennessee Constitution limits the General Assembly to ninety legislative days. As the volume and complexity of legislative issues expanded, the legislature adopted increasingly creative ways of interpreting this limitation. "Legislative days" is now defined as days when the House or Senate are actually in floor session, meaning that days when only legislative committees meet do not count against the Constitution's ninety-day limit. In addition, "legislative days" is construed to mean days in floor session for which legislators can be paid. These two innovative interpretations of the Constitution have enabled the General Assembly to extend its working time by about a third, a practical policy given the move to annual sessions and the enormous expansion of the legislature's agenda.

The General Assembly convenes in regular session on the first Tuesday after the adjournment of the Organizational Session. Most regular sessions conclude their business in May, though on occasion adjournment has occurred as early as April or as late as mid-June. On average, the legislature uses about fifty days of its official legislative days during the odd-numbered year of its two-year session and about forty days the second year, thus providing about three extra weeks for campaigning in an election year. The expiration of the two-year limit of ninety "legislative days" does not require the General Assembly to adjourn or prohibit enactment of legislation. Rather, it simply prohibits the members from being paid while in Nashville. While the legislature on occasion works a much-publicized day or two without pay at the conclusion of the session, the constitutional limit acts as a strong motivation for members to conclude their work and leave town.

The legislative week begins on Monday evening, when the Senate and House convene in floor session. Committees and subcommittees hold meetings throughout the day on Tuesday and on Wednesday morning until about noon. The Senate and House usually meet in floor session on Wednesday afternoon and again on Thursday morning before adjourning for the week. This somewhat unconventional schedule reflects the fact that the Tennessee General Assembly strives to remain a "citizen legislature" in which a large majority of its members have some kind of employment in their hometowns. By beginning the legislative week on Monday night and ending most weeks by noon Thursday, a sizable number of legislators can devote at least a portion of the week to their non-legislative duties.

The Tennessee Constitution authorizes that Extraordinary, or "Special Sessions," of the General Assembly may be convened by the Governor under Article III, Section 9, or by the speakers if they receive a petition signed by two-thirds of the House and Senate members. Unlike many states, Tennessee has rarely convened special sessions of the legislature. Special sessions were called by Gov. Lamar Alexander in 1984 and 1985 to address education and corrections legislation, by Gov. Ned McWherter in 1992 for a joint package of education and tax reform, and by Gov. Don Sundquist in 1999 and 2000 to address tax reform.

Legislative Powers and Functions

Enacting laws and appropriating state funds are the two most important functions of the General Assembly. In addition to these responsibilities, Tennessee's balance of constitutional power provides the legislature oversight of the executive branch, selection of certain public officials, and the discipline of public officials who violate the law.

Fig. 3.2. Chamber of the Tennessee House of Representatives. Photo by John M. Scheb II.

Growing Volume of Legislation

Two facts are central to understanding the role of the Tennessee legislature. The last quarter of the twentieth century witnessed an explosion in the volume of legislation that paralleled an increased willingness by the legislature to become involved in disputes among the state's commercial and local government entities. Second, this surge of legislative activism did not extend to the state budget, where the Governor retained a highly disproportionate influence in determining budget priorities.

In the 85th Session of the General Assembly in 1965–66, 1,078 bills were introduced and 364 were enacted into law. By the Bicentennial Session of 1995–96, the number of bills introduced had tripled to 3,332 and the number enacted to 1,083.[5] No single factor explains this increase in the volume of legislation. The move to annual sessions produced an immediate growth in the number and scope of bills. The creation by the Congress of large federal programs (such as the Clean Air Act, the Clean Water Act, and Medicaid) that were managed by state government introduced new areas of legislative activity. A larger and more professional legislative staff made it possible for legislators to keep up with more bills and undertake more initiatives. Finally, a steady growth in the number of full-time lobbyists contributed to what some contend was a parallel growth in the volume of legislation. Although some of this increase was a natural result of Tennessee's economy becoming more complex, it is fair to say some lobbyists sought to justify their existence by generating issues and legislation that in turn required lobbying services.

A legislator may introduce two kinds of legislation. The most common is a general bill, defined as legislation that applies to all persons and localities in the state. The General Assembly spends approximately 90 percent of its time addressing general bills. In the average session, about 20 percent of the legislation enacted consists of local bills, or private acts, that apply only to a single county or municipality. Private acts are usually introduced by a legislator at the request of the local governing body, such as the city council or the county commission. Examples of private acts might be a proposal to raise a county's restaurant tax or adjust the salaries of a local official. Some view as outdated the requirement that local governments must seek legislative approval for what are essentially local decisions. One finds divided opinions among legislators, some of whom would like to avoid being caught in the middle of local controversies and others who relish their influence and leverage over local policies. Because protocol urges unanimity among a county's legislative delegation prior to passage of a private act in the House or Senate, the objection of a single legislator at times can impede the passage of a local bill.

State Budget

The single most important item of any legislative session is the Appropriations Bill containing the Governor's proposed budget for the coming fiscal year. The Appropriations Bill is co-sponsored by senior legislators from the Governor's party. In the event the budget is predicated upon passage of a tax increase, the Appropriations Bill and the tax legislation travel in tandem through the legislative process. Although the Appropriations Bill is subject to extensive discussion and hearings, the history of both the House and Senate is that only the most senior Democrat and Republican legislators participate in budgetary decision making. Legislators file hundreds of budget amendments, knowing they likely will not be adopted but hoping they will be interpreted by the folks back home as a good-faith effort. Most public budget debates become focused on one or two high-profile issues, such as whether state employees receive a 2 or 3 percent raise or whether the Governor is permitted to reduce the Housing Development Authority budget by $75 million or $45 million. On such issues, the legislature usually prevails. Meanwhile, the hundreds of remaining items in the Appropriations Bill, including billions of dollars for schools, roads, health care, prisons, and state parks, go essentially unchanged by the legislative process. This legislative deference to the Governor on budgetary matters is the single most defining characteristic of the Tennessee General Assembly (fig. 3.2).

Oversight of the Executive Branch

The legislature devotes a significant portion of its time to oversight of the executive branch, or, more accurately, to oversight of specific programs in the executive branch. The earliest formal approach to legislative oversight was the creation in 1967 of the Fiscal Review Committee, composed of senior Democrats and Republicans elected by their peers from the House and Senate. With a full-time nonpartisan staff, the Fiscal Review Committee meets monthly throughout the year to examine policy concerns or the fiscal status of various state programs. Coinciding with the administration of Republican Governor Lamar Alexander, the legislature established a new entity, the joint oversight committee, to monitor on a regular basis large areas of executive branch policy. Oversight committees have both House and Senate members, and thus to some extent lessen the proliferation of staff and the number of committee meetings. The first such effort, the Education Oversight Committee, was created in 1984 after enactment of Alexander's education reform package and the accompanying one-cent increase in the state sales tax. Created ostensibly to monitor the implementation of Alexander's controversial teacher evaluation plan, the Education Oversight Committee evolved over time as a legislative vehicle to address all aspects of K–12 and higher education. The federal court's takeover of Tennessee's prisons in 1985 led to the creation of the Corrections Oversight Committee. Established initially to oversee major policy decisions such as prison construction and prison industries, the Corrections Oversight Committee later attracted national attention during attempts to privatize much of the state's prison system. The TennCare Oversight Committee was established in 1992 after Democratic Governor Ned McWherter's radical reform of the state's Medicaid program. Although other standing and select committees from time to time review and comment on executive branch initiatives, only one—the Joint Government Operations Committee—has developed the stature and influence approaching that of the Fiscal Review Committee and the three oversight committees.

The Joint Government Operations Committee saw its importance and influence on executive branch policy rise and fall in the decade after it became a standing committee. When first established by the General Assembly in 1977, the House and Senate Government Operations committees represented the boldest effort yet to exercise legislative authority over the administration. Meeting monthly, the Joint Government Operations Committee was empowered to approve or reject any of the hundreds of proposed rules and regulations from state agencies or higher education institutions. The aim was to curb the proliferation of regulations that had the force of law but which may have been outside the intent of the authorizing legislation. The committee took its mandate seriously. Dozens of rules were rejected, a process that in turn motivated agencies to reduce the volume and scope of rules with marginal justification. However, in Tennessee as elsewhere, the rule-making process did not withstand a constitutional challenge to its infringement on the powers of the executive branch.

The elimination of its rule-making powers left the Government Operations Committee to shift its emphasis to the "sunset review" process, another effort by the legislature to extend oversight to the executive branch. In theory, state government would be reduced if every state agency, from the Board of Cosmetology to the Department of Correction, was required every seven years to undergo a thorough examination of its purpose and the extent to which it had fulfilled its statutory obligations. Although its goals were noble, the attempt to take on such an enormous task meant that few agencies could receive a meaningful evaluation. Minor recommendations were adopted and implemented, but on the whole the work of the Joint Government Operations Committee and its influence over the executive branch never met the expectations that accompanied the committee's creation.

Election of Constitutional Officers and Ratification of Nominees

Unlike some states, Tennessee does not conduct popular elections for its Treasurer, Comptroller, and Secretary of State. Each of these important posts is filled through an election held in joint session by the House and Senate. For obvious reasons, the persons who occupy these constitutional offices are close to the legislative leadership, particularly of the majority party. They are, in effect, senior advisors to the legislature, and their staffs are available to assist in a host of legislative activities.

Discipline of Public Officials

While the Tennessee legislature has rarely used its power to disapprove gubernatorial nominations, the legislative branch on occasion has exercised its authority to discipline members of the executive, legislative, or judicial branches. Since 1975, the House has expelled one member for criminal violations and forced two others to resign in the face of imminent expulsion. Two judges have been impeached for breaches of ethical conduct, including a member of the state Criminal Court of Appeals who wrote to a pornographic magazine on court stationery. What was easily the most famous case of legislative "discipline" occurred in 1979, when the speakers of the Senate and House joined to administer the oath of office three days early to Governor-elect Lamar Alexander. The extraordinary event was designed to revoke the powers of outgoing Gov. Ray Blanton, who had vowed to pardon dozens of incarcerated criminals before leaving office.

How Laws Are Made

The process of enacting a law in Tennessee is complex and slow, as it was designed to be by the Founding Fathers, who feared the impulsive nature of democracy. Most bills go through the following procedure.

Introduction of Bills

A bill must be filed with an identical "caption" and text in the House and Senate, where it is assigned a bill number by the Chief Clerk. The term "caption" refers to a citation of the Tennessee Code Annotated to be changed by the proposed bill. Unlike Congress, any amendments to a bill must be related to the specific purpose contained in the bill's caption. A bill whose caption pertained only to speed limits, for example, could not be used to sneak in an exemption to the sales tax or raise benefits for retired teachers. A legislator who wishes to protect a bill from amendments drafts a very narrow, or "tight," caption. A legislator who desires for strategic purposes to disguise the intent of a bill files what is termed a "broad" caption that covers large portions of the Code.[6]

First and Second Readings

In the nineteenth century, when each legislative session might consider as few as forty to fifty bills, the legislature required that all bills be read in their entirety three times on three different days prior to passage. The increased volume and complexity of legislation eventually made this rule impractical. Bills today are passed routinely as a group on first and second readings, usually at the end of a day's floor session. The purpose is not to debate their merit, but to make members and the public aware of their introduction. After passage on second reading, the Speaker assigns a bill to a standing committee.

Committee Deliberation

A bill is placed on the committee's calendar at the request of the sponsor and with the approval of the chair. Non-controversial bills may encounter less than a minute's discussion before receiving a recommendation for passage. For more controversial or complicated bills, the chair may invite witnesses to participate in the committee's deliberation. A sympathetic committee may choose either to recommend the bill for passage or to recommend the bill for passage with amendments. If the bill generates or spends state revenues, the bill is sent to the Finance Committee for further consideration. Bills in the House also require approval by the Committee on Calendar and Rules. A cultural legacy of the Tennessee legislature is the unwillingness to embarrass a colleague by openly killing legislation. Although the results are the same, committees often go to great lengths to avoid the appearance of discourtesy by deferring unpopular bills to subcommittees that will never meet. While transparent, such efforts help a legislator save face and thus ease the tension in a process that by its nature can generate personal bitterness.

Floor Deliberation

After receiving a recommendation for passage by the appropriate committees, a bill is scheduled for consideration on the floor calendar. With rare exceptions, no persons other than legislators are allowed to address legislation on the House and Senate floors. If amendments were adopted in committee, each amendment must be taken up and voted on separately. Additional amendments may be proposed on the floor. Passage of amendments requires a majority of those members present and voting. Passage of the complete bill on third reading requires a majority of the entire body—seventeen in the Senate, fifty in the House.

Consideration by the Second Chamber

After passage by either of the chambers, a bill is transmitted to the other chamber, where it lies on the Clerk's desk until receiving a recommendation for passage by committee. To speed up an already laborious process, the Senate and House employ a rule that allows each chamber to consider a bill in its complete form if the bill has already been passed by the other body. For example, if a bill has been passed by the Senate with thirteen amendments, the House may move to "substitute and conform," thus allowing debate to begin on the entire bill as amended instead of requiring debate on each individual amendment. Each chamber retains the right to change any portion of the legislation prior to a vote on third reading.

Conference Committee

If the versions of the bills passed by the two chambers are not identical, one of the chambers must either "recede" or "concur" in the differing language before the bill is enacted. If the differences cannot be reconciled by the full bodies of the House and Senate, the speakers may appoint a conference committee with members from each chamber to resolve disagreements. In Tennessee, unlike many states, a conference committee's authority is not limited, thus allowing the committee if it chooses to rewrite the bill completely. A conference report may not be amended on the Senate or House floor and must receive a majority vote of each chamber.

Consideration by the Governor

If identical versions are passed by both chambers, the bill is sent to the Engrossing Clerk, where all amendments from the House and Senate are inserted to place the bill in its final form. After being officially signed by the House and Senate speakers, the bill is transmitted to the Governor. The Governor has ten working days to sign the bill, veto the bill, or let the bill become law without signature. Vetoed bills are returned to the Senate and House, where they require a majority vote—not the two-thirds required by most states—from both chambers before becoming law.

The Committee System

On spring days in Nashville, when the dogwoods are in bloom, the streets around Capitol Hill are lined with yellow school buses carrying school children to see their state government in action. Many of the children are coming to the State Capitol for the first time. In the case of some rural students from outlying counties, it may also be the first time they have ridden in an elevator. The students usually are taken by their teachers to view the House and Senate in floor session. In the majority of instances, they leave puzzled and a bit cynical. Most of the activity they witness involves mundane issues that the students do not fully understand and which are, frankly, boring. The process rarely includes passionate debate. Legislators frequently read newspapers or walk around the chamber talking to their colleagues. The attention span for the average student visiting the House and Senate chambers is about twenty minutes.

Most students who visit the Capitol do not realize the blandness they see on the House and Senate floors occurs because proposed legislation is subject to an elaborate committee process. In theory, the process is designed to accomplish two goals. First, through a division of labor and expertise, committees provide a mechanism for sifting out the hundreds of bills judged not worthy of consideration by the full House and Senate. The second goal involves a recommendation of remaining bills for passage, either with or without changes. In practice, committees are the true battleground of the legislative process. For a majority of legislative issues, committees are the place where ideologies, special interests, and legislative ambitions collide. Bills are seldom rejected by majority vote of the ninety-nine House members or thirty-three senators. Unsuccessful bills more often fall victim to negative votes in committee, meaning that on occasion a bill's fate may lie in the hands of as few as four or five legislators. The committee system is complex, made more so by the fact that the House and Senate operate with different committee rules. For the legislator who fears the opposition may have more votes, a knowledge of how to manipulate the rules has more than once served to overcome a disadvantage. Until these rules are mastered, no legislator or lobbyist can be fully effective.

Committee Rules

The Senate and House are responsible for establishing committees and adopting the rules and procedures under which they operate.[7] Some aspects of the committee system are common to the House and Senate. Each body has a small number of standing committees, ten in the Senate and thirteen in the House. Standing committees have nine members in the Senate, but House committees vary in size from nine members to more than thirty. Most committees meet once a week. With the exception of the Finance and Calendar committees, standing committees are created to consider legislation limited to specific areas such as education, transportation, or state and local government. The respective speakers assign members to committees and designate the committee officers, comprised of the chair, the vice chair, and the secretary. Most legislators serve on two committees, except for House committee officers, who also serve on the House Committee on Calendar and Rules. The relatively small number of standing committees in Tennessee enables committee schedules to be arranged so that legislators avoid assignment to two committees that meet simultaneously. All bills are assigned to a standing committee by the respective speakers.

The Tennessee legislature has taken strides since the early 1970s to shed the image of back-room deals. Meetings of all standing committees are open to the press and the public. To avoid last-minute surprises, legislators wishing to have their bills considered must file formal notice the previous week with the committee chair. Committee calendars are posted in the halls of the Legislative Plaza and on the Internet to inform legislators, the press and the public about legislation to be considered the following week.

Although the committee system of the House and Senate has a number of relatively minor variations in its rules and procedures, three significant differences illustrate how the two chambers have taken separate paths in the development of the legislative process. In the Tennessee House, as is the case in Congress, all committee chairs and officers are members of the majority party. The tradition dates to 1973, when Ned McWherter needed to promise enough leadership positions to oust an incumbent Speaker.[8] The policy was institutionalized during McWherter's fourteen-year tenure. In the Senate, Republicans have consistently chaired three to four committees since 1987, when their support enabled John Wilder to retain his position as Speaker. A committee chair's authority to create subcommittees, appoint their membership, assign bills to subcommittee, and schedule bill calendars can bring into play the chair's party loyalty as well as relationships with the Governor, the Speaker, and other legislators. While House Republicans have more or less adapted to Democratic dominance in the committee system, Senate Democrats have been known to chafe under a process that, in the name of bipartisan collegiality, at times ignites more partisan sparks than its House counterpart.

The committee system of the House and Senate differs in a second important respect. The Senate Calendar Committee is strictly a scheduling committee for the Senate floor. Made up of three senators, the Calendar Committee cannot block consideration of bills recommended for passage by a standing committee. In contrast, the House Committee on Calendar and Rules must also recommend for passage each bill before being scheduled on the House floor calendar. Because the committee is comprised of officers from the standing committees, the practical effect is that Democrats—or, more accurately, the House Speaker—have enormous leverage over any bill introduced in the General Assembly. The rule is another put in place by McWherter, who used it sparingly but effectively to strengthen his leverage with two Republican governors. An equally important but generally less recognized benefit is the Speaker's ability to hold in check special interests that may succeed in overpowering a standing committee. Successive House speakers have generally refrained from abusing the power of the Calendar and Rules Committee, most often using it to delay bills until obtaining concessions on other legislative matters from the Senate or Governor.

Subcommittees

A third major difference between the House and Senate committee systems centers on the use of subcommittees. The expanded use of subcommittees did not occur until the late 1980s, and they play a much greater role in the House than in the Senate. A rapid increase in the volume of legislation, especially in standing committees such as Education, Judiciary, and State and Local Government, led to a further division of labor. The Education Committee, for example, was broken down into subcommittees for K–12, Higher Education, and Vocational Education. One key difference separated the Senate and House. The Senate did not grant subcommittees the power to kill legislation, reserving that right to the full committee. In the House, subcommittees gradually became a primary vehicle for stopping legislation, whether by the leadership or by lobbyists.

The growth in the number and influence of subcommittees has been a two-edged sword. Highly charged issues such as abortion can he disposed of in subcommittees, thus avoiding the need to put all ninety-nine members on record. Similarly, all House bills with a fiscal impact are first referred to a Finance subcommittee unaffectionately known as the "Black Hole." The seven members of the Black Hole subcommittee are vested with enormous influence, but in turn save the state hundreds of millions of dollars by rejecting expensive "apple pie" bills that the full House would have a difficult time defeating. The down side of the subcommittee process lies in the extent to which it compromises the notion of a full and fair debate on each bill. When subcommittees can kill bills, proponents of legislation must acquire at least fifty votes in the House and seventeen votes in the Senate, while opponents can prevail simply by acquiring only three or four key votes in a subcommittee. Such a system invites abuse by special interests willing to concentrate large contributions on a handful of legislators important to a subcommittee. When this occurs, the entire system ceases to function on behalf of those it was intended to serve.[9]

The question of how best to operate subcommittees is unresolved and remains perhaps the most divisive procedural issue among members of the Tennessee legislature. Invariably, each legislative session will witness an attempt in the full House or Senate to bring to the floor a bill that was defeated in committee or subcommittee. Proponents argue on behalf of fairness. Opponents argue with equal conviction that the committee system, despite the rigid nature of its rules, provides the only effective barrier against the political anarchy that could result in its absence. Bringing a bill to the floor over the objections of a committee requires a two-thirds majority vote. So long as this rule prevails, the legislature will likely continue to support a delicate process balanced between fairness and stability.

Finance Committees

The most important committees in the House and Senate are the Finance committees, formally known as the Finance, Ways and Means committees. In years of strong revenue growth and in years of shortfalls and budget cuts, one constant in the Tennessee legislature has been the ability to provide a balanced budget before the end of the regular session. One need look only to the Congress or to a number of states that routinely must convene special budget sessions to appreciate the importance of this tradition.

Every bill that either costs or saves state funds must be referred to the Finance committees and recommended for passage before consideration on the House and Senate floors. Each year dozens of bills receive approval from standing committees, such as Education or Judiciary, only to die in the Finance Committee. The most common tactic is to refer spending bills "behind the budget," meaning bills that would spend unbudgeted state funds may not be considered until the Finance Committee recommends in final form the Appropriations Bill. Because the state Constitution requires the annual state budget to he balanced, most unfunded bills "behind the budget" are allowed to die quietly en masse without further discussion. Most legislators do not object to this process, even though at times it may impede passage of their personal legislation. They realize the considerable power they defer to the members of the Finance Committee serves two important functions. The role of the Finance Committee relieves legislators of the pressure of having to pick and choose among a host of popular but unaffordable bills. In addition, it provides a stability and predictability critical to Tennessee's budget process. This stability, which was a constant until the 1999 and 2000 sessions, has been the envy of some states where budget arguments routinely lead to legislative gridlock among the House, the Senate, and the Governor.

If the budget problems of 2000 prove to be an aberration, the historic absence of legislative gridlock in Tennessee's budget process can in large part be traced to a unique and somewhat controversial feature that has been in place since the early 1970s. Usually about two weeks before the end of the annual session, the House and Senate Finance committees complete work on their respective versions of the Appropriations Bill. The two Finance committees recommend the Appropriations Bill for passage after considering some two thousand to three thousand amendments. Most legislators file their amendments knowing that chances of approval are slim. In an average year, the Finance committees enter the final stages of the budget process with some $10 million to $20 million in one-time money available to add or move around within the Governor's multi-billion-dollar proposed budget. The money is customarily used to fund fifty to one hundred small projects for individual legislators, including both Democrats and Republicans. Those critical of such projects as lighting for Little League ball fields or supplements for local museums refer to the budget amendments as "pork barrel." Others view the projects as a relatively cheap way of providing the public with tangible and popular evidence of their tax dollars. The unique feature of Tennessee's budget process emerges after the differing versions of the Appropriations Bill are passed on the House and Senate floors. For about two days, Democrat and Republican leaders from the House and Senate join the Constitutional Officers and the Governor's Finance Commissioner in an unknown location—usually a hotel suite—to debate budget amendments contained in either but not both of the two Appropriations bills. Since 1973, this custom in most years has produced a workable budget compromise, often without the need for a formal Budget Conference Committee to hash out the differences in public. Each year the press produces an obligatory condemnation of the "secret meetings." And indeed, some legislators voice complaints from time to time about the exclusionary nature of a process that is, quite literally, a backroom deal. Such criticism ignores the important role of the secret meetings in maintaining a level of civility crucial to the success of the budget process and to continued confidence in the bipartisan culture of Tennessee's legislative system.

Like a host of other political issues, one must weigh the virtue of Tennessee's budget process against the quality of the end product. So long as it continues to provide balanced budgets that are perceived to be fair, the seemingly ad hoc approach to the annual distribution of billions of dollars will likely remain a fixture in the Tennessee legislative process.

Study Committees

In addition to the committees and subcommittees that have permanent standing, the legislature each year creates a dozen or so temporary committees directed to study specific issues. These study committees usually have their origins in one of three purposes. On occasion an important legislative proposal is so complex or far-reaching in its scope that all of its ramifications cannot be fully examined during the hectic pace of a legislative session. In such cases, the legislature will often create a special committee directed to study a specific issue and report its recommendations by the next year. One of the most notable such committees was created in 1983 to study Gov. Lamar Alexander's controversial proposal to implement a performance-based pay plan for teachers.

More common but less serious are study committees created as a means of "deflating" bills that are hastily drafted and introduced by a legislator more concerned with publicity than policy. In the past such legislation has been introduced, for example, after well-publicized incidents of child abuse or alcohol-related traffic deaths. By creating a study committee that examines the bill months later, legislators sometimes can avoid making a lasting decision in a highly emotional atmosphere.

A final use of study committees is one that offers a chance to educate legislators on an issue that would not pass in the absence of more extended discussion. One of the best examples of this process involved an effort in 1995 to reform Tennessee's adoption laws. Proponents who wanted to open up adoption records faced complicated legal issues and a bureaucracy that resisted change. By creating a study committee, a loosely organized group gained publicity and over time convinced skeptical legislators of the merits of their bill. The study committee recommended substantial changes to adoption laws that eventually were enacted by the full legislature and used as a model by other states.

Less Rural and Less Rigid

Slightly more than two-thirds of the membership of the Tennessee legislature turns over every ten years. The effect of this change is so gradual as to be almost imperceptible without the perspective of time. In yet another unique characteristic of Tennessee's political process, the legislature's leadership has remained remarkably stable during a period that has witnessed significant changes in the profile of its members.

Changing of the Guard

Some might say that Joe Fowlkes personifies the gradual changes that have reshaped the face and philosophy of the Tennessee legislature since the early 1970s. Unfailingly polite and respected by his colleagues, Fowlkes was first elected to the House of Representatives in 1991 at age forty-three. Married with three children, he received a law degree from the University of Tennessee. He is a member of the Lions Club and attends the Church of Christ in his hometown of Cornersville in rural Middle Tennessee.

Joe Fowlkes won his seat by defeating a longtime incumbent in the Democratic primary. His opponent was a farmer born before the Depression who did not attend college. Unopposed in a series of elections, his tenure had enabled him to become a committee officer. Though many considered the incumbent unbeatable, Fowlkes ran an aggressive campaign, stressing the need for new ideas and focusing on the perks his opponent had gathered during his tenure in Nashville. Overconfident and unable to respond to Fowlkes's modern campaign techniques, the incumbent lost by a two-to-one margin.

In Joe Fowlkes's district, his victory represented a changing of the guard. A representative whose perceptions and priorities were molded in a time before most Tennessee homes had electricity was replaced by someone a generation younger, better educated, and more responsive to issues beyond those that directly affected his rural district. With subtle variations, the kind of change reflected in the election of Joe Fowlkes was repeated in dozens of legislative districts—both urban and rural—across Tennessee since the early 1970s. In district after district, today's legislators of both parties are generally better educated and less provincial than their predecessors. Joe Fowlkes was the primary force behind efforts in 1998 to adopt a phased-in process for the issuance of driver's licenses, a creative initiative that would have been unthinkable for Fowlkes's predecessor. Observers debate the effect of legislative

Stable Leadership

Most legislative bodies reflect to a large extent the personalities and philosophies of their leaders. Frequent changes in leadership often produce accompanying changes in style and priorities. Likewise, when key leaders hold power for an extended time, their philosophies tend to be institutionalized. Few state legislatures in the last quarter of the twentieth century witnessed the continuity of leadership found among seven key positions in Tennessee. These leaders, both Democrats and Republicans, shared similar values of fiscal conservatism and bipartisan cooperation. None was touched by scandal. While long terms in public office may prove at times an impediment to new ideas, there is little debate about the stability and predictability they provide the political process.

- John Wilder, thirty-two years: First elected Senate Speaker in 1971, he served for three decades as one of Tennessee's most influential leaders.
- Ned McWherter, twenty-two years: His record tenure of fourteen years as House Speaker was followed by eight years as Governor.
- Bill Snodgrass, forty-four years: Elected State Comptroller in 1955, he served until 1999 as a senior financial advisor to the legislature and seven governors.
- Harlan Mathews, twenty-six years: One of Tennessee's leading fiscal experts, he served ten years as Finance Commissioner, ten years as State Treasurer, and six years as Deputy Governor before his appointment in 1993 to the United States Senate.
- Ben Atchley, eighteen years: Republican Leader of the Senate elected in 1985, he was a chief advisor to a Democratic speaker and two Republican governors.
- Douglas Henry, twenty-six years: Appointed Senate Finance Chairman in 1977, he felt it his responsibility to support budgets of both Democratic and Republican governors.
- John Bragg, twenty-four years: Appointed House Finance Chairman in 1973, his efforts to implement conservative policies for lower debt and a sound pension system strengthened Tennessee's financial reputation.

turnover on specific legislative issues, but few deny it has resulted in a less passive, less provincial, and more productive legislature.

Representative Ronnie Davis might be seen as the Republican counterpart to Joe Fowlkes. A bit older than Fowlkes, Davis has represented the small East Tennessee mountain town of Newport for two decades. A director of vocational education in Newport, Davis was elected by his party as House Assistant Majority Leader for twelve years.

Joe Fowlkes and Ronnie Davis represent an aspect of the Tennessee legislature that is important to understanding the nature of its political decision making. Both are fiscally conservative. In other respects both are moderates who share a commitment to public education, strong environmental standards, and a desire to make sure both urban and rural Tennesseans have access to primary health care. Although Fowlkes comes from a historically Democratic region and Davis from an equally Republican district, each would probably concede that party loyalty was determined more by place of birth than by philosophical differences. Fowlkes supported the far-reaching welfare changes of a Republican Governor in 1996. Likewise, in 1992 Davis made the motions on the House floor to defeat efforts by more conservative Republicans to derail the education reform package of a Democratic Governor. Each action would be unimaginable in legislatures dominated by more partisan considerations.

An Institution of Bipartisan Moderation

At the close of the twentieth century, the Tennessee General Assembly, despite acrimonious debates about tax reform, was an institution characterized by a philosophy of bipartisan moderation. Unlike many states, Tennessee legislators still arranged their seats in the Senate and House the old-fashioned way, by region instead of party. Reflecting on his ten years in the House, former Majority Leader Bill Purcell stated, "There were only two issues that broke along party lines. Literally, only two out of thousands."

Part of the explanation for Tennessee's cooperative culture is found in the relative absence of rigid ideology. Conventional liberals comprised a distinct minority among Democrats. Among Republicans, the faction committed to defunding and dismantling government that achieved dominance in other state legislatures had not acquired senior leadership positions in Tennessee. Having few legislators on the extremes of the political spectrum makes it easier to find consensus.

Although rural interests—particularly in West Tennessee—retained an influence disproportionate to their numbers, the legislature in several ways reflected a diversity and tolerance unknown in earlier times. From 1968 to 2000, the number of black legislators increased from two to seventeen, the latter representing a percentage close to that of Tennessee's 16 percent black population. The legislature's occupational profile at the end of the century showed only twelve farmers, most of whom generated more money from second jobs other than agriculture. The legislature's twenty-six attorneys wielded more influence in the Senate than in the House, where much of the leadership came from small business.

Interestingly, at the turn of the century the Tennessee Senate and House still did not have the numbers of women increasingly found in other legislatures. The small percentage of female legislators was not a result of any conscious effort to deny them access to a male-dominated power structure. Indeed, Democrats in both the House and Senate achieved electoral success in the 1990s by recruiting female candidates against Republican incumbents. Despite these efforts, by 2000 there were only three female senators and fifteen female representatives, seven of whom were in the House Black Caucus.

One of the most significant changes in the Tennessee legislature has been a gradual growth in the number of legislators representing suburban districts. The relative absence of partisan politics over the years meant that many legislative issues divided along urban and rural lines. A population shift in the 1970s and 1980s created a large number of suburban districts that introduced a third major force in legislative decision making. Based primarily in the bedroom communities around Memphis and Nashville, the suburban districts often hold the balance of power in debates that historically would have been cast exclusively in urban and rural terms. Suburban legislators have been particularly concerned with the distribution to cities, counties, and school districts of sales tax revenues collected in urban malls from suburban shoppers. Because many voters in these districts have no tradition of party loyalty, the suburban districts often are the scenes of intense campaigns waged by both parties.

Despite demographic changes in both the state's population and the make-up of the General Assembly, by the turn of the century the changes had not yet produced a complete shift of power away from rural interests. Without exception, both the House and Senate since 1973 repeatedly elected rural speakers. The continued presence of rural speakers acted as a moderating influence on efforts by Governors and others to implement major policy changes in areas such as education or transportation spending. How long the rural interests could hold on to their disproportionate influence was unclear. More certain was the fact that less and less would important legislative debates divide along lines of party or geography. Increasingly, a younger and better educated group of legislators would produce shifting coalitions, whose temporary nature reflected a new era and a new approach to the legislative process

The "Almost" Independent Legislature

As a young freshman legislator in 1955, I thought I ought to read the Governor's proposed budget before I voted on it. I went to the Governor's Office and asked if I might see the budget. A list was produced, and I was told my name was not on the list, whereupon, I went back upstairs, voted "yes" on the budget, and went home.

Sen. Douglas Henry, Chairman, Tennessee Senate Finance Committee, in remarks to the Tennessee Bicentennial Celebration, 1996

While the term "balance of power" is frequently used by Americans to describe the relationship between the executive and legislative branches of government, one must keep in mind that no such perfect balance exists, either in Washington or in any of the fifty state legislatures. Each relationship is unique, evolving over the decades in response to a multitude of influencing factors, not the least of which are the personalities of the men and women who occupy leadership positions. In states such as Texas or North Carolina, the legislature could be argued to hold more power than the Governor. The reverse is true in Tennessee, where, despite significant strides toward greater balance, the scales of political power remain tipped in favor of the Governor.

Rise of a Two-Party System

Lasting changes in the legislative process are frequently the product of a single event that shakes up the political status quo. The Tennessee legislature's move toward greater independence from the executive branch had its origins in such an event, the inauguration of Winfield Dunn of Memphis as Governor in January 1971. The first Republican Governor elected in a half-century, Dunn followed an eighteen-year period during which two rural Democrats, Frank Clement and Buford Ellington, swapped occupancy of the Governor's Office.

While it would be misleading to suggest that the legislature was merely a rubber stamp for Clement and Ellington, it would be accurate to say that the two governors wielded enormous influence in legislative affairs. Contemporary legislators find it difficult to comprehend that in the 1950s and 1960s it was common for the Governor to announce his selections for the House and Senate speakers, whereupon the respective bodies voted accordingly. The Governor's influence in choosing the legislative leadership was also evident in a similar deference to the Governor's budget proposals. Legislators of the era recall when only those "on the list" were permitted to view the budget document. In those days, the Governor's Appropriations Bill often was enacted without amendments after less than five minutes of discussion.

Though less important than Dunn's landmark victory, the 1970 legislative elections brought another change that temporarily injected a more partisan tone into the political process and ultimately played a role in efforts to establish greater legislative independence. Much of the national debate in the late 1960s focused on race relations, urban violence, and the Democratic administration's handling of the war in Vietnam. Alabama Governor George Wallace's 1968 presidential bid as an independent had given expression to the frustration of many Democrats, especially in West Tennessee, who for the first time began in large numbers to part from traditional voting patterns and vote for independents and Republicans.

As national forces propelled a shift in state politics, other factors also were transforming the political landscape in Tennessee. Suburban communities outside Memphis and Jackson, as well as the bedroom communities in the counties surrounding Nashville, were rapidly becoming dominated by young middle-class white families, many of whom were the first generation with a college education and the promise of long-term prosperity. These demographic shifts coincided with the emergence of a new generation of more sophisticated Republican candidates seeking to take advantage of the dissent within the ranks of Tennessee Democrats by running for local and statewide offices. The changes culminated in November 1968, when Republicans, bolstered by a surge of victories in Memphis and surrounding Shelby County, held an even number of seats with Democrats in the House of Representatives for the first time since Reconstruction. The following January, with the support of the body's single independent member, Republicans elected a Speaker and organized the House for the 1969 and 1970 legislative sessions.

Moves toward Legislative Independence

Ironically, on the day in November 1970 when Tennesseans elected Winfield Dunn as the first Republican Governor in modern history, Democrats retook control of the House of Representatives. Unaccustomed to their two years in the political wilderness and smarting from the loss of the Governor's Office, the Democratic House majority adopted a decidedly more partisan and confrontational stance toward the new Republican Governor. Most partisan of all was House Speaker Jim McKinney of Nashville, whose conduct was openly contemptuous of the administration. The deterioration of relations between the legislature and the Governor produced a tone of sarcasm and distrust that troubled even Democrats concerned about the impact of such behavior on larger issues. McKinney's partisan leadership style was found so distasteful that House Democrats rejected him for reelection after a single term. Despite his defeat, his brief tenure had put in motion forces that would lead to a more professional, more self-confident, and more independent legislative branch of government. These forces were not ideological. Rather, they reflected the General Assembly's heightened desire to acquire the tools needed to establish a legislative process less dominated by resources under the Governor's control.

Among the legislature's most significant steps toward independence in the early 1970s was the construction of the Legislative Plaza, located underground and connected by escalators and a three-hundred-foot marble tunnel to the Capitol across the street. Some three football fields in length, the Legislative Plaza houses leadership offices for the House and Senate, committee offices, a cafeteria, hearing rooms, and facilities for the press. Prior to construction of the plaza, many legislators literally were forced to work out of their hotel rooms. A shortage of legislative offices and committee hearing rooms made scheduling a constant source of irritation and confusion and limited efforts to review administration proposals. The Legislative Plaza gave Tennessee one of the nation's most spacious and convenient legislative facilities. The convenience it provided enabled the legislature for the first time to develop a more coordinated response to bills, budgets, and initiatives from Capitol Hill.

The Legislative Plaza also provided space for the House and Senate to hire more professional staff. Previously, legislative staff consisted of

Fig. 3.3. Back side of the Tennessee State Capitol. Photo by John M. Scheb II.

a few secretaries and the Legislative Council (later named the Office of Legal Services), a small nonpartisan staff whose primary function was the drafting of legislation for the House and Senate. The notion of partisan staffing found in other states was alien to Tennessee. Beginning in the 1970s, Senate standing committees employed full-time staff to provide analysis to bills assigned to the committee. The House eventually followed suit, beginning with the Finance Committee and expanding gradually to provide a research analyst for most standing committees. The Democrat and Republican leadership of the House and Senate also acquired professional staff, although most outsiders are surprised to find the respective staffs of the House and Senate speakers remain quite small compared to other states.[10]

A third important step toward legislative independence was the expanded role of the Fiscal Review Committee, comprised of members elected by their peers from the House and Senate and supported by an Executive Director and staff. The committee staff's primary responsibility is assigning a fiscal impact to any bill or amendment filed in the House and Senate. Prior to this review, the legislature was as the mercy of the administration to provide accurate and timely information. Fiscal notes carry substantial weight in legislative debate and often are used as pretexts for defeating otherwise popular bills whose costs are not provided for in the budget. The Fiscal Review staff strives for political neutrality, although on occasion some have been accused of succumbing to the pressure of legislative leaders and fashioning a fiscal note to further a political agenda.

Legislative independence received an indirect assist from an idea in vogue nationwide during the mid-1970s. Called "sunset review," its goal was to reduce the size and cost of government by a periodic review designed to challenge the justification of each state agency's performance and policies. Like most such political fads, sunset reviews did little to reduce the size of government. One unintended result in Tennessee, however, was a growth in the size and scope of the Comptroller's staff assigned to conduct the sunset reviews. Because the Comptroller is elected by the majority party of the House and Senate, it followed that this expanded staff expertise would be utilized by the legislative leadership seeking greater analysis of administration programs. The practice of "borrowing" the Comptroller's staff was accelerated in 1979 with the inauguration of Lamar Alexander and institutionalized during the Republican Governor's two terms. By the end of the 1990s, the Comptroller's staff influenced legislative policy as much as any group in the General Assembly.

Indeed, staffing remains one of the unique characteristics of the Tennessee General Assembly, an odd blend of old and modern approaches. More than in most states, staffing is a hodgepodge of committee staff, Fiscal Review staff, partisan leadership staff, nonpartisan Office of Legal Services staff serving both the House and Senate, and staff employed by the Constitutional Officers. Despite this somewhat disjointed arrangement, total staffing remains small compared to levels found in most state legislatures. The process is inefficient and on occasion inhibits the kind of aggressive analysis—especially in regard to complex interdisciplinary issues—needed to establish the legislature as a truly coequal branch of government. The result is a tendency for the legislature to focus upon a few major issues for extensive review in addition to a large number of lesser issues that do not require detailed analysis.

While some criticize this approach as an abdication of the legislature's responsibilities, others view it as a more practical philosophy of "do a few things and do them well." The experience of other states demonstrates that large legislative staffs and full-time legislators do not ensure better legislation or a more efficient legislative process. This issue was addressed in 1997, when *Governing Magazine* compared the Minnesota and Tennessee legislatures. The author observed that while Tennessee spends less than half of what Minnesota—a state of comparable size—spends on staff and legislative expenses, the Tennessee legislature (fig. 3.3) has displayed "a consistently impressive record of substantive work throughout the 1990s." Noting that "all sense of collegiality had vanished from the full-time Minnesota legislature," the author stressed that Tennessee annually conducts "efficient, productive and thoroughly civilized sessions" while "holding to a level of comity and bipartisanship that is foreign to most chambers these days." The author concluded, "While Tennessee's legislature is far from perfect, it speaks to the value of simple qualities such as civility that have largely been lost in the legislatures that have rushed headlong toward professionalism."[11]

Staking Out Its Territory

The Tennessee legislature has traveled a great distance toward political independence since the days when governors named its leaders and legislators worked out of hotel rooms. Despite this progress, the Tennessee General Assembly does not exercise the same degree of power and influence as a great number of state legislatures across the country. The most significant evidence of this gap is the legislature's continued deference to the Governor in the design of a multi-billion-dollar state budget. Year after year, under both Democratic and Republican governors, the legislature leaves approximately 98 percent of the administration's proposed budget untouched. This tradition is a legacy of the philosophy of Senate Speaker John Wilder and House Speaker Ned McWherter, as well as the fact that the lack of adequate staffing leaves the legislature at a great disadvantage when seeking to develop comprehensive alternatives to administration budget proposals.

In the evolutionary process of establishing its identity, the legislature has staked out policy prerogatives that, although ambiguous to outsiders, are relatively clear to those who participate on a regular basis. High-profile but straightforward issues such as criminal penalties, abortion, gambling, annexation, gun control, and alcohol clearly lie within the legislature's domain of influence. Likewise, the legislature increasingly has attempted to referee complicated disputes stemming from the deregulation of the communications industry or the eternal fight between the insurance and health-care industries. With a handful of notable exceptions, the Governor traditionally has received approval for major reforms in areas such as education, health care, or welfare after the legislature has placed its "thumbprint" on the proposal in the form of minor modifications. The legislature seldom initiates changes in tax policy, though legislators are very much involved in efforts by the Governor to enact legislation that includes tax increases, exemptions, or fundamental changes in the state's tax structure.

Students of political theory find interesting the unique relationship that exists in Tennessee between the Governor and the legislature. Proponents of the illusive "balance of power" contend that the disproportionate influence of the Governor, particularly in budgetary matters, leaves the Tennessee process flawed. Others note that Tennessee has succeeded in implementing far-reaching reforms in education, health care, and welfare programs that probably could not have survived a legislative process in which political power was more evenly distributed. Stated differently, this view places a higher value on a political process that functions effectively and responsibly than on one that aspires to a precise balance of power between the executive and legislative branches.

Do Political Parties Still Matter?

The locations are well known in Nashville. In a ballroom of the Sheraton Hotel or a private dining room at Jimmy Kelley's restaurant, the ritual takes place each year in the weeks just before the start of the January legislative session. Dozens of lobbyists, political aspirants, and assorted hangers-on attend the fund-raisers of the Democratic and Republican legislative caucuses. The price of admission is usually five hundred dollars, although the money raised is far more important than the size of the crowd. One year the invitation to a Senate Democratic fund-raiser read, "You Need Not Be Present to Attend." With the exception of legislators themselves, the list of those attending is remarkably similar at all the events. Most lobbyists attend all legislative fund-raisers. A large number give about the same to both parties.

The aggressiveness and sophistication with which both parties raise campaign funds has increased sharply, beginning in the early 1970s and accelerating in the 1980s. In 1978 the House Democratic Caucus had a campaign budget of less than $100,000. By 2000, the figure had grown to more than $1,500,000 with no end in sight. Even these sums represented a small portion of the cost of campaigns by the end of the century. Candidates in hotly contested legislative races routinely spent $75,000 in the House and $200,000 in the Senate. Figures three times that high were not uncommon.[12] Increasingly, campaigns were no longer civil affairs marked by speeches at the Rotary Club or shaking hands at the county fair. Parties fought ferociously for every marginal seat. Direct mail, radio ads, and negative research for every candidate were organized from Nashville. Unlike elections in previous years, both parties tried to convince voters the choice was one between a rising, shining Tennessee and the abyss.

Agreements and Differences in Party Ideology

The tenacity with which the Republican and Democratic parties wage legislative campaigns raises a fundamental question about the Tennessee legislature: If the culture of the Tennessee political process is grounded in nonpartisan cooperation, why does it matter which party is elected? A question that at first glance appears absurd is worthy of more thoughtful examination. By many standards, few ideological differences distinguish East Tennessee Republicans from West Tennessee Democrats. Most Tennesseans would be hard pressed to name significant philosophical differences among the three Republican and two Democratic governors since 1971. Despite predictions to the contrary, the legislature and the state witnessed no major policy changes when Republicans gained brief control of the Senate from 1995 to 1997.

In some respects, the philosophical common ground of the two parties is more important than their differences. Virtually no distinction separates the commitment by both parties to the sanctity of fiscal conservatism and low taxation. Both parties are rigid in their support of Tennessee's Right to Work Law, which prohibits workers from being forced to join a union. Large majorities in both parties oppose the use of federal funds for abortion. Historically, support for the death penalty and opposition to the income tax have been strong among Republicans and Democrats. The tradition was turned on its head, however, in 1999, when Republican Governor Don Sundquist advocated a state tax on income, a proposal that attracted more support from Democrats than Republicans.

While the philosophical gap between Democrats and Republicans in the Tennessee legislature is not as wide as in some states, important differences do exist. Democrats as a group have been more reluctant than Republicans to encourage the privatization of state services. Republicans on occasion have demonstrated an almost reflexive opposition to unions, while Democrats have generally been supportive of union activities such as increased benefits for unemployed or disabled workers. Republican antipathy to employee organizations often has extended to the Tennessee State Employees Association and the forty-thousand-member Tennessee Education Association, leading both groups to gravitate by default toward Democrats. Perhaps most significant, Republicans, particularly in the House, have had difficulty relating to and working with Tennessee's black community. Sporadic attempts to reach out to the Black Caucus were so half-hearted that by the 1990s Republicans seemed to have abandoned the effort altogether. As the emotional debates of 1999 and 2000 demonstrated, significantly more support existed among Democrats to lower the state sales tax in exchange for a tax on the income of the wealthiest Tennesseans.

Why the Parties Are Similar

At least three reasons offer an explanation for the similarity of Democratic and Republican agendas in the Tennessee legislature. Democrats were the majority party for more than a century in every southern state following the Civil War. The eastern third of Tennessee, however, had opposed secession in 1861 and thus had existed as a Republican stronghold long before the development of competitive Republican parties in most other southern states. Tennessee Republicans were ready to challenge successfully for statewide offices in the mid-1960s, roughly two decades earlier than a majority of other southern states. The party's relative maturity enabled it to field well-known candidates such as Howard Baker, an East Tennessean who eventually became Majority Leader of the U.S. Senate and White House Chief of Staff. Most Republican candidates of that period probably would not have appealed to Tennesseans with a platform of radical change. Although by 1970 Republicans held the Governor's Office and both Senate seats, their victories had not been the result of ideological wars that characterized many Republican gains in other states in the 1980s and 1990s. Voter backlash to racial integration was a factor, but in most cases Republicans simply had offered better candidates and run better campaigns than their Democratic opponents.

A second reason for the centrist flavor of the Tennessee legislature may lie in the fact that Republicans have not had much experience in leadership positions. Despite frequent victories in statewide elections, Republicans in the last half of the twentieth century held majorities in the House for only two years, from 1969 to 1970, and in the Senate for only two years, from 1995 to 1996. In the House, the likelihood of continued Democratic dominance was probably a subtle factor in the willingness by many Republicans to seek accommodation rather than confrontation with their Democratic colleagues. This attitude was cultivated during the tenure of Speaker Ned McWherter, who co-opted large numbers of moderate Republicans into the working Democratic coalition. The process evolved differently but produced much the same result in the Senate, where after 1987 the sharing of committee chairs between Democrats and Republicans encouraged the two parties to work together. One could argue that, if given a prolonged chance to develop an agenda, a Republican majority might generate different policies and priorities. Given that both parties have pursued a moderate path for more than three decades, such a change would likely occur only if preceded by a dramatic upheaval in the current leadership.

Indeed, it was not ideology but the influence of strong personalities that was most responsible for the philosophy of fiscal conservatism and moderate populism that characterized the Tennessee legislature at the close of the century. Though listed on the ballot as a Democrat, there is nothing about Senate Speaker John Wilder that identified him as distinctly different from Republicans. He sponsored fund-raisers for both Democratic and Republican senators and appointed members of both parties to leadership positions. While House Speaker Jimmy Naifeh was more clearly identified with the Democratic Party, his leadership style was a legacy of his mentor, former Speaker McWherter. The House leaders on occasion would close ranks to oppose a Republican initiative they thought ill-conceived. At no time, however, did the process move toward consistent partisan confrontation.

Why Parties Are Needed

As is the case with all democratic institutions, the Tennessee legislature is in a state of constant evolution. One must always keep in mind that the attitudes and culture present at any particular moment will eventually change. Economic depression, urbanization, scandal, fiscal crisis, the influence of powerful personalities, and events such as the Civil War have changed the Tennessee legislature in the past and will do so again.

Political parties play a crucial role in providing a measure of stability through these changes. They offer a vehicle for men and women to participate in their government in an orderly manner. To a degree, they prevent a political system from being dominated exclusively by the aristocracy. Parties provide a valuable forum for debating new ideas that might not otherwise receive a fair hearing. In their absence, the attempt to sort out good candidates and good ideas would be extraordinarily difficult.

Parties play a different but equally important role in the legislature itself. The fact that parties do not take sides on every issue does not imply they are irrelevant. They provide a mechanism for organizing the complicated and potentially divisive process of making laws. Choosing speakers, committee chairs, and constitutional officers would be chaotic without the party structure. Perhaps most important, the task of raising and allocating the funds for a multi-billion-dollar state budget is inconceivable without the discipline provided by political parties. The fact that legislators often concede an extra portion of budget funds to the districts of legislative leaders underscores the importance of this function.

As time goes by, it is possible that political parties will once again represent differing sides of great social issues in the Tennessee legislature. The debate over changing Tennessee's tax system generates a level of emotion that threatens not only relationships between the parties, but also the cohesion of the parties themselves. At the close of the century, a growing segment of the Republican Party was increasingly supportive of private education at the expense of public schools. If these trends continue, ideological debates over the future of taxation and public education might redefine the direction of political parties for the next generation.

The Process Works, but Can It Last?

The evolution of the political process during the last quarter of the twentieth century produced a Tennessee legislature unique in several respects among its national and regional counterparts. A traditionalist Senate coexisted with a more diverse and activist House. The legislature's most prominent characteristics were its bipartisan civility, fiscal conservatism and openness to innovative and ambitious social policy initiatives. On most fiscal matters, the legislature deferred to the Governor, who in turn stayed out of legislative squabbles. Even on the explosive issue of tax reform, partisan agendas rarely intruded on substantive legislation.

The legislature's political culture made possible the enactment of several innovative and far-reaching initiatives in the 1980s and 1990s. Tennessee's radical experiment in 1992 with health-care reform resulted in TennCare, a replacement for the federal Medicaid program that, despite management problems, moved more than a million participants into managed care, extended health-care insurance to more than a half million working poor, and saved the state

$1 billion during its first three years. A 1996 overhaul of the welfare program put in place time limits and work requirements for welfare recipients. Education initiatives in 1984 and 1992 raised the state sales tax 1.5 cents for education, redistributed the state funding formula to assist poorer counties, and put in place a performance-based salary plan for teachers. A corrections system once among the nation's worst became the first to have all of its prisons accredited. Serious challenges remain, including a tax system that continues to be one of the nation's most regressive and threatens the state's financial stability. Despite the considerable work still unfinished, one could argue that the ambitious policy initiatives implemented by Tennessee are a testimony to the state's unique legislative environment.

Whether the culture of bipartisan cooperation survives in the twenty-first century will depend on its ability to withstand several threats to its traditions. The Senate has been guided for thirty-two years by John Wilder, the House for thirty years by Ned McWherter and two speakers who trained as his lieutenants. When these rural West Tennessee leaders step down, it is impossible to predict whether their coalitions will survive or whether they will be replaced by a total upheaval of the leadership structure. Tennessee's overall population growth is not occurring in West Tennessee, a signal that five decades of leaders and coalitions from the rural counties between Nashville and Memphis may be drawing to a close. The growth of the Republican Party's ideological right wing, particularly in the Senate, may make it more difficult to achieve compromise on a variety of issues. Finally, Tennessee's outdated tax structure captures an ever-decreasing portion of the state's economy, threatening to make the state budget process a more difficult and acrimonious exercise with each passing year.

Few legislators wish to see the Tennessee General Assembly change in a way that would introduce a more partisan and more confrontational tone to the process. Unfortunately, such forces have often proved impossible to control.

4

The Governor

Governor McWherter and his two staffers grew quiet as the National Guard helicopter hovered over the fifty-yard line of the little high school stadium in Hohenwald, the county seat of Lewis County. Down below, bleachers on both sides of the field were filled with students and townspeople, many of whom had waited more than an hour in the hot September sun. Cheerleaders from the high school led chants of "Go Big Ned!" as the 270-pound Governor climbed out of the helicopter and walked toward the end zone where state troopers waited with his car. Overwhelmed by the enthusiasm of the unplanned reception, the Governor turned and "worked the rope" down each sideline, touching and being touched, first by squealing elementary students, then by women from the shops and businesses on the nearby courthouse square. A small group of severely retarded children had been placed in the shade of an oak tree close to the Governor's motorcade. Bending to his knee, Tennessee's most powerful politician spoke one by one to children who could not understand his words. After a one-hour meeting staged to highlight a local mental health clinic, the Governor was clearly uplifted as the motorcade returned to the stadium for the fifty-minute trip back to Nashville. The Governor stopped in mid-sentence as the car turned the corner and pulled into the steaming parking lot. Up ahead, sweating in the sun, the crowd was still there, hoping for a last look at their Governor.

In Tennessee, the Governor is still a big deal. Certainly this is true in the political sense, but also as measured by the basic respect and good feelings that a majority of Tennesseans have about the office of the Governor. A substantial portion of the large crowd in Hohenwald that turned out for Ned McWherter more accurately came to see "the Governor," not McWherter, a distinction that is important to keep in mind when studying the role of Tennessee's modern Governor. Beginning in 1954, Democrats Frank Clement and Buford Ellington were elected by large margins to serve alternating four-year terms in a leapfrog process that lasted until 1970. By 1978, Tennesseans had approved a constitutional change allowing the Governor to serve two consecutive four-year terms. In the twenty-two years from 1978 through the end of the century, Tennessee had only three governors. Republicans Lamar Alexander and Don Sundquist served two-term bookends around the two terms of Democrat Ned McWherter. Each was elected by comfortable margins and reelected in landslides over underfunded opponents who enjoyed only half-hearted support from their respective parties. Each of the three governors enjoyed high popularity ratings throughout most of their administrations.

In addition to Governors Alexander, McWherter, and Sundquist, Tennessee during the period produced Republican Senate Majority Leader and later White House Chief of Staff Howard Baker, and Democratic Vice President of the United States Al Gore Jr. Alexander served as Secretary of Education under President George Bush. McWherter was a close insider of President Bill Clinton's "kitchen cabinet." One could argue that Tennessee's voice in the nation's political and economic circles was greater during the last two decades of the twentieth century than at any time since the days of Andrew Jackson and James K. Polk in the 1830s and 1840s. After decades at the back of the political and economic lines, Tennesseans had a renewed pride in their state that played a significant part in the exceptional support for governors of both political parties.

Most likely some evolving combination of individual leadership, economic growth, and civic pride in Tennessee's new image explains the "era of good feeling" that characterized much of state politics from 1978 until the close of the century. As occurs in most political systems, a byproduct of good feeling was increased political power and opportunity for the chief executive. In part, the legacies of Tennessee governors during the last half of the twentieth century are judged by the extent to which they were willing and able to use their power to bring about lasting changes. While the precise reasons remain subject to debate, since the mid-1950s Tennessee's governors have consistently enjoyed a combination of legislative influence and general public support unmatched in all but a few states. Even during Ray Blanton's highly controversial tenure from 1975 to 1979, the administration maintained the ability to enact budgets that were largely unchanged by the legislature. This uncommon level of influence and support during the "era of good feeling" serves as a backdrop to many of the issues and events encountered in the study of Tennessee's Governor.

Deceptively Vague: The Governor's Constitutional Powers

The general public confidence extended to Tennessee's governors in the late twentieth century was not reflected in the state's first Constitution. Significantly, Article III, which addresses the Governor, is about one-third as long as the enumeration of powers to the legislative branch contained in Article II. As would be expected, the document revealed a widespread disdain for executive authority, a philosophical legacy of the recent War of Independence from the British Crown. Requirements to be Tennessee's Governor were few in 1796 and have not changed. The Governor must be thirty years of age, a United States citizen, and a resident of Tennessee for seven years. For 158 years until 1954, the Governor was limited to a term of two years, though eligible for reelection.[1]

In a time when the national government was weak and the safety of the citizenry from Indian hostility was a priority, the 1796 Tennessee Constitution assigned the Governor command over the state militia. Until curtailed after the Civil War by the 1870 Constitution, the Governor's military role was among the most important functions of the office. Motivated by memories of British abuses from the colonial period, Tennessee's constitutional framers also granted the Governor authority to grant clemencies and absolute pardons to persons convicted of crimes. The use and misuse of this extraordinary power over the years often provided insight into a Governor's most basic values. Governor Frank Clement granted numerous pardons and is known to have agonized over whether to stay executions of Death Row inmates. Ned McWherter, despite overcrowded prisons, could not bring himself to grant clemency to more than two or three inmates during his eight-year term. Ray Blanton had a less complicated philosophy; he sold pardons to make money for his friends.

Beyond commanding the militia, granting pardons, and filling judicial vacancies, the specific role of Tennessee's early governors was vaguely defined by modern standards. The original Constitution was silent even on whether the Governor should prepare a state budget, stating in Section 11 only that the Governor "shall, from time to time, give to the General Assembly information of the state of government, and recommend for their consideration such measures as he shall judge expedient." The document does not mention the Governor in regard to building roads, prisons, schools, or a multitude of other activities that over time became central functions of the executive branch. Section 18 gave the Governor authority to veto legislation enacted by the legislature, but constrained the Governor's power by allowing the legislature to override the veto with a simple majority. This language still exists in the Tennessee Constitution. From time to time various authors will incorrectly note the veto process as evidence that Tennessee is a "weak Governor" state. While more accurate in the state's earlier history, this assessment is not valid today.

Power Shifts

The role and relative influence of the Tennessee Governor have expanded greatly since statehood in 1796. For roughly 150 years, state government was small and, with infrequent exceptions, issues were relatively uncomplicated. Creative, activist governors were rarely sought by either the public or by the banks, railroads, and mining interests that dominated much of state politics. While governors on occasion emerged as leading players in such high-visibility issues as prohibition, women's suffrage, and child labor, the balance of power remained tilted toward the General Assembly well into the 1920s. A landmark change in the power balance occurred during the administration of Gov. Austin Peay, who in 1923 reorganized state government functions and restructured the state's tax system[2] and in 1925 implemented education reforms as progressive as any in America.[3] Yet despite the expanded influence of the executive branch in tax policy, building roads, and funding schools, the fact remained that large areas of Tennessee did not have electricity, telephones, or decent roads until the late 1930s. The Governor's role continued to be defined largely as it had been since the Civil War—the head of a small government in a poor state. Indeed, the first book published about Tennessee's political system stated in 1940, "The legislative branch of the state government is undoubtedly the most important of the three departments of government."[4]

Tennessee's governors served until the early 1950s against the backdrop of an agrarian economy and a still-small federal government, neither of which required an activist Governor with broad powers. The growth of federal government that began with President Franklin Roosevelt's New Deal programs in the 1930s continued to accelerate in the decade after the Second World War ended in 1945. In particular, cheap electrical power resulting from Roosevelt's creation of the Tennessee Valley Authority led to the development of manufacturing and service industries in Tennessee and raised the importance of building roads, expanding and managing the higher education system, and recruiting industrial investment. All of these were government functions a part-time legislative body was never designed to do. The federal government's decision in the mid-1950s to construct the interstate highway system provided an enormous boost to the influence of governors who would choose the routes, exits, and—in some cases—the contractors for large sections of the new highways. A similar increase in the size of state government was an unintended byproduct of the GI Bill. In the span of a single generation after 1945, the University of Tennessee's Knoxville campus grew from three thousand to more than thirty thousand students, a spectacular increase repeated throughout the state's

Fig. 4.1. A piano duet played by Gov. Lamar Alexander and rock-and-roll musician Jerry Lee Lewis. *Source:* Governor Alexander Papers, Tennessee State Library and Archives.

entire system of higher education. One of the most visionary and successful government programs in American history, the GI Bill's free college tuition for war veterans was the vehicle to the middle class for hundreds of thousands of Tennesseans who otherwise might have continued working in the state's mills and small factories. Highways and higher education are but two examples of the explosion of federal laws and programs regarding preschool education, health care, environmental regulation, economic development, worker safety, and other items that produced a parallel expansion of state government agencies needed to implement the new laws.

One unintended result of these federal initiatives in Tennessee was a historic shift in political power from the legislative branch to the executive branch. In the way that water fills an empty pitcher, the infusion of federal funds filled the political vacuum in a state whose leaders had not clearly foreseen the implications of such growth on political relationships. Ironically, at the moment when forces demanded the legislature adapt to keep pace with the Governor, the state Constitution presented two of the biggest obstacles. The document's limitation of the General Assembly to ninety-day sessions every two years presented the worst possible handicap to efforts by legislators to keep up with events. With most of the interstate highway projects still on the drawing board in the mid-1950s, getting to Nashville on a regular basis was impossible for dozens of legislators. A second obstacle to legislative change was the difficult process of amending the Constitution itself. The laborious process meant that it was 1968 before the General Assembly could convene each year. By then, power had shifted so far and so fast toward the Governor that it would take decades to restore greater balance to the system.

Because the tiny staff in the Tennessee General Assembly did not grow appreciably during this period, the vast majority of information—and thus political power—came to reside with the Governor. Put simply, by the 1950s Tennessee had, over a span of about three decades, become too big and too complex for the gears of government to remain in the hands of rural legislators who came to Nashville only in January, February, and March of odd-numbered years. No one had planned the change, but by 1955 one could argue the Governor *was* state government in Tennessee. State budgets, measured in hundreds of millions of dollars and later billions, had become documents which for the next three decades an overwhelmed legislature could only rubber stamp. For legislators, road projects became favors instead of requests from the Governor. Legislative leadership positions at times in the 1950s and 1960s were chosen by the Governor as routinely as if required by the Constitution. Although beginning in the 1970s the General Assembly made gradual strides in reversing the trend (see chapter 3), as the century came to a close the political balance of power between the executive and legislative branches resembled nothing like that envisioned by the state's founding fathers two hundred years earlier. Unlike states such as Texas and North Carolina, in Tennessee the Governor, with vaguely defined constitutional powers, was clearly the dominant force in state government.

Roles of the Modern Governor

A much larger crowd than usual nearly filled the auditorium of the Kingsport Middle School. The local symphony, although modest in size and repertoire, had generated considerable publicity with the appearance of a guest pianist. His very presence was a response to decades of jokes from television comedians about the state's intelligence and sophistication. To a person, the audience was impressed by his image—educated in New York, trained in classical piano, articulate, and self-assured. With a former Governor in prison, in a state accustomed to ranking near the bottom in many categories, his frequent participation with local symphonies had restored to many Tennesseans a measure of badly needed confidence. After his performance of a piece by Chopin, the sustained applause had little to do with an appreciation for piano technique. The crowd rose to its feet in recognition of a performance by the Governor of Tennessee, Lamar Alexander (fig. 4.1).

In Tennessee, as in all states, the outline of a Governor's role and responsibilities is defined by the state constitution and decades of statutes enacted by the legislative branch. While the outline of responsibilities is much the same for all governors, the political canvas on which each must work varies greatly. Some governors enter office during periods of economic expansion, while others must plan initiatives with budgets that project little or no growth in state revenues. To a great extent, the policy agenda is shaped by the successes or omissions of preceding governors. Even if a new Governor cares little about programs such as corrections or mental health, problems inherited from previous administrations can force those issues onto the priority list. Issues also can take on a different perspective if governors confront a legislature dominated by the opposing party. The perspective evolves yet again if the legislature contains one or more members who have their eyes on the Governor's office. High-profile crimes, natural disasters, even collegiate athletics are forces beyond the Governor's control that nonetheless can influence the public's collective attitude and generate demands for action. Each Governor must shape an agenda in the context of circumstances that vary greatly through the years. Indeed, one could argue that these inherited circumstances more than any other factor drive the Governor's political and legislative agendas.

If governors have agendas that are greatly influenced by external forces, the individual styles with which they pursue these agendas are products of more personal characteristics. Among the governors, it is a mixture of loyalties, ego, ambition, skills, and priorities that places a unique signature on each administration. Governors with ambitions of becoming U.S. Senator or even President find themselves weighing in a different way the political considerations of each major decision. Friendships and jealousies lead governors of both parties to have relationships ranging from warm to merely polite with members of the state's congressional delegation. Within the General Assembly, some governors have close, longtime friends, while others, particularly Republicans, come to the office as outsiders from the Nashville power structure. While by definition all persons who want to be Governor have strong egos in the positive sense, the willingness to address specific issues often is related to a Governor's confidence in the ability to control events. Because dedicating a new road project will always be easier than managing the state's health-care system, all governors are sometimes irresistibly pulled toward the path of political least resistance.

Another important individual characteristic that defines governors is the collection of intellectual and political skills that each brings to the job. Among governors of the modern era, Frank Clement had a remarkable ability to grasp and retain information about complicated issues. Lamar Alexander possessed the distinct but equally important skill of knowing how to communicate ideas to the public through the media. Governors approach issues from a broad range of educational, business, and political experiences that affects how a problem is addressed, or if it is addressed at all. The composite of these experiences, when combined with personal style and external forces, produces the priorities that ultimately form the agenda and legacy of each Governor. Don Sundquist came into office the first day wanting to reform an outmoded welfare system. Ned McWherter looked at most major issues in the context of his desire to bring rural Tennessee back into the economic mainstream. Lamar Alexander wanted Tennessee to enter more aggressively the high-stakes competition for foreign and domestic investment.

Although over the decades the Tennessee Governor has taken on a rather standard set of roles and responsibilities, governors have performed each with varying degrees of interest and skill. If the right combination of priorities, skills, and circumstances is aligned, a Governor can pass on, at least in regard to selective issues, a lasting legacy. Time and political capital both have limits that make it unfair to expect all governors to undertake bold initiatives on all fronts. Indeed, if accompanied by honesty and good fiscal management, the ability for a Governor to be identified by historians with only one or two major program initiatives can be argued to be a reasonable standard for success. The history of Tennessee's modern governors is the story of the issues and responsibilities chosen by each, and whether they proved to have chosen wisely.

Policy Leader

Since the 1920s, the vast majority of major policy initiatives in Tennessee state government have originated with the Governor. Beginning with the administration of Gov. Austin Peay, a handful of the most activist governors have proposed successful initiatives in several areas of state government. Other governors, for a variety of reasons, have been more passive and thus have generated few new legislative proposals. On this point, one should take care not to evaluate a Governor solely by the volume of policy initiatives. Some proposals are ill-conceived, often taking the form of an impractical idea motivated by a political agenda. At times governors who have worthwhile ideas do not have the political skills to guide the initiative through the legislative process. Perhaps the most frustrating category contains the governors who had good ideas, got them enacted by the legislature, but did not have either the focus or administrative skills to meet the challenge of implementing the new program on a statewide basis. By one standard, the best Tennessee governors have generally been those who aggressively addressed two or three major problems, achieved legislative approval for the solution, and implemented the policy changes in a way that had lasting benefits.

While the Tennessee Governor has historically been assigned the role of policy leader, one must keep in mind that in this context the "Governor" is not a single person but a group of senior advisors who work under the Governor's direction. This important distinction has much to do with the nature and relative success of policy initiatives. Several factors that have little to do with political philosophy make the policy process one that requires the right balance of discipline and collegiality. In most cases, the Governor's staff come from different backgrounds, with some members never having met until after the election. Too often key positions in the Governor's Office are awarded to top campaign staff, sometimes ignoring the fact that the jobs require entirely different skills. Most governors give a portion of key positions to political friends with little regard to how they will fit into the larger process. To the extent that the Governor's staff do not know—or trust—one another, communication can break down in a way that inhibits the development of sound policy. More important than not knowing one another, some of the staff will not know instinctively how the Governor will approach or react to a given issue, a situation that, particularly in the heat of the legislative process, can impede action and generate bad decisions. This general unfamiliarity is complicated by the inevitable power struggle among the staff who, insecure in their position, disparage their colleagues in an effort to gain the Governor's favor and attention. Finally, the Governor and staff of virtually every new administration fall victim for a time to the rhetoric of their recent election campaign. Hard-fought campaigns by their nature overstate the virtue of the candidate's ideas and the shortcomings of the preceding administration. The tendency is harmless unless a Governor and staff members move into their new offices with the arrogant belief that every existing program is flawed and that only they have the intellectual capacity to make things right again. Such an attitude on more than one occasion has led to the abandonment of good programs for no other reason than the program was identified with a previous administration.

A Governor's chance to be an effective policy leader depends to a great degree on the ability to gather a talented staff and maximize their talents. A good Governor does not have to be exceptionally smart if the self-confidence is present to hire a staff that is bright and allowed to generate creative ideas. Either the Governor or a senior staff person in whom the Governor places absolute trust must organize the duties of the staff and the process by which communication flows to and from the Governor. If a priority is placed on talent and creativity while jealousies and arrogance are held in check, the chances of the Governor emerging as an effective policy leader are greatly enhanced.

Spokesperson for the State

One role thrust upon every Governor is that of spokesperson for the state at a broad range of events and ceremonies. The guarantee of publicity from the Governor's presence generates hundreds of invitations each month asking the chief executive to cut a ribbon, dig a ceremonial shovel of dirt, dedicate a new industry, or speak at a college graduation. Because the glamour brought to an event by the Governor's entourage is usually more important than what is actually said, all governors have performed the role more or less adequately. With the exception of Memphis and Nashville, a visit by the Governor invariably will produce a picture and small story in the local newspaper. The importance of these events lies in their ability to provide Tennesseans a critical feeling of connection with their government.

The generally pleasant role of state spokesperson on occasion brings the Governor a darker, more emotionally challenging duty. When sudden tragedy strikes, it is usually the Governor to whom citizens look to express their grief or anger. In much the same role President Bill Clinton assumed after the 1994 bombing of a federal building in Oklahoma City, governors are expected to be counselor and comforter when a tornado, a nursing home fire, or the collapse of a bridge produce fatalities and destruction too overwhelming for citizens to absorb alone. Few governors likely think about this aspect of the job when they contemplate seeking the office. Some ultimately carry the responsibility with grace. Others treat it as an uncomfortable burden of office.

"Foreign Affairs" Diplomat

In contrast to their predecessors, Tennessee governors since about 1980 have devoted a significant portion of their time to issues and relationships that extend beyond the state's borders. The activities divide loosely into political, policy, and business categories. How governors allocate their time among numerous multi-state associations is an indicator of not only their interests but also how they see, or wish to see, themselves viewed by the public and their peers. Lamar Alexander is the only Tennessee Governor to have chaired and effectively used the National Governors Association as a forum to showcase policy initiatives. Ned McWherter chaired the Atlanta-based Southern Regional Education Board and used the board as a resource for plans to equalize funding among Tennessee's 139 local school districts. Don Sundquist served as chair of the Southern Growth Policy Board located in Raleigh, North Carolina. Critics contend that many of these and similar organizations contribute little beyond expensive conventions and the efforts of staff to justify their existence. While the quality and relevance of these organizations vary from very good to very bad, the astute Governor understands that each group, fairly or not, often shapes the national image a state develops with a particular issue. The actual success or failure of a Governor's new "reforms" back home matters little in the public relations sense if the reforms are marketed convincingly on the national or regional stage. Conversely, some noteworthy policy initiatives have gone largely unnoticed because Tennessee governors did not cultivate relationships with those in and near the national media.

If national and regional associations provide little of substance, Tennessee governors on occasion must interact with other states on matters of the highest priority. These encounters can test a Governor's skills in solving problems and negotiating deals with others of equal rank and status. Most discussions among governors take on the air and style of diplomatic relations, unfailingly cordial and laced with gratuitous compliments. One of the most notable exceptions to this diplomatic formality arose from a dispute in the late 1980s between Ned McWherter and North Carolina Governor Jim Martin. The issue involved a public outcry in Tennessee over discharge from a Canton paper mill that polluted the Pigeon River just before it crossed the state line into Newport. McWherter's Christmas Eve decision to deny the mill a water-quality variance sparked months of sniping and threats from Martin, including a clumsy and ineffective effort to ban the sale of Tennessee-produced Jack Daniels whiskey in North Carolina.[5] Most interstate policy issues have been resolved under more friendly terms. Among the most significant is the Interstate Hazardous Waste Compact, in which Tennessee joined Alabama, Kentucky, and South Carolina in a twenty-year plan to manage industrial wastes safely and more cost-efficiently.[6]

Investment Recruiter

Writing in an age when virtually everyone in Tennessee lived on a farm, the framers of the state Constitution never dreamed that recruiting industrial investment one day would be among the leading items in the Governor's portfolio of activities. That the state should have a formalized plan to attract new factories, distribution centers, or service industries was largely an alien notion until the early 1970s, when Gov. Winfield Dunn established the first Department of Economic and Community Development. Despite this important first step, a lack of state resources and lack of a sophisticated recruitment strategy prevented Tennessee from competing on a level field with a

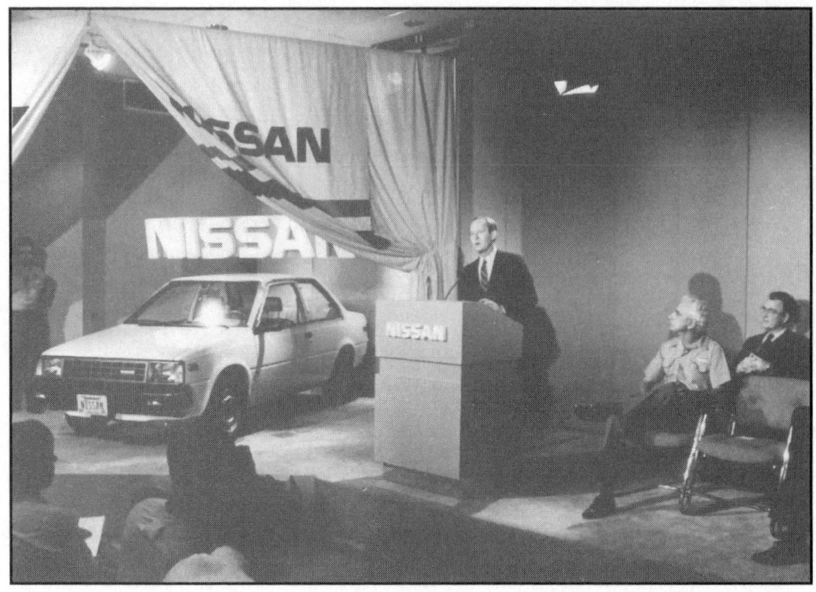

Fig. 4.2. Gov. Lamar Alexander announces the arrival of the new Nissan plant at Smyrna. *Source:* Governor Alexander Papers, Tennessee State Library and Archives.

number of other states, particularly in the North and Midwest. While the state did an increasingly better job of providing information to companies that inquired about possible investments in Tennessee, efforts to solicit such investments too often consisted of little more than the "cold calls" associated with those who sell encyclopedias door to door. If domestic recruitment was haphazard, attempts to attract foreign investment were even more primitive. Few persons in Nashville had even the vaguest idea how to move among the financial corridors of London, Frankfurt, and Tokyo. Until the early 1980s, industrial recruitment in Tennessee was a hit-or-miss activity in which the Governor played only a minor role.

As they often do, attitudes and policies changed as the result of a single event. Perhaps because he served his political apprenticeship in Washington, Lamar Alexander brought to industrial recruitment a different perspective for the roles of both the Governor and state government. Taking a cue from some of his northern and western colleagues, Alexander elevated the priority of industrial recruitment among the items that competed for time and attention on the Governor's schedule. Alexander correctly determined that Tennessee's cheap labor, cheap land, and cheap electrical power would be strong incentives for industries, especially foreign ones, looking for expansion in the American market. He marshaled all the resources of state government—roads, higher education, environmental regulation—in developing bids for major projects. In effect, the traditional process was transformed from a negotiation between a large company and a small community to a much different one in which the state of Tennessee, led by the Governor, could bargain on behalf of the community with a wide range of financial incentives.

The first major success of Tennessee's new economic development strategy occurred in 1982 with the announcement by the Japanese Nissan Corporation of plans to build a $500 million assembly plant employing four thousand workers in the small town of Smyrna, located about twenty miles south of Nashville. The announcement was a landmark event that represented a number of "firsts" for Tennessee. For the first time, Tennessee had beaten a large number of other states in a spirited competition noted by the national media. The announcement signaled that Tennessee had gained the confidence of the tight-knit Japanese corporate community, the beginning of a long-term relationship that over the years saw Tennessee recruit dozens of companies from Japan.[7] Equally important, Nissan's investment led a parade of automotive manufacturers and their suppliers to the South, where Tennessee was well positioned to attract a disproportionate share of the new jobs. Alexander recognized the political as well as the economic value of the Nissan investment. By clever marketing of Nissan's choice of Tennessee, Alexander defined himself in the national media as a "New South" Governor, bold and future-oriented. While his opponents challenged the substance of the image, it was one welcomed and embraced by most Tennesseans.

Alexander's successful recruitment of Nissan (fig. 4.2) was followed in 1986 by the announcement from General Motors that Spring Hill, Tennessee, would be the site of the company's billion-dollar investment for its new Saturn automobile. Saturn's decision was the highest-profile recruitment victory in Tennessee history, accelerating the growth of the state's automotive industry and solidifying Tennessee's reputation as a new economic player on the national scene. The economic benefits to Tennessee and the political benefits to Alexander assured that future governors would make industrial recruitment a priority on their agendas. In addition to several international recruitment trips to Europe and Asia, Ned McWherter devoted as much personal time to "working the phones" with investment prospects as any single aspect of his administration. Don

Sundquist also traveled extensively to Europe and Asia to call personally on domestic and foreign prospects. While governors would adopt different styles and the quality of their recruitment personnel would vary, one fact was indisputable. In less than a decade, industrial recruitment had gone from the back burner to a primary responsibility of the Tennessee Governor.

Commander-in-Chief

The Governor's role as Commander-in-Chief of military forces is an example of a constitutional power that has changed dramatically from its original intent yet still has a relevant and important place in state government. The 1796 Constitution envisioned a Governor who needed authority to raise and lead a militia against Indian hostilities. The Governor's modern role as Commander of the Tennessee National Guard comes into play in a variety of circumstances involving natural disasters, domestic disturbances, and engagements by the American military overseas. While an adjutant general appointed by the Governor runs the National Guard on a day-to-day basis, it is the Governor who issues orders to mobilize the Guard and assign them to various duties. Governors Frank Clement and Ned McWherter, who had close prior association with the Guard, predictably gave more attention to Guard issues. For most governors, the Guard usually occupies a lower priority.

Decisions to activate the Guard have placed a mark on some extraordinary events in Tennessee's history. Gov. Frank Clement in 1956 left no doubt about his intentions to obey the federal court's integration orders when he sent the Guard into Clinton the morning after segregationists exploded a bomb in the local high school. Gov. Buford Ellington ordered the Guard into Memphis and Nashville in 1968 to quell rioting in the wake of the assassination of Martin Luther King Jr. During a 1993 ice storm that shut down power for days over some two-thirds of Tennessee, the Guard in many communities was a critical lifeline for the delivery of food and medicine.

Tennessee's early governors would be amazed at a third responsibility for the Guard that resulted from the downsizing of the American armed forces following the collapse of Soviet communism and the contraction of the Russian military in 1989. The modern Tennessee Guard plays a major part in the transport of soldiers and equipment when the United States becomes engaged in a foreign conflict. Thousands of Tennesseans were called up as part of Guard units that served in Saudi Arabia and Kuwait during the Gulf War with Iraq in 1991.

Tennessee units also were sent to Rwanda in 1994 as part of U.S. efforts to prevent widespread starvation caused by civil war. Regardless of whether governors assign much importance to the task, the Governor's role of Commander-in-Chief has changed greatly over two centuries yet remains a vital component of the constitutional powers granted to the office of Governor.

Sources of the Governor's Power

In the natural ebb and flow of influence that democracy produces between the executive and legislative branches of government, the modern Tennessee Governor has accumulated political power from several advantages unique to the office. Most of these contemporary sources of power have little to do with responsibilities granted the Governor by the state Constitution. Rather, the Governor benefits from the way in which seemingly unrelated parts of the political process have evolved over time.

The Governor's greatest single advantage stems from Tennessee's continuing commitment to a part-time legislature. Apart from the House and Senate leadership, senior members of the respective Finance Committees, and some Nashville-area legislators, few senators and representatives have much of a presence on Capitol Hill from May to January. While numerous legislators develop a good knowledge of selected state programs, only a handful have the experience to understand and debate the hundreds of funding items in the state budget. As the primary source of information about departmental budgets, personnel, federal policies, and simply how programs operate, the administration has a huge advantage over legislative committees with minimal staff and part-time legislators. The culture of the General Assembly's part-time "citizen legislature" results in the Governor being clearly the dominant player in a budget process that shapes the size and direction of state programs. This fundamental distinction, more than any other over the long term, is the most important defining element in the Governor's political relationships with the General Assembly.

This is not to suggest that Tennessee would necessarily be better off with a full-time legislature similar to those found in a number of northern and midwestern states (see chapter 3). Political changes of this magnitude come with tradeoffs that might or might not be acceptable to most Tennesseans. If the experiences of other states offer a guide, the additional staff that invariably accompanies a full-time legislature would contribute to making the legislative process more partisan and less civil.

To the extent such partisanship might jeopardize efforts to preserve a conservative fiscal policy or address pressing legislative problems, attempts to make lasting changes in Tennessee's part-time legislature will encounter serious reservations from legislators as well as governors.

In addition to having a vast advantage of information in the budget process, the Governor can be expected to use other advantages of office that together offer the potential to govern effectively. New governors and their senior staff require varying amounts of time to understand these sources of power and appreciate their political dimensions. Once again, whether the sources of executive power are used to their maximum benefit has a lot to do with the Governor's experience and interests, as well as the competency and continuity of the Governor's staff. The depth of a Governor's political influence at any moment in history can largely be determined by observing whether the following resources at the Governor's command were used often and well.

Allocating Budget Funds

The Governor's dominant role in the budget process is the single most distinguishing feature of the power balance in Tennessee's state government. Dozens of constituencies, from farmers to college students to local governments, are far more concerned with the level of annual state funding for their respective programs than with most issues that fill media accounts of the political process. Citizens often forget that the majority of state programs do not make frequent changes in mission or management policy. Year after year, the quality of state programs is more likely to be affected by levels of funding in the state budget than by bills debated in the legislature.

Although the General Assembly has made significant strides in becoming a more equal partner in the budget process, the tendency remains for legislators to concentrate on just a few of the hundreds of items contained in the budget document. The result is that in any given budget proposed to the legislature by the Governor, only a few funding items are changed in a substantial way before being enacted. The highly visible arguments that take place around these limited issues distract attention from the fact that some 98 percent of the Governor's budget is regularly approved by the legislature without change and with little discussion.[8]

Each side knowing this to be the case, the savvy Governor has the opportunity to use the budget to build coalitions for a variety of policy initiatives. The most common strategy uses "capital," or state-funded construction projects, as political leverage. A Governor can, for example, promise a legislator a new library at the local college in return for an "open mind" on health-care legislation. For decades governors also have used road projects to persuade a legislator to be more "flexible" on an issue of importance to the administration. Most Tennesseans never see or recognize the subtlety of such legislative deals. To some citizens, this kind of political horse-trading is ethically, if not legally, inappropriate. In a political world dominated more often by practicality than philosophy, such deals are an integral part of a legislative process whose very survival depends upon compromise. Some legislators, it should be emphasized, do not participate in trading support of one issue for another. These legislators, however, are seldom found in the inner circle of political decision making. An astute Governor can look at the state budget as a whole, carefully distribute needed projects, and in so doing build a working coalition for most issues within the legislative process.

Dispersing State Grants

Few Tennesseans are aware that governors have discretionary control over tens of millions of dollars in state and federal grant monies. Ranging in size from several thousand to several million dollars, these grants are available to colleges, local governments, and a variety of groups associated with state programs. Governors discover that these grants often can be used as effective leverage in the political process.

Some grants are developed with a great deal of thought and planning, while others appear more as an afterthought. Grants generally can be divided into two categories. The first allocates grants as a means of learning more about specific problems or ideas. Grants have been used, for example, to examine policy issues such as student testing or the care of juveniles with mental disorders. Agencies such as the Department of Transportation allocate millions of dollars annually to universities to conduct research on topics such as bridge construction or the composition of roads. Grant funds also are spent for pilot projects in attempts to test policy changes in selected communities before attempting to implement the changes statewide.

A second category of state grants involves federal funds allocated by the Governor for a wide variety of projects that otherwise would rarely be priorities in the state budget. These grants have been used to fund recreational greenways, urban trolleys, riverfront parks, and a broad range of other projects with only a marginal relationship to programs and services traditionally associated with state government. While most of the grants have some form of application process that involves competitive proposals, governors in fact usually have wide latitude in choosing the grant recipients.[9] Each grant is worth a story in the local newspaper and a political chip with local legislators and public officials. Used wisely, the grants serve to bolster the Governor's popularity among the public and solidify political relationships with legislators and local officials.

Coordinating Industrial Investment

The Governor's expanded role in recruiting business investment, while giving local communities a larger arsenal of resources with which to compete for new jobs, also greatly enhanced the Governor's political leverage with communities eager for assistance. Increasingly, companies considering a Tennessee investment approach the state Department of Economic and Community Development for guidance in identifying locations suitable for new plants and for financial incentives to make them more profitable. All things being equal, the Governor can point industrial prospects to any one of several communities and accompany the suggestion with several hundred thousand dollars worth of incentives. Ned McWherter in particular had a conscious strategy of guiding industries to rural counties in an effort to disperse jobs to the state's pockets of unemployment. Don Sundquist succeeded in greatly increasing legislative appropriations for industrial incentives and as a consequence expanded still further the Governor's role as an agent between local communities and prospective investors.

More than many observers realize, the new dynamics of industrial investment have had a substantial impact on the power of the Tennessee Governor. Mayors, county executives, and other local officials desirous of state assistance with business prospects cross the Governor at great risk. The Governor's annual Economic Development Conference has become one of the largest conventions in Tennessee, attended by virtually every local chief executive and chamber of commerce official in the state. Each person in attendance understands the rules of the game have changed in a fundamental way that channels increased political power to the first floor of the state Capitol.

Raising Political Campaign Funds

No one in Tennessee, including members of the United States Senate, can match the fund-raising capacity of an incumbent Governor. While senators might on occasion be able to raise substantial amounts for their personal campaigns, none has the time or influence to raise large sums for a variety of candidates in the manner available to the Governor. Although few legislators will admit it publicly, the awareness of the Governor's fund-raising potential, either for them or against them, is always a serious consideration when deciding whether to support or oppose an initiative important to the Governor.

As is the practice in many states, it has become customary for governors in Tennessee to begin their terms with a large fund-raising effort that accompanies the inauguration festivities. A host of special interest groups that wish to have access to the Governor and senior administration officials over the next four years willingly give amounts up to five thousand dollars. The Governor's fund-raisers generally are not so crude as to threaten those whom they solicit for contributions. The process is a subtle one understood by most of those involved. As expressed succinctly by one lobbyist, "No pay, no play."

Apart from the ethical issues raised by this practice, the large sums raised by the Governor have a direct political significance. If raised in a Governor's first term, the political war chest is a factor used to intimidate potential opponents in the next election. This fact, perhaps more than any other, contributed to the minimal opposition enjoyed by incumbent governors in the reelection campaigns of 1982, 1990, and 1998. The Governor can use campaign funds in a different but equally important way during the second term. Tennessee election laws allow the Governor to allocate personal campaign funds to assist other candidates throughout the state. The knowledge that the Governor is capable of writing a check for twenty thousand pieces of negative direct mail will give pause to even the most partisan legislative opponent.

Even if the Governor decides to keep most or all personal campaign funds, as some do, the opportunity still exists to raise large sums on behalf of other candidates. This type of fund-raising is usually done in one of two ways. A few telephone calls from the Governor or a senior staff member can be counted on to generate checks for a candidate. As an alternative, most candidates are happy just to have the Governor attend a fund-raising event, knowing that the Governor's presence will enlarge the crowd and contribute to the candidate's credibility. For a candidate, the best of all worlds occurs when the Governor agrees to host a fund-raiser at the Executive Residence in Nashville, an event guaranteed to produce several thousand dollars in contributions.

Most governors grow weary of the constant demand to raise money for themselves and others. They all realize, however, that their fund-raising potential is one of the greatest advantages they enjoy in the political process. So long as campaign laws make the advantage possible, they likely will continue to exploit its considerable leverage.

Dominating the Media

Communicating to the public through the media is an opportunity open to every legislator and, at least in theory, to all persons involved in the political process. In practice, few individuals in Tennessee ever come close to having either the access to the media or the public relations resources at the Governor's disposal. This fact often stacks the political deck in favor of governors, including those who are not particularly adept at understanding the nature and potential of public relations. For governors skilled in the art of using the media to convey messages to the public, the resources inherent in the Governor's office provide an enormous advantage in any political debate.

Unlike in Washington, where over time legislators as well as reporters achieve broad name recognition, the Tennessee Governor is the only individual in state government whom most citizens can name. Regardless of how influential a legislator may be in the halls of the Legislative Plaza, the influence can rarely compete with the Governor's credibility with newspapers or television stations hundreds of miles away. Most legislators do not have the staff, the media experience, or the "star power" enjoyed by the Governor. Moreover, political arguments simply do not resonate with most citizens when they come from unknown persons. Confronted with a statement by the Governor and a rebuttal from an unknown legislator living two hundred miles away, most Tennesseans consciously or unconsciously side with the person whom they feel they know best—the Governor.

Fortunately or unfortunately, depending upon one's point of view, most Tennessee governors have rarely maximized the potential of the public relations resources at their command.

Assessing Tennessee's Governors

As the roles and responsibilities have changed, so too have the power and influence of Tennessee's Governor undergone a remarkable evolution since 1796. From the early 1920s until the late 1960s, Tennessee's shift from an agrarian to a complex industrial-service economy combined with the oversight of expanded federal programs to transform state government. As in private enterprise, the day-to-day management of large programs in education, corrections, health care, transportation, and economic development demanded a strong executive. Recognizing this fact, Tennesseans twice amended the Constitution, in 1954 to give the Governor a four-year term and in 1978 to allow the Governor to run for reelection. The amount of attention and information required to plan and operate multimillion-dollar programs made it impossible for a part-time legislature with limited staff to remain on an equal footing with a rapidly growing executive branch. Other changes, including more sophisticated use of the media, the ability to raise large amounts of campaign funds, and the state's emerging influence in local economic development, all served to increase the power of the Tennessee Governor. Even as the legislature in the early 1970s began a gradual effort to restore the balance of power, Tennessee's economic prosperity in the 1980s and 1990s produced an era of good feeling that, in terms of political influence, generally benefited Tennessee's governors more than the General Assembly.

As one would expect, Tennessee's governors used this increased power and responsibility in different ways and with varying degrees of success. Each Governor was forced to work within unique political and economic constraints that formed agendas and shaped legacies. During the twentieth century's last three decades, most major state programs—education, health care, roads, environmental protection, welfare, prisons, mental health—experienced periods of dramatic improvement as the result of initiatives from respective governors. Unfortunately, many of these impressive strides came only after the public became aware of serious problems caused by years of benign neglect. Throughout the modern period, one finds governors with good ideas but poor management skills, and others who understood the levers of power but demonstrated little creative initiative. Some made bad decisions because they could not escape a rigid political philosophy and open their minds to new ideas. A couple experienced a profound change of mind on issues that led to bold proposals. With the exception of tax reform, most governors could get legislative approval for major policy initiatives. Most were honest. All were fiscal conservatives who tried to protect the state's financial reputation.

Despite the numerous advantages afforded the Governor by Tennessee's history and political culture, it remains unrealistic to expect the Governor to solve all problems and win all political battles. Even the most extraordinary skills sometimes cannot overcome the state's economic climate, the longtime neglect of a particular state program, or incompetent managers inherited from previous administrations. The brightest and most adept Governor has a limited amount of political capital that can be spent quickly and replenished only if invested wisely. A Governor's greatest challenge is understanding how to invest political capital. Rather than attempting to address every problem at once, the Governor must carefully construct a multi-year strategy that takes into account limits on the resources of time and energy and the ability of the legislature to absorb multiple policy changes. Much like a poker player in a high-stakes game, a Governor must not attempt to win every hand. Knowing when the political cards provide the winning odds and playing them aggressively are the secrets that enable governors to make lasting contributions. If played well, the Governor's "political chips" accumulate in a manner that offers the possibility of more winning hands. Conversely, by being reckless or timid, a Governor can squander much of the legislative influence inherent in the office.

Decades of political history and tradition might be turned upside down by one issue that threatens the power and influence of Tennessee's Governor and the alignment of the state's political institutions. Changes in Tennessee's economy, especially the growth of catalog sales and Internet commerce, have made it increasingly difficult for state government to capture enough sales tax revenues needed to fund basic services.[10] As the twenty-first century opened and other states accrued large budget surpluses, an antiquated tax structure in Tennessee based disproportionately on sales taxes produced enormous revenue shortfalls in a state accustomed to conservative fiscal policy. Efforts by Democratic and Republican governors and some legislators to join forty-two other states and implement a tax on income has met with ferocious opposition from much of the public. If and how the state resolves the issue of tax policy will define for years to come the quality and progress of a multitude of important state programs. Equally significant, the aftermath of the tax debate could fashion the state's political forces for the first part of the twenty-first century. Included in this historic process is a potential realignment of the state legislature and, depending upon circumstances yet to unfold, the evolving balance of power between the executive and legislative branches of Tennessee government.

5

The State Bureaucracy

They are the faceless image of state government, rarely seen on television or in the newspaper. Some go to work in suits, some in uniforms, others in overalls. They are often the target of Tennesseans who know little about state government but are quick to express criticism. On talk radio and in political commercials, they hear themselves referred to disparagingly as "bureaucrats," always in a tone meant to convey the image of lazy and overpaid state employees eating doughnuts in a Nashville office tower. Year after year, they endure such insults, knowing that the great majority of state workers live outside Nashville and make less money than the average Tennessean. They also know that none of these critics has walked the cellblocks at Brushy Mountain Prison or pulled bodies from a three-car wreck on Interstate 40.

Day after day, thirty-five thousand essentially anonymous people quietly turn the gears of state government. Despite the size and scope of state government, few Tennesseans have a clear idea of what it does. When a chemical truck overturns on a bridge or a highway is closed by a rockslide, citizens have—if only temporarily—an immediate sense of what the state bureaucracy means to their lives. On a daily basis, the presence and the importance of state government are more remote. Even education, the largest and most visible of state programs, is generally viewed by most citizens as one defined by local issues and personalities. In much the same way that a river makes news only when it overflows its banks, the mundane nature of most state government services makes it more likely to attract attention when bad things happen. The single prisoner who escapes generates far more reaction than the twenty thousand who are incarcerated without incident. On a personal level, a foul-up with the renewal of a driver's license can shape for years an individual's attitude about the competency of the entire state bureaucracy.

It is important to understand the ways in which government programs relate to a multitude of activities that affect the daily quality of life for more than five million Tennesseans. Some state agencies—education, health care, corrections—administer multi-billion-dollar programs that warrant individual chapters in this text. As important as these programs are, they only begin to reflect the scope of state government. In this chapter, we examine a portion of the remainder of the state bureaucracy, with particular attention to the manner in which the style and purpose of state agencies reflect the philosophy of Tennessee's political system.

Constitutional Officers

Crowded around the door to Hearing Room 30 in the Legislative Plaza, the four architects make nervous small talk as they wait their turn on the agenda of the State Building Commission. The represent the leading architectural firm in their community, with a combined experience of more than one hundred years. Despite their prominence back home, their palms are sweaty as they go over last-minute details for the presentation of plans for a new $20 million building at the University of Tennessee. To a great extent, the future reputation of their firm will be determined by a fifteen-minute presentation before three Constitutional Officers.

Four important leadership positions in the state bureaucracy were established by the Tennessee Constitution. Referred to as the Constitutional Officers, those holding these positions are the Comptroller, the Treasurer, the Secretary of State, and the Attorney General. Each position is independent of the Governor. All serve functions as staff and advisors to the legislative leadership and, depending on relationships, to the Governor. The Comptroller, the Treasurer, and the Secretary of State are elected in joint session by the House and Senate. The Attorney General is elected by the Tennessee Supreme Court.

Although the four Constitutional Officers employ staffs that are relatively small compared to those of agencies such as the Department of Human Services, they are among the most influential players in state government. Despite their influence, outside of the financial, legal, and architectural professions, few Tennesseans know their names. The Constitutional Officers operate most effectively out of the limelight, rarely seeking to embarrass or upstage the Governor or legislators. They wield their influence as central figures on a number of state boards and commissions that function with a lengthy and rigid set of procedures. Depending upon one's point of view, these procedures are seen as cumbersome red tape or as necessary to guard the state's moral and financial integrity.

Comptroller

The Comptroller is one of the least visible yet most influential individuals in Tennessee state government. Although the Comptroller sits on a multitude of state boards and commissions, the office has a single overarching mission: ensure that the financial business of state and local governments is conducted in a fair and honest manner. The Comptroller is elected in joint session of the Senate and House, usually during the second day of the January Organizational Session that follows legislative elections in November. The term of office is two years.[1]

Among the most important functions of the Comptroller's Office are the three divisions of State, County and Municipal Audit, a world of accountants who are the financial watchdogs of every state agency, every state college and university, and every local government. Persons in state or local government who entertain the idea of stealing money, giving state contracts to a friend, or otherwise abusing the public trust must do so with the expectation that one day an auditor from the Comptroller's Office likely will review their financial records. The staff also conduct periodic performance audits of various state agencies to determine if their programs reflect the legislative intent of the laws that created them years earlier (see chapter 3). Collectively, the staff of these three audit divisions include some of the most competent members of the state bureaucracy.

The Comptroller participates as a member and provides staff support for four other important state boards and commissions, all of which are largely unknown to most Tennesseans. The State Funding Board is responsible for issuing hundreds of millions of dollars in state bonds authorized by the General Assembly and for administering the payment on the state debt.[2] The Tennessee School Bond Authority oversees the issuance of bonds to state colleges and universities for the construction of revenue-producing facilities such as dormitories and arenas. The Tennessee Local Development Authority sets policy for issuing bonds to make loans to local government for water, sewer, and solid waste treatment facilities.[3] The State Board of Equalization is assigned the difficult task of seeing that property in Tennessee's ninety-five counties is valued and assessed fairly for purposes of taxation.[4]

The work of these boards represents the ultimate in "inside baseball," a maze of financial activities that few on the outside notice and even fewer understand. Despite the fact that the media rarely cover them and that governors and legislators seldom make public mention of what they do, the members and staff of these boards in one sense represent the essence of what the bureaucracy of a democratic government should be—honest and competent civil servants. On a weekly basis, their decisions have a multi-million-dollar impact on interest rates for state bonds, bids on large state construction projects, and the ability of local governments to raise funds for important initiatives.

The average citizen who attends a public meeting of these boards and commissions is often left numb by the detail of their procedures and the laborious manner in which they function. Not apparent to most, however, is the irresistible temptation for corruption that would occur in the absence of the rules and processes demanded by these boards and commissions. Whether through fear or moral persuasion, the Comptroller's Office during the last half of the twentieth century helped instill a culture of basic honesty that runs through most of state government and much of local government in Tennessee. In the context of governments throughout America and the world, that achievement is no small thing.

Treasurer

Although fewer than one Tennessean in a hundred could name the state's Treasurer, the office is one of the most important in state government. The Comptroller is joined on most state boards and commissions by the Treasurer, who also has a single guiding responsibility: sound management of the state's money. The Treasurer has served for decades as the financial confidant of speakers and senior legislators. Like the Comptroller, the Treasurer is elected for a two-year term by the General Assembly meeting in joint session.[5]

Most Tennesseans give little thought to precisely what happens to the billions of dollars collected in tax revenues before the money is actually spent on a state service or project. Through the Investment Division, the Treasurer adds billions of dollars, both to the state budget and the State Retirement Fund, from the investment of tax revenues. The Treasurer also invests money from the pension fund in a broad variety of stocks and bonds. Cash from tax collections is invested in certificates of deposit in banks and savings and loan institutions across Tennessee. The ability to direct the flow of millions of dollars on a weekly basis makes the Treasurer an influential voice among the state's financial industry.

A second important responsibility of the Treasurer is managing a pension fund that at the end of the twentieth century had some 170,000 active members and more than 60,000 retirees receiving monthly benefits.[6] Although few governors or legislators across the country talk about retirement systems when they run for office, measuring the strength of a state's pension system is an excellent way to tell how well a state manages its fiscal affairs. In the 1980s, states such as Alabama and Louisiana were forced to spend millions from their annual budgets to prop up retirement systems that did not have enough money to pay for the benefits of retirees. Through the Division of Retirement, Tennessee during the 1990s joined South Dakota as one of only two states that could boast of a state retirement system more than 100 percent funded. In other words, Tennessee's pension system actually took in more money each year than it paid out to retirees. That the Tennessee Treasurer has been able to build and maintain such a strong pension system is a reflection of two traits found throughout state government: a philosophy of fiscal conservatism coupled with a belief by both parties that some programs should be kept off limits to partisan meddling.

Using reams of economic data compiled by the University of Tennessee, the Treasurer is a lead player in a third activity crucial to the state's financial stability. Each fall the State Funding Board adopts a formal recommendation to the Governor and General Assembly that establishes the anticipated growth in state tax revenues for the coming year. To casual observers, whether this projected growth rate is 4.5 percent or 5.2 percent is of little interest. When applied to a multibillion-dollar budget, a variance of 0.1 or 0.2 percent in the growth rate translates into tens of millions of dollars up or down for state programs. The Governor and the General Assembly cannot by law adopt a state budget based upon revenue projections higher than those recommended by the State Funding Board. If, for example, the Board's maximum projected growth rate for the Tennessee economy is 4.1

percent, then the budget adopted by the General Assembly cannot contain programs and services representing a combined cost increase of more than 4.1 percent. Such a policy makes it extremely difficult for governors or legislators to adopt a budget loaded with pay raises or other items that likely would create a budget deficit. Thus, while the Treasurer is involved in few decisions about how the budget pie is sliced, the office has enormous influence on determining the size of the pie and, through this process, reinforcing a conservative approach to state finance matters.

Secretary of State

At most political and social functions where the Comptroller and Treasurer are present, one can usually also find the Secretary of State. The Secretary of State is the third Constitutional Officer on a number of boards and commissions dealing with financial matters. The Secretary of State is selected in the same manner as the Comptroller and Treasurer, the most significant difference being that the term is for four years.[7] Perhaps more so than the other two offices, the nature of the Secretary of State's responsibilities has changed over time. In the early years of the state's history, the Secretary of State's chief function was serving as the official repository of all state records. The broad range of records included laws enacted by the General Assembly, pardons issued by the Governor, and contracts entered into by the state. While the Secretary of State still provides this important function, the office expanded its duties during the last quarter of the twentieth century.

The Division of Administrative Procedures operates much like a judicial system to arbitrate disputes regarding the administration of policies in a multitude of state agencies. The division employs dozens of administrative law judges who conduct hearings on issues ranging from personnel complaints to disagreements between a business and the Department of Revenue over the interpretation of tax policy. The Division of Charitable Solicitations is responsible for keeping a registry of the hundreds of organizations seeking to raise funds in the name of charity. Protecting the public from fly-by-night operations is a constant challenge and is critical to the reputation of legitimate charities. Since 1959 the Division of Elections has sought to maintain a uniform policy of election procedures in every county for federal, state, and local elections. Few elections go by without a ruling by the State Election Coordinator about the qualifications of a candidate or the official vote tally in some Tennessee community. The Division of Libraries and Archives, in addition to housing official copies of state laws and documents at the State Library and Archives adjacent to the Capitol, also oversees sixteen regional libraries. In recent years the Tennessee Library and Archives has been used by thousands to study their family genealogy.

Although none of the state's founding fathers would have anticipated it, perhaps the most popular function of the Secretary of State is the biennial publication of the Tennessee Blue Book, an excellent and concise summary of Tennessee history and government. The Blue Book has become the gift of choice from legislators to thousands of Tennessee teachers and school children.[8]

State Building Commission

In most every state, the enormous amount of money involved in the construction and leasing of state property historically has been an irresistible temptation for graft. In Tennessee, the success of one state commission in stemming such corruption warrants special mention. Every purchase or lease of property, as well as all construction or renovation of state facilities, must receive approval from the State Building Commission.[9] Comprised of the two Speakers, the Comptroller, the Treasurer, the Secretary of State, and the Commissioner of Finance, the purpose and procedures of the Building Commission are a statement about Tennessee's approach to reducing corruption in an area of state government susceptible to inappropriate influence. Meeting publicly each month in the Legislative Plaza, the Building Commission selects architects for all construction projects, reviews design and cost proposals, and examines bids for all major contracts. Department commissioners and contractors are often scolded if projects are over budget or behind schedule. Architects have been shamed publicly for proposing flat roofs or otherwise unacceptable designs for a host of state projects.

The process is not perfect. Because the selection of architects for major projects must consider quality as well as cost, the process is perceived as arbitrary by some of those not chosen. The commission also has been accused of being unduly partial to those architects who make political contributions. These criticisms aside, the State Building Commission has made a lasting contribution not only to government integrity but also to the quality and cost efficiency of Tennessee's capital construction program.

Attorney General

The Attorney General is in some respects unique among Tennessee's Constitutional Officers. In duties and method of selection, the Attorney General differs from most others throughout the country. Whereas in most states the Attorney General is chosen in a statewide election, Tennessee is the only state in which the Attorney General is elected by the Supreme Court.[10] In a majority of states, the Attorney General is empowered to prosecute a variety of crimes. In Tennessee, during the eight-year term the Attorney General's authority to prosecute is confined to securities and state contract fraud.

The Attorney General's chief responsibility is to represent state government in a variety of areas, including all civil litigation before state and federal courts and all criminal cases in the appellate courts. Such cases often involve a constitutional challenge to laws recently enacted by the General Assembly. Other cases, such as those in the 1980s and 1990s that challenged the constitutionality of conditions in the state's schools and prisons, are high-profile events conducted personally by the Attorney General. The great majority of cases are important but relatively minor matters handled by a staff of more than one hundred attorneys in fifteen administrative divisions. During the 1990s, the office was in danger of being overwhelmed by the explosion of litigation in every area of government, from prisons to state hospitals.

Among the Attorney General's most important functions is interpreting the intent of statutes enacted by the General Assembly. Each year the Attorney General will be asked by legislators or other public officials to "opine," or provide formal written rulings clarifying questions about the intent of a statute or article of the Tennessee Constitution. The consequences of these rulings range from the insignificant to the far-reaching, such as whether the state Constitution prohibits the legislature from enacting a tax on income.

Legislators, editorial writers, and others periodically debate whether the Attorney General should be chosen in a statewide election instead of being selected by the five-member Supreme Court. Both sides make a compelling argument. Opponents of the current system contend that an individual with such influence should not operate insulated from the public will. Others point to a number of states where persons often view the office of Attorney General as a stepping stone to a candidacy for governor. In seeking high-profile issues and cases for political visibility, these persons are tempted to place politics ahead of other, more important functions of the office.

Antiquated or Efficient?

While most Tennesseans do not have an informed opinion about the selection and duties of the Constitutional Officers, many who do believe the present system is an antiquated process that does not reflect the bipartisan nature of the state's modern political culture. They point out that among the four Constitutional Officers, not a single Republican was elected to serve during the last half of the twentieth century. They note further that a single individual served as Comptroller from 1953 until 1999, and that only two persons served as Treasurer from 1976 through the close of the century. Supporters of changing the process suggest that a different method of selection might introduce new personalities and philosophies to what they view as a rigid political system

As with many issues of Tennessee state government, the debate eventually gravitates to the question of how one balances the priorities of process and results. Some would argue that the unique longevity of Tennessee's Constitutional Officers has owed less to political influence than to the simple fact that they did a good job. Supporters contend a process that produced the nation's highest bond rating, a strong pension system, an efficient capital construction program, and a general culture of honesty throughout state government is one that should not be tinkered with carelessly. So long as these factors exist, one should not anticipate serious efforts to amend one of the least understood yet most important parts of Tennessee's bureaucracy.

Executive Departments

She knew from fifteen years' experience that a phone call at 1:30 A.M. meant bad news. A single mother from East Tennessee, Nancy had been given a small promotion to move to the Nashville office of the Department of Human Services. The voice on the phone gave her instructions similar to those she received about twice a month. On this evening, she would drive to a housing project in North Nashville and attempt to take custody of an abused child from a drunk and belligerent mother.

The executive branch of state government is closely identified with the comments and initiatives of the Governor. While the Governor is the person best qualified to express government's priorities and direction, the image of state government ultimately is determined by the performance of thousands of workers in the executive branch bureaucracy. They work for twenty-one separate departments, some of which have

Fig. 5.1. Tennessee State Office Building, Nashville, 2001. Photograph by John M. Scheb II.

offices in each of Tennessee's ninety-five counties.[11] A relatively small number of executive branch employees—many fewer than in the past—received their jobs as a result of political connections. Many entered state government by scoring well on civil service examinations. The remaining portion of state employees is comprised largely of low-wage workers who perform unskilled labor in state institutions.

Contrary to frequent criticisms, most state workers are competent and qualified for their jobs. Still, the overall quality of state government often suffers when measured against comparable parts of the private sector. With very few exceptions, salary compensation for state jobs is not competitive with private salaries that are determined more by the market and less by political considerations. Indeed, one of state government's secondary functions is to serve as a training ground for employees who work a few years and then offer their experience for higher pay elsewhere. The salary-related turnover among lower-level management is accompanied by similar turnover among top-level management that occurs after a change in administrations. Winning candidates for governor who pledged during the campaign to "run government like a business" often have eliminated many of the bureaucracy's most experienced employees during the first month in office, an act most successful businesses would question.

The twenty executive branch departments can be divided roughly into three categories that, with a bit of overlap, can be used to help understand their missions. The first group manages large facilities and is responsible for the custody of adults or juveniles. The second group provides a variety of distinct services to citizens and communities. The third group could be defined as quasi-regulatory in nature.

A final thought is helpful in understanding the executive branch. The twenty departments and their respective commissioners are not equals in the eyes of the Governor. Depending on the Governor's priorities and the Governor's personal relationship with the commissioner, the departments inevitably fall into a pecking order. To the consternation of many commissioners, the unwritten pecking order determines face-time with the Governor and staff, which in turn affects legislative emphasis and budgetary support for the department.

Custodial Agencies

Most Tennesseans are aware that state government's responsibilities include the operation of prisons. The sheer size of the prison system, coupled with the visibility given by the media to crimes and criminal trials, contribute to this awareness. These responsibilities are exercised by the Department of Correction (see chapter 13). Far less attention is given by the media and, unfortunately, by the Governor and the legislature to two other state agencies assigned the twenty-four-hour custody of human beings: the Department of Children's Services and the Department of Mental Health and Mental Retardation.

The Department of Children's Services has a mission in some respects more complex than its adult counterpart.[12] The expansion of the department's mission in the mid-1990s to include a variety of child-related services such as foster care, protective care, and adoption placed a strain on the ability to evaluate and provide appropriate services to youth who in many cases have multiple problems. Still, the department's most challenging function remains the custody of about five hundred juveniles, most of whom have committed multiple felonies and are committed by the courts to state custody with a combination of psychiatric and education needs.

Federal law and judicial rulings have determined that an individual's eighteenth birthday is a threshold that delineates the responsibilities and management options for the adult and juvenile correctional systems. Those under eighteen years of age are considered by definition "children," capable of having their minds educated and their behavior transformed. As they perhaps should be, Tennessee's four juvenile corrections facilities are held to far higher standards of education, treatment, and supervision than the adult prisons. Strict policies limit the ability to punish misbehavior or segregate those incarcerated on the basis of age and gender. Many of these policies were designed for facilities that in the past operated more like schools, not fully taking into account that contemporary fifteen and sixteen year olds often are as hardened and dangerous as twenty year olds three decades ago. To a great degree, facilities and treatment programs developed for burglars and runaways must attempt increasingly to integrate a population filled with juveniles convicted of murder and other violent offenses.

In the 1950s thirty-two-year-old Gov. Frank Clement made an impassioned plea for Tennessee to abandon the notion that persons with psychiatric or developmental problems should simply be warehoused in medieval conditions. His leadership led to the creation of the Department of Mental Health and Mental Retardation, a department that on the whole has maintained high standards of care at its nine residential facilities. The department operates four mental retardation facilities for adults and children in Greeneville, Nashville, Arlington, and Bolivar. Five facilities for persons with mental illness are located in Knoxville, Nashville, Chattanooga, Bolivar, and Memphis.[13]

Like states across the country, Tennessee has struggled with the debate between those who support the institutionalization of persons with serious psychiatric problems and others who advocate releasing the majority of patients to a variety of programs in the community. Even the best of psychiatric hospitals are depressing by nature, leading many outsiders to endorse efforts to "deinstitutionalize" as many patients as possible in favor of group homes and other assisted living programs. Three problems have impeded this movement. While paying lip service to the notion of group homes for the mentally ill or mentally retarded, few communities are actually willing to accept the facilities in desirable neighborhoods. The issue is compounded by the occasional disturbance of a former psychiatric patient whose behavior becomes violent after forgetting or refusing to take prescribed medicine. Ironically, just as efforts to establish new group homes have met with resistance, so too have attempts to close state institutions encountered legislative opposition from those concerned about the loss of jobs and payroll in the surrounding area. The result is a state policy that is neither fish nor fowl. No state mental health institution has been closed despite greatly reduced patient populations, while mental health advocates claim resources for community facilities on the whole have not kept pace with needs.

Agencies That Provide Services

The Tennessee bureaucracy contains nine departments for which the primary mission is the delivery of services to various segments of the public and business community. They are the departments of Agriculture, Economic and Community Development, General Services, Health, Human Services, Military, Safety, Tourism, Transportation, and Veterans Affairs. The agencies range in size from the Department of Human Services, with more than five thousand employees who manage food stamps and other programs for the poor, to the Department of Veterans Affairs, with fewer than one hundred employees.

Some of these departments receive only sporadic attention from the Governor or the media, usually in the case of minor corruption or a major vacancy. The Department of General Services has the

Fig. 5.2. On left, Tennessee State Office Building; and on right, Shelby County Office Building; both in Memphis. Photo by William Lyons.

responsibility of purchasing, managing, and disposing of everything from computers to state vehicles, a task that in the past has been involved in abuse and corruption. Located in each county, the Department of Health provides thousands of immunizations, prenatal care, and other health services, largely to the poor. The Department of the Military houses the Tennessee National Guard, an agency that despite its highly politicized culture is one of the largest and best guard units in America. The Department of Tourism does little more than place television and magazine ads, often sharing a fee with advertising agencies that supported the Governor's election campaigns. The Department of Agriculture is an advocate for a diminishing but still important and politically active portion of the state's economy.

Among the state departments that deliver services, three occupy a separate plateau of special importance to most governors. Although most Tennesseans primarily think of the Highway Patrol when they drive too fast or witness a wreck, a legacy that goes back more than a half-century makes this division of the Department of Safety among the most politicized agencies in state government. In many of Tennessee's counties, one finds troopers divided—sometimes openly—into Democratic and Republican factions. Early commitment to a candidate for Governor, especially in the primaries, can lead to rapid advancement in the event one bets on the winning horse. Meanwhile, those on the losing side can look forward to working the night shift on Interstate 65.

Even more political in a different way is the Department of Transportation, a massive agency with an annual budget in excess of one billion dollars. A community's economic future can depend on the location of a new road or even a new exit on an existing road. For all but a few legislators, the widening of an existing road or the construction of a new one is the most visible and convincing evidence to voters of legislative effectiveness. Legislators find it possible to be "flexible" toward a host of otherwise distasteful bills if support for the Governor's position is linked to a road project needed back home. Construction can be separated into numerous annual segments, either to extend a legislator's ability to demonstrate "steady progress," or, conversely in some cases, to send voters a message that the incumbent does not have the political clout "to get the job done." The department's influence in the legislature is accompanied by the ability to raise large amounts of campaign contributions from the state's road contractors. Taken together, these factors underscore the unique importance placed on state road projects and make the Department of Transportation a major player in Tennessee's bureaucracy.

During the 1980s and 1990s, the Department of Economic and Community Development rose to the top tier among executive branch agencies in terms of political importance. Nationwide, governors increasingly view the recruitment of large, high profile new industries as a means not only of generating political support but also of leaving a lasting monument to their administrations. The decision by the automotive industry to build a series of large assembly plants in the South accelerated a trend by southern governors to begin offering tax breaks, roads, water and sewer infrastructure, job training, and other inducements to industries thinking of moving South. Tennessee was among the first to play the game successfully. During the administration of Lamar Alexander, both Nissan in 1982 and Saturn in 1986 chose Tennessee as the site for a major manufacturing plant. To a large extent, these plants constitute Alexander's political legacy.

On occasion, governors competing for such "marquee investments" have been accused of being financially reckless in their zeal to lure new companies. Such criticisms were leveled at Kentucky Governor Martha Layne Collins's inducements for Toyota in the mid-1980s and at Alabama Governor Jim Folsom's successful bid in 1993 for Mercedes, an unprecedented incentive package that dwarfed a very competitive proposal from Tennessee.[14] Folsom was so eager to win that he promised to install the three-pronged symbol of the German corporation atop Birmingham's Legion Field, a stadium named in honor of the American Legion that defeated Nazi Germany in World War II.

When and how the state should extend companies inducements to come to Tennessee—or to stay there—is a matter of growing debate among both legislators and economists. Tennessee has been relatively conservative in regard to such inducements, believing that there is a threshold beyond which the state does not receive a net revenue return on tax breaks and other investments. To this concern is added the resentment of existing Tennessee companies that do not share in the incentives offered to companies locating in the state for the first time. As other states become ever more aggressive, Tennessee governors and legislators will repeatedly need to determine how best to navigate a process with no rules and no guidebook.

Policy and Regulatory Agencies

The final category of agencies that make up the Tennessee bureaucracy contains departments that are far from equal in status and scope. The Department of Financial Institutions, formerly the Department of

Banking, is charged with oversight of Tennessee's state-charted banks. Beginning in the mid-1980s, the department's scope of responsibility gradually diminished as liberalized banking laws resulted in the acquisition of small, locally owned banks by regional holding companies located in Atlanta, Charlotte, and Richmond. A traditionally unnoticed department was thrust onto center stage in early 1983 when the collapse of the Butcher banking empire, headquartered in Knoxville, led to the subsequent closure of dozens of small banks across Tennessee. The department received substantial criticism from legislators and the media for allowing widespread corruption in the Butcher banks to go undetected for years.

The Department of Revenue, while often mistaken for the federal Internal Revenue Service, is an important though much less aggressive agency than its federal counterpart. The department's mission is to collect the sales, franchise, excise, gasoline, and other taxes owed the state, mostly from businesses. Citizens who believe the tax laws to be clear and straightforward are surprised to learn that the commissioner must frequently rule on complex interpretations of the Tennessee tax code. The media seldom notice such decisions, but whether, for example, Memphis-based Federal Express pays tax on jet fuel purchased in Indiana and transported to Tennessee is of great financial consequence to all involved.

A third quasi-regulatory agency is the Department of Labor and Workforce Development, created in theory to protect the health and safety of workers while taking into account the rights and needs of the state's employers. The department inspects work sites to make sure conditions are safe, employees are compensated without regard to gender, and minors are not subjected to excessive hours on the job. An important but little understood agency responsibility is the administering of workers' compensation laws that govern if and how much employees are paid for being injured on the job. The workers' compensation program illustrates why the Department of Labor, perhaps as much as any in state government, reflects a genuine philosophical difference between Democrats and Republicans. Democratic governors traditionally have appointed Labor commissioners from the ranks of organized labor, while Republicans have just as frequently filled the post from the ranks of business. In an effort to consolidate job training and job placement activities, the Sundquist administration in 1998 combined the departments of Labor and Employment Security.

While some state departments have a narrow and well-defined focus, the Department of Commerce and Insurance at times appears to be the repository of any program discarded or not coveted by other parts of the bureaucracy. The department was created in 1873 as the Bureau of Insurance to regulate the licensing and standards of the state's growing insurance industry. In addition to housing the Insurance Division, the department also is home to the diverse regulatory boards and commissions, the state's Consumer Affairs Division, the State Fire Marshall's office, and TennCare, the state's multi-billion-dollar indigent care program left on the agency's doorstep in 1995 by the Department of Finance and Administration. Despite the size and scope of the department's portfolio, the Commissioner is rarely a part of the Governor's inner circle.

Another department with a strange blend of responsibilities is the Department of Environment and Conservation. Some political activists historically have maneuvered for appointments as Commissioner, attracted by the department's relatively pleasant mission as steward of Tennessee's state parks and natural areas. The sober reality they inevitably encounter is that the Commissioner and staff devote a disproportionate amount of time to the department's broad array of environmental responsibilities. Many who would expect the department to regulate air and water pollution are surprised to learn its responsibilities also include cleanup of hazardous waste sites, regulation of landfills, and tracking of the movement and disposal of toxic wastes, all complex programs involving federal, state, and local governments. The controversial nature of the department's mandate often forces the commissioner and, indirectly, the Governor to referee emotional disputes among the interests of business, environmental, and local government groups. The task is sometimes complicated by sharp philosophical differences between a politically appointed Commissioner and a career staff identified more strictly with environmental concerns.

For every governor, the Department of Education is among the most visible and important agencies in the Cabinet (see chapter 11). Citizens and legislators alike devote more attention to Education's budget and policy questions than to those of any other department in the bureaucracy. Performance expectations are higher, and, more so than with other departments, expectations are annually measured in great detail—in the form of student test scores. The Commissioner of Education is frequently called to testify in the legislature and speak to a variety of education and civic groups across the state.

Most governors at some point undertake a significant education initiative, making it imperative that the Commissioner and staff work closely and effectively with the Governor, the Governor's staff, and education leaders in the General Assembly. To an extent not appreciated by many outsiders, a Governor's education reputation is tied to the talents of the Education Commissioner and a bureaucracy that in the past was often a dumping ground for local superintendents who had been defeated for reelection. A governor with no particular background in education policy can still succeed if assisted by a talented and effective Education Commissioner. The reverse, however, is seldom true. Even a pro-active and knowledgeable governor has difficulty achieving meaningful changes in the education bureaucracy without a respected and energetic Commissioner.

First among Equals: Department of Finance and Administration

The high-profile nature of departments such as Education and Transportation disguises the fact that within Tennessee state government, the Department of Finance and Administration, commonly referred to as F&A, is undisputedly first among equals. The department's mission can be summarized in two simply stated functions: allocate the state's resources in such a way as to recognize the priorities of the Governor and the legislature and keep the state budget in balance. The execution of these two goals is enormously complex and demands great political skill, so much so that only the most talented of Finance Commissioners have left office with their reputations fully in tact.

Placed in context, Tennessee's Finance Commissioner oversees a budget with cash flow greater than all but a few of America's largest corporations. Within the budget is a multitude of programs, services, and contracts, most of which involve millions of dollars. Unlike most corporations, a majority of the programs and services have constituencies that are not reluctant to make their needs known to governors, legislators, and, on occasion, the media. Also unlike the private sector, the Finance Commissioner must develop a budget and sell it in through public discussion to 132 legislators who have a variety of priorities, loyalties, and ambitions. The state budget, once approved, must be sustained by revenues that are not contingent upon a good product or the ability to develop an effective marketing campaign. Rather, the Commissioner is at the mercy of an economy that, because of Tennessee's heavy reliance on sales tax revenues, is subject to fickle and unpredictable shifts in consumer attitudes toward the purchase of durable goods such as cars and furniture.

The demands of the job require a Commissioner with unique talents. Foremost is a good chemistry with the Governor, an absolute requirement for daily conversations about difficult decisions. An effective Commissioner must blend a sound knowledge of finance matters with equally good personal skills. An absence of the latter is the most common reason some Finance Commissioners from the business world have failed in state government when they could not accommodate the compromise required of legislators and other state officials. This talent is frequently put to the test in the Commissioner's role as the person who, instead of the Governor, must say no to an endless series of budget requests. The practice became so common under Gov. Ned McWherter that his Finance Commissioner, David Manning, was unaffectionately known within the state bureaucracy as "Dr. No."

Located about one hundred feet from the Governor's office, the Commissioner's office on the first floor of the Capitol is the initial battleground of political infighting in state government. All state agencies must run their budget proposals through F&A, and it is rare indeed for another Commissioner to prevail in an argument with a Finance Commissioner who sees the Governor on a daily basis. Some Finance Commissioners are content to stay in the background and confine their roles strictly to managing state finances. Others on occasion have sought a more visible role as policy makers. They are rarely loved and often loathed by their colleagues in the administration and the General Assembly. In either case, they are among the most important components to the relative success or failure of Tennessee's modern governors.

Boards, Commissions, and Agencies

After patiently waiting his turn, Jeff entered and sat down in the sparsely decorated office. He had driven 250 miles to see the Director of the Governor's Transition Office, the person largely responsible for recommending many of those who would receive appointments or jobs in the new administration. Jeff had been a loyal and effective county coordinator in the 1986 governor's race. He had come to Nashville to ask a favor of the new Governor. The Transition Director was surprised when Jeff professed no interest in a state job. "What I've always wanted," Jeff said, "is a position on the Pest Control Board."

Like every state in the country, the Tennessee bureaucracy contains an array of boards and commissions created over the decades by the General Assembly. Within each profession are members for whom appointment to the governing board represents the achievement of status among their peers and in their local community. A major criterion for most appointments is friendship with the Governor, a member of the Governor's senior staff, or a legislator from whom the Governor seeks or owes a debt of gratitude. At century's close, dozens of separate boards and commissions were in existence. A few of these boards, such as the Boxing and Racing Commission, had little business and did not meet regularly. A larger category of boards was created to regulate specific professions, such as doctors or realtors. A third category, smaller in number but more far-reaching in scope, actually makes policy decisions as important as many of those debated in the legislature. While it is impractical to examine each board and its functions, a general sense of their collective role is a vital part of understanding the nature of Tennessee state government.

The Professional Regulatory Boards: Protecting the Consumer or the Profession?

Virtually every business profession in Tennessee has convinced the General Assembly to establish a state board dedicated ostensibly to developing and maintaining standards for the profession. Critics would argue that the real function of these boards is to protect existing professions from competition.

The vast majority of professional boards are comprised of persons who are selected by the Governor and whose compensation is limited to travel expenses. The larger boards have a full-time Executive Director, while some smaller boards in related professions share an Executive Director. Apart from hosting annual meetings and occasional educational seminars, the boards have two primary functions, both of which from time to time generate controversy. The first involves establishing standards for obtaining and renewing a professional license, usually in the form of written and sometimes oral examinations given once or twice a year. Each board confronts the challenge of developing licensing standards that are rigorous enough to protect the quality of the profession, while not so high as to make it unreasonably difficult for new persons to obtain a license. Every few years the legislature is presented with complaints about a licensing board with standards so high that few, if any, new applicants can pass its examination and thus provide competition to existing members. In most instances, a public scolding before the legislature's Government Operations Committee serves to resolve this problem.

A second and much more sensitive function of the professional boards is a greater source of concern among citizens and legislators. Most boards have a mechanism established, at least on paper, to sanction members of the profession who engage in inappropriate behavior, either during or apart from the performance of their professional duties. Most boards agree in theory that whether it be doctors, lawyers, realtors, or any other group, it is in the best interests of the public and the profession to revoke the license of those guilty of unethical behavior. In practice, it has proved very difficult in Tennessee, as it has in most states, for professional boards to impose even minimal sanctions against one of their own. Even after discounting confirmed complaints that are only "unethical" as opposed to allegedly "illegal," many close to the process have doubts as to whether Tennessee's professional boards are as diligent as they should be about ridding their professions of unscrupulous practitioners. While it is true that the staff for these boards are woefully ill-equipped for the volume and complexity of complaints, it remains that some boards with thousands of members go for years with few or no sanctions.

Other Regulatory Agencies

While the work of the licensing boards is confined largely to developing standards and monitoring the activities of their respective professions, the General Assembly assigns a more policy-oriented function to a number of regulatory boards.[15] As in most states, the regulatory boards exist to help apply to specific cases guidelines established by the legislature for a host of important and often complicated issues. For example, despite the best efforts of the legislature and the Department of Conservation and Environment to define lengthy standards required to operate a landfill, each year witnesses several local governments attempting to defend operations or permit applications before the Water Quality Control Board. In much the same way, the Air Pollution Control Board is empowered to levy fines on Tennessee's largest industries in the event the board determines emission standards have been exceeded. The ability to deny a landfill permit or fine a major corporation means that the meetings of the regulatory boards, while rarely covered by the media, are frequently attended by some of the most expensive legal and professional consultants available.

The activities of two regulatory boards warrant special mention. In a move that represented a significant philosophical shift, the Health Facilities Commission was created in 1973 by the General Assembly in an attempt to provide a more rational process of growth for the hospital and nursing home industries.[16] Without such oversight, the legislature feared that the competition for each hospital to provide a comprehensive array of services would lead to an escalation of health-care costs and the financial collapse of hospitals and nursing homes in both urban and rural communities. The Health Facilities Commission served to reduce somewhat the overbuilding of beds and the unnecessary duplication of expensive equipment. Critics complained, however, that inappropriate influence applied to commission members too often compromised the commission's mission and integrity. Moreover, the growing number of hospital and physician alliances resulting from the 1993 implementation of competitive managed-care contracts in the state TennCare program raised a fundamental question about the continued need for state regulation of health-care facilities.

An entirely different constituency group, many wearing orange hunting vests instead of tailored suits, follows closely the decisions of the Tennessee Wildlife Resources Agency (TWRA). With more than five hundred employees across the state, the eleven-member TWRA is responsible for developing and enforcing policies governing wildlife, fishing, and boating. In many areas of Tennessee, a vote for a sales tax increase will bring a legislator less grief than votes by TWRA to change the deer season or introduce an unpopular species of fish into an area lake. Appointments to TWRA are among the most coveted a governor can dispense.

Too Many Boards and Too Few Resources

This section has examined only a handful of the dozens of state boards and commissions that are an important part of responding to the public's desire for increasingly high standards of health and safety in their daily lives. Indeed, the sheer number of boards, coupled with their respective responsibilities, has made it impossible for governors and legislators to keep up in a meaningful way with the daily activities of all but the most visible. Governors are overwhelmed simply with filling the multitude of vacancies that must constantly be awarded to persons they hope are at least moderately competent and loyal to the administration. Professional boards likewise are overwhelmed by an avalanche of complaints and license renewals that must be handled by staff that are undermanned and subject to frequent turnover. In the absence of close oversight, some boards find themselves more influenced by relationships within the profession than an obligation to serve the public interest.

None of this suggests that Tennessee's boards and commissions are fundamentally flawed or that they should be eliminated. They exist to serve what in most cases is a mission understood and supported by the public. What Tennesseans must also understand and accept are the limitations imposed by resources and circumstances, and the fact that in a government with limited resources some functions will be held to lower expectations than others.

Openness in State Government

One of the expectations of modern democratic government is that the decision-making process should be open to public view. Anyone can watch the debate on the floor in the Tennessee House or Senate or listen to oral arguments before the Tennessee Supreme Court. All meetings of county commissions, city councils, and local school boards are open to any member of the public. The phrase "sunshine" is used to express the requirement of open meetings for all government entities in Tennessee. Although not all of the important decision making of state government takes place in the "sunshine," much of what goes on in contemporary Tennessee government is visible to the public. Government in Tennessee is generally more open than in most states, a fact established by the state's open meetings and open records laws.

Open Meetings

Tennessee public agencies, including universities and all departments of state, city, and county governments, must conduct their business subject to the provisions of the state's open meetings law.

The preamble of the bill states clearly the law's intent: "The General Assembly declares it to be the policy of this state that the formation of public policy and decisions is public business and shall not be conducted in secret." The law reaches beyond elected officials to include any nonprofit agency where public funds make up at least 30 percent of the agency's budget. A meeting is defined as any assembling of the members of any public body that "consists of two or more members, with the authority to make decisions for or recommendations to a public body on policy." The translation of this law prohibits, at least technically, two school board members or two members of a city council from having a private telephone conversation about public business. In contrast to the tradition of closed-door meetings that historically characterized much of state and local government, the implications of the law were extraordinary. While Tennessee's open meetings law does not include inspections of public projects or the chance meeting of individuals, its authors were explicit in pointing out that electronic communications and "informal" gatherings should not be used to circumvent the spirit of the act. The law is far-reaching, applying even to labor negotiations between agencies and public employee unions, a fact that has a particular impact on Tennessee's school boards and local teachers organizations.

All meetings covered under the open meetings law must be publicly announced with appropriate notice, usually at least a week, provided for both regular and special meetings. Minutes of meetings must be fully recorded and open for public inspection. The law does not allow secret votes and requires that all votes must be publicly recorded. The law also stipulates that actions taken by any affected agency not in compliance with the procedures of the open meetings law become null and void.

On paper, Tennessee's open meetings law is an excellent attempt to provide the public a better understanding of their government and put in place a more meaningful process of accountability for those who make decisions. Despite its noble goals, many who work in government on a daily basis are cynical about the law's methods and unintended results. Critics contend it is impractical and foolish for important decisions to be made without discussion among the parties beforehand. Legislators argue that airing disputes and ideas in private leads to a better product than one produced by those who fear every word might be published in the newspaper. Many school board members believe it absurd to think parties can enter negotiations involving millions of dollars without prior and candid discussions. Regardless of whether these arguments are valid, such discussions take place on a regular basis as a part of the political process. Legislators in their right minds do not schedule a bill for a committee vote without having discussed it beforehand with committee members. University board members do not arrive in town to vote on million-dollar projects without some prior conversation. To think otherwise is hopelessly naive.

From time to time various citizens or groups wish to challenge government decisions on the basis of a perceived violation of the open meetings law. In many cases, their suspicions are valid but incapable of being proved. Challenging actions or even laws for violations of the open meetings law requires filing a suit in circuit or chancery court, an act that involves considerable time and expense. The court has the power to enjoin any violator not to violate the act further as well as to impose penalties beyond the nullification of any action taken. Such suits are not frequent. At the local level, the threat of suit sometimes involves a game of bluff, each side hoping the other will fold before going to court.

While the purpose of Tennessee's open meetings law is clear, its enforcement and practical benefits are less so. The law is a burden to many honest government officials who believe some problems can be best addressed through candid and private discussions. The law is equally burdensome to citizens who, believing that an agency or employee has acted improperly, must file suit to seek redress. Despite these and other examples of unintended consequences, few can argue that the law has brought Tennessee government miles from the days of secret meetings, secret votes, and a total absence of accountability to the public it exists to serve.

Open Records

In 1977 the General Assembly codified a thorough set of procedures to ensure that any state agency's records are open to the public for inspection.[17] These records include all books, papers, and correspondence of the offices covered in the open meetings law. Exceptions include interoffice memos by the director and staff, along with similar materials from another agency considered confidential. A limited number of records from specific agencies also are considered confidential. For instance, the records of all Tennessee students, communications within the office of the Attorney General relative to pending legal action, and information concerning industrial prospects in the Department of Economic and Community Development are not open to public inspection.

Individuals can review open records by showing a valid driver's license when requesting access. Personnel records are not exempted, including records of applications for open positions. This requirement has led Tennessee colleges and universities to hire consulting firms to identify candidates for positions as presidents and chancellors. This expensive backdoor process is needed to allow potential candidates for these positions to express interest privately, without the risk of exposure to their current employers.

Tennessee's open records laws on occasion are burdened with problems of cost and the invasion of personal privacy. As the 1990s drew to a close, one wanting to obtain an employee's telephone number could do so by requesting personnel records. More troublesome were broad requests for information that required large amounts of staff time and photocopying. Determining appropriate costs and the line between reasonable and unreasonable requests for information remained a challenge. These issues aside, the intent of the law is very clear. The business of the state is to be conducted in the open.

Understanding the Limitations

The Tennessee state bureaucracy, like most governments across the nation, suffered a significant loss of public confidence during and after the anti-government rhetoric of the Reagan administration in the 1980s. As is often the case, some of the criticism was valid and much was overblown. A fair assessment would probably conclude that the Tennessee bureaucracy's strengths and weaknesses are mirrored in most large and diverse private corporations. Most of the thirty-five thousand or so state employees are competent and perform well. A small percentage does not. Some divisions and programs function with impressive efficiency. Others are plagued by a lack of initiative or a failure to understand the "big picture"—the fact that each agency is part of a larger whole with multiple priorities.

The most common misconception of the Tennessee bureaucracy is that it is grossly overstaffed. While this charge may have been valid in some departments in the mid-1980s, an extended period of attrition during the McWherter and Sundquist administrations sharply reduced the number of state employees in virtually all departments other than the Department of Correction.[18] Indeed, by the close of the twentieth century one could argue that some programs were understaffed to the point their purpose and worth were in question.

During a period when governors were indicted in Alabama, Arkansas, Oklahoma, and Louisiana, with a single exception involving the Secretary of State, Tennessee state government did not have a major corruption scandal since road contractors were caught rigging construction bids in 1983. Largely because Tennessee for the most part has enjoyed honest leaders, a culture of honesty has developed throughout most of state government.

Finally, a fair judgment must take into account three handicaps that make it impossible for Tennessee state government to function with maximum efficiency. Senior managers turn over in wholesale numbers at each election and frequently are forced to change course to suit the priorities of the new chief executive. Second, these managers are not and never will be paid salaries remotely competitive with their private industry counterparts, making it impossible to recruit talent in adequate numbers. Perhaps most important, the bureaucracy in effect works for a governing board with 132 independently elected members, a challenge faced by no corporation in America.

Given these obstacles, the state's ability to build a bridge, clean up a landfill, operate a prison or mental hospital, manage universities, or renew a driver's license takes on an entirely different perspective. From this perspective, one should be less surprised at the Tennessee's bureaucracy's shortcomings than at the fact that it works as well as it does.

6

The Judiciary

In August 1996, Tennessee voters ousted Justice Penny White from the state supreme court. White was running unopposed in a merit retention election in which voters were asked simply to vote "yes" or "no" on the question of whether she should be retained in office. The election was not a recall referendum, but rather the first application of a new system for judicial selection and retention known as the "Tennessee Plan." Although the Tennessee Plan has some unique features, the process is basically a form of merit selection and retention that originated in Missouri in 1940 and later was widely adopted by the states.[1]

Nationally, the overwhelming majority of judges who stand for merit retention are retained. Justice White, however, had the distinct disadvantage of being the first Tennessee Supreme Court justice to be subjected to merit retention. Undoubtedly, many voters in 1996 did not understand the new system. Indeed, because the system was new and because Justice White's name stood alone on the ballot, many voters may have assumed that she was being subjected to some sort of recall effort. Actually, in a way, she was. The Tennessee Conservative Union had targeted White for defeat, charging her with being "soft on crime." More significantly, the Republican Party saw an opportunity, for the first time in modern history, to defeat an incumbent Democrat justice, and, with the aid of Republican Gov. Don Sundquist, secure a Republican appointment to the court.

Justice White, an appointee of Democrat Gov. Ned McWherter and the court's first female member (fig. 6.1), was viewed by her detractors as one of the Tennessee Supreme Court's more liberal justices. As evidence, White's adversaries pointed to her alleged "soft" record on crime. Specifically, opponents objected to a handful of White's votes involving death penalty cases. Much of the discussion on editorial pages and talk radio centered on one very controversial decision. White had joined two other justices who, on grounds of improper procedure, voted to reverse the death sentence in a grisly case involving the rape and murder of an elderly Memphis woman.[2] By focusing public attention on this unpopular decision, opponents were able to frame Justice White's merit retention election not as a referendum on her competence or diligence, as the new law intended, but as an expression of support for the death penalty. The strategy sealed White's fate, even though on numerous occasions she had voted to uphold death penalty convictions. In trying to defend herself against harsh and often inaccurate criticism, White was hampered by the canons of judicial ethics, which prevented her from explaining decisions delivered from the bench.[3] The fact that

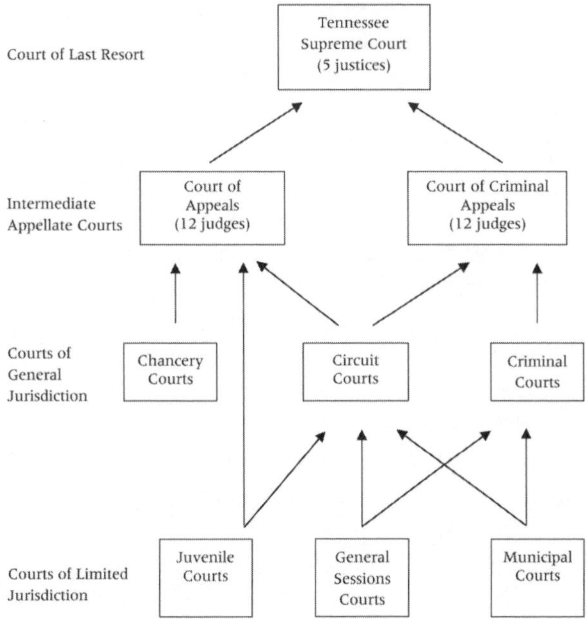

Fig. 6.1. Tennessee Court System.

Tennessee had not carried out an execution in thirty-six years also seemed to have little impact on an electorate that at times appeared transfixed with the death penalty issue. Ultimately, the voters opted for White's ouster by a margin of 55 percent to 45 percent. Only 19 percent of the state's registered voters cast ballots in this election. Had the turnout been higher, the outcome might have been different.

In the wake of Penny White's ouster, appellate judges in Tennessee perhaps became more attentive to public opinion and less assiduous in applying unpopular legal rules. Such sensitivity may or may not have been the objective of many who targeted Justice White in the merit retention election. It is equally likely that the death penalty rhetoric was a device employed by Republicans to defeat an otherwise competent Democratic justice. While Justice White and her supporters objected to what they perceived as the "politicization" of the judiciary, the episode's irony lies in the fact that White was not defeated, as judges have been in other states, because she was guilty of attempting to make policy from the bench. Rather, she found herself placed on the wrong side of a highly emotional issue in a period of increased visibility for the court. After decades as a secondary player in Tennessee politics, the Tennessee Supreme Court since the mid-1980s had moved closer to center stage. Since this shift, students of modern Tennessee government and politics cannot afford to ignore the state judiciary.

Tennessee Court Structure

Alexander Hamilton once characterized the judiciary as the "least dangerous branch" of the federal government.[4] In Tennessee, the judiciary is not only the "least dangerous" but also the least intelligible branch of state government. Unlike the executive and legislative branches, Tennessee's judicial branch in several respects is as much a reflection of the nineteenth century as the twentieth century. The Tennessee court system (if "system" indeed is the appropriate term) is a confusing patchwork of specialized courts, overlapping jurisdictions, and local variations in rules and procedures. Average Tennesseans, most of whom are poorly versed in any aspect of government, find the state judiciary particularly impenetrable.

The first Tennessee Constitution, adopted in 1796, empowered the state legislature to create circuit and chancery courts in each of the state's ninety-five counties, as well as a three-judge state supreme court. Not until the Constitution of 1835, however, were the state courts recognized as an independent branch of government. The courts acquired equal constitutional status, including the power to interpret statutes authoritatively and to declare unconstitutional legislation null and void.[5]

Today's Tennessee court system is based on Article VI of the Constitution of 1870, the charter that remains in effect at the beginning of the twenty-first century. Article VI, Section 1, of the Tennessee Constitution declares: "The judicial power of this State shall be vested in one Supreme Court and in such Circuit, Chancery and other inferior Courts as the Legislature shall from time to time, ordain and establish." Over the years, the General Assembly has availed itself of this authority, establishing a number of specialized tribunals and modifying the jurisdictions and procedures of various courts.

Much of the complexity of the Tennessee court system is attributable to the legislature's frequent use of private acts (laws that have only local applicability) to create particular local courts and make

Fig. 6.2. Justices of the Tennessee Supreme Court, 2000. Standing, from left, Associate Justices Frank F. Drowota III, Adolpho A Birch Jr., William M. Barker, Janice M. Holder; seated, Chief Justice E. Riley Anderson. *Source:* Administrative Office of the Tennessee Courts.

changes in the jurisdictions of existing tribunals. A century of creating such courts produced an inefficient judicial system in which it was difficult to determine which court was responsible for what cases. During the early and mid-1970s, experts on judicial administration called for the system to be overhauled.[6] In 1977, a limited constitutional convention adopted a proposed revision of the judicial article of the state constitution. For a variety of reasons, voters ultimately rejected this attempt to reform the court system.[7] One of the main sources of opposition to the amendment was the Tennessee Trial Lawyers Association, which maintained that the current system was not in need of overhaul. Additional opposition came from various judges who perhaps felt threatened by the proposed change. Since then, the legislature has accomplished a number of reforms by statute. Nevertheless, compared with other state court systems, Tennessee's still ranks as one of the most complex and archaic.[8]

Every state has a court system with individual features. While these unique aspects of judicial structure and process vary greatly, most state judicial systems share a number of common principles and procedures. Every state, for example, has a collection of trial courts and one or more appellate courts. Trial courts make factual determinations and settle disputes by applying applicable principles of law. Appellate courts review the decisions of trial courts, correct errors, and settle legal questions that are in doubt. In every state, there is one tribunal with final authority on matters of state law; in most instances it is called the state supreme court. Many states, including Tennessee, have intermediate appellate courts directly below the Supreme Court to handle routine appeals. This approach seeks a division of labor that permits the state supreme court to focus on the most important and difficult questions of law. At the trial level, most states differentiate between courts of general jurisdiction and courts of limited jurisdiction. The former are the "major" trial courts; they conduct civil and criminal trials in more serious cases. Courts of limited jurisdiction handle less serious matters such as misdemeanors and small claims, and often they conduct preliminary hearings in cases that will be tried in the courts of general jurisdiction. Courts of limited jurisdiction also include specialized trial courts, such as municipal and juvenile courts.

Figure 6.1 depicts the structure of the Tennessee courts. The structure has four levels: trial courts of limited jurisdiction; trial courts of general jurisdiction; intermediate appellate courts; and, at the apex of the judicial hierarchy, the Tennessee Supreme Court.

Courts of Limited Jurisdiction

Often called "local courts" because they are funded exclusively by city and county governments, the courts of limited jurisdiction have jurisdiction to try minor civil and criminal matters. Local courts also handle preliminary matters in major civil and criminal cases.

Courts of General Sessions

The most important of the courts of limited jurisdiction is the Court of General Sessions. The general sessions courts were created by the state legislature in 1960 to replace the antiquated justice of the peace system. Justices of the peace were judges of limited jurisdiction; often they were not formally trained in the law. As law became more complex, especially in the area of criminal procedure, justices of the peace became increasingly dysfunctional.

General sessions courts function in all of Tennessee's ninety-five counties, although two counties in East Tennessee refer to these courts as "trial justice courts." The jurisdiction of the general sessions courts varies from county to county, based on private acts adopted by the General Assembly. Essentially, general sessions courts handle preliminary matters in major criminal cases and have jurisdiction to try minor criminal and civil matters.

General sessions judges have the authority to issue search and arrest warrants. The judges also have power to set bonds for persons released from custody pending resolution of their case. General sessions courts also conduct preliminary hearings to determine whether there is probable cause to believe that a defendant is guilty of the crime charged. If the court makes a finding of probable cause, the defendant is bound over to the grand jury (see discussion of grand juries below). In Tennessee, a defendant cannot be found guilty of a felony unless he or she is first indicted by a grand jury. Persons accused of misdemeanors also have the right to grand jury indictment but can waive this right, in which case they are tried by the sessions court. Minor misdemeanors, which Tennessee law calls "small offenses," do not require indictment by the grand jury. These cases are tried by the sessions court. General sessions courts do not impanel juries, so any trial in this court is before the bench (judge). Sessions court judges also serve as juvenile judges, except in those counties for which the legislature has established a separate juvenile court.

In terms of civil jurisdiction, the general sessions courts are authorized to try small claims.[9] They also have jurisdiction over suits to recover personal property with no limit on dollar value. Because the sessions courts are not courts of record, appeals from their judgments take the form of *trial de novo* (basically, a new trial in which testimony is taken again for the record) in the courts of general jurisdiction.

Juvenile Courts

Beginning in the late nineteenth century, states established juvenile courts as an alternative approach to dealing with crimes committed by juveniles. Juveniles are defined in Tennessee as persons less than eighteen years of age. The idea was to remove juveniles from the harsh system of criminal justice for adult offenders and place them in a system that emphasized rehabilitation rather than punishment. Tennessee first established juvenile courts in 1905, but only in the three most urbanized counties of the state.[10] Today, there are nearly one hundred juvenile courts in the state.[11] These courts have exclusive jurisdiction in proceedings involving minors alleged to be delinquent, unruly, dependent, or neglected. Juvenile courts also have concurrent jurisdiction with circuit, chancery, and probate courts in some areas. In districts lacking juvenile courts, jurisdiction over juvenile cases is vested in the general sessions court. In Tennessee and elsewhere, it is increasingly common for juvenile courts to waive jurisdiction when minors are charged with serious criminal offenses such as murder or rape. The transfer of a juvenile to an adult court is especially likely in the case of older juveniles with previous criminal offenses. Waiver of jurisdiction occurs on the motion of the district attorney general. If the motion is granted, the case is transferred to the criminal (or circuit) court, so that the juvenile can be tried and sentenced as an adult.

For most of the twentieth century, juvenile courts existed in loosely defined legal territory. Juvenile judges, for example, were not required to be attorneys until the 1980s. Judges exercised wide discretion over sentencing, with punishments for similar crimes varying greatly in different parts of the state. A surge in violent crimes by juveniles in the 1970s and 1980s led to expansion of the juvenile detention system and growth in the number of juveniles tried and sentenced by adult courts.

Municipal Courts

Also known as "city courts," municipal courts have geographical jurisdiction within their particular cities. About three hundred of Tennessee's cities have municipal courts. Their substantive jurisdiction extends to the violation of city ordinances. The most common matters these courts deal with are parking and traffic violations. Many cities in Tennessee have adopted ordinances that mirror state criminal law in the area of misdemeanor offenses. The purpose is to have such offenses, when committed within city boundaries, tried by municipal courts in a process that provides an additional revenue stream to cities. Generally, a municipal judge may assess fines up to fifty dollars and jail sentences up to thirty days. However, such powers vary widely from city to city. Decisions of the municipal courts are subject to review via trial de novo in the courts of general jurisdiction.

Municipal courts are constituted by city charters that set forth the qualifications for city judges. For example, the Knoxville city charter provides:

> There shall be a judge of the municipal court of said city who shall be elected by the qualified voters of said city, and shall hold office for a term of four (4) years, and until a successor is elected and qualified. Said judge shall be not less than thirty (30) years old, and shall have been a resident of said city for three (3) years immediately prior to election, and shall be licensed to practice law in the State of Tennessee.[12]

Ostensibly, municipal courts serve as a convenient means of disposing of minor matters. They have been criticized for the informality of their procedures, which at times compromises the integrity of the court. Certainly a disproportionate number of complaints filed with Tennessee's Administrative Office of the Courts relate to the municipal courts. Some would go so far as to characterize the municipal courts as revenue-raising agencies rather than judicial tribunals. Without question, the municipal courts would be prime targets for abolition if reformers could remake the state judiciary.

Trial Courts of General Jurisdiction

Tennessee's ninety-five counties are divided into thirty-one judicial districts. Within each district are circuit courts and chancery courts, as provided by the state constitution. About one-third of these districts also feature specialized criminal courts, and a few even have separate probate courts to handle estates. Since 1984, trial judges in each district have elected one of their number to serve as presiding judge for that district.

Circuit Courts

Tennessee's circuit courts are courts of general jurisdiction, which means that they hear both civil and criminal cases. In thirteen of the state's thirty-one judicial districts, separate criminal courts relieve the circuit courts from hearing criminal cases. The civil jurisdiction of the circuit court is quite broad, encompassing torts, contract disputes, condemnations, worker's compensation claims, and divorces. Circuit courts also have jurisdiction over probating wills, although in two districts separate probate courts have been established. More commonly, the circuit courts establish divisions to deal with probate and divorce cases. For example, the circuit court in the twentieth judicial district (Davidson County) is comprised of eight divisions; of these, one deals exclusively with probate, and another handles all divorce cases. Circuit judges also hear appeals from courts of limited jurisdiction. These appeals take the form of trial de novo (a new trial).

Chancery Courts

Chancery courts are exclusively civil courts. They were established as "courts of equity" (as distinct from "courts of law") to handle matters falling outside traditional common-law actions. Chancery courts reflect the court system's English origins. Traditional equity courts are based on the English system, in which the Lord High Chancellor acted as the "King's conscience." The Lord High Chancellor could modify the application of strict legal rules and adapt the relief given to the circumstances of individual cases. Until recently, Tennessee's chancery courts maintained this distinctive character. Cases were heard by chancellors (as distinct from "judges"), in whom considerable discretion was vested. Chancery courts did not conduct jury trials. Today, the chancery court is very similar to the circuit court (their jurisdictions overlap substantially and in some districts are coextensive).

Although still presided over by "chancellors," chancery courts now operate according to procedures essentially the same as in the circuit courts; they even conduct jury trials.[13] Given that the jurisdictional and procedural differences between the chancery and circuit courts have been largely eliminated, the justification for maintaining these courts separately is not readily apparent. Because both the circuit and the chancery courts are mentioned in the state constitution, arguably it would require a constitutional amendment to consolidate these tribunals, not an easy thing to obtain in Tennessee.[14] Add to this difficulty the considerable political influence of chancellors and a general lack of public concern about the courts, and it becomes even less likely that legislators or Governors will undertake the kind of initiative needed to reform these two antiquated remnants of the state's judicial system.

Criminal Courts

Criminal Courts were established by the General Assembly to relieve circuit courts in areas burdened by heavy caseloads. Criminal courts exist in thirteen of the state's thirty-one judicial districts. In addition to having jurisdiction over criminal cases, the criminal court judges hear misdemeanor appeals from the general sessions courts. Criminal cases are handled at the trial level by circuit court judges in districts without criminal courts. Because criminal courts specialize in criminal cases, which differ significantly from civil cases in both substantive law and procedure, there is some justification for maintaining these separate tribunals. Certainly most of the judges now serving in Tennessee's criminal courts would have some difficulty adjusting to a circuit judgeship, and most are quite content to specialize in criminal jurisprudence.

Intermediate Appellate Courts

One of the features that distinguishes the Tennessee court system is the divided structure of intermediate appellate courts. In 1895, the General Assembly created the Court of Chancery Appeals. In 1907, this tribunal, renamed the Court of Civil Appeals, acquired appellate jurisdiction over the circuit as well as the chancery courts.[15] In 1925, the name was changed to the Court of Appeals.[16] In 1967, the legislature established the Court of Criminal Appeals to handle routine appeals in criminal cases.[17] Thus, at present two intermediate appellate courts exist, one for civil cases and one for criminal cases. Tennessee is one of only two states with such a structure at the intermediate appellate level.[18]

Court of Appeals

Currently composed of twelve judges, the Court of Appeals hears most appeals of civil cases from lower courts.[19] The Court of Appeals meets in Knoxville, Nashville, and Jackson. When meeting in one of these cities, the court hears cases originating in the lower courts of the corresponding grand division of the state. A panel of three judges normally hears cases in the Court of Appeals. A strictly appellate body, the Court of Appeals does not take testimony or admit evidence. The judges review the records of lower courts to determine whether errors exist that warrant reversing the lower court's decision. The judges begin by examining the briefs submitted by counsel for both parties to a case. Review of the written briefs is followed by the appearance of counsel representing both parties, to make arguments orally and answer questions from the bench. As in most court proceedings, oral arguments are open to the public, although people seldom attend. Cases are decided in private conferences among the judges. The court's decisions, justified by written opinions, are reported publicly. Decisions of the Court of Appeals may be appealed to the Tennessee Supreme Court, which hears such appeals at its discretion. The Court of Appeals renders the final decision in a great majority of the cases it hears.

Court of Criminal Appeals

In the 1960s, when the Tennessee Supreme Court needed relief from a growing number of routine criminal appeals, the General Assembly might have expanded the jurisdiction of the Court of Appeals to deal with this caseload. However, the Court of Appeals judges, not wishing to broaden their responsibilities or increase their workload, persuaded the legislature to create a parallel tribunal exclusively for routine criminal appeals. Also composed of twelve judges, the Court of Crim-

Fig. 6.3. Fayette County Courthouse, Summerville. Photo by William Lyons.

inal Appeals operates in essentially the same way as its civil counterpart, with jurisdiction limited to:

(1) Criminal cases, both felony and misdemeanor;
(2) Habeas corpus and Post-Conviction Procedure Act proceedings attacking the validity of a final judgment of conviction or the sentence in a criminal case, and other cases or proceedings instituted with reference to or arising out of a criminal case;
(3) Civil or criminal contempt arising out of a criminal matter; and
(4) Extradition cases.[20]

As with the Court of Appeals, panels of three judges sit monthly in Jackson, Knoxville, and Nashville to hear cases from the corresponding grand divisions. The Tennessee Supreme Court retains discretionary jurisdiction to review decisions of the Court of Criminal Appeals.

Tennessee Supreme Court

The party was hosted by one of Nashville's prominent socialites at her home in Belle Meade. Among some one hundred persons in attendance were legislators, members of the Governor's cabinet, and various leaders of the city's business community. Most of those present ambled from room to room, mingling and chatting easily with friends and strangers. One group, however, did not mingle with the crowd. The five men congregated in the study, sitting in a closed circle with glasses of Scotch. Seemingly oblivious to the commotion surrounding them, they turned their attention and quiet conversation toward each other. Even at a party, no one present, including leaders of the state's legislative and executive branches, thought it proper to invade the discussion of the Tennessee Supreme Court justices.

At the apex of the judicial system is the Tennessee Supreme Court. Composed of five justices (fig. 6.2), not more than two of whom can live in any one of the state's three grand divisions, the Supreme Court has the final word on all questions of state law.[21] The state constitution requires the court to meet in Knoxville, Nashville, and Jackson. While sitting in one of these cities, the court hears appeals from that grand division of the state.

The creation of the intermediate appellate courts to handle routine civil and criminal appeals has enabled the Supreme Court to concentrate on the most important issues of state law. The only cases that may bypass the appellate courts are those in which the principal question has to do with the constitutionality of state statutes, or with local ordinances when "there is a special need for expedited decision and which involve (A) state taxes; (B) the right to hold or retain public office; or (C) issues of constitutional law."[22] In such cases, the Supreme Court may assume jurisdiction directly, assuming that one of the parties to the case requests it to do so. The only cases in which the Tennessee Supreme Court must grant review are those involving the death penalty, disciplinary actions against attorneys, and tenure of teachers. The ability to control its agenda enables the Tennessee Supreme Court to avoid much of the case volume found in other state supreme courts and focus its energies on issues of significance to state and local governments.

In addition to interpreting state law, the Supreme Court also plays an important role in supervising the administration of the state court system.[23] The Supreme Court determines the rules of procedure for itself and all other courts of the state, although these rules are subject to approval by the General Assembly.[24]

Judicial Review

Like the federal courts, Tennessee's courts of law exercise the power of judicial review—that is, the authority to rule on the constitutionality of governmental action. This power is not recognized explicitly in the Tennessee Constitution or the U.S. Constitution. Rather, in Tennessee as in the federal system, judicial review has been established through judicial assertion, the accumulation of precedent, and the acquiescence of the political community. Just as the Governor and the legislature have seen their powers and responsibilities evolve over time, so the judicial branch has changed in ways that, if they have not made the judiciary an equal branch of government, at least have rendered the Supreme Court a more serious player in Tennessee's political system.

At the trial level, the chancery court often exercises the power of judicial review because that is usually where plaintiffs seek injunctive relief against unconstitutional governmental actions. However, all courts of record can declare laws unconstitutional if that is necessary to the resolution of cases before them. For example, in 1995, the Davidson County Circuit Court struck down a state statute prohibiting private, consensual homosexual acts. The court found that the Homosexual Practices Act violated the right to privacy implicit in the state constitution. The Court of Appeals affirmed the circuit court, and the Tennessee

Supreme Court denied review.[25] Accordingly, the act was stricken from the Tennessee Code.[26]

Judicial Activism and Restraint

For the most part, the Tennessee courts have shown considerable restraint in the exercise of judicial review. In some instances, the state courts could be faulted for showing too much deference to the other branches of government. For example, in *Kidd v. McCanless* (1956), the Tennessee Supreme Court refused to review the constitutionality of the malapportionment of the General Assembly, saying that courts "have no power to compel either the legislative or the executive department to perform the duties committed exclusively to their respective domains by the fundamental law."[27] Of course, aggrieved citizens turned to the federal courts and ultimately found relief.[28]

A more activist judicial posture is seen in the more recent "Small Schools Case," filed in 1987 by seventy-seven rural school systems arguing that the state's educational funding system was unconstitutional (see chapter 11). In a landmark decision with far-reaching consequences, the Tennessee Supreme Court held that "the Tennessee Constitution guarantees to the school children of this State the right to a free public education and imposes upon the General Assembly the obligation to maintain and support a system of free public schools that affords substantially equal educational opportunities to all students."[29] In what for Tennessee was a bold use of judicial review, the court found "constitutionally impermissible disparities" in the funding of school districts across the state and ordered the legislature to remedy the situation. However, the court gave the legislature considerable leeway in redressing the problems, which helped to mute criticism that the court had gone too far in its use of judicial review.

Correcting Legislative Malfunctions

Sometimes the legislature must turn to the courts to correct blunders in the legislative process. A good example of this is the Toy Towns case.[30] During its 1997 legislative session, the General Assembly passed a statute that became known as the "Toy Towns law."[31] When introduced in the legislature, the bill's caption indicated that the proposal amended the Tennessee Code "relative to the distribution of situs-based tax collections after new municipal incorporations and the timing of elections to incorporate new municipalities." Unknown to all but a few legislators, a key provision of the legislation dramatically reduced the population requirements for municipal incorporation. This made it likely that tiny towns would spring up in suburban areas wishing to block annexation by larger cities. Not surprisingly, Tennessee's cities were alarmed by this development, which had moved through the legislature almost unnoticed. The reaction of opinion leaders across the state to the legislation was almost uniformly negative. The law immediately was challenged by the Tennessee Municipal League and a number of cities. The chancery court rejected the challenge, ruling, in effect, that the General Assembly has the constitutional right to enact a bad law. The plaintiffs, increasingly desperate, took the case to the Court of Appeals. At this point, recognizing the unusual circumstances involved and under intense private pressure from political leaders, the Tennessee Supreme Court intervened, using its "reach down" power granted by the legislature.[32] This unique feature of Tennessee's legal system permits the Supreme Court to expedite an appeal in order to determine a question of "unusual public importance." Relying on Article II, Section 17, of the Tennessee Constitution, the court held the act invalid, not because the content of the new law was unconstitutional but because the bill enacted by the General Assembly dealt with a topic that was not included in the bill's caption (see chapter 3). Writing for a unanimous bench, Chief Justice Riley Anderson observed that

> [t]he purpose of Article II, §17, is to prevent "surprise and fraud" and to inform legislators and the public about the nature and scope of proposed legislation. The constitutional purpose is effectively thwarted when a restrictive caption is employed and then legislation is adopted which is broader than the caption. In this case, although we are convinced the General Assembly's action was in good faith, the restrictive caption failed to adequately inform the members of the General Assembly and the citizens of this state about the nature and scope of the legislation that eventually passed.[33]

The court's decision raised eyebrows among legislators and legal scholars. In rescuing the legislature from a tight spot, the court relied upon a constitutional provision frequently ignored by the General Assembly. If some observers believed the court had invoked a seldom-used provision of the Tennessee Constitution to correct a breakdown in the legislative process, they were right. Employing a highly creative interpretation of the constitution did not mean, however, that the court had acted irresponsibly. Each branch of government has a dual responsibility to foster laws that are sound as well as legally on firm ground. In the instance of the Toy Towns law, both legislative and judicial branches had the good sense to recognize that a mistake had been made and the good judgment to correct the mistake before irreparable harm could be done to the state. The court's decision left the General Assembly free to enact the measure again, although all parties involved knew that the issue was effectively dead. More important, the turmoil and embarrassment aroused by the issue insured that, at least for a time, the legislature would be more diligent in monitoring so-called "housekeeping" bills.

Politics of Judicial Selection

The state constitution requires that Tennessee judges be elected to eight-year terms, then leaves it to the General Assembly to determine the process under which such elections take place.[34] Until the 1970s, all state judges were elected on partisan ballots. Partisan elections continue today at the trial court level, where candidates run as Democrats or Republicans. State law requires that candidates be lawyers and meet certain residency requirements. Those wishing to be judges campaign much as people run to be elected county sheriff or county executive, the only real difference being that judicial candidates are somewhat limited in their campaign rhetoric by the canons of judicial ethics. Partisan judicial elections are controversial, in Tennessee and elsewhere. Many judges dislike having to run for office and deplore the fundraising, handshaking, and endless social functions that campaigning requires. For several decades, reformers in Tennessee and elsewhere have criticized the partisan election of judges, leading many states to abandon or modify the traditional model in favor of a more "merit-based" approach. As early as 1940, two scholars of Tennessee government observed, "If the popular election of judges is to be retained, methods should be devised that would insure the selection of men properly trained for the judicial offices."[35] Concern over judicial qualifications, as well as the politics of judicial selection, has led reformers to propose merit selection and retention of state judges.

Tennessee Plan

In 1971, the General Assembly adopted an alternative mode of selection for the judges of the intermediate appellate courts.[36] Patterned after a model first deployed in Missouri in 1940 and now widely used among the states, this new approach represented an attempt to reduce the effect of partisan politics and increase the emphasis on merit in judicial selection and tenure decisions. Under the so-called "Tennessee Plan," when a vacancy occurs in the appellate courts, a judicial selection commission takes applications, interviews applicants, and ultimately submits a list of three names to the governor, who then appoints one of these individuals to fill the vacancy. When that judge's term has expired, he or she runs unopposed in a "retention election," in which voters vote "yes" or "no" on the issue of whether the incumbent should be retained. If the majority votes in favor of retention, the incumbent serves an entire eight-year term, after which another retention election is held. If not, the merit selection process begins anew.

In 1994, the General Assembly extended the Tennessee Plan to cover the Tennessee Supreme Court. As noted above, Justice Penny White, who had been appointed by Gov. Ned McWherter to fill an interim vacancy, was the first Supreme Court justice to run for retention under the new system. Justice White's name appeared by itself on the ballot in the context of the question "Should Justice Penny White be retained?" This may have led some voters to assume that Justice White was being subjected to a recall vote. Two years later, all five members of the state supreme court came up for retention. Despite some opposition to Justice Adolpho A. Birch Jr., all of these incumbents were retained by comfortable margins.

Advocates of merit selection and retention contend that the system removes "politics" from the selection and tenure of judges. More accurately, the newer process only changes the nature of the political forces at work.[37] The Governor, for example, still can be expected to fill numerous judicial vacancies with persons supportive of the party in power. State and local political leaders, as well as interest groups such as labor or the district attorneys, still lobby the Judicial Selection Commission and those involved in a merit retention election on behalf of particular candidates. The key to the Tennessee Plan, as with any similar system, lies in the choice of Judicial Selection Commission members. In many states, the Governor and the organized bar dominate the selection of the commission. In Tennessee, both the leadership of the state legislature and the Governor have substantial input into the process. By statute, appointments to the commission are made by the Speaker of the Senate and the Speaker of the House. The state's legal community also plays an important role, however. The Tennessee Bar Association, the Tennessee Trial Lawyers Association, the Tennessee Defense Lawyers Association, and the Tennessee Association of Criminal Defense Lawyers all submit lists of names from which most of the commissioners must be chosen. State law provides for input by the general conference of Tennessee district attorneys. Lest lawyers totally monopolize the commission, the statute also provides for the appointment of three members who are not lawyers. Finally, the speakers are constrained to "appoint persons who approximate the population of the state with respect to race, including the dominant ethnic minority population, and gender."[38] Each appointment of commission members, as well as each name nominated to the Governor for consideration, is the product of dozens of telephone calls and political considerations. The Judicial Selection Commission submits to the Governor a list of three nominees for each vacancy. The Governor is not bound to accept any of the nominations and may require the commission to provide a new list until an acceptable name is submitted. Behind-the-scenes conversations, usually with the Governor's legal counsel, typically yield the result desired by the Governor.

Considerable debate remains as to whether the Tennessee Plan, or any system of merit selection and tenure, actually produces a better qualified appellate judiciary. While the process certainly is not apolitical, it is designed to introduce a measure of expertise into judicial selection, along with assurance that the interests of minority groups are not ignored.

Judicial Discipline and Removal

One of the problems that any court system must address is how to discipline judges who engage in unethical or inappropriate conduct. The time-honored mechanism for judicial discipline is impeachment and removal from office, but in recent years many states have moved to supplement this cumbersome process.

Impeachment

According to Article V, Section 4, of the Tennessee Constitution, judges who "commit any crime in their official capacity which may require disqualification" may be impeached by a majority vote of the House of Representatives. If the House returns one or more articles of impeachment, a trial is held in the Senate, with the Chief Justice of the Tennessee Supreme Court presiding. The Senate must achieve at least a two-thirds majority to convict the accused.[39] Upon conviction, the accused is removed from office and disqualified from holding public office in the future. The impeached judge also may be subject to subsequent criminal prosecution, if appropriate, according to the normal process.[40] The lengthy and complicated impeachment process, which mirrors the procedure specified in the U.S. Constitution, is seldom utilized. The last time it was invoked to remove a state judge was in 1958, when a criminal court judge was impeached and convicted on several charges.[41]

The impeachment process described above applies not only to judges, but also to Constitutional Officers (see chapter 2). This general impeachment process applies only in cases of criminal misconduct and not ethical lapses or conduct unbecoming a judge. However, Article VI, Section 6, contains an additional removal provision applicable only to the judges and attorneys general. It states: "Judges and Attorneys for the State may be removed from office by a concurrent vote of both Houses of the General Assembly, each House voting separately; but two-thirds of the members to which each House may be entitled must concur in such vote." This section does not make reference to criminal misconduct, suggesting that judges could be removed for essentially any reason that the legislature determines to be just cause. The two-thirds majority vote required in each chamber acts as a safeguard against removing judges for strictly political reasons.

Court of the Judiciary

In 1979, the General Assembly created the Court of the Judiciary to assist in cases involving the removal of judges. Composed of judges, attorneys, and laypersons, the Court of the Judiciary reviews complaints about judicial conduct, often from disgruntled litigants or attorneys. Where these complaints are determined to have merit, the Court of the Judiciary may issue a reprimand, issue a cease-and-desist order, suspend the offending judge for a period of thirty days, or recommend the judge's removal altogether. If the Court of the Judiciary recommends removal, the matter is referred to the General Assembly, where a two-thirds majority in both houses is required to remove a judge from the bench. At the close of the twentieth century, only three judges had been removed through this process. One was Shelby County's General Sessions Judge Ira Murphy, who was convicted in federal court of mail fraud, perjury, and obstruction of justice. Murphy, who previously had served as chair of the House Judiciary Committee, unsuccessfully challenged the constitutionality of the Court of the Judiciary in the Tennessee Supreme Court.[42] The case involving the most outrageous behavior was that of Chancery Court Judge David Lanier of Dyersburg, who was removed after being convicted in federal district court of civil rights violations involving extortion of sex from female employees and litigants before his court.[43]

Ancillary Offices

Every state has a number of offices that perform auxiliary functions for the courts. Chief among these are state attorneys general, district attorneys, public defenders, and grand juries. Every state also has a set of ancillary boards and commissions that perform quasi-judicial functions or assist the judiciary in some respect. In Tennessee, there are more than twenty-five such bodies (listed in table 6.1).

TABLE 6.1

TENNESSEE'S JUDICIAL BOARDS AND COMMISSIONS

Advisory Commission on Rules of Civil and Appellate Procedure
Advisory Commission on Rules of Criminal Procedure
Board of Law Examiners
Board of Professional Responsibility
Child Support Guidelines Commission
Commission on Continuing Legal Education
Commission on Dispute Resolution
Commission on the Future of the Tennessee Judicial System
Commission on Gender Fairness in the Courts
Commission on Racial and Ethnic Fairness in the Courts
Commission to Review the ABA Model Code of Judicial Conduct
Commission to Study the Appellate Courts
Committee to Study Integrated Court Computer Systems
Commission on Uniform Legislation
Court Improvement Commission—Foster Care Review
Court of the Judiciary
General Sessions Judges Forms Study Committee
Indigent Defense Commission
Judicial Council
Judicial Ethics Committee
Judicial Selection Commission
State Law Library Commissions
Supreme Court Building Commissions
Tennessee Code Commission
Tennessee Judicial Conference Committees
Tennessee Lawyers Fund for Client Protection
Tennessee State/Federal Judicial Council

SOURCE: Tennessee Blue Book, 1900–2000 (Nashville: Tennessee Office of Secretary of State).

Tennessee Attorney General

The Attorney General is the chief lawyer for the state. In Tennessee, the Attorney General's Office represents the state in the appellate courts when criminal defendants seek to challenge their convictions or sentences. Officially, the Attorney General's office conducts investigations, renders advisory opinions on legal questions that are not before the courts, and represents the state when the state is a party to litigation. Unofficially, the Attorney General, despite being appointed by the Supreme Court, often privately gives legal advice to the Governor and members of the legislature on matters involving the state. This relationship is unique among the fifty states and is responsible for an equally unique line of communication among Tennessee's three branches of government.

In most states, the Attorney General is appointed by the Governor or elected directly by the people. To some, it may seem that having the Supreme Court choose the state's chief attorney is at odds with the fundamental constitutional principle of separation of powers. Because the Attorney General represents the state's legal interests before the Supreme Court, many view it as odd or even inappropriate that the Attorney General would be selected by the same court. Observers must keep in mind, however, that another feature unique to Tennessee affects the balance of power. Almost alone among the states, Tennessee's Attorney General has very limited powers of prosecution. Historically, the public's right to elect or remove such officials is tied to the enormous power of a prosecutor to take away a person's property or freedom. One can argue that, since this power is not present in Tennessee, it is less important for the Tennessee Attorney General to be chosen by the voters or by the voters' elected Governor. Most citizens in the state seem to believe that, as a practical matter, Tennessee's unique arrangement works reasonably well.

District Attorneys General

In Tennessee, the District Attorney General is an elected official responsible for prosecuting criminal cases in a particular judicial district. The District Attorney serves an eight-year term and is elected on a partisan ballot. The District Attorney has considerable discretion regarding whether to prosecute a given case and present it to the grand jury. Without a grand jury indictment, there can be no prosecution. In exercising this discretion, District Attorneys are guided not only by their own predilections, but also by the resources of their offices and the expectations and preferences of their constituencies. The prosecution of mundane cases often is delegated to an assistant, while high-profile cases, usually involving murder or drugs, are handled personally by the District Attorney. Winning or losing such cases more often than not determines whether a District Attorney wins reelection.

Public Defender System

In 1963, the United States Supreme Court held that indigent persons accused of felonies in state courts must be provided counsel at public expense.[44] Subsequently, the Court extended that holding to misdemeanors.[45] In Tennessee, these constitutional mandates originally were implemented by trial judges, who appointed counsel from the private bar to represent indigent defendants on an ad hoc basis. In 1989, the General Assembly created a public defender system to handle indigent defense, which brought Tennessee into line with the approach followed in most states.[46]

Each of the judicial districts elects a public defender who in turn appoints a staff of assistant public defenders and investigators to handle criminal cases assigned to the office. Occasionally, however, a criminal court judge still appoints private counsel to represent an indigent defendant. A criminal judge may appoint counsel because the local public defender's office is backlogged or has a perceived conflict of interest in the case. The latter occurred in 1998, when a criminal court judge in Knoxville appointed two members of the local bar to represent Thomas "Zoo Man" Huskey, who had been charged with the murder of several prostitutes near the Knoxville Zoo. The public defender's office was precluded from representing Huskey because previously the office had represented some of the victims when they were prosecuted for prostitution.

Grand Juries

The grand jury is an institution deeply rooted in Anglo-American legal tradition. The grand jury's purpose is to provide a safeguard against arbitrary or overzealous prosecution. It reviews evidence obtained by a prosecutor and decides whether sufficient evidence exists to hand down an indictment against an accused. The Fifth Amendment to the U.S. Constitution states, "No person shall be held to answer for a capital, or otherwise infamous crime, unless on a presentment or indictment of a Grand Jury." That provision applies only to prosecutions in federal courts. The Tennessee Constitution parallels the federal Constitution by providing that "no person shall be put to answer any criminal charge but by presentment, indictment or impeachment."[47] Impeachments are acted upon by the state legislature; presentments and indictments are functions of grand juries. Before an individual can be tried for any criminal offense other than minor misdemeanors, a grand jury must review the case and return a "true bill."

In Tennessee, the grand jury consists of twelve persons. All adult residents of Tennessee who are U.S. citizens are eligible for service on a grand jury, unless they are deemed incompetent under a provision of the Tennessee Code. Grand juries are impaneled twice a year at times determined by the presiding judge of the district. Grand jurors serve a term of six months. In addition to reviewing criminal cases, grand juries have the power to investigate allegations of misconduct in county government.

Many District Attorneys probably would prefer a system in which they could charge defendants through an "information" filed in a court of law. Such a process is a less cumbersome system used in a number of other states. The wishes of District Attorneys notwithstanding, grand juries, in Tennessee and elsewhere, do not pose a serious obstacle to prosecutors. Because grand jury proceedings are secret (fig. 6.4), and because defendants and their attorneys are not present to rebut testimony, prosecutors typically have little difficulty securing indictments. The odds are stacked so heavily in favor of the prosecutor that there is an old saying: "A good prosecutor could get a grand jury to indict a ham sandwich."

Assessing the Court System

Like many other aspects of Tennessee government, the state's courts today reflect the evolution of a system originally designed for a different era. While it might be argued that the system "works," it probably would work a lot better if its functioning were clearer. Still, as Thomas Van Dervort has observed, "Tennessee's judicial system has come a long way toward modernizing its institutions to meet the changes of modern society."[48] Judicial administration certainly has become more professionalized, and rules of procedure have become more uniform.

Changes implemented in the latter part of the twentieth century made Tennessee's judicial system a bit less subject to partisan politics. The modified Missouri Plan for the Supreme Court and the appellate courts protects judges from partisan elections, but not, as Penny White's experience demonstrates, from partisan efforts to remove them from the bench. Penny White's defeat underscored the vulnerability of a sitting judge targeted by skillful opposition interests. Her defeat also pointed out the difficulty faced by incumbent judges in responding to vicious or inaccurate political attacks. As intended, reelection under the Tennessee Plan is not automatic, but most appellate judges in fact are retained. Ultimately, the system provides a balance between the desire to have judges reflect popular will and the need for a judicial system insulated from the unpredictable swings of the public mood. The only mechanism that would protect judicial independence completely is the federal model of giving judges lifetime appointments. Of course, the political culture of Tennessee never would support this alternative.

In Tennessee, the judicial "system" is less a system than a hodgepodge of laws and courts piled up over the decades. Tennessee's culture, a product of its own history and political personalities, never has demanded a clearly ordered system of courts. Stakeholders in the Tennessee legal system—primarily lawyers and judges—have adapted to this culture, learning its rules and participating in its often confusing process. The public has expressed no great concern with the system. Until it does, Tennessee's judicial system likely will remain much as it has been for decades. Like a grandfather's car, it is outdated but still functional.

Part III

TENNESSEE POLITICS

7

Political Parties and Interest Groups

It is October 1991. More than twelve hundred Democrats are gathered in a ballroom of Nashville's Opryland Hotel for the party's annual Jackson Day Dinner. The featured speaker is Sen. Jay Rockefeller of West Virginia. During the dinner, Senator Rockefeller chokes on a chicken bone and is rushed by ambulance to Vanderbilt Hospital. As the ambulance leaves the hotel, Gov. Ned McWherter huddles frantically with his aides in an effort to find a last-minute replacement for the keynote speaker. With few options, McWherter turns to a fellow governor, who by coincidence had visited McWherter that afternoon and who had accepted an invitation to stay over and attend the dinner with his wife. Although many in the room are more interested in getting the score from the World Series, the visiting Governor quickly captures their attention with a rousing thirty-minute speech that has the crowd cheering and on its feet. By the time he leaves the stage, Tennessee Democrats who did not know him before he spoke are repeating his name: Gov. Bill Clinton of Arkansas.

A political party is "any continuing organization, identified by a particular label, that presents candidates for public office at mass elections."[1] In Tennessee, as in the United States generally, we have two major political parties—the Democrats and the Republicans. Both parties routinely nominate candidates for public office. Thus, in most general elections, voters are asked to choose between Democratic and Republican candidates.[2] Of course, the parties do much more than simply nominate candidates; they help to recruit political leadership, organize the political process, and help structure the process of governance as well.

In Tennessee, as in the rest of the nation, a person does not so much "join" a party as identify with one, with the ultimate goal of seeing that candidates from his or her party are successful in making decisions about what government eventually will do. Those who win public office become part of the "party in government." Those who identify with the party are the "party in the electorate."

Tennessee's two-party system is characterized by broad-based parties, each encompassing a wide range of interests. This necessarily prevents any party from becoming too narrow or exclusionary, either of which would doom a party to failure. While often they stake out opposing policy positions that involve disagreements on major issues, parties usually do not define themselves in terms of a single issue. Rather, in order to win, they put together coalitions of voters attracted to a number of issues. Thus, parties have a vital function in any democratic system. They promote compromise and cooperation among various interests. They allow a multiplicity of interests to speak and be heard, even though their voices may be somewhat muted. The parties' tendency to promote compromise helps to insure stability within the political system.

Interest groups are private organizations formed to advance the shared interests of their members. In political science, an interest is simply something that someone wants to achieve—a goal or desire. Often, the shared interest that brings people together is economic—a desire to get a larger slice of the pie. But the interest of the group may be purely ideological—a wish to see public policy in a given area move in a liberal or conservative direction. To qualify as an interest group, an organization must have an objective and be able to articulate that objective publicly. Interest groups attempt to advance their members' interests by influencing the public policy making process. Politics, from the perspective of interest groups, is basically a struggle to determine "who gets what, when and how."[3]

Although most of the publicity surrounding interest groups focuses on the national political scene, interest groups are active at the state level as well. In Tennessee, interest groups maintain an ongoing presence, usually in the form of lobbyists, in the state capital. For the most part, their work goes on behind the scenes, insulated from public view. But occasionally an interest group will enter the public arena, as in the fall of 1999, when a group calling itself Tennesseans for Fair Taxation ran a television ad exhorting the public to support "tax reform."

Political parties and interest groups are both important vehicles through which citizens can participate in the political process. Both serve to articulate interests—that is, both speak publicly on behalf of certain issue positions. Both can be viewed as intermediary institutions that help link the public to its government. Yet there are profound differences between parties and interest groups. Interest groups tend to focus on one narrow or "special" interest; parties bring various interests together under one umbrella. Interest groups tend to work directly on desired public policy outcomes; parties focus on winning elections. Interest groups have to answer only to their members. Political parties have to answer to the electorate.

In this chapter we concentrate much more on political parties than on interest groups. While both are important, political parties are more central to political and governmental processes. Parties are quasi-public organizations that serve to organize the political process in a fundamental way. Interest groups are, by their very nature, more peripheral. An interest group may be extremely important on one issue and completely irrelevant on another. An interest group may become extremely influential at one point in time and cease to exist altogether a few years later. Moreover, because interest groups typically are private organizations, their activities are less subject to observation.

Development of the Tennessee Party System

To a great degree, the development of Tennessee's parties parallels that of the nation as a whole. Neither the Tennessee Constitution nor the United States Constitution mentions political parties. The founders of our country were wary of the influence exerted by any organized group on the political process. The first real attempt at organizing various interests for the purpose of affecting an election was in regard to ratification of the U.S. Constitution. The Federalists, including George Washington, John Adams, and Alexander Hamilton, strongly supported ratification. Those who opposed ratification of the Constitution were known as Anti-Federalists. The Anti-Federalists represented a diverse set of interests whose only common thread was opposition to the Constitution.

The first President, George Washington, sought to avoid the formation of political parties by including diverse interests in his administration.

What he got instead was severe factionalism within the administration. Alexander Hamilton, Washington's Secretary of the Treasury, was the major proponent of Federalist ideas. The Federalist program strongly supported banking and business and, by extension, the interests of the major cities. The main instrument of business and banking interests would be a national bank, which was a centerpiece of Federalist thinking.

Thomas Jefferson, whose views diverged sharply from those of Hamilton, was Washington's Secretary of State. Jefferson became the spokesman for opposition to Hamilton's program within the administration. James Madison, who also opposed Hamilton's policies, led the opposition in Congress. Within a few years, the followers of Jefferson and Madison organized a political party under the name "Democratic-Republicans." By 1796, both Federalist and Democratic-Republican candidates were presenting themselves to voters as members of opposing political parties. These party labels provided a cue to the voters. The voters quickly could determine the candidates' basic approach to government by their party affiliations. These early parties greatly simplified the task of voting in the fledgling Republic. They reduced the complexity of issues to a simple choice. This reduction was vital if the government was to make rational decisions on major issues. The function of parties is the same, whether at the national or state level—to structure choices for voters.

After the disintegration of the Federalists, there was a brief period (known as the "Era of Good Feelings") in which there was little expression of factionalism. However, following the election of 1824, the Democratic-Republicans split into the National Republicans, championed by John Quincy Adams; and the Democratic-Republicans, led by Andrew Jackson of Tennessee. The Jackson wing, which later would evolve to become the "Democrats," became the dominant party, while supporters of Adams continued to offer competition. This period helped to redefine cleavages in the country. Jackson had appealed to working persons, exploiting class divisions and establishing the Democratic Party as the party of the "common man." In addition, the Democrats established a regional base in the South and the West, and became the "majority party." This party began to develop an organizational base as candidates ran under its banner for state and local offices throughout the country. This party base was strengthened to some degree by the "spoils system" that Jackson championed. The spoils system is a system of staffing government that rewards supporters with jobs and contracts.

After Jackson came back to beat Adams in the election of 1828, a permanent split occurred in the former Democratic-Republican Party. This split provided an opportunity to redefine the party landscape. The Whig Party emerged from this realignment. The Whigs represented eastern and business interests, as opposed to the Jacksonian Democrats, who appealed to the "common man" and made structural changes to open the party up to wider participation.

The legacy of Jackson had a pronounced effect on Tennessee party politics. In many ways, the period following the ascendancy of Jackson saw the first real party movement in the state. The divisions in the 1830s revolved around Jackson's Vice-President, Martin Van Buren, and Hugh Lawson White. Both men were candidates for the Democratic presidential nomination in 1836. Although Van Buren ultimately received the nomination, Tennessean White received the support of Tennessee delegates. White's support, based largely in East Tennessee, became the basis for the growth of the Whig Party in the state. White's success in the state was interpreted as tarnishing the reputation of Jackson. The next two years would witness the beginnings of modern parties in Tennessee.[4]

Slavery and Party Realignment

The slavery issue split the parties much as it divided the nation. Nowhere was the split more pronounced than in Tennessee. In East Tennessee, where slavery was impractical because of the mountainous terrain, most citizens remained loyal to the Union. Middle and West Tennessee, on the other hand, were overwhelmingly committed to the Confederacy. The only exception was the Highland Rim area on the border between Middle and West Tennessee. These divisions were reflected in the results of a referendum on whether the state should withdraw from the Union.

This support for separation from the Union long undergirded partisanship in the state. The Republican Party became indelibly etched in the public mind as the party of Lincoln and the North. Those wanting to remain in the Union were expressing the sentiments of Republican President Abraham Lincoln. Those wanting to leave the Union were expressing antipathy to the Republican position. East Tennessee became solidly Republican; Middle and West Tennessee became part of the Democratic "Solid South."

Following the Civil War, the Republican Party became known as the Party of Reconstruction. This assured its minority status in Tennessee for almost one hundred years. The geography of support for the Republican position in 1861 continued until the last third of the twentieth century, when it began to erode somewhat.

A Modern Two-Party System

While national changes in the locus of support for the parties took place following the Civil War, Tennessee remained solidly in the Democratic fold. This continued through the Great Depression that began with the stock market's Great Crash in 1929. That cataclysmic event brought about major shifts in the national parties. These shifts set the stage for the eventual return of the two-party system in Tennessee. The South, including Tennessee, remained solidly in the Democratic Party camp. However, union members, Catholics, minorities, and northern big-city residents joined them in what became known as the New Deal coalition. From the perspective of the twenty-first century, this coalition seems problematical at best, with the South as "odd group out." The pressures of the Depression and World War II and the country's support for Roosevelt kept the fabric from unraveling. But by the 1940s and early 1950s, the growing civil rights movement had begun to threaten the New Deal coalition. This was true in Tennessee before the rest of the South, perhaps because the state always had had a Republican base in East Tennessee.

Parties in Tennessee since 1932

Tennessee Democrats dominated the state's politics in the 1930s. When any party enjoys such control, the battles take place within that party rather than between it and the minority party. Mayor Edmund Crump of Memphis was the dominant player within the Democratic Party. He operated mostly behind the scenes in supporting candidates for office throughout the state. In order to win a statewide position such as Governor or United States Senator, a politician would need to be a Democrat and, as such, would need to court "Boss Crump." Crump could deliver large numbers of votes, especially from the state's largest city—Memphis—to his chosen candidate. He clearly was the state's most powerful politician for many years.

As the 1950s approached, Tennessee Republicans faced a dilemma. Would they accommodate to the Democrats and not challenge the majority party's statewide control? The Republican Party of the 1940s was a conservative organization, with most of its power based in East

Boss Crump

E. H. Crump, better known as "Boss Crump," was the most powerful politician in Memphis for a good part of the twentieth century. In the traditional manner of the machine politician, he built a political machine in Memphis by providing benefits to those who supported him with their votes. While his influence began to wane in the late 1940s, his rhetoric remained as fiery as ever. When his political enemy, Gordon Browning, sought another term as Governor in 1948, Crump took out a newspaper ad reading: "Browning, as governor for one term, converted the proud capital of Tennessee into a regular Sodom and Gomorrah, a wicked capital reeking with sordid, vicious infamy. His handy vultures were also there. One may re-brand a hog with a smooth crop, a fork in the end of its ear, or a bit out of the bottom of its ear, yet it remains the same hog."

Crump's political demise coincided with the onset of changes in the state's Democratic Party. Estes Kefauver, a Crump enemy, was elected to the United States Senate from Tennessee in 1948. Kefauver was a major figure in the national party as it moved to a more liberal position on civil rights. Soon it became clear that one could win the Democratic Party nomination, and the general election, without the support of Mr. Crump.

Crump died in 1954, his influence having faded considerably, along with his now obsolete political style.

SOURCE: Wilma Dykeman, *Tennessee: A Bicentennial History* (New York: Norton, 1975), 109.
Fig. 7.1. E. H. (Boss) Crump.

Tennessee, and existing largely for purposes of patronage (rewarding supporters with jobs). This system had a certain appeal for the Republicans, who were in a position to gather in some rewards if they agreed to stay in their place.

Those controlling the federal government are in a position to dispense rewards to those who show loyalty to their party. Thus the Republican Party could offer positions to those willing to field candidates in state and local races where there was no chance of winning. When Republican Dwight Eisenhower was elected United States President in 1952 and 1956, for example, there were plenty of appointments to be made. Loyal Republicans throughout the South were in a position to receive these appointments (hence the term "Post Office

Republicans"). This system left in place a Democratic Party which dominated the major statewide offices. Between the end of Reconstruction and the 1960s, very few Republicans were elected to statewide office. In fact, the real election for these offices was the Democratic primary in August. The Democratic nominee was, for all practical purposes, the winner.

National trends in the late 1940s began to sow the seeds for a revitalization of the two-party system in Tennessee. The break in the Democrats' dominance of the Volunteer State began with the presidential election of 1948. President Truman's progressive stance on civil rights issues produced a rift in the Democratic Party. A number of Southern Democrats, who came to be known as Dixiecrats, defected from the party. Strom Thurmond of South Carolina ran for President as the Dixiecrat candidate and got 2.4 percent of the popular vote nationwide. In Tennessee, the Dixiecrat revolt had some popular appeal, as Thurmond garnered 13.4 percent of the popular vote in the Volunteer State. President Truman was reelected in a close vote. The Dixiecrat Party disappeared from the scene, with its leader and many of its supporters joining the ranks of the Republicans.

The 1952 presidential election further loosened the Democratic Party's iron grip on Tennessee politics. Tennesseans broke the almost century-long Democratic Party domination in contests conducted across the state. The Republican war hero, Dwight Eisenhower, edged the Democrat, Adlai Stevenson of Illinois. For the first time, many outside the state's traditionally Republican area, East Tennessee, split their tickets, voting for a Republican for President while continuing their strong support of Democrats for statewide and local offices. In 1952, for instance, 84 percent voted for the Democrat Albert Gore Sr. for U.S. Senator, while 59 percent voted for Stevenson. In Shelby County, the falloff was even greater, with 86 percent voting for Gore and only 52 percent for Stevenson.

Four years later, President Eisenhower captured the state's electoral votes with a narrow victory over Stevenson. From that point on, Tennessee became a "two-party" state, at least in presidential elections. It was not until 1966, however, that the Tennessee electorate was willing to elect a Republican to statewide office. Howard Baker, who had made a strong effort in the special election two years prior against Ross Bass, easily was elected U.S. Senator with 56 percent of the vote. In 1970, Republicans Winfield Dunn and Bill Brock were elected Governor and Senator, respectively. Now all three statewide offices were in Republican hands. Republicans made serious gains in the General Assembly as well. Tennessee had become a two-party state.

Ascendancy of the Republican Party

Two related factors made possible the revitalization of Tennessee's Republican Party. The first was the change in the national Democratic Party, which had become the champion of activist government and civil rights for African Americans. While many in the South were lifelong Democrats, they were "Southern Democrats," much less supportive of civil rights than those in the national party. Prior to the 1960s, a truce between the wings of the party held, with many Southern Democrats holding key U.S. House and Senate positions, while other party members actively sought the Presidency.

In 1964, a conservative Republican, Barry Goldwater, sought and later won the Republican presidential nomination. He captured the nomination largely through grassroots efforts around the country, involving many people in politics for the first time. Many Goldwater supporters ran for office at the local level or sought nomination as delegates to the Republican National Convention. Goldwater's nomination made the Republican Party more conservative ideologically. He was suspicious of large government programs, including the Tennessee Valley Authority. This proved to be disastrous to the party in the fall elections, where Lyndon Johnson won a landslide victory, both nationally and in Tennessee. However, it set the stage for many in the South to enter politics at the local level and to begin to organize viable Republican parties in areas, even states, where the party had been moribund for nearly a century.

These Republican organizational efforts also occurred in Tennessee. Soon many Tennessee voters, lacking traditional Republican roots but comfortable with the new Republican message, found this new Republicanism to their taste. Even many conservative Democrats, unwilling to change their long-standing party identification, found themselves considering voting for Republican candidates for state and local offices for the first time. As part of this movement, a number of candidates in traditionally Democratic areas in Middle and West Tennessee made serious attempts to seek office under the Republican banner. Much of this movement took place in suburban Memphis and Nashville. This produced results over the next decade, establishing the Republican Party as a viable force in Tennessee politics.

These changes were reflected in a changed political landscape. The changes became pronounced first in West Tennessee. Democrat Clifford Davis long had held the Ninth Congressional District seat. He often ran without opposition both in the Democratic primary and the November general elections. In 1960, his Republican opponent was George W. Lee, an African American who mounted no campaign at all. Following Davis's retirement, Democrat George Grider was elected in 1964. Grider aligned himself with the more liberal wing of the national Democratic Party and was one only a few Southern Democrats to vote for the Civil Rights Act of 1964. The emergence of the conservative wing of Republican Party in West Tennessee in the early 1960s allowed Dan Kuykendall, a conservative Republican, to seek and win Grider's seat in 1966. This election was a true landmark. A Republican had contested and won a congressional election in a district that routinely had been conceded to the Democrats, a district only a few years earlier almost bereft of people willing to call themselves Republicans. The basis of this breakthrough was clear; it was traceable to ideological shifts in the national parties and to grassroots movements among conservatives whose thinking was not in agreement with the philosophy of the national Democratic Party. This movement soon saw Republicans elected as Governor and as both U.S. Senators.

Dual Base of Tennessee's Republican Party

It may be said that two distinct wings of the Republican Party had emerged. The first, more traditional and a bit more moderate, was centered in East Tennessee and in the Highland Rim counties between Middle and West Tennessee. The second, more ideological than traditional in focus, was centered in the suburbs and small towns of Middle

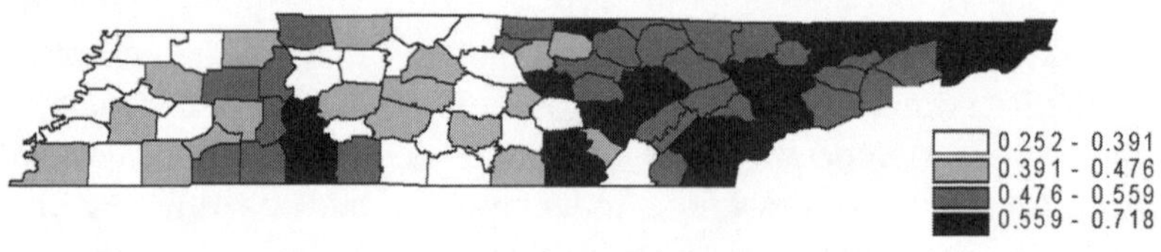

Fig. 7.2. 1976 Presidential Primary: Vote for Gerald Ford.

and West Tennessee, especially the suburbs outside Memphis. The dual but complementary bases of the party occasionally are revealed in contests within the party. Consider the 1976 Republican Presidential primary (fig. 7.2).

Parties in Government

Tennessee parties are recognized throughout the laws that govern the state. A party has certain rights if its officers file with the Secretary of State and the Coordinator of Elections.[5] No political party may have nominees on a ballot or exercise any of the rights of political parties under this title until its officers have filed on its behalf with the Secretary of State and with the Coordinator of Elections.

Elected officials are part of the party in government in Tennessee. The party in government consists of those officeholders from a particular party and deals with their efforts to organize the government and develop public policy—in the General Assembly, throughout the executive branch, and, to some degree, throughout the state. Of course, parties are formed with the purpose of winning elections to staff government. Thus winning of elections and staffing of government have a goal—implementing the winners' policy preferences. Much of what parties do once the election is over is to staff Tennessee government so as to make it work to achieve the winners' goals. Ultimately, this is what elections are about and why parties are formed in the first place.

Parties in the General Assembly

Democrats controlled both state houses throughout almost all of the twentieth century. However, beginning in the late 1960s, Republicans became much more competitive. Whereas Democrats had captured 70 to 80 percent of the seats in previous decades, Republicans closed the gap in both houses. In fact, by 1970 the Republicans had captured half the seats in the Tennessee House. But the Democrats managed to hold majorities in the crucial years following the federal census count, when the General Assembly draws the all-important lines for new House and Senate districts, as well as those for the U.S. House of Representatives. This ability to draw district lines is very important. In these cases, as in many others, the party with the majority agrees to act in a unified manner, through its meeting or "caucus."

The process of redistricting has become very sophisticated technologically. Staff are able quickly to move voting precincts from one district to another and to gauge the impact on each district's population size and the likely effect on future elections in districts they might create. There is reasonable leeway in constructing new districts, as long as state constitutional guidelines are observed, the districts are approximately the same size, and federal court guidelines regarding majority and minority districts are met. The party with a majority in the General Assembly has a real advantage in seeing that its members are kept in "safe" districts where they are likely to have continued electoral success.

Organizing the General Assembly

The party holding the majority in each house meets in caucus during the Organizational Session following the state elections in even-numbered years. In the state House, the majority party's leader can count on all members of his caucus to support him or her for the important position of Speaker. The Speaker appoints the committees and their respective chairs.

While the Senate usually works in the same way, Democrat John Wilder remained in control in the 1990s by putting together a coalition of Conservative Democrats and Republicans to keep his position. Wilder then appointed Republicans to chair some key committees. This arrangement continued despite the Republican victory in 1994, when Republicans rewarded Wilder for his nonpartisan stance.

While parties may be important in the legislature (and especially in the House), they do not play the role in Tennessee that they do in many states or in the national Congress. Rather, the main cleavages here are ideological and personal, more than partisan, in nature. Tennessee Republican and Democratic office-seekers usually do not differ on fundamental issues when they seek office. Much of the campaigning, especially for the House, is based on personal contact with the voter, either door to door or on the telephone. Often a substantial portion of the constituency personally knows the candidate. However, once candidates reach the legislature, they think of themselves in partisan terms, most notably when organizing the assembly.

The Speaker of the House and Speaker of the Senate (Lieutenant Governor) appoint committees and committee chairs. In making these appointments, the Speaker is supposed to consider the members' abilities, preferences, and seniority in the legislative body. Obviously, appointment power gives the Speaker, who almost always is chosen by the caucus of the majority party, tremendous ability to affect the flow of legislation. This can be accomplished by sending a bill to a hostile committee or subcommittee for a quick death.

The parties play a direct role in the legislative process, apart from the Speakers. In the House and Senate, the members of each party meet in caucus during the Organizational Session of the General Assembly, held in January following elections for the assembly, to choose their own party leaders. Those selected are known as the Majority Leader and Minority Leader, depending on which party has a majority of seats in the General Assembly. Each party's leaders work with party members in each chamber to insure that legislation sees the party leadership's desired end—death in subcommittee, perhaps, or successful passage. The leaders are important in managing debate concerning legislation in the two chambers.

The Democratic and Republican caucus chairs, chosen in their respective party caucuses during Organizational Sessions, help the Majority Leader and Minority Leader direct the role of the parties in the legislative process. The caucus leaders preside over party meetings in which members of each party discuss the party's role, if any, in pending legislation. The caucus chairs also play a key role in getting members of their parties elected to the General Assembly. They recruit candidates and help with fundraising.

Party Influence

In Tennessee, the parties are woven throughout the fabric of legislation and government. One example is the State Election Commission, which appoints a local election commission in each county. County election commissions oversee the time and place of local elections and the ballot form. The party controlling the General Assembly is given majority status on the three-member State Election Commission, which in turn appoints each county's five-member election commission. These county election commissions can have no more than three members from each party. Thus county election commissions are controlled by the majority party in the state, regardless of the partisan makeup of the county. In reality, appointing members of the local election commission is a task deferred to elected state legislators from that area. This is the case even in areas dominated by the opposition party. With the Democrats controlling the General Assembly through the late 1990s, the election commissions in East Tennessee counties were still controlled by local Democrats. This gives Democrats not only the ability to decide locations of polling places and early voting procedures, but also some appointment power. Each local election commission chooses the local registrar of elections, a highly paid post.

Choosing a Registrar of Elections in Knox County

In the fall of 1996, Knox Countians voted on a controversial proposal to unify their city and county governments. In order to pass, the proposal had to be approved by those living inside the city limits as well as those dwelling outside. This necessitated tabulating the votes separately for the two areas. On election night, the election commission discovered that there was no way to separate the votes of those who had voted in the early voting period. The voting machines had not been programmed correctly. As it turned out, this mistake did not matter. The proposal lost the combined county vote. But a major part of the foul-up was laid at the hands of the outgoing registrar of elections, who is in charge of overseeing voter registration, voting, and counting votes under the guidance of the county election commission. The commission also was criticized for failing to oversee the preparation of the machines properly.

Even though Knox long has been a Republican county, local Democrats who controlled the county election commission effectively chose the new registrar. This is because the state law governing appointments assigns the majority party in the state three of the five local commissioners. In 1997, the Democrats controlled the process. The leading Democrat in the Knox County delegation played a major role in the choice of the commissioners and subsequently in the choice of the new registrar. This process demonstrates the importance of party in staffing government and the importance of a party's controlling the General Assembly and being in a position to dispense jobs to supporters.

Party in the Electorate

The term "party in the electorate" refers to all those voters who identify with a party. Party identifiers represent the base upon which candidates hope to build a winning electoral coalition. In many states, voters choose a party or opt for independent status when they register to vote. These states have "closed primaries," in which only those registered with a party are allowed to participate. In other states, including Tennessee, there is no registration by party. Thus Tennesseans express their party preferences indirectly, by choosing to vote in a party's primary. This decision, which becomes part of the voting records kept in each county, does serve as a good mechanism for identifying those who are strong partisans. But it is not a particularly good measure of overall party strength, because a much smaller proportion of registered voters participates in primaries than votes in general elections.

Trends in Party Identification

Most Americans do not join political parties, but rather identify with them. The best way to ascertain the nature of support for each party is to tally answers to the question, "Do you consider yourself a Democrat, a Republican, or an Independent?" This measure, called party identification, probably is the best indicator of the status of the party in the electorate. When Americans answer this question, they are not necessarily indicating their voting preference in any particular election. Rather, they are expressing their affinity with one or the other party or a lack of affinity with either party. In many elections, voters choose a candidate from the opposite party. However, over the long term, one's party identification is the best available indicator of how that person would vote in any election.

While there is a wealth of survey data regarding the preferences of Americans, there is much less information available about Tennesseans' party identification. However, beginning in early 1980, a picture began to emerge. The picture is of a slowly diminishing Democratic majority (fig. 7.3). By 1997, the Republicans had pulled even with Democrats in partisan identification.

TABLE 7.1
TENNESSEE PARTY IDENTIFICATION BY REGION, 1997

	Total	*East*	*Middle*	*West*
Republicans	30	33	27	28
Democrats	29	23	31	35
Independents	41	44	41	36

SOURCE: Tennessee Poll, Social Science Research Institute, University of Tennessee, Knoxville.

The regional basis of party identification is shown in table 7.1. East Tennessee remains the stronghold of Republican identification in the state. Democrats enjoy slight majorities in the middle and western divisions of the state, sufficient to create a dead heat statewide when balanced against the Republican advantage in East Tennessee.

Clearly, an ideological basis exists for Tennessee partisan attachment (table 7.2). Democrats are much more likely to consider themselves

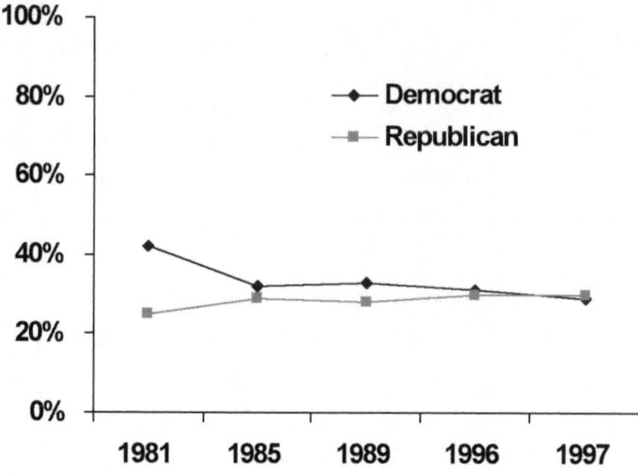

Fig. 7.3. Party Identification in Tennessee, 1981–1997. ***Sources:*** **For 1981, statewide survey conducted by Department of Political Science, University of Tennessee, Knoxville. For remaining years, statewide surveys conducted by the University of Tennessee Social Science Research Institute.**

liberals than are either Independents or Republicans. However, in 1997, one in five Democrats still classified himself or herself as a conservative. It is clear that Tennessee Republicans are much more unified in their outlook than are Democrats. There are very few liberal Republicans. Tennessee Democrats can expect to win their share of state and local elections as long as their candidates are not perceived as excessively liberal. Likewise, it would be difficult to get a majority of votes for any Democratic presidential candidate who might be considered too liberal.

TABLE 7.2
TENNESSEE IDEOLOGY BY PARTY IDENTIFICATION, 1997

	Total	*Democrats*	*Independents*	*Republicans*
Liberal	17	31	15	5
Moderate	48	47	52	44
Conservative	36	22	33	51

SOURCE: Tennessee Poll, Social Science Research Institute, University of Tennessee, Knoxville.

Racial differences clearly exist between the supporters of the two major parties in Tennessee (table 7.3). African Americans are much more likely to be Democrats; a plurality of whites consists of Republicans. In fact, in Tennessee as in much of the South, the Democratic Party has become the minority party among whites. While we do not have access to survey data from before the 1960s, we have every reason to believe that there has been a gradual shift among Tennessee's whites away from the Democratic Party. This shift does not imply that Democrats are headed to the point where they cannot win a statewide race. It does suggest that Democrats who aspire to win the white vote must appeal strongly to the moderate and conservative wings of their party.

TABLE 7.3

TENNESSEE PARTY IDENTIFICATION BY RACE, 1997

	Total	*Blacks*	*Whites*
Democrat	30	65	24
Independent	29	26	43
Republican	41	9	34

SOURCE: Tennessee Poll, Social Science Research Institute, University of Tennessee, Knoxville.

Structure of Tennessee's Political Parties

The political parties are organized around the American federal model. However, in the federal party system, unlike the federal system of government, almost all of the power is at the state level. In fact, national party offices are quite limited. There is very little that the national party offices can force the state or local parties to do. The national party has no control over who is nominated to run for an office under the name of the party. Each state party controls the method of candidate nomination within the state. Furthermore, once an individual is elected under the party banner, there is little that the party can do to force the member to comply with the party's policy preferences.

Governing the Parties

The state parties each have a governing structure known as the Executive Committee. These committees are based on the state's thirty-three Senate districts. A state committeeman and committeewoman are elected from each district. The executive committees can make

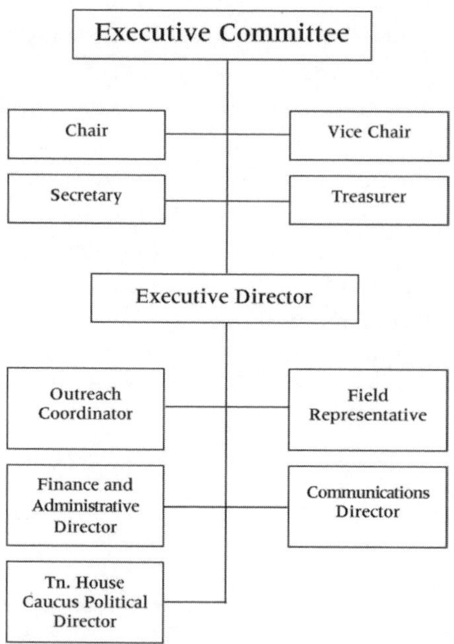

Fig. 7.4. Tennessee Democratic Party Structure.

statements on behalf of the party on state and national issues. They also coordinate fundraising for candidates and provide assistance for those seeking office under their party's labels. The executive committee elects a chair and hires a staff. The chair serves as spokesperson for the party. He or she also performs a major role in party fundraising and in recruiting candidates for state and local office. The leadership structure of the Tennessee Democratic Party is shown in figure 7.4. The Republican Party has a similar organizational structure.

The leadership of the parties in Tennessee often has a dual orientation—toward Washington and toward Nashville. The Washington perspective is guided by the state's representatives in the U.S. House and especially the U.S. Senate, as those in Washington invariably face a set of issues different from those confronting people in Nashville. This is especially true if the U.S. Senators have attained important party posts. For instance, during the 1980s, Sen. Al Gore and Sen. James Sasser were leaders of the national Democratic Party. During that time, the Tennessee party's leadership had a distinctly Washington slant. In the mid-1990s, on the other hand, state party chair Houston Gordon was much more oriented toward Nashville and issues within the state, such as prison privatization.

At the county level, each of the parties has an executive committee and a chairperson. The county chairperson has responsibility for recruiting candidates and coordinating campaigns for partisan contests. The county party chairperson is particularly active in county-level races for county commission, judicial contests, and the constitutionally mandated offices of county executive, sheriff, trustee, register of deeds, and district attorney general (DAG). The DAG contest, of course, crosses county lines in all but the largest counties.

Informal Party Activities

In addition to the formal party governing structures, there are functioning informal party organizations across the state. The local parties have "clubs" in many counties. These clubs meet regularly and provide forums for potential candidates or those who aspire to leadership in the party or candidacy in local elections. They also sponsor events to raise funds for the party. A staple of most Republican organizations is the annual "Lincoln Day Dinner" held annually on Lincoln's birthday. Likewise, Democrats hold Truman or Jackson Day dinners. These dinners serve to energize the core of the parties and to raise funds for local elections. Local candidates already holding office regularly participate in these informal party activities to keep in touch with the party's most active members and to maintain an electoral base against potential challengers from within their own parties.

Party Fundraising

The parties raise funds through a variety of sources. The point of these funds is clear—to support the parties' candidates to win elections. Each party maintains mailing lists of those who have contributed to the parties in the past or to candidates running under their party label. Each party uses these lists to solicit cash contributions and to invite potential contributors to give money and to attend dinners and receptions for party luminaries.

Party Assistance in Elections

The parties play a major role in elections, not only in statewide contests, but also in local races and those for the Tennessee General Assembly. While the state parties tend to steer clear of involvement in primary elections, once the nominee is chosen, they often play an active role. This role is not limited to financial support, but extends to dispatching professionals to assist with the campaign. This assistance is supplemented by providing polling data and computerized voter lists that can be used to target the voters most likely to turn out in a primary election.

While Tennessee parties play a role in elections at the state and local level, they can do no more than assist candidates in campaigns that center largely on characteristics of the candidates. Candidates are still at the center of the campaigns. They must put together their staffs, define their issue positions, do the legwork to raise money and contact voters, and project a winning image to the electorate.

Presidential Nominations

Among the many functions performed by political parties, arguably the most important is choosing nominees to seek office. The United States does not have a strong central party system. Rather, the national parties are loose federations of state parties. The national parties assert themselves strongly every four years when they gather at national conventions to choose their nominees for President and Vice President and write the platforms on which these nominees will run.

Tennessee parties must choose their delegates to the national conventions every four years. The procedure for doing this is very complicated. This complication is largely a function of the national parties' evolving rules for insuring that party leaders, minorities, women, and candidates obtain a certain threshold of votes in a portion of the state or the state as a whole. Delegates to national political conventions are chosen from each state according to laws passed by state legislatures. These state laws must be consistent with guidelines of the national political parties, or the state risks not having its party delegations accepted by the national conventions.

In Tennessee, the Secretary of State determines who are serious candidates for each party's nomination for President and submits their names to the State Election Commission no later than the first Tuesday of the year when the election will be held. If 2,500 registered voters file a petition (fig. 7.5) with the State Election Commission, the Secretary of State informs the prospective candidate that, unless the candidate withdraws, his or her name will be placed on the ballot of the party in the upcoming presidential preference primary. The Secretary of State then certifies the names to be placed on the primary ballot and forwards these to each county election commission.

Tennessee's presidential preference primary is held on the second Tuesday in March in the years when presidential elections are held.

Tennessee has participated in "Super Tuesday" since its inception in 1988, when many party activists in many southern states decided to hold their primaries on the same day, early in the primary season, in order to have greater clout in the choice of parties' nominees. Many Southern Democrats were interested in using this leverage to move the national party toward the middle of the political spectrum.

FORM OF NOMINATING PETITIONS

We, the undersigned registered voters of the state of Tennessee and members of the (respective) party, hereby nominate (candidate's name), (address) of ____________ County, as a candidate for delegate to the national convention of the (respective) party to be voted in the presidential preference primary election to be held on the ____ day of March. We request that the above nominee's name be printed on the official ballot as a candidate for delegate (at large) or (from the ____ congressional district).

Fig. 7.5. Form of Nominating Petitions.

Choosing Convention Delegates

The national parties determine the number of delegates that each state can send to the national convention. This is done by a formula that takes into account the state's population, its support for the party's nominee in the previous presidential election, and the total number of delegates to be seated at the convention. The chair of each party must forward this number to the Secretary of State in January of the primary election year. In 1996, for example, Tennessee was allotted eighty-three delegates to the Democratic National Convention and eleven alternates.

The actual selection of delegates is quite complex. The national parties require that a number of those going to the national convention be chosen at the congressional district level. The state law defers to the parties in this selection process. However, it dictates that there shall be at least three delegates chosen from each congressional district. Also, at least one-third of the delegates not elected at the district level must be elected by those voting in the presidential primary. Despite the freedom left to the state parties in determining who the delegates are, they are required to select delegates for specific candidates, so that delegations to national conventions reflect the proportions of the votes cast statewide for the candidates for the nomination.

This process of delegate selection is one of the most important tasks performed by state parties. It gives party leaders a chance to reward those who work on behalf of the parties with a trip to the national convention. Moreover, given Tennessee's participation in the Super Tuesday primary process, it gives the state substantial clout in selecting the party's eventual nominee. This process reflects the federal nature of the parties and emphasizes that the state is the basis of party organization. The national parties come together every four years, but the foundation of this process is at the state level.

Assessing the Party System

In Tennessee the parties have taken on a different texture than they have at the national level. Tennessee parties cannot be understood apart from the state's unique political history. The geography of the state, having given rise to the state's internal divisions over secession from the Union, formed the character of Tennessee's two parties. The Democratic Party was long the dominant party, literally running the state from the period following the Civil War to the early 1960s. In fact, both the Democratic Party in the electorate and the Democratic Party in government often diverged widely from the national Democratic Party. The Republican Party, on the other hand, while alive in East Tennessee, where Union support ran high, was virtually nonexistent throughout the rest of the state until the mid-1960s.

Support for the Republican Party began to appear in the middle and western parts of the state in 1952, in connection with the presidential candidacy of Dwight D. Eisenhower. It would be another decade before that support would extend to Republican candidates at the state and local levels. With Barry Goldwater's 1964 presidential campaign, a new, ideologically oriented Republican Party began to take hold in Middle and West Tennessee. For the first time, many Middle and West Tennesseans began to think of themselves as Republicans, rather than as Democrats who sometimes voted Republican in presidential elections.

As the end of the twentieth century approached, the Democrats were still the majority party in the state, especially in terms of organization and strength in the General Assembly. However, a good case could be made that Republicans could hold their own, if not triumph, in statewide races. There are good reasons for this apparently dual notion of party dominance.

Many Republicans are motivated by ideology more than by tradition. They do not share the long-term commitment to the party as an institution that Democrats tend to have. Without this long-term attachment, they are less likely to participate in party-building activities, especially at the local level. East Tennessee, however, continues to provide a wellspring of support for Republicans. East Tennessee Republicans have been loyal to the traditional wing of the Republican Party. While certainly conservative, they are driven not so much by ideology as by history and heritage.

In terms of popular party identification, Tennessee has evolved into a competitive two-party state. Republicans can compete successfully for statewide office, as well as for enough seats in the General Assembly to threaten Democratic control. Most of those who observe state politics would say that it is better to have competitive parties than to have a one-party state. This is because the political process is invigorated by two strong parties articulating different policy positions. While Tennessee's parties do not differ greatly on matters of policy, they do provide a structure for presenting issues and positions. In elections for President, U.S. Senator, and, to a lesser degree, the U.S. House of Representatives, Tennessee's parties normally stake out positions like those of the national parties. However, in elections for Governor, General Assembly, and local offices, Tennessee parties do not oppose each other with the vigor displayed by their national counterparts. There is a simple reason for this: in their stands on state and local issues, Tennessee parties do not differ very much. Their candidates tend to sound similar themes—smaller government, low taxes, and support for traditional values. To be sure, there are some differences. Tennessee Republican leaders have been somewhat more pro-business and somewhat less supportive of organized state employees and teachers. But the differences are clearly marginal.

Tennessee Republicans and Democrats can live with each other and can tolerate each other in powerful positions. This willingness, especially when combined with the advantages of incumbency and the cost of running for office, has led the parties to "concede" many elections, perhaps to run for the office another day. How else could one explain the majority Democratic Party's lack of a strong candidate to oppose Governor Sundquist in 1998?

Actually, Tennessee parties have come to an unofficial treaty of sorts. Ever since Lamar Alexander was elected Governor in 1978, soon after Governors became eligible to succeed themselves, the party in opposition has not made a serious effort to challenge a Governor who seeks a second term. Following Republican Alexander, Democrat Ned McWherter and then Republican Don Sundquist were elected and reelected with minimal opposition as they sought second terms. Thus, for twenty-four years of eight-year terms, the incumbent ran without strong opposition when seeking reelection.

While no case could be made that the parties have made any "deal" guaranteeing not to mount strong opposition to a sitting Governor, it is obvious that both Democrats and Republicans tend to work with a Governor of the opposite party. This cooperation is possible because of the lack of strong ideological differences between the parties. Tennessee parties are pragmatic. Each wants to control the Governor's mansion, and each would love to control both houses of the General Assembly. Neither, however, wants to take on tasks unlikely to succeed, such as taking on an incumbent with high name recognition and a substantial war chest of campaign funds. So they seem to find that getting along with the other party is preferable to fighting, when the fight seems very difficult.

While this strategy may serve party leaders, it often leaves the voters with very little to vote on. Most House and Senate seats are considered safe, with the incumbent having such an advantage that there is only a minimal campaign, if any. If there is no contested statewide race, voters often find very little to draw them to the polls. Unsurpris-

John Jay Hooker Challenges Gov. Don Sundquist

Many observers were surprised on the morning of August 7, 1998. Perennial candidate and political maverick John Jay Hooker had won the Democratic Party nomination to run against the incumbent Governor, Don Sundquist. Hooker had expended no money and little effort in seeking the nomination. But he was better known than any other candidate. In fact, there was no serious Democratic attempt to field a candidate capable of taking on the Governor. In this case, the Democratic Party failed to do one of the most important things that parties do: recruit a strong candidate. What happened? How could the party holding a majority of seats in both houses of the state legislature fail seriously to contest an election for Governor? The answer is complex but goes to the heart of the political party system that exists in Tennessee today.

ingly, many do not vote. Such was the case in 1998, when incumbent Republican Gov. Don Sundquist, with $5 million in the bank, faced maverick Democrat John Jay Hooker. Only about 25 percent of registered voters turned out, and Sundquist won reelection in a landslide of epic proportions, receiving 68 percent of the vote. Obviously, John Jay Hooker was not a credible challenger. Simply put, no Democrat wanted to take on the popular Governor, leaving the gadfly Hooker to run almost a non-campaign, with virtually no funding.

The Democrats' decision to concede the 1998 governor's race, like the Republicans' decision not to challenge Ned Ray McWherter eight years earlier, did not serve the cause of strong parties. Moreover, these decisions did not serve the cause of democracy at the state level. In a strong party system, the parties are obligated to provide the voters with choices. Tennessee parties often fall short in meeting this obligation.

Interest Groups

In recent decades, American politics has witnessed the proliferation of interest groups—private organizations that attempt to shape public policy according to the interests of their members. To some extent, interest groups have assumed some of the traditional functions of political parties.

Organized interests play a major role in determining the policy agenda, and to some degree, policy outcomes in Tennessee. Many states have a dominant industry, and in such a case it almost always plays a significant—even a controlling—role in state politics. Michigan has the automobile industry; Texas has oil. Tennessee has no such dominant industry, but rather has a group of influential interests. These interests pursue their agendas in a variety of ways in the political arena. Not only do they have great concern as to who will staff government, but also they feel the need to communicate their preferences to elected and appointed officials.

There is no clear consensus about the strength of various groups in Tennessee politics and certainly no clear way to measure that strength. But some groups clearly stand out as having a good deal of influence in the Tennessee political system.

Tennessee Education Association

The Tennessee Education Association (TEA) is the professional organization representing Tennessee's public school teachers. The TEA may well be the most influential of all organizations lobbying the General

Assembly. As an affiliate of the National Education Association, it takes an active role in supporting increased funding for public education and enhanced pay for teachers. Moreover, the TEA supports professional standards for teachers.

TEA communicates with its members by means of its *Legislative Report*. TEA's power derives from the size of its membership and its effective organization. It does not always get its way, however. TEA objected strenuously to Gov. Lamar Alexander's "Career Ladder" program in the 1980s. However, despite that opposition, the General Assembly approved the program. Later Governor McWherter was successful in altering some of the aspects most objectionable to teachers.

State Employees

Tennessee's state employees are major players in many policy arenas. Their organization, the Tennessee State Employee Association (TSEA), advocates for professional compensation and opportunities for those working for the state. The TSEA is particularly active when the General Assembly is considering legislation that would privatize a function of state government. For example, in 1998, the legislature considered but rejected a proposal to allow private industry to operate much of the state's prison system. The legislature was acting with at least some understanding that the prisons likely would be operated under a contract with Corrections Corporation of America, a Tennessee company.

Farm Bureau

The Tennessee Farm Bureau (TNFB) provides an array of services to Tennesseans involved in agriculture. By the end of the 1990s, the TNFB claimed almost a half-million members and their families. The services, which range from providing insurance to tax assistance, also include lobbying the General Assembly on behalf of agricultural interests. For instance, in the early 1970s, the bureau helped push a bill through the General Assembly that reduced property tax rates for farmers.

Tennessee Municipal League

The Tennessee Municipal League (TML) represents the interests of Tennessee's cities and towns. It has long played an active role in the Tennessee General Assembly. TML was founded in 1940 to lobby the General Assembly on behalf of Tennessee's incorporated places. Prior to coming under criticism for its handling of the 1997 "Toy Towns" legislation, it had been viewed as one of the most effective organizations lobbying state government. As noted in chapters 2 and 6, the General Assembly in 1997 adopted a measure that dramatically reduced the requirements for municipal incorporation, a measure that alarmed cities across the state. Of course, the measure ultimately was nullified when the state supreme court declared the act unconstitutional.[6] Still, many city leaders wondered how the legislation could have been enacted without TML's knowledge. Widespread member dissatisfaction with the organization led to a shakeup in TML's leadership.

Business and Professional Interests

A large array of business and professional interests are active in Tennessee politics and play a major role in the policy process. Some groups, such as the Tennessee Manufacturers Association, the Business Roundtable, and the Tennessee Association of Business, are umbrella organizations representing companies or industries with common positions on taxation, education, or other issues. Organizations such as the Tennessee Trial Lawyers Association, the Tennessee Retail Merchants Association, the Tennessee Medical Association, or the Tennessee Malt Beverage Association represent a single group or industry. Both categories are well funded, have full-time Nashville offices, give large amounts of campaign funds to Republicans and Democrats, and have a permanent lobbyist on Capitol Hill. A third group consists of professional and nonprofit organizations, such as cosmetologists or Common Cause, which are concerned about specific issues but generally lack the funding and staff available to some other groups. Finally, Tennessee has a large number of individual companies, such as Saturn, Federal Express, or Eastman Chemical, that employ their own lobbyists. All of these groups from time to time have an impact on legislation, although organizations with the largest staffs and the ability to provide campaign funds wield a comparable level of political influence. Many groups join with other associations or organizations to support or oppose a specific bill, knowing that they may be on different sides on another bill the next day.

Ad Hoc and Single-Issue Groups

Often interest groups form in response to a changing political landscape. An ad hoc umbrella collection of various conservative organizations and interested citizens formed to oppose Supreme Court Justice Penny White's reelection to the Supreme Court. In 1999, when it appeared likely that the State of Tennessee actually would execute a Death Row inmate for the first time since 1960, a number of groups opposing the death penalty suddenly appeared on the scene.

Interest groups played a prominent role in battles over the state income tax in 1999 and 2000. A small but persistent group called Tennesseans for Fair Taxation for years had lobbied for enactment of a state income tax. When the issue actually made it onto the legislative agenda in 1999, this group finally had some cause for optimism. On the other side of the issue, a group called the Free Enterprise Coalition, led by former Republican state chair Tommy Hopper, placed ads on the radio countering the "lies" of Gov. Don Sundquist and his "tax thieves."[7] Groups opposing the income tax enjoyed a tremendous advantage—their position was largely supported by public opinion (see chapter 8).

Regulating Campaign Contributions

One way that organized interests operate in Tennessee is through political action committees that funnel money to political candidates. State law and rule-making authority limits their contributions to candidates for state and local offices. While individual contributions are limited to one thousand dollars for any primary or general election, political action committees can contribute up to five thousand for each election. The rules governing campaign finance are posted by the office of the Secretary of State.[8] A candidate must form a campaign committee and keep records for public disclosure at specified dates. All candidates must report any campaign contributions greater than one hundred dollars.

Regulating Lobbying

While interest groups realize an obvious benefit from seeing that candidates they support are put in office, many see the electoral process as only the beginning. Most certainly would like to have access to elected officials so that they might lobby them on potential legislation. The Tennessee General Assembly regulates lobbying,[9] the rules being posted by the Tennessee Secretary of State.

A lobbyist communicates directly or indirectly with any official in the legislative or executive branches of government with the intention of influencing a legislative or executive action. If one wants to lobby, he or she must register with the Registry of Election Finance within five days of taking on lobbying duties. Any person registering as a lobbyist must show written documentation of his or her authority to represent each organization on whose behalf work will be done. Lobbyists are prevented from providing gifts to any government official, candidate for public office, or person in the official's or candidate's immediately family. The exception is purchases of food and beverages, which are allowable but subject to a dollar limit.[10]

It would be a mistake to conclude that those who seek actively to influence public officials operate under the watchful eye of the law. Some observers have noted that the flaw in Tennessee's regulation of lobbyists is that one can act like a lobbyist without registering as a lobbyist. One can merely claim to be a "consultant," "government affairs specialist," or the like. The Registry of Election Finance lacks the ability effectively to investigate anyone who acts as a lobbyist but does not register as such.[11]

Assessing Parties and Interest Groups

As it has for two centuries, the relative strength of Tennessee's two political parties continues to evolve in response to the state's demographic changes and the new priorities of a generally wealthier population. One party dominates for a decade or more, then the other. Modern Tennessee is a state with a genuine two-party system, although the parties often do not offer a genuine choice among ideas or candidates.

Increasingly, the political system is defined more by personalities and less by parties. As Tennessee's parties have declined in importance, the number of influence or interest groups has expanded rapidly. In a state in which issues and ideology are blurred, most interest groups support both political parties. A political culture that clings to the notion of a part-time citizen legislature struggles to stem the tide of full-time, well-funded special interests. With each passing year, that task becomes more difficult.

8

Public Opinion

Its name is Public Opinion. It is held in reverence. It settles everything. Some think it is the voice of God.

Mark Twain

Like Mark Twain, political scientists long have recognized the importance of public opinion in American politics. They are not alone. Incumbent politicians and those who would unseat them rely heavily on polling. Media outlets routinely sample public opinion, as do government agencies interested in public attitudes on specific policy issues. This is true at not only the national level, but also the state level and, increasingly, the local level. Tennessee has seen a proliferation of polls conducted by government, news media, academia, and, of course, politicians. In short, everyone involved in politics or engaged in observing politics is interested in public opinion. Even those politicians who do not rely upon survey research usually have their own informal methods of gauging what their constituents think.

"Public opinion" is the aggregation of all the values, beliefs, attitudes, and opinions held by individuals on questions of public concern. Much of this tends to be ephemeral stuff—opinions on issues that may be here today and gone tomorrow. While these short-term aspects of public opinion may be important in determining outcomes of elections or policy problems, long-term elements of public opinion shape the environment in which politics takes place.

The most important of these enduring elements of public opinion are party identification and ideological self-identification. Party identification and ideological self-identification are examples of reasonably stable attitudes that are linked both to issue positions and to candidate evaluation.[1] Party identification long has been recognized as the main long-term force underlying voters' positions on policy issues and ultimately influencing their decisions in the voting booth.

Party Identification

As noted in the previous chapter, party identification simply refers to a citizen's feeling of attachment (or lack thereof) to one of the political parties. In the United States (and certainly in Tennessee), we have a two-party system. Although there are a number of minor third parties, the Democratic Party and the Republican Party define the political landscape (tables 7.1–7.3, fig. 7.3). Virtually all elected officeholders identify with one of the two major parties. In the electorate, however, party identification tends to be softer and more fluid. There is no formal party membership. Rather, party identification refers to psychological attachment to one party or simply to a tendency to vote for the candidates of one party rather than the candidates of the other party. This may be based on conscious decision making, or it may be a function of parental example. The attachment may be hard and fast, as in the case of the "rock-ribbed Republican" or "yellow dog Democrat," or it may be soft and tentative, wavering according to issues and events of the day.

Over the past few decades, more and more citizens have become disenchanted with the two-party system and have come to identify themselves as "Independents." However, many of these Independents, when pressed, reveal that they lean in the direction of one of the two major parties. This is because they tend to prefer the policies endorsed by one party to those espoused by the other. Thus, when measuring party identification, political scientists often use a scale like that presented in figure 8.1.

Ideology

"Ideology" refers to a reasonably well-organized set of views on questions of policy. In American political discourse, these sets of views

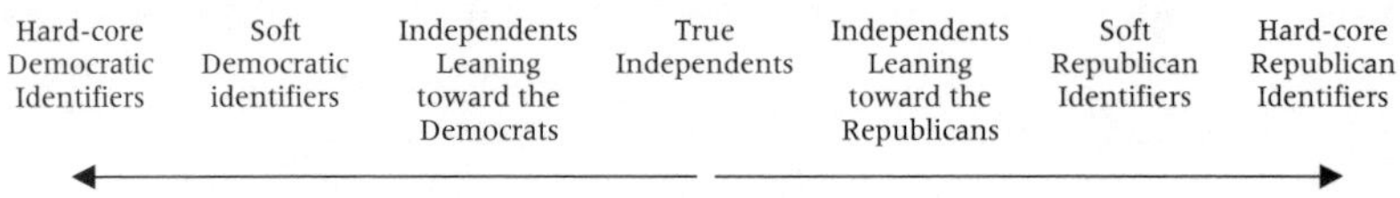

Fig. 8.1. Party Identification Scale.

usually are denominated "liberal" or "conservative," with the term "moderate" used to indicate a middle point in the spectrum. The terms "liberal" and "conservative" are not easy to define, but it is possible to sketch the broad contours of their meaning.

Liberals believe that people are fundamentally good and reasonable and that society can be improved significantly. Conservatives take a less benign view of human nature and thus have a more pessimistic attitude toward the possibility of progress. Liberals are more likely to be associated with various "reform" movements, whereas conservatives often regard such movements with skepticism.

Conservatives tend to stress the importance of traditional values and institutions; liberals are more likely to see them as oppressive. In what they sometimes characterize as a "culture war," conservatives find themselves defending monogamy, marriage, and the nuclear family against what they perceive as threats to these institutions. Liberals counter that they are not attacking traditional values and institutions per se, but only an oppressive orthodoxy that denies the legitimacy of alternative lifestyles.

Conservatives generally defend free-market capitalism, the right to unlimited accumulation of property, and the right to control one's private property. Liberals often point out the shortcomings of the capitalist system and typically support government intervention in the economy to protect the natural environment, ameliorate poverty, combat discrimination, and achieve other socially desirable goals. Liberals tend to be more favorable toward taxation, which obviously is necessary to support government programs. Conservatives tend to be pessimistic about the ability of government to address social problems and usually prefer that government confine itself to its more traditional functions, such as protecting national security and maintaining law and order. Conservatives usually oppose higher levels of taxation.

With regard to the justice system, liberals generally are more sympathetic to the rights of persons accused and convicted of crimes, whom they often regard as victims of poverty, discrimination, and injustice. Conservatives, on the other hand, usually take a "get-tough" approach to issues of criminal justice, supporting harsh punishments and opposing efforts to "handcuff" the police.

Having offered these general definitions, we hasten to add that many people who would identify themselves as liberal or conservative would take exception to some elements of our definitions. Indeed, the terms *liberal* and *conservative* may be the most frequently distorted and misunderstood words in the political dialogue. Because *liberal* and *conservative* are used every day by pollsters, commentators, and candidates, and because they can mean entirely different things to different people, the reader must pause to take a special look at two of the most important words in the vocabulary of Tennessee politics.

In some respects, the use and misuse of the words *liberal* and *conservative* come from a desire to simplify ideas and personalities that sometimes are very complicated. When asked to describe a political figure or to identify one's own political philosophy, it is easier to assign a conservative or liberal label, even if a multitude of exceptions exist that make the label meaningless. The value of the terms *conservative* and *liberal* is diluted further by the presence of voters who avoid choices and fear the consequences of being associated with a particular political party, individual, or position on an issue. In numbers that never can be counted with certainty, these individuals attempt to split the difference by telling pollsters they are "moderates" or "independents," confusing themselves with genuine moderates and making it impossible to tell whether, in the voting booth, the respondent might support some specific candidate or issue.

Even among voters who choose to identify themselves with a label, the terms *liberal* and *conservative* convey different things, in part because the meanings of the words have changed over time, along with the issues that defined those meanings. In the early 1960s, for example, supporting the right of African Americans to eat beside whites in restaurants would have placed one on the extreme "liberal" end of the political spectrum, whereas today in Tennessee such a position has no meaning at all in defining ideology. Within the Republican Party, many believe that being a fiscal conservative means keeping a balanced budget, while others insist true fiscal conservatism requires not just balancing, but also cutting, government spending. Many women who identify themselves to pollsters as "conservative" feel strongly that government should be more active in enforcing environmental standards and increasing spending for education—two positions generally associated with "liberals." The fact that two-thirds of Tennesseans favor state-promoted gambling in the form of a lottery raises questions about characterizations of Tennessee as a "conservative" state. In Tennessee, a proposal to tax personal incomes (long regarded as a litmus test for liberalism) is supported by much of the state's leading "conservative" business community. Another major state program, TennCare, also confounds those who want to assign philosophical labels. In extending health care coverage to four hundred thousand previously uninsured Tennesseans, TennCare seems to be a most liberal program. But by moving $4 billion from the public to the private sector, TennCare simultaneously is one of the most conservative initiatives in America.

When subjected to close examination, few issues in state government fall cleanly into ideological boxes. Yet even when issues (the death penalty or the income tax, say) are relatively easy to categorize, one finds large numbers of Tennesseans who take a "conservative" stance on one issue and a "liberal" position on another. Despite the challenges these and other examples pose to labeling, reporters, pollsters, and the public continue to use "conservative," "liberal," and "moderate" as terms to define issues, candidates, and the electorate. They do so largely for two reasons. Virtually all the data collected over the last five decades have used the terms "conservative" and "liberal," making it extremely difficult to establish points of reference with the use of any other terms to describe voters. Second, all shortcomings aside, few alternatives would provide pollsters and voters anything more meaningful than "liberal" or "conservative" to describe how voters view themselves and others. Those who conduct polls and those who read them must understand the limitations and potential inconsistencies contained in the data. Used carelessly, polls can produce a highly distorted view of people and issues. Used wisely, polls can be a revealing snapshot of who we are and what we want from those who seek to lead us.

Intersecting Party Identification and Ideology

In analyzing political tendencies, it is useful to examine how the concepts of party identification and ideology intersect. In talking about tendencies within the two parties, we often use ideological labels, as shown in figure 8.2. On the whole, Republicans tend to be more conservative than Democrats, but there are many exceptions to this tendency. At the state and local levels, especially, ideological differences between the parties can be quite blurry. In Tennessee and throughout the South, a substantial number of citizens can be described as conservative Democrats. Although liberal Republicans are increasingly rare (especially in the South), within the GOP a real divergence of opinion exists between conservative and moderate wings of the party. This divergence is especially pronounced on socio-moral issues like abortion; to a great extent, it reflects differing attitudes toward the so-called "Religious Right."

	Liberal	*Moderate*	*Conservative*
Democrat	Liberal Democrat	Moderate Democrat	Conservative Democrat
Independent	Liberal Independent	Moderate Independent	Conservative Independent
Republican	Liberal Republican	Moderate Republican	Conservative Republican

Fig. 8.2. Intersection of Party and Ideology. *Source:* Tennessee Poll, University of Tennessee Social Science Research Institute.

Issues

A large part of politics is about *issues,* which are differences in opinion about how government should address particular problems or concerns. Issues are important at the state and local levels of politics, but not always the same issues that are commanding the national spotlight. This chapter examines Tennesseans' attitudes on three important policy issues: abortion, the state income tax, and the state lottery. Abortion rights have not been a particularly visible issue in Tennessee politics, because much of the debate concerning it is grounded in decisions of the U.S. Supreme Court, and because Tennessee leaders of both parties consciously have attempted to avoid a divisive fight. Still, examining the abortion issue provides an opportunity to see how attitudes of Tennesseans compare with attitudes of Americans generally.

Tennessee Poll

The data upon which this chapter is based are derived from the Tennessee Poll, a statewide survey of adults conducted periodically by the Social Science Research Institute (SSRI) at the University of Tennessee, Knoxville.[2] Over the years, the Tennessee Poll has attempted to gauge public opinion on a variety of issues, including crime, education, health care, welfare, gun control, prisons, and many other important questions.

The chapter will focus on five variables for which we have data over a substantial period (1993–98): party identification, ideological self-identification, the state lottery, the state income tax , and abortion rights (table 8.1). Partisanship and ideology are fundamental to any analysis of public opinion. Over the last several years, the lottery, the state income tax, and abortion rights are issues that have been discussed frequently and about which most Tennesseans had a firm opinion. While far from a complete mapping of the opinion landscape of the state, these data provide insight into the state's political culture.[3]

TABLE 8.1
TRENDS IN TENNESSEE PUBLIC OPINION, 1989–1998 (PERCENTAGE)

	1989	1990	1991	1992	1993	1994	1995	1996	1997	1998
PARTY IDENTIFICATION										
Democrat	31	32	30	31	34	35	33	31	33	33
Independent	40	41	43	39	38	33	33	36	36	37
Republican	30	27	27	30	28	32	34	33	31	30
IDEOLOGY										
Liberal	15	14	17	15	12	17	17	17	17	15
Moderate	54	51	51	50	45	38	45	43	45	42
Conservative	31	35	32	35	43	45	38	40	38	43
STATE LOTTERY										
Favor	60	62	70	70	72	71	67	68	68	68
Not Sure	6	6	6	8	4	6	6	7	26	27
Oppose	34	32	24	22	24	23	27	25	6	7
STATE INCOME TAX										
Favor	30	30	34	32	31	26	31	24	27	24
Not Sure	11	12	10	10	8	15	10	11	9	12
Oppose	59	58	56	58	61	59	59	65	64	64
ABORTION LAW										
Easier	5	7	9	7	10	n/d	8	5	5	5
About Right	49	50	47	49	43	n/d	46	50	47	50
Harder	46	43	44	44	47	n/d	46	45	48	45

Trends in Party Identification

In the late 1940s, political scientist V. O. Key observed that "the forces of history . . . may have destined Republicans to a minority position" in Tennessee politics.[4] As we noted in the previous chapter, recent decades have seen the level of party competition in Tennessee increase significantly. In 1981, UT-Chattanooga political scientist Robert Swansborough found that 25 percent of Tennesseans identified with the Republican Party, although he noted that support was substantially higher than in the South generally.[5] As of 1998, the Tennessee Poll indicated that Tennessee had become a very competitive partisan environment (fig. 8.3).[6] On average, over the eight-year period, 30 percent of those surveyed identified themselves as Republicans, as compared with 32 percent as Democrats and 38 percent as Independents. This level of Republican identification represented a significant increase

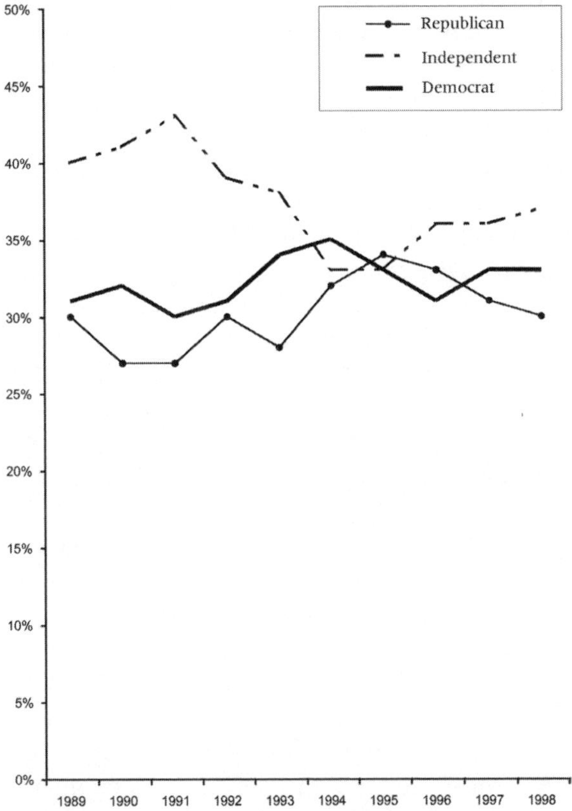

Fig. 8.3. Party Identification, 1989–1998. ***Source:*** **Tennessee Poll, University of Tennessee Social Science Research Institute.**

over the 25 percent level found by Swansborough in 1981, although it was still a long way from a majority. The Independents, the largest bloc of voters, dictated which party would control government and were the focus of intense effort in statewide elections.

In terms of mass party identification, Tennessee in the late 1990s was reasonably consistent with the national picture. Trends differed slightly, in that Tennesseans were a bit less likely to identify as Democrats and a bit more likely to identify as Independents. Tennessee was indistinguishable from the nation with respect to the proportion of Republican identifiers.

In 1994, Republicans Don Sundquist, Bill Frist, and Fred Thompson were elected to the post of governor and the two U.S. Senate seats, respectively. This sweep, as well as Thompson's reelection in 1996, clearly demonstrated the viability of Republicanism in Tennessee. The resurgence of the Republican Party certainly was not unique to Tennessee, as indicated by the Republican takeover of Congress in 1994. Indeed, the shifting party loyalties of Tennesseans paralleled what was happening throughout the South, as whites en masse defected from the Democratic Party. This development obviously was related to race, but it also was related to ideology. In Tennessee, as throughout the South, many whites left a Democratic Party they perceived to be too liberal. Indeed, the 1998 Tennessee Poll data showed that only 27 percent of white respondents identified themselves as Democrats. As a group, these white Democrats tended to be less educated, less affluent, older citizens. They also were more comfortable with the "liberal" label.

One should not interpret the Republican successes in the 1990s as predicting the death of the Tennessee Democratic Party. Democrat Bill Clinton carried Tennessee in the presidential elections of 1992 and 1996. Despite a series of well-financed campaigns by the Republicans, only one Democratic incumbent was defeated in the 1998 legislative races. At the end of the twentieth century, Democrats were mayors in Memphis, Nashville, and Chattanooga, and in the Republican stronghold of Knoxville, a Democrat held the position of county executive. Tennessee was, indeed, a two-party state in which a campaign victory depended as much upon the quality of the candidate and the funds expended as upon party loyalty.

Ideological Trends

In the 1998 Tennessee Poll, only 15 percent of respondents identified themselves as liberals. This figure contrasted sharply with the national population, where, during the late 1990s, as many as one-third identified themselves as liberals (fig. 8.4). Like Democratic identifiers, liberals in Tennessee tended to be less educated and less affluent than other citizens. The Tennessee Poll showed that, while African Americans were much more likely than whites to call themselves Democrats (67 percent to 27 percent), they were only marginally more likely than whites to self-identify as liberals (21 percent to 17 percent).

The proportion of self-identified conservatives increased substantially throughout the ten-year period (fig. 8.4). Whereas in 1989 about 31 percent identified as conservatives, in 1994 the number had grown dramatically, to 45 percent. Those calling themselves conservatives decreased significantly in 1995 to 38 percent, perhaps in reaction to perceived excesses of the national Republican agenda. In 1996, the proportion of conservatives bounced back to 40 percent. The average for the entire period was 37 percent—remarkably close to the national norm.

The percentage of Tennesseans identifying themselves as moderates dropped significantly from 54 percent in 1989 to 38 percent in 1994, the year Tennesseans gave the Republicans huge electoral victories that helped the GOP take control of Congress. In 1995, Tennesseans pulled back to the center, as the proportion of moderates

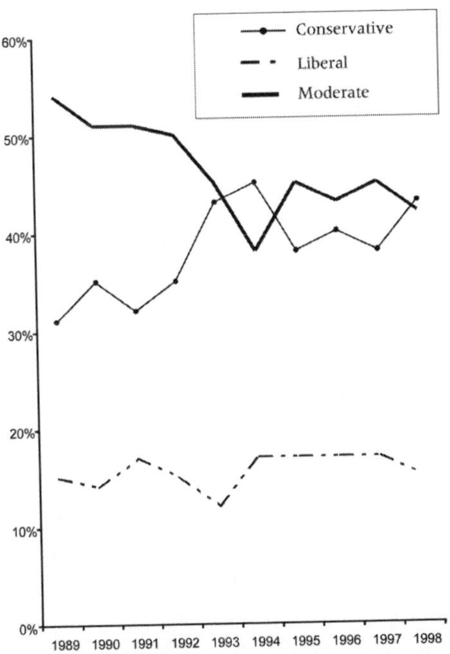

Fig. 8.4. Ideological Self-Identification, 1989–1998. ***Source:*** **Tennessee Poll, University of Tennessee Social Science Research Institute.**

jumped from 38 percent to 45 percent. The proportion of conservatives dropped from 45 percent to 38 percent, while the proportion of liberals remained constant at 17 percent. Since 1996, figures for ideological self-identification have been fairly stable.

At the close of the 1990s, Tennesseans were more likely than Americans generally to self-define as moderates, just about as likely to identify as conservatives, but considerably less likely to adopt the liberal label. The data suggest that Tennesseans are somewhat more conservative than Americans generally. Thus we can characterize the Tennessee political environment as moderately conservative. This label is consistent with the observation that most, if not all, successful statewide Republican candidates—including Lamar Alexander, Bill Frist, Don Sundquist, and Fred Thompson, have run fairly moderate campaigns and certainly have avoided making obvious appeals to the far right.

Intersection of Party and Ideology

In Tennessee, as in national politics, ideology and party identification often are related, though the correlation between party and ideology is far from consistent. Reflecting national trends, conservatives are more likely to be Republicans, and liberals are more likely to be Democrats. However, in Tennessee, Democrats are much more conservative than the national Democratic Party.

TABLE 8.2
INTERSECTION OF PARTY IDENTIFICATION AND IDEOLOGY IN TENNESSEE, FALL 1998 (PERCENTAGE)

	Liberal	*Moderate*	*Conservative*
Democrat	9.3	13.6	9.3
Independent	7.4	17.4	12.6
Republican	2.7	10.4	17.3
Total Percent	19.4	41.4	39.2

SOURCE: The Tennessee Poll, University of Tennessee Social Science Research Institute.

NOTE: Percentages add to 100 for the entire table.

Tennessee voters also include significant numbers of conservative Democrats and even a few liberal Republicans. Table 8.2 shows how the electorate breaks down when we intersect these variables. The modal category is "moderate Independent" (17.4 percent), followed closely by "conservative Republican." In Tennessee, Democrats are most likely to prefer the "moderate" label. They split evenly between liberals and conservatives. Clearly, Tennesseans who identify with the Democratic Party are, on the whole, more conservative than Democrats nationwide. This helps to explain the fairly cozy relationship that has existed for some time between Democratic and Republican leaders in the state. The parties in Tennessee simply are not that different ideologically and therefore are less antagonistic than in many states across the country.

Public Attitudes on Policy Questions

During the 1980s and 1990s, Tennessee state government addressed but never finally resolved the issues of a state lottery and a state income tax. Throughout this period, the Tennessee Poll measured public opinion on the state lottery and the state income tax, as well as attitudes about abortion, which has been a controversial issue among Tennesseans since *Roe v. Wade* was decided by the U.S. Supreme Court in 1973.

State Lottery

In the mid-1980s, many Tennesseans became interested in the possibility of establishing a state lottery to supplement or replace other sources of state revenue. As adjoining states Georgia, Kentucky, and Virginia adopted lotteries, concern mounted that Tennessee was losing sales tax revenue as consumers near the border crossed state lines to buy gasoline and groceries at stores where they could also purchase lottery tickets. Increasing numbers of Tennesseans, many of whom identified themselves as conservatives, viewed a lottery as an acceptable alternative to increases in the state sales tax. Since 1989, the Tennessee Poll included the following question: "Some have suggested a state lottery for Tennessee. How do you feel? Would you favor or oppose instituting a lottery in Tennessee?" The Tennessee Poll consistently found high levels of public support for the lottery (see fig. 8.5). On average over the ten-year period, about two-thirds of respondents indicated support for the lottery; about one-quarter expressed opposition. Opposition to the lottery was most intense among strong conservatives, the elderly, people in rural/farming areas, fundamentalist Protestants, and, interestingly, those with the highest levels of education.

Until 2001, the state legislature steadfastly refused to allow Tennesseans to vote on whether the state constitutional prohibition of lotteries should be removed. Given the strong public support for the lottery, how could this refusal be explained? To some extent, it reflected the sincere personal views of legislators. But for some Republican legislators, there were practical political reasons. Republican primary voters tend to

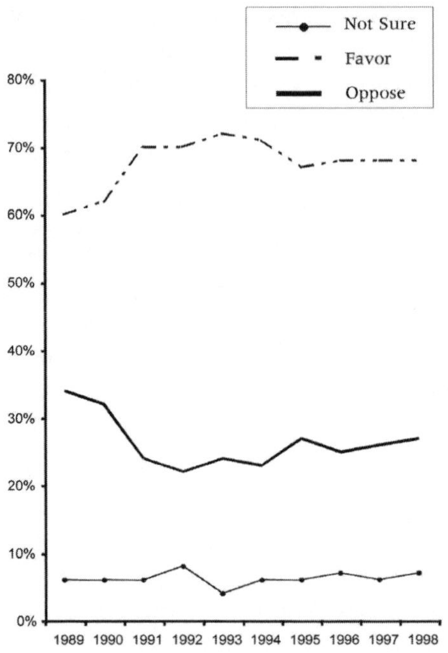

Fig. 8.5. Views on the State Lottery, 1989–1998. ***Source:*** **Tennessee Poll, University of Tennessee Social Science Research Institute.**

be more conservative, and it is among conservatives that opposition to legalization of the lottery is the strongest. In November 2000, the complexion of the state senate changed as two anti-lottery senators were replaced by more sympathetic members. In February 2001, faced with a fiscal crisis and strong public opposition to an income tax, the state legislature reversed course and approved a resolution calling for a statewide referendum on the lottery question to be held in November 2002. The measure would change the state constitution to allow a state lottery to be established, the proceeds of which would go to higher education. Given the strong public support for the lottery, most observers expected that this measure would pass, but in politics intensity can make a huge difference. And the intensity factor favored those who opposed the lottery.

Abortion Rights

Although the question of abortion rights remains one of the most hotly contested policy issues on the national scene, in Tennessee the debate has not been nearly as contentious as it has been in many other states. The issue rarely has figured prominently in campaign rhetoric. Anti-abortion protests in Tennessee have not been characterized by the violence witnessed in several states. The lack of confrontation, however, does not imply that Tennesseans do not have opinions on this divisive national issue.

As figure 8.6 indicates, very few Tennesseans want abortions to be more accessible. A substantial minority, very nearly approaching a majority, would like to see abortions made harder to obtain. Does this mean that Tennesseans would support a fundamental change in policy on this issue? Probably not. The Tennessee Poll of fall 1995 asked respondents: "Do you think that the United States Supreme Court should overturn or uphold its 1973 decision in *Roe v. Wade*, which effectively legalized abortion in this country?" Although a substantial minority (39 percent) favored overturning *Roe*, a greater percentage (49 percent) preferred that the decision be upheld; 12 percent were unsure.[7] Like Americans generally, Tennesseans are troubled by the abortion issue and would like to see the number of abortions reduced, but most do not support a fundamental change in public policy in this area.

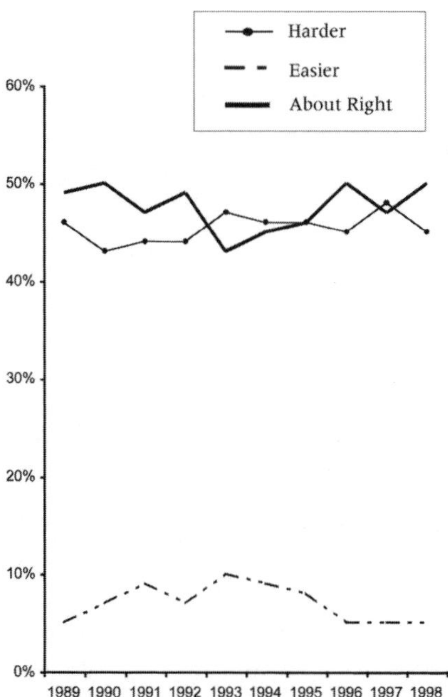

Fig. 8.6. Views on Abortion, 1989–1998. ***Source:*** **Tennessee Poll, University of Tennessee Social Science Research Institute.**

In many ways Tennessee has been spared the most divisive political battles on the abortion front. The anti-abortion movement has become increasingly active in attempting to elect lawmakers who support its agenda. These candidates do not represent a majority of legislators, although anti-abortion legislators are a growing force within the Republican Party. Organizations such as Operation Rescue have not undertaken major efforts within the state. Perhaps the even split in public opinion, in a broader climate of more moderate conservatism, has injected a bit of caution into the thinking of any politician who risks alienating opponents on either side of the issue.

State Income Tax

A trio of Tennessee political scientists once observed that, "if controversies are lacking, a fight can always be stirred up on taxes."[8] A longstanding question in this state has been whether to institute a personal income tax. Writing in 1975, Greene, Grubbs, and Hobday expressed the view that "the insatiable demand for governmental expenditure" might lead to adoption of such a tax, although the authors admitted, "By all signs it is unwelcome at present."[9] Tennessee relies primarily on a very high sales tax to generate revenue. This system is often criticized as regressive and unstable. At times, as during Ned McWherter's and Don Sundquist's second terms as governor, the issue actually has made it onto the public agenda, but strong public opposition prevented the legislature from enacting an income tax. In fact, a strong expression of negative public opinion caused the General Assembly to adjourn two special sessions in 1999 without voting on the tax question. Similarly, in the year 2000, despite the intensive efforts by the Governor, the General Assembly refused to adopt an income tax (see chapter 14 for more discussion).

Between 1989 and 1998, the Tennessee Poll found consistent public opposition to an income tax. Although a substantial minority of Tennesseans favored such a tax, the weight of public opinion clearly was with opponents (see fig. 8.7). By the end of the 1990s, despite Governor Sundquist's best efforts (including a $1 million "public education" campaign), little prospect existed for change in the climate of public opinion. The number of Tennesseans who believed the state faced a fiscal crisis was inadequate to overcome emotional opposition to an income tax. Moreover, there was reason to believe that Tennesseans did not trust their state government to use the proceeds of any new tax wisely.

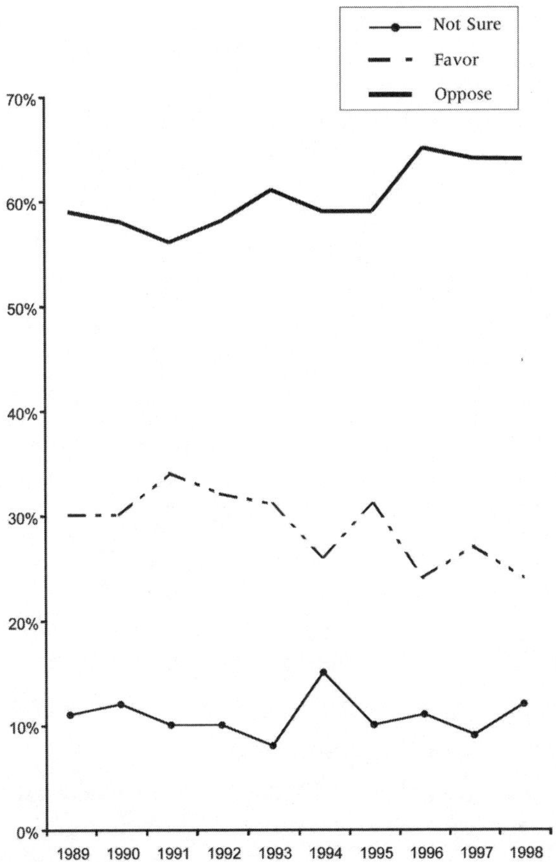

Fig. 8.7. Views on State Income Tax, 1989–1998. *Source:* Tennessee Poll, University of Tennessee Social Science Research Institute.

Ideology, Partisanship, and Policy Issues

Issue positions are often grounded in partisanship and ideology. The Tennessee Poll of fall 1998 showed that Republicans and conservatives were much more likely to favor toughening abortion laws than others (see table 8.3). Both groups also manifested higher levels of opposition to the lottery and the income tax. However, the relationship between ideology and the income tax issue was very weak, suggesting that ideological orientations among modern Tennesseans may have more to do with social and moral values (e.g., gambling and abortion) than with pocketbook issues. The data also suggested that opposition to government taxation was fairly widespread in Tennessee.

TABLE 8.3
ISSUE POSITIONS, BY PARTY IDENTIFICATION AND IDEOLOGY, FALL 1998 (PERCENT)

	Democ	*Indep*	*Repub*	*Lib*	*Mod*	*Conserv*
State Lottery						
Favor	72	70	52	79	71	51
Oppose	24	25	45	18	26	45
Not Sure	4	5	3	3	3	4
State Income Tax						
Favor	34	28	18	28	28	24
Oppose	59	65	70	67	65	65
Not Sure	7	8	12	5	6	11
Abortion Law						
Easier	6	5	2	15	2	2
About Right	60	50	38	62	57	35
Harder	34	45	60	23	41	63

SOURCE: The Tennessee Poll, University of Tennessee Social Science Research Institute.

Regionalism within the State

As we pointed out in chapter 1, Tennessee is divided into three grand divisions, each of which is culturally and politically distinctive. However, Tennessee Poll data from 1989 suggested that regionalism was becoming less significant as a determinant of public opinion (see table 8.4). While East Tennessee remained the most Republican of the three grand divisions, the differences in partisan identification across the state were less pronounced. The same trend was true of ideology. The three regions were indistinguishable in terms of their collective sentiments regarding the lottery and were only marginally different on the abortion and income tax issues. The data suggest that the state's political culture, once regarded as tripartite in character, had become more homogeneous.

Race, Gender, and Socioeconomic Status

Racial differences in American public opinion are well documented. Tennesseans are no exception. The Tennessee Poll revealed clear differences between white and black voters (see table 8.5). By far the most pronounced racial differences were in the area of partisanship, with blacks more than twice as likely as whites to identify as Democrats and whites more than three times as likely as African Americans to self-identify as Republicans. Blacks also were somewhat more likely to see themselves as liberals but, interestingly, almost as likely as whites to self-define as conservatives. On the lottery issue, there were no racial differences. On abortion, blacks were somewhat more likely to favor the pro-choice position. As a group, African Americans were significantly more supportive of instituting a state income tax, a reflection of the notion that lowering the sales tax in favor of a tax on incomes would help most black families.

TABLE 8.4
PARTY IDENTIFICATION, IDEOLOGY, AND ISSUE POSITIONS, BY REGION, FALL 1998 (PERCENT)

	East Tenn	*Middle Tenn*	*West Tenn*
Party Identification			
Democrat	25	35	36
Independent	40	41	37
Republican	35	24	27
Ideology			
Liberal	21	14	18
Moderate	34	50	43
Conservative	45	36	39
State Lottery			
Favor	66	68	61
Oppose	30	28	35
Not Sure	4	4	4
State Income Tax			
Favor	25	31	23
Oppose	66	62	65
Not Sure	9	7	12
Abortion Law			
Easier	2	6	6
About Right	49	53	44
Harder	49	41	50

SOURCE: The Tennessee Poll, University of Tennessee Social Science Research Institute.

The Tennessee Poll also reveals something of a "gender gap" with respect to party identification (see table 8.5). Women were significantly more likely to embrace the Democrats and slightly less likely to adhere to the Republican Party. In terms of ideology, women as a group were less conservative than men, but the gap was fairly narrow here. On the policy issues, there were some differences, but none was especially dramatic.

TABLE 8.5

PARTISANSHIP, IDEOLOGY, AND ISSUE POSITIONS, BY RACE, GENDER, AND SOCIOECONOMIC STATUS (PERCENTAGE), FALL 1998

						Income	
	Male	*Female*	*White*	*Black*	*Low*	*Mod*	*High*
Party Identification							
Democrat	27	35	27	67	37	37	21
Independent	37	42	40	28	44	32	43
Republican	36	23	33	5	19	31	36
Ideology							
Liberal	16	20	17	21	19	14	25
Moderate	44	40	43	35	45	47	35
Conservative	40	40	40	44	36	39	40
State Lottery							
Favor	67	64	64	79	69	67	66
Not Sure	30	31	32	18	27	30	30
Oppose	3	5	4	3	4	3	4
State Income Tax							
Favor	24	28	26	25	31	28	22
Oppose	69	61	65	67	64	59	72
Not Sure	7	11	9	8	5	13	6
Abortion Law							
Easier	4	5	4	6	6	4	3
About Right	51	47	49	53	39	49	63
Harder	45	48	47	41	55	47	34

SOURCE: The Tennessee Poll, University of Tennessee Social Science Research Institute.

As one might expect, there was a relationship between income and party identification. Democrats, on average, had smaller incomes than Republicans. This difference in partisanship did not translate into dramatic ideological differences across income levels, although there were some significant policy differences across the income groups (especially on the abortion issue).

Assessing Public Opinion

Public opinion data collected throughout the 1990s painted a picture of a population almost evenly divided between Republicans and Democrats, with Independents holding a slight plurality. During the 1990s, Tennesseans cemented their opposition to an income tax and solidified their support for a lottery, but they remained sharply divided on abortion. Differences in political culture among the state's traditional divisions showed signs of easing. Overall, Tennessee remains a moderately conservative state whose people harbor considerable skepticism of government.

9

Campaigns and Elections

The scene takes place every two years. In and around the offices of the House Speaker, the Majority Leader, and the Democratic Caucus Chairman, groups of staff, lobbyists, and other political hangers-on assemble at the Legislative Plaza in Nashville as the returns of legislative elections come in from across the state. Most make nervous conversation while they drink wine from paper cups, watch the three televisions set up in the Speaker's conference room, and wait for voting results called in from key districts. From the Speaker and Constitutional Officers to the secretaries, all realize what is unspoken. Power, prestige, and jobs for the next twenty-four months depend upon phone calls received over the next two hours.

Elections provide the mechanism through which the electorate communicates its preferences to government. Elections also hold public officials accountable to the people whom they govern. If officials do not perform to the satisfaction of a majority of the electorate, they will lose their jobs. Finally, elections perform the function of conferring legitimacy upon the political system. If rulers are chosen in elections perceived as free and fair, people are far more likely to extend the right to govern.

Anyone considering running for office must be aware of the variety of forces that converge during an election. Who else will be a candidate? How much money will it take to run a successful campaign? What groups are most likely to vote? What will the overall level of voter turnout be? What are the key issues in the race, and how do these issues affect the groups likely to vote? What interest groups have a stake in the contest, and how will they seek to influence the outcome? Will the campaign be covered by the news media? If so, will the media focus on issues or personal scandals? Who can be counted on to help? Is the election important enough to the state political party for it to provide assistance? The answer to each of these questions has a bearing on the outcome of the race.

Elections are divided into two categories: primary and general elections. Primary elections are designed to choose each party's nominees for the general election. The general election determines who will hold office. Parties are not required to hold primary elections in Tennessee, but for state and federal offices almost always opt to do so.[1] Indeed, from the 1920s until the 1960s, victory in a Democratic primary was tantamount to a general election victory in statewide races and in local elections in most of Middle Tennessee and West Tennessee. In similar fashion, the Republican primary victor was virtually guaranteed success in local elections in many areas of East Tennessee.

Tennessee Elections in the Federal System

The complexity of the American federal system produces a great number of elections, held at different times for different offices. In a given year, a citizen may be asked to vote in both nomination contests and general elections for offices at the local, state, and national levels. Some of the state and national elections occur on the same dates, while elections for local offices are held at different times. Turnout, especially for state and local elections, tends to be quite low (see fig. 9.1). If as many as 50 percent of eligible voters turn out to vote in a state or local election, commentators are likely to pronounce the turnout "high."

Three elections are conducted at the federal level: President and Vice President, U.S. Senator, and U.S. Congressional Representative. Together, these elections dominate the national political agenda. Elections for federal office are held in even years, with a presidential election held every four years. More citizens vote in elections when

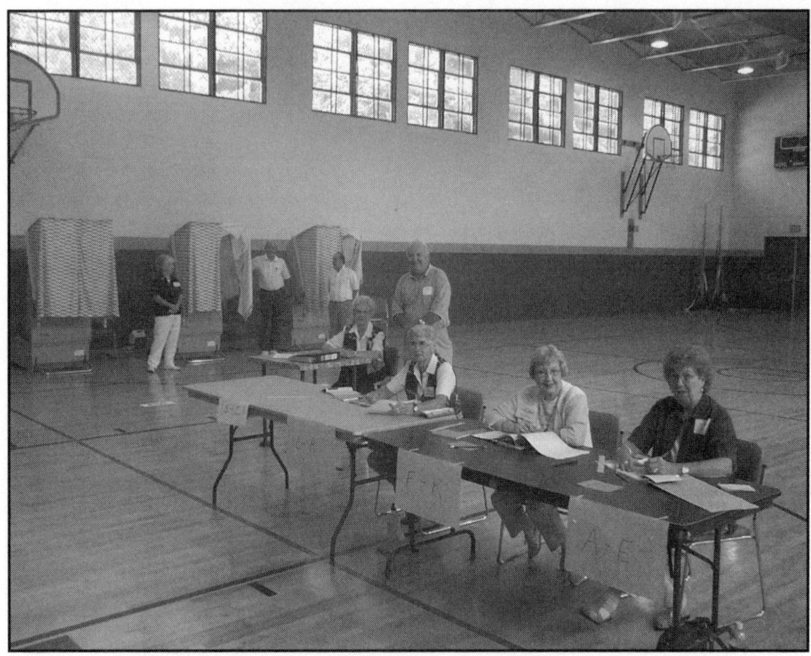

Fig. 9.1. Idle election workers in a West Knoxville precinct waiting for voters to appear during the state primary in August 2000. In Knox County, turnout was only about 10 percent of registered voters. Photo by John M. Scheb II.

the President is being chosen. Since the early 1970s, voter turnout for federal elections has declined. Today fewer than half of American adults choose to participate in presidential elections. Only about a third of eligible voters participate in elections held in the even years between presidential elections, when a third of the state senators and all U.S. Congressional Representatives are elected. In Tennessee, participation in national elections mirrors national norms (see fig. 9.2). Keep in mind that the chart's increase in the volume of turnout reflects growth in Tennessee's population, and not growth in the percentage of eligible voters who choose to vote.

Tennessee state elections are held every two years in even years. Every four years, in the even year between presidential elections, Tennesseans select the Governor, who can hold office for no more than two consecutive terms. The gubernatorial election coincides with the election of all members of the Tennessee House and half the members of the state Senate. Primary elections for these elections are held in August, with the general elections following in November. Elections for the U.S. House and the U.S. Senate (when occurring)

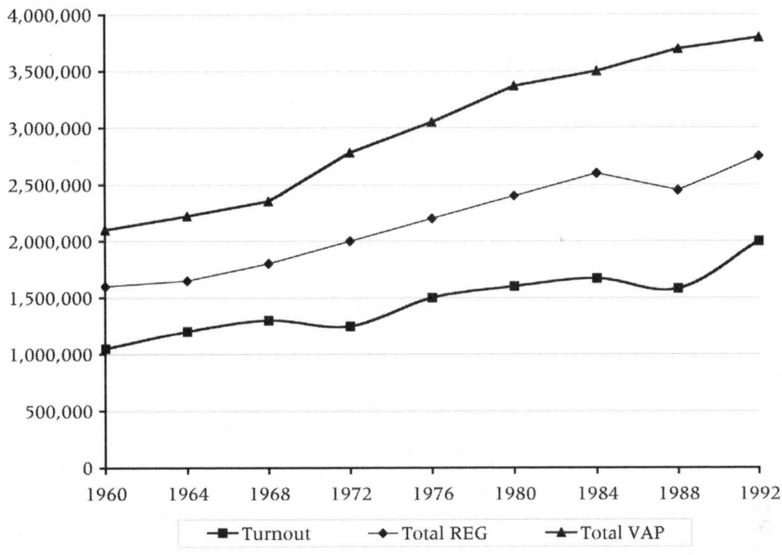

Fig. 9.2. Turnout in Presidential Elections in Tennessee, 1960–1992. ***Source:*** **Federal Election Commission.**

are held on the same dates. The state also holds retention elections for the Tennessee Supreme Court and the Court of Appeals in the November cycle.

Another category of elections at the county level includes offices created by the state legislature. Elections for the local offices of county executive, sheriff, trustee, court clerks, and register of deeds are held every four years.[2] Elections are conducted on eight-year cycles for trial court judges and District Attorneys General. For Tennessee's local offices, primary elections are held in May. General elections for local offices are scheduled in August, coincident with the primary elections for state offices. Tennessee's campaign process effectively stretches the electoral cycle, even in years where there is no presidential election, from May to November. Serious campaigning begins in February or March—sometimes much earlier—and does not cease until Election Day in November. This protracted campaign season, at times involving dozens of candidates for various offices, may induce confusion and fatigue in much of the electorate. Turnout in the May primary elections for local offices often is quite low and usually is not much better in the August general elections, unless a competitive primary election for Governor or U.S. Senator stirs things up (see table 9.1).

TABLE 9.1
TURNOUT IN TENNESSEE GENERAL ELECTIONS, 1992–1998

	Percentage of voting-age population voting in general election
1992	47
1996	44
1998	22

SOURCE: Center for Voting and Democracy.

Municipal Elections

The time for municipal elections is established in a city's charter. Most towns and cities opt to hold their elections in odd years. Many cities and towns also have chosen to hold nonpartisan elections, in which candidates do not run as Democrats or Republicans. By removing party labels and holding elections without competition from statewide or national elections, those writing city charters insured that local issues would be the focus of the elections. Separation of city elections from state and national forces was advocated by the reform movement in American politics.[3] This movement of civic reformers had the goals of making city government more professional and of removing corruption. One unanticipated negative effect of these "reforms" was a drop in turnout for city elections. In Knoxville, the decline in turnout has led the city to consider amending its charter to place its elections back on the even-year cycle, so that mayoral elections would coincide with the statewide gubernatorial election.

"One Person, One Vote"

Elections for the Tennessee General Assembly, as in most state legislatures, are conducted by electing one person for each Senate district and one for each House district. The Tennessee Constitution gives the General Assembly the responsibility for drawing boundaries for these districts. Every ten years, after the new federal census data is released, the Tennessee General Assembly convenes in regular session to redraw the lines for the districts that elect ninety-nine members of the state House of Representatives and thirty-three state senators. The redistricting process seeks to reflect shifts in the state's population while maintaining districts of roughly equal size. The process is extremely complicated and can become highly emotional, especially when moving district boundaries puts two incumbent legislators in the same district. Legislative leaders who draw the lines are guided by two conflicting forces. First, they wish to draw districts that give their party the best chance to gain seats. At the same time, they are aware that any redistricting plan approved by the legislature and the Governor also must be approved by federal and state courts, each of which has different and sometimes contradictory standards. The difficulty of the task is compounded when the legislative leadership and the Governor represent different parties. Not only political careers, but also at times control of the political process, are at stake.

The Tennessee Constitution sets the number of representatives at ninety-nine and senators at thirty-three. If a legislative district is composed of two or more counties, the counties must adjoin each other. Because it is more practical for smaller counties to have a single representative or senator, the Tennessee Constitution states that no county shall be divided if it is in a multi-county district. This provision against dividing counties has been overruled by the federal courts. In its famous "one person, one vote" decision, *Reynolds v. Sims*,[4] the United States Supreme Court held that state legislative districts had to be equal in population. While legislators understood that the Supreme Court did not mean that districts must have exactly equal populations, the decision did not provide guidelines as to what the population variance could be. The issue was of great significance when placed against the Tennessee Constitution's clear intention not to split county lines. In other words, with a population variance of 15 percent, legislators could draw lines that split few counties. If, however, the required standard for population variance was closer to 5 percent, it would become necessary to split perhaps two dozen more counties in order to satisfy the federal Court. Each alternative has enormous consequences for legislators and their respective parties. Moreover, failure to meet the Court's expectations can result in the majority party's worst nightmare. The Court reserves the right to throw the plans out, as it has in other states, and draw its own redistricting plan for the General Assembly.

Minority Representation and the Voting Rights Act

Every ten years, the General Assembly's redistricting process is subjected to close scrutiny by federal and state courts. Under the 1965 federal Voting Rights Act, state legislatures must insure that minority voters have an equal opportunity to participate in the electoral process. This statute has been interpreted by the Supreme Court to mean that states cannot draw legislative district lines in such a way as to prevent blacks from being elected. Minorities who challenge a redistricting plan must demonstrate that district lines deprive them of an equal opportunity to elect candidates of their choosing. The Voting Rights Act does not guarantee minorities a number of legislators directly proportional to their percentage of the state's population. From the opposite perspective, neither the law nor the courts allow the legislature to draw bizarre districts solely for the purpose of electing minorities.

The federal rules regarding voting rights are not at all clear, and, when coupled with the constitutional requirements and partisan politics, lead lawmakers to confront a very difficult task when new lines are to be drawn. Following the 1990 reapportionment, a group of African American voters brought suit in federal court under the Voting Rights Act to challenge the reapportionment of the state Senate.[5] The state's plan called for the creation of three majority-black districts in West Tennessee, which probably would have led to the election of three black state Senators (9 percent of the Senate). Because the state's voting-age population was 14 percent black, and because two more majority-black districts could have been drawn in West Tennessee, plaintiffs argued that the state had failed to live up to its obligations under the Voting Rights Act. A three-judge panel in the federal district court in Memphis agreed and ordered the state to prepare and submit a new reapportionment plan. However, the state appealed. The district court agreed but was overturned by the U.S. Supreme Court.[6] The Supreme Court held that states do not have a duty to maximize the number of majority-black districts.[7] On remand, the district court in Memphis upheld the state's plan.[8]

In evaluating the political influence of the African American electorate, one needs to consider a number of factors, only one of which is the number of districts in which African American voters elect a senator or representative. Often overlooked are the so-called "influence districts." Although represented by white legislators, such districts include sufficient numbers of minority voters to influence elections and the policy decisions of those elected. A good example of such a district is the state Senate district long occupied by Memphis Democrat Steve Cohen. Cohen, who is white, represents a district in which the voting-age population is one-third black. Without the overwhelming support of blacks in his district, Cohen might well have been defeated in 1988,

1992, and 1996. Had most of those black voters been used to create a new majority-black district, Cohen likely would have been defeated by a conservative white Republican. Indeed, this phenomenon has taken place in states where legislatures have redrawn district lines with the goal of increasing the number of black legislators. Tennessee Democrats (who, being the majority party, have always drawn the redistricting lines) have taken great care to make sure that, as they make it possible for more black Democrats to be elected to the legislature, they do not end up with a net increase of white Republicans. Such a result would dilute not only the Democratic Party's influence but also the aggregate influence of blacks on issues of importance to the minority community. Thus, African American political influence is maximized when there is an optimal combination of majority-black districts and influence districts.

Governing Elections

Under the U.S. Constitution, states are given responsibility for conducting federal, state, and local elections.[9] They must conduct these elections in a manner consistent with the applicable provisions of the federal Constitution and statutes.[10] In addition to redrawing congressional and state legislative district lines after each federal census, the state's responsibility includes setting the time and place of elections, overseeing registration and voting, keeping records of election results, and determining procedures for qualifying to run for state or local office.

State Election Commission

The State Election Commission regulates state-level elections in Tennessee (i.e., the Governor, state legislature, and retention of appellate judges). The State Election Commission is housed within the offices of the Secretary of State. The commission is made up of five members: three from the party holding a majority of seats in the General Assembly, and two from the minority party. Commissioners, who are chosen by a combined vote of the House and Senate, serve four-year terms. No more than two can reside in any grand division of the state, assuring representation of each grand division.

Local elections are governed by county election commissions. The State Election Commission appoints each of the five-member county election commissions and monitors its activities. The county election commissions must be composed of three members of the party holding the majority in the state legislature. This allows the majority party in the General Assembly to control the county election commissions

Major Duties of the Division of Elections

1. Generally supervises all elections;
2. Authoritatively interprets the election laws for all persons administering them;
3. Prepares instructions for the conduct of registration;
4. Advises election commissions, primary boards, and registrars-at-large as to the proper methods of performing their duties;
5. Investigates the administration of the election laws and reports violations to the district attorney general or grand jury for prosecution;
6. Publishes training materials for the use of election officials;
7. Furnishes instructions for election officials as to their duties in the conduct of elections, and furnishes copies of the election laws manual and updating materials to election commissions, primary boards, and registrars-at-large;
8. Reviews all bills affecting the election laws and reports in writing to the General Assembly on them individually; reports to each General Assembly with any recommendations the coordinator of elections may have for improvements in the election laws or their application;
9. Ensures that all election commissions within the state shall prohibit any person from becoming qualified to have such person's name placed on any ballot wherein such person is seeking to be nominated or elected to more than one state legislative office, voted on by voters during any primary or general election;
10. Properly files and keeps up to date the information supplied by the county election commissions; and supplies that information, within a reasonable time, to any member of the General Assembly upon request;
11. Develops a uniform petition form for use by persons seeking to qualify to run for public office and furnishes such form to county election commissions for distribution to such persons;
12. Devises and furnishes to the clerks of the circuit and criminal courts a form to be used for notifying county election commissions of the fact that a registered voter in their county has been convicted of an infamous crime and therefore should be purged from the registration records; and instructs the registrars in each county that they are to purge the registration of any person appearing on the infamous crime list who is registered to vote in their county;
13. Conducts a training seminar for registrars-at-large, deputy registrars-at-large, and county election commissioners at least once per calendar year;
14. Keeps accurate records of those registrars who do and do not attend training seminars and transmits these records to the state election commission;
15. Prepares and administers a written examination on election laws to any registrar-at-large who desires to take the exam at least once per calendar year.

Source: Adapted from Tennessee Code Annotated §2-11-201.

even in counties dominated by the other party. Because Democrats almost always have held the majority of seats in the General Assembly, election commissions even in staunchly Republican East Tennessee counties have been controlled by Democrats.

The State Election Commission reviews petitions filed by candidates for state office. The county election commissions do the same for candidates for county office. Each county election commission appoints a registrar, who is the chief administrative officer of the election commission. In rural counties the position is considered a good job and is a political plum for the party holding the majority in the state legislature.

Division of Elections

The Division of Elections supervises the conduct of elections under the direction of the State Election Coordinator.[11] The election process is tightly prescribed at the state level and at the county level is administered within these prescribed rules. Even though the local election commissions appoint registrars, they are provided training at the state level.

Early Voting

"Early voting" refers to the process of voting prior to the designated day of election. Although early voting is conducted in a variety of ways in different states, the common purpose is to make it easier to vote for citizens who, because of health or business conflicts, find it hard to get to a polling site between 7:00 A.M. and 7:00 P.M. on Tuesdays. Early voting first was tried in Texas in 1991, and it was implemented in Tennessee in 1994. Each county was instructed to establish a two-week period for early voting to begin twenty days prior to any election. Most counties designated the county courthouse as the early voting site. Larger counties set up satellite voting sites at malls and other centers of activity.

Early voting has changed the dynamics of voting in Tennessee and forced candidates to alter their strategies. In some communities, early voters exceed 15 percent of total turnout. Faced with this trend, campaigns cannot wait until the last week to run radio spots and send direct mail. Budgets and strategies, including efforts to reach groups such as nursing home residents, must be designed to accommodate a voting schedule that begins weeks earlier when early voting is an option. Early voting does not change the nature of the electorate so much as it does when people vote.[12] In particular, people over age sixty-five are most likely to take advantage of early voting. These and other consequences of early voting have brought about changes in campaign activities that typically took place in the last two weeks of an election.

Unfortunately, the one change early voting has not brought about is a significant increase in the number of persons who vote. People who must get their children to school and go to work find it very inconvenient to vote in Tennessee and in most states. Some have suggested that changing the two-hundred-year-old tradition of voting on Tuesday to Saturday might make voting easier and more attractive. Until these and other changes take place, early voting will have little impact on the level of voter participation.

Election Laws and Unforeseen Circumstances

From time to time, strange events result in unexpected and undesired consequences for the election process. In such instances, election procedures are forced to deal with situations such as a nominated candidate's inability to serve if elected, due to either disability or death. One of the most bizarre and tragic examples of such events occurred in 1998, when longtime Democratic state Senator Tommy Burks was opposed for reelection by a Republican nominee, Byron Looper, who legally had changed his middle name to "(Low-Tax)." About three weeks before Election Day, the heavily favored Burks was murdered. The person arrested and indicted for the murder was Burks's opponent, Looper. Tennessee had no law dealing with replacement of a nominated candidate who died after being nominated in the primary election or of a candidate jailed and accused of a crime. To the horror of the citizens in Burks's Senate district, Looper remained the only candidate on the ballot despite his incarceration. The situation was resolved by an eleventh-hour write-in campaign for Burks's widow, Charlotte, who won with virtually all of the votes cast.

Statewide Campaigns

The process of actively seeking public support for office is known as a campaign. Campaigning has taken on many forms over the years. The idea always has been the same for any candidate: to reach potential voters and convince them to vote for that candidate. How candidates attempt to contact voters and how they attempt to gain their confidence have changed greatly over time, influenced to an enormous degree by two technological innovations, the television and the personal computer. Whether personal or technological, contact has been, and likely will continue to be, the essence of campaigning.

Foreshadowing the Modern Campaign Era: 1960

By the late 1960s, television had become a staple of national political campaigns. The power of television had become clear in the 1960 presidential election, with John Kennedy's victory over Richard Nixon. Many attributed the narrow Kennedy triumph to his performance in a memorable debate during the campaign. Kennedy was conscious of his image when preparing for this debate, which was the first to be televised to a mass nationwide audience. Nixon barely considered the effect of the cameras and their ability to shape his image for millions of viewers. Kennedy was tanned and rested, while Nixon was fighting a cold. Where Kennedy applied makeup, Nixon had a "five o'clock shadow." Kennedy remained cool under the hot stage lights. Nixon perspired heavily. Although a slight majority of Americans who listened on radio thought Nixon had won the debate, a much larger majority of the record number of television viewers were attracted to the image of the "cool" and confident Kennedy. Analysts disagree over the debate's ultimate impact on voters, but most acknowledge that it was a significant factor in Kennedy's victory in the closest election in modern history.

While television came to dominate presidential campaigns during the 1960s, the technique and scope of modern television campaigning took a little longer to evolve in Tennessee and other states. By 1974, candidates for statewide office were making use of television ads, as the only effective way to reach large portions of the electorate in a state with more than four million people. The new campaign strategy was particularly important to Republicans, who needed television to overcome the Democrats' advantage in party identification. Since it is much easier to communicate a candidate's image than a party platform, a minority party often will find skillful use of the mass communications media critical to victory.

Republican Breakthroughs: Howard Baker and Winfield Dunn

The development of the Republican Party in Tennessee finally led to truly competitive two-party races for statewide office. The breakthrough occurred in 1966 in the contest for the U.S. Senate, when Republican Howard Baker (fig. 9.3) defeated Democrat Ross Bass. Republicans repeated the feat four years later in the race for the Governor's seat, with Winfield Dunn's triumph over John J. Hooker and a divided Democratic Party. Both campaigns foreshadowed a developing trend in Tennessee electoral politics. The strategy used in these two races became a Republican blueprint for successful campaigns: nominate an articulate, somewhat moderate candidate, and hope that the Democrats lack the unity, the money, or the candidate to exploit their advantage in party identification.

Lamar Alexander and the Birth of the Modern Statewide Campaign

Lamar Alexander, following an unsuccessful effort as the Republican nominee four years earlier, again became a candidate for the Governor's office in 1978.[13] His victory was a landmark in Tennessee politics. The significance of his victory was not just that a Republican had won in a state long dominated by Democrats. Rather, having lost to a traditional rural candidate in 1974, Alexander's second attempt in 1978 redefined the style of Tennessee political campaigns. Guided by a media consultant from Washington, D.C., Alexander skillfully established an image, communicated it through skillful use of the free and paid mass media, and established a core issue around which to build his candidacy.

Alexander could not have asked for a better set of circumstances around which to build his campaign. His predecessor, Gov. Ray Blanton, was so plagued by scandals that he did not seek a second term, despite being the first governor eligible to do so following a recent change in the Tennessee Constitution. The Democratic nominee, Knoxville banker Jake Butcher, had spent lavishly during a tough primary campaign. Labeled by Alexander as a "millionaire banker," Butcher was dogged by concerns about his banking practices, leaving many Independents leery after the Blanton years.

Alexander had problems of his own. In his prior election bid in 1974, Alexander had had "image problems." Blanton's folksy style contrasted sharply with what he termed Alexander's "country club" background at Vanderbilt and New York University. A native of East Tennessee, Alexander had worked as a member of the staff in the Nixon White House. That experience and a rather stiff demeanor combined to create the impression of a very conservative, young Republican who was out of touch with average Tennesseans, especially those in the middle and western parts of the state.

In 1978, both Butcher and Alexander employed media consultants to shape political advertising campaigns and to exploit television as an increasingly important tool in politics. Alexander and his staff created an event that would serve as the basis for his paid advertising, while also garnering much coverage in local news media. This event was a "walk" across Tennessee, beginning at his parents' home in Maryville in East Tennessee and ending in Memphis.

Fig. 9.3. From left, Howard Baker, Ray Blanton, and Jim Sasser. *Source:* Tennessee State Library and Archives.

The walk and Alexander's red and black plaid shirt formed the centerpieces and the imagery of Alexander's campaign. Both became important symbols that helped Alexander counter his image as an elitist who was out of touch with average Tennesseans. By appearing in all the towns along the walk, Alexander came to seem accessible rather than aloof. Likewise, by appearing in casual attire, he shed his upper-class image and appealed to the mainstream voter.

By contrast, the Democratic nominee, Jake Butcher, never could escape the pall of the lingering Blanton scandals or shake his image as a "millionaire banker." Toward the end of the campaign, Alexander's victory seemed inevitable. He had done what a statewide Republican candidate had to do: hold his Republican base in East Tennessee; project an image persuasive to independent voters; and, most important, exploit a weakened Democratic candidacy.

McWherter Campaign: Unifying the Democratic Party

In terms of preparing them for a future run at the Governor's office, the successes of the Alexander years probably did more to prepare Democrats than Republicans. By 1986, the Democrats, after a half-century in power, had been on the outside looking in for twelve of the previous sixteen years. While the Dunn success could be written off as a temporary setback, eight years under Governor Alexander had made clear one sobering point. Republican support had expanded to the point that, given a well-funded and competent Republican challenger, a divisive Democratic primary likely would bring defeat for the Democrats.

Ned McWherter, Speaker of the Tennessee House for fourteen years, had been encouraged to run for Governor against Alexander in 1978 and 1982. Sensing that the political stars were not aligned, he instead had concentrated on enhancing his visibility and strengthening the party during Alexander's two terms. McWherter's activities included frequent speaking engagements around the state and support for Democratic candidates for office at all levels. In his role as Speaker, McWherter developed vital name recognition among much of the public and, more important, influence and support among a host of interest groups, including teachers, sheriffs, and farmers.

Following disastrous showings in the two Alexander victories, Tennessee Democrats were more interested in fielding a consensus candidate than they had been in the past. While others were likely to consider the race, Speaker McWherter was better positioned than most to be the candidate around whom Democrats could rally. In November 1984, far in advance of his likely opponents, McWherter held the first meeting to lay the groundwork for his race for Governor in 1986. As a result of the meeting, official campaign papers were filed, a statewide poll was conducted, and State Treasurer Harlan Mathews was placed in charge of raising funds for the campaign.

The McWherter campaign, hoping to avoid an expensive and potentially divisive primary election, sought to raise enough money early in the process to discourage primary opponents. In March 1985, McWherter held a highly successful fund-raiser at Nashville's Opryland Hotel, bringing in $700,000 and establishing himself as the candidate to beat. In the summer of 1985, McWherter visited all ninety-five Tennessee counties, appearing at various low-key events, raising money, and building his organization. While his potential opponents were still deciding whether to run, McWherter's efforts provided critical experience for his staff and developed a system of advance work and communication that would prove invaluable later, in the heat of a campaign.

Two other serious candidates sought the Democratic nomination for Governor in 1986: Nashville's Mayor Richard Fulton and Public Service Commissioner Jane Eskind. Both candidates had statewide name recognition from previous campaigns. Eskind had the advantage of substantial personal wealth to fund her campaign. Neither, however, had the organizational skills or the statewide network of personal commitments that characterized the McWherter campaign.

Despite credible candidates and adequate financial resources, the Eskind and Fulton campaigns were incapable of challenging McWherter on a county-by-county basis. McWherter had developed a staff able to organize multiple events on a daily basis, raise money, and respond to the jabs of opponents and the news media. McWherter's early lead in the polls lessened in June but held steady in the weeks before the primary election. Unable to mount a campaign outside Nashville, Fulton faded in frustration. Eskind's personal wealth made possible a campaign consisting largely of a heavy media blitz, something the McWherter camp took seriously. Alexander had demonstrated how a media-savvy candidate could use image politics to win against a candidate reliant upon conventional campaigning. Moreover, McWherter—a bald, 275-pound beer distributor—was hardly an ideal television candidate. But Eskind was unable to communicate a reason to vote for her. Finally, in the second debate among the contenders, McWherter underscored his strengths and her weaknesses when he asked, "Jane, have you ever been to Hancock County?" His connection to grassroots Tennessee, especially the state's rural areas, earned him a clear victory in the Democratic primary.

In concept, McWherter's task, if not easy, was simple. Victory over former Gov. Winfield Dunn in the general election required that McWherter bring together the factions of the Democratic Party. Both Eskind and Fulton endorsed McWherter and agreed to participate in a statewide unity tour. The Fulton and Eskind campaigns had concentrated on attracting black voters, especially in the urban centers. Black voters not only were crucial to McWherter's success, but they constituted the one group with whom he had done poorly in the primary election. To defeat Dunn, it was imperative that McWherter attract black voters in numbers large enough to offset anticipated Republican majorities in suburban Memphis and East Tennessee.

The 1986 Governor's election disproved the conventional wisdom that any Republican automatically would garner massive electoral support in the East. Winfield Dunn's record as Governor, while positive in the broad sense, had angered many citizens in northeastern Tennessee. During his term from 1971 to 1975, Dunn had vetoed funding for a medical school in Johnson, vetoed funds to widen a dangerous highway, vetoed funds for vocational education, and attempted, over public opposition, to locate a prison in Morristown. Dunn hoped that time and the region's Republican heritage would be enough to overcome this legacy against McWherter. In this hope, Dunn was whistling in the dark.

McWherter's message was straightforward. In one community after another, he stated his belief that state government should make it possible for every region of Tennessee to share in the state's economic prosperity. Dunn had difficulty articulating a clear message and soon found himself on the defensive, attempting to explain complicated investments and his failure to pay income taxes for two years after he left the Governor's Office. McWherter shrugged off charges that he was too heavily connected with the beer industry by pointing out that some of the state's largest beer retailers were among Dunn's leading financial contributors.

Dunn's problems in northeastern Tennessee were compounded by Republican Congressman James Quillen, who made little secret of his anger at Dunn and his support for McWherter. Dunn's candidacy thus had no strong base beyond hard-core Republicans. On election day, McWherter recaptured the black vote, broke even in Memphis and Chattanooga, won Nashville, and stormed through the rural counties with huge margins. The lesson from this campaign was clear. With a strong candidate and a unified party, the Democrats were still a strong force in Tennessee politics. To win against a strong Democratic opponent, even an attractive and well-funded candidate like Winfield Dunn needed a unified Republican Party and a clear message.

Statewide Campaigns: National Forces

Identifying the precise relationship between national issues and Tennessee statewide elections is difficult. Although dominated by local issues and personalities, statewide elections still do not occur in isolation from public attitudes about the President, the Congress, and the general state of affairs nationally. Just as both parties at times have welcomed the assistance of their President or presidential nominee in statewide elections, at other times the Tennessee candidates have turned and run away from the national ticket. President Ronald Reagan in 1984 and Vice President Al Gore in 1996 were viewed as very helpful to local candidates. President Jimmy Carter in 1980 and Republican nominee Bob Dole in 1996 were not.

In Tennessee, races for Governor and U.S. Senator tend to focus to a great extent on personalities. Despite all the speeches, debates, and press releases, most Tennesseans who voted for Democrat Ned McWherter for Governor and Republican Fred Thompson for the U.S. Senate did so for reasons that had little to do with policy platforms. McWherter's compelling rural persona and Thompson's motion-picture fame were factors far more important to voters than tax or education policies. In a different but related way, Tennessee voters are not unique in their tendency to vote against an incumbent as often as in support of a challenger. In 1978, Lamar Alexander capitalized on public disgust with the Blanton administration. In one of Tennessee's most significant elections, voter disapproval of President Bill Clinton in 1994 had an enormous impact on the election of a Republican Governor and two Republican U.S. Senators. Analysis of the election indicated that a major reason for the Republican landslide was not so much a shift toward Republican policies as a sharp rise in the number of Democrats who, dismayed by national events, failed to vote. By 1996, a majority of Tennessee voters, like their national counterparts, demonstrated the volatility of politics by supporting Clinton in his reelection bid. The 1990s illustrate how national issues can have a substantial, albeit indirect, influence on Tennessee politics.

Governors' campaigns in Tennessee tend to be less influenced by national events. As one would expect, a Governor's race deals with issues of state interest, although the issues seldom are discussed in detail. An examination of the successful campaigns of Lamar Alexander, Ned McWherter, and Don Sundquist reveals no lengthy platforms filled with specific proposals. The reasons are obvious. The news media do not report on complicated proposals, and the public in general does not understand them. Moreover, each detail of a proposal gives the opponent another opportunity to find fault and place the candidate on the defensive. Armed with public opinion polls, candidates find it safer and easier to pledge support of public education, economic development, and a "get-tough" policy for criminals. Whether the candidates actually have plans for these initiatives is a question unanswered until after the election. Tennessee history proves that some winning candidates indeed did have policy initiatives, while others did not.

Those attempting to identify precise relationships between national events and state politics will encounter as many exceptions as examples. An analysis of campaign success always must include not only the basic quality of the candidate and the campaign staff, but also the amount of money available to deliver the candidate's message in a technology-centered age. Since all these factors are never identical, one must take great care to avoid jumping to a conclusion about the importance of external influences in a given election. History suggests that, with only a few significant exceptions, Tennessee statewide elections are won and lost on the basis of qualities and circumstances only marginally influenced by national events.

Candidate-Centered and Party-Centered Campaigns

Television, direct mail, and rapid communication all lessened the influence of party organizations. Since that occurred, Tennessee statewide campaigns have become centered much more on the personalities of the candidates and much less on the policy positions or influence of the Democratic or Republican parties. Beginning in the primary season, the candidates establish their own staffs and campaign organizations that operate independently of the state party. Even after winning the party nomination, the campaigns remain more a reflection of the candidate than the party. All significant decisions, from campaign strategy to fundraising, are made by the candidate and not the party organization. In Tennessee, as in many states, the state party does not have large amounts of cash available for candidates. This is true partly because Governors and other elected officials do not wish to see the party organization become strong enough to meddle in their affairs. Since the 1960s, state parties have tended to concentrate on providing "in-kind" assistance to candidates for state legislative seats, while avoiding making large contributions to statewide campaigns for Governor or the U.S. Senate.[14] In addition to names of local persons who will put up yard signs and work the polls, the most valuable in-kind contributions are lists of individuals who, on the basis of their primary voting records, are likely to support the candidate. A second practice, consistently denied by party officials, involves funneling campaign contributions from political action committees to candidates whose "independence from special interests" prevents them from taking such contributions directly.

Running for Local Office

In Tennessee, as in most other states, Democrats and Republicans conduct primary elections, usually in May of even-numbered years, to choose their nominees for county executive, district attorney general, and other local offices. The nominees from the two parties, assuming each party fielded candidates, meet in a general election held in August. County and state level elections are conducted in years when there is not a presidential election.

County Primaries

Winning election or reelection to a county office is different in important ways from running for Governor or the U.S. Senate. While the state party occasionally may have an interest in a high-profile office such as the county executive of Knox County, the local party takes the lead in recruiting candidates for such county offices as county clerk or trustee. With the demise of party influence at the state level, recruiting candidates for local office has become one of the major duties of the county Democratic and Republican party organizations. Involvement in candidate selection varies greatly with a party's relative strength in the area. Party leaders usually find it easier to recruit a high-quality candidate if the party has dominated recent county elections. Indeed, too much success can produce a surplus of candidates and lead to an expensive and divisive primary fight. In contrast, years of domination by one party, such as by the Republicans in East Tennessee or by the Democrats in West Tennessee, can make it hard for leaders of the minority party to recruit candidates.

The decision to run for office is, in most cases, a private one, although examples exist in which large companies or wealthy individuals have sponsored candidates. While the personal decision may be complicated, the actual process of becoming a candidate is relatively simple. The first official step involves filing a qualifying petition with the local election commission. For each election, there is a date several weeks prior to Election Day that represents a deadline for candidates who wish to run. The purpose of such deadlines is to minimize confusion and allow the local election commission to prepare official ballots. Qualifying petitions are available at the local election commission office. The petition must be returned prior to the filing deadline, accompanied by the candidate's signature and the signature of twenty-five registered voters eligible to vote in the candidate's election. No filing fee is required, making it easy to place one's name on the election ballot in Tennessee. One unfortunate result of Tennessee's lax election laws is that many people file qualifying petitions with no intention of conducting a campaign or winning the election.

Early Campaign: Fundraising

State laws regarding the raising and reporting of money, while never satisfactory to everyone involved, nonetheless are an important part of the campaign process. The Tennessee Registry of Election Finance requires candidates to file extensive information designed to reveal who gives the campaign money and how the money was spent. Candidates for every state office, from Governor to state Senator, state Representative, and major judicial offices, must file reports with the Registry of Election Finance. Candidates for city and county offices must file their disclosures with local election commissions. Candidates for state Senator and Representative must file locally as well as at the state level. A candidate does not have to file campaign financial disclosure statements if seeking an office for which service is part-time, compensation is less than one hundred dollars a month, and the campaign does not spend more than five hundred dollars.

Despite frequent complaints from candidates about the volume and burdensome detail of financial disclosure, the process is an important protection against corruption. In the absence of such disclosures, wealthy groups or individuals certainly would seek to influence elections in ways that many voters would view as inappropriate. If, for example, drunk driving laws are an issue in the election, voters have a right to know if the alcohol industry gives campaign funds to either or both of the candidates. Similarly, many voters wish to know if a large portion of a candidate's funding comes from outside Tennessee.

Organizing the Campaign

Soon after a statewide election has taken place, one can expect newspaper columnists and other political pundits to speculate about persons likely to be candidates in the next election. Political analysts look for several features in a potential candidate. This is not to suggest that all these features must be present for a candidate to win. They do, however, reflect the profile of candidates who, based on Tennessee electoral history, most frequently have achieved success in statewide campaigns.

Observers look first for potential candidates with national or regional stature, or at least wide name recognition. Fred Thompson's election to the U.S. Senate in 1994 had much to do with the fame he gained starring in successful motion pictures. Similarly, Al Gore's rise to the vice presidency began in his twenties, with the name recognition developed while his father was a U.S. Senator from Tennessee.

Another important consideration involves the incumbent. If the incumbent is popular, the chances of a serious challenge from within the incumbent's party are virtually nonexistent. Given the extraordinary challenge of raising several million dollars, even the most qualified candidates from the other party may decide that the campaign is not worth the risk. Before a candidate comes close to filing a qualifying petition, considerable time must be devoted to determining two things: how much money can be raised, and whether the opponent is so popular or so wealthy that the amount raised will be insufficient.

Assuming the availability of sufficient money and an opponent whose popularity is not overwhelming, several other factors influence the decision to enter a political campaign. What are the relative strengths and weaknesses of the candidate and the opponent? Is either a good speaker? How will both appear on television? Does the candidate enjoy broad name recognition? Does the candidate have family members who can assist in the campaign? Does the candidate enjoy good relationships with party and elected officials? Does the candidate have the physical stamina for a prolonged campaign? To develop a meaningful sense of a candidate's viability, each of these questions must be addressed from the perspective of both the candidate and the opponent.

In addition to questions that involve assets for a campaign, an objective candidate must be able to weigh these assets against potential liabilities. Political liabilities tend to be identified more with a specific candidate than with either party. "Job performance" certainly is a relevant factor, although a vague term in the minds of many voters. Job performance can be measured in terms of an incumbent's support of an unpopular position or simply the failure to attend the Paris Fish Fry or the Columbia Mule Day celebration. Each example can be damaging to the voters' image of job performance. In addition to job performance, the potential candidate must take into account political land mines (such as the failure to pay income tax) or personal problems (such as a contested divorce or a drunk-driving arrest) that would provide the news media with an opportunity for a "feeding frenzy" of "attack journalism."[15] Finally, the candidate must recall all previous slights to prominent persons—politicians, newspaper reporters, business leaders—who relish the chance to get even. Among the most common mistakes in politics is the inability of persons caught up in the excitement of contemplating office to consider thoroughly the potential liabilities that certainly will surface during a campaign.

Ultimately, a potential candidate's choice to take the plunge into the political waters is a personal one. The local party cannot draft nominees. The national parties, whose fundraising capacity gives them a voice in recruiting candidates, still cannot dictate who runs for office. Potential candidates must launch their campaigns expecting little assistance from the party in the nomination process and, at best, only a fraction of the funds needed for a general election battle. After all the encouragement, candidates running against incumbents quickly discover that a campaign can be a lonely experience.

Raising Money

Sometimes referred to as the "first primary," raising money for a campaign has become the most crucial aspect of a candidate's nomination strategy. Two facts—that campaigns cost so much money and that raising money is so hard—explain why so many of Tennessee's incumbents of both parties seldom face strong opposition for reelection. Fundraising is called the first primary because the process of raising money weeds out candidates before the actual primary election takes place. A candidate often begins an "exploratory campaign" with campaign funds called "seed money." The funds may be personal or, just as frequently, donations obtained from a relatively small group of individuals closely associated with the candidate. For example, early in the process, an attorney is likely to rely on other attorneys to provide money that makes it possible to travel the state and set up a more sophisticated fundraising operation.

The process of using seed money to generate more resources has encouraged some candidates to rely increasingly on direct mail. Fundraising through direct mail involves developing a list of potential contributors or obtaining such a list from the party or another campaign. The campaign sends out as many requests to the targeted individuals as can be afforded. The letter typically makes a dramatic appeal, overstating the problems and the ability of the candidate to resolve them, and concluding with a request for a donation. If the mailing is large enough, a response of only 2 or 3 percent can generate net income. While direct mail is used by the national parties and from time to time by statewide candidates, its value in Tennessee is limited. The strategy does not raise nearly enough funds to make a campaign viable, and it is rare for any Tennessee candidate to employ the method more than once during an election cycle. The process is expensive and, because the market is crowded, the return is minimal.

Candidates needing money rely on other methods. Fundraising events routinely receive five hundred dollars per person at dinners and cocktail parties. Celebrity galas have become standard fare for serious statewide candidates. Depending upon the candidate's stance on issues, appeals to specific groups, such as teachers, doctors, or labor, can generate funds. Having a network that includes these groups is extremely important to a candidate with little campaign experience.

In the modern era, unless the candidate has great personal wealth, raising campaign funds is arguably the single most important activity for any candidate. The cliché that it takes money to make money is appropriate in describing the crucial need for seed money in a campaign. Whether from direct mail, chicken dinners, interest groups, or one-on-one solicitation, the ability to raise millions of dollars in a period of months unfortunately has become the bar that every candidate who hopes to run successfully for statewide office in Tennessee must clear.

Putting Together a Staff

Most modern statewide campaigns rely heavily on paid consultants. These professionals, many of whom do not live in Tennessee, have particular expertise that they make available to candidates at substantial cost. Campaign consultants include experts on media relations, polling, advertising, campaign strategy, and fundraising. One of the first competitions among candidates involves assembling a team of consultants who bring credibility as well as expertise to the campaign. In an effort to buy such credibility, a candidate sometimes foolishly pays large sums for a consultant's reputation, without regard to whether the consultant has the time, interest, or skills needed for a particular race. Consultants who have managed winning races in Boston, for example, may not do so well in rural West Tennessee. Despite the fact that reputations in the industry rise and fall with each election cycle, early "handicapping" of political races is based, as often as not, largely on the perceived skills of the consultants and not on the qualities of the candidate.

In Tennessee as in most states, consultants tend to work with candidates of only one party. Many consultants operate as individuals with the capability to provide a full-service support service, including development of image items such as yard signs and bumper stickers, speech themes, and television and radio advertising. Because polling data dictates the purchase of advertising, polling services are usually, but not always, contracted with a firm separate from the media consultant whose fees involve sale of the candidate's ads. Ideally, a consultant will hold weekly meetings with a media buyer, a pollster, a fund-raiser, and other major players in the campaign, including the candidate. The purpose of these strategy meetings is to determine the nature and timing of any advertisements, upcoming campaign events, and strategies for obtaining maximum positive coverage in the free media. An experienced and attentive political consultant can make an invaluable contribution to a campaign. In contrast, more than one campaign has faltered when its resources were squandered on consultants who, because of bad judgment, too many clients, or a willingness to put profits above the cause, led the candidate down the wrong path.

In addition to paid consultants, campaigns require other talents, some modern and some as old as campaigns themselves. At the top is the campaign manager, who, if the candidate is wise, is given authority to make most day-to-day decisions involving personnel, finances, and strategy. Most young persons do not have the experience to run campaigns, while those with the experience usually cannot or will not leave high-paying jobs for the hassle and uncertainty of a campaign. Advances in computer technology since the 1980s have mandated that at least one member of the campaign team have information technology skills capable of organizing voting lists, campaign contributions and expenditures, and an issue data base. Campaigns need a press aide to field inquiries from the news media accurately and tactfully. A very important position, and one often overlooked until problems mount, is the campaign scheduler responsible for juggling multiple events in a brief period. Equally important is the ability to plan events so that crowds are large, the sound system works, and the right people are seated on stage with the candidate. A good campaign has a policy coordinator who knows enough facts about issues to make the candidate sound credible. Campaigns also need persons to coordinate volunteers, distribute materials, interpret a host of election laws, and organize efforts to get out the vote on Election Day. Few campaigns, organized as they are quickly and somewhat haphazardly, perform all of these functions flawlessly. Yet, unless most of the so-called "secondary" campaign slots are filled with competent persons, even campaigns with the best candidates and the best consultants will encounter serious problems.

Running Alone

From the outside looking in, many voters might conclude that candidates from the same party run together as a team. Despite occasional appearances together and a general rhetoric of party unity, the fact remains that, in modern Tennessee, political candidates run their own races. More often than they wish to admit, they argue behind the scenes about a host of major and minor issues. Senators argue with Governors about scheduling fundraising events and who is raiding the other's financial base. Elected officials bicker over who did or did not endorse a candidate in a previous election. Governors and U.S. Senators look over their shoulders at members of Congress whom they suspect of harboring ambition for higher office. At the legislative level, candidates frequently cut deals with the other party to avoid competition. Except for candidates who are clearly behind, few want to be identified with another campaign, fearful that another candidate's real or imagined problems somehow will be transferred to them by association.

As a result of a process that is part practicality and part paranoia, candidates and their campaigns go it alone to a far greater extent than most observers realize. While there is considerable overlap among contributors to the various campaigns, virtually every other aspect of the campaigns is done independently. When a candidate steps out and declares a bid for office, the decision should be accompanied with the understanding that modern democracy at times is not so far removed from medieval Europe, where power and influence rested with leaders bound by a loose political alliance.

Assessing Campaigns and Elections

Campaigns and elections are vital to any democracy. They are the mechanisms for placing individuals and ideas in government. Perhaps more important, elections offer the chance to remove bad officials without resorting to violence. Despite the importance of elections to the health of the political system, most Tennesseans do not take the campaign process seriously. Fewer than half bother to vote. Even fewer are familiar with the issues that define candidates and elections.

Some observers contend that public apathy concerning elections is a natural product of economic prosperity. Perhaps. However, voters may have become alienated from the political process for other, more disturbing reasons. The enormous cost of statewide campaigns now prevents all but the wealthy, or those with access to wealth, from running for office. The fact that the great majority of campaign funds are spent for shallow and often negative advertising is a trend not lost on voters. The decline of political parties and the competition of ideas has given rise to the cult of personality. An inability to find meaningful distinctions among candidates and parties can only reinforce public cynicism about the value of elections.

Despite its many shortcomings, the election process in Tennessee should be viewed in its historical context. Elections have been framed around personalities since the days of Andrew Jackson. Money always has been a dominant factor in successful campaigns, and it can be argued that, with the revitalization of the Republican Party in the

1960s, Tennessee enjoys a more vigorous debate of political ideas than at any time since the Civil War.

Whether Tennessee's political system is in a period of decline, or simply in another stage of a development more than two centuries old, is a question that in time will be measured by the safety and prosperity secured for the people by their elected leaders.

10

The Media

The Capitol Hill Press Corps is as interesting a group of people as one would ever want to meet. About half of them look as if they slept in their clothes. They are smart, irreverent, and often profane. Most drink too much coffee and many drink too much alcohol. Unlike their counterparts in Washington, most make substantially less money than the persons they cover. They are expected to produce accurate and interesting stories under the pressure of deadlines that few outsiders understand or appreciate. All are interested in politics, but few care about ideology. They are objects of praise, hatred, and manipulation, sometimes all in the same day.

In some respects, the shortcomings of the press are remarkably similar to those of the government officials they cover. Neither group is held in high regard by the public. Both are frequently forced to make quick decisions on the basis of inadequate or inaccurate information. Perhaps the most disturbing similarity is a sensitivity to criticism, making each party defensive and capable of comments they later regret.

Some members of the Capitol Hill Press Corps last no more than a year or two in the political furnace. Others occupy their cubicle in the Legislative Plaza for three decades. As a group, they are indispensable to the operation of state government (fig. 10.1).

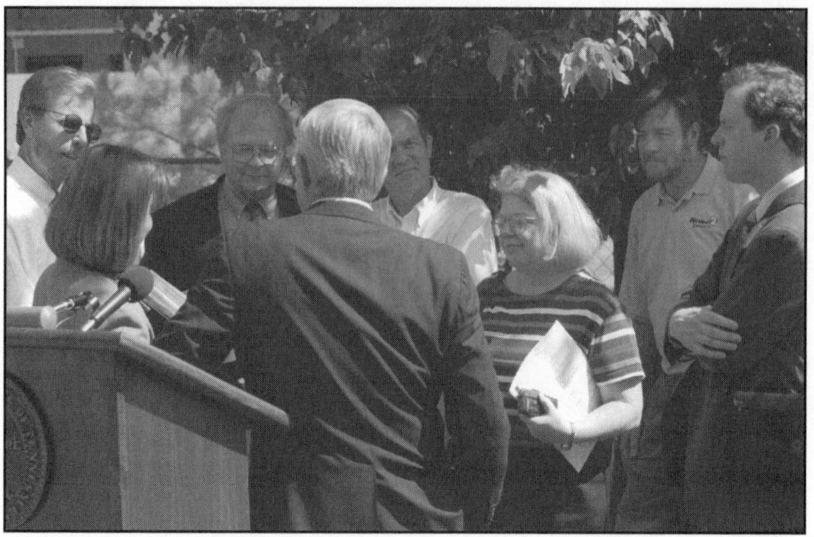

Fig. 10.1. After an address, Gov. Don Sundquist chats with members of the Capitol Hill Press Corps. *Source:* State of Tennessee Photographic Services.

What most of us call "the media" consists of people and organizations that disseminate information to the public. The media are generally divided into two categories. The print media include newspapers, journals, tabloids, and magazines. The electronic media encompass radio, television, and the Internet. While the media are often referred to as the "fourth estate," some have gone so far as to call the media the "fourth branch of government." More accurately, the organizations that constitute the media should be viewed as institutions much like political parties and interest groups. Far from being mere conduits of information, however, the media help form public perceptions of issues, elected officials, and candidates for office. Ultimately, the media have a significant impact on American political culture by shaping the values, beliefs, and expectations of the citizenry.[1]

A New Breed

In many places they are called "the media," but as a practical matter Tennessee governors and legislators still refer to the collection of newspaper, television, and radio reporters as "the press." Like the political institutions it covers, the press underwent significant changes in the last quarter of the twentieth century. Some changes were the products of technologies developed in the 1980s that revolutionized the storage and dissemination of information. Other changes resulted from cultural forces and events that were reshaping every aspect of Tennessee society, including the political process.

From Typewriters to Terminals

For the majority of newspaper reporters, or "pencils" as some call them, the move from typewriters to computer terminals was the most important change in political coverage since the invention of the telephone. No longer did reporters have to run from a press conference to a telephone to call in a story. The ability to add information and quotations to stories up to the last minute enabled reporters to acquire more sources and check more facts. Changes demanded by editors could be incorporated in minutes instead of hours. Computer disks replaced many of the documents and papers that cluttered the reporter's desk. The computer retrieved old stories and old press releases with the touch of a finger. Breaking stories coming across the wire could be reviewed instantly.

Changes of a different kind revamped the process of television reporting. Smaller and lighter cameras, or "mini-cams," freed reporters from the need to find a single stationary location from which to film events. By the early 1980s, a reporter's ability to take a camera anywhere at any time became a blessing or a curse, depending upon one's point of view. The perfection of videotape and the subsequent replacement of film also expanded the options of television reporters. The process of editing was faster and the quality of presentation far better with videotape. A third technological advance broadened the range of stories that could be covered by television. Satellite uplinks provided for the first time the ability to report events live from even the most remote locations. Reporters who previously had to "bicycle" film footage over long distances could now cover an event live—whether in the state Capitol or a maximum-security prison—on the six o'clock news through a satellite feed.

Changes in Attitude

Cultural trends produced different changes for the press that were just as important, if more subtle. Photographs of the Capitol Hill Press Corps from the 1950s and 1960s show a group that would be unrecognizable in today's Legislative Plaza. The group was composed entirely of white males. Each was dressed in a white shirt, tie, and suit. The contrast of such a group to the modern press corps could not be more stark. Today's contingent is more than half female. Black reporters are not uncommon, especially among television and radio crews. Both ties and jeans are optional. Openly contemptuous of decorum, individual reporters in recent years have been known to light cigarettes during press briefings in the Governor's Office. During one notable legislative session in the 1980s that dragged on longer than expected, one senior reporter demonstrated his frustration by refusing to shave until legislators adjourned and went home.

The modern Capitol Hill Press Corps differs from its predecessors in ways more significant than diversity or dress codes. Their informal style and appearance are visible evidence of a more fundamental change that occurred in the relationship between the press and government. The close familiarity and deference to political leaders that characterized much of the Tennessee press corps in the 1950s and 1960s were transformed over a period of about seven years in the 1970s into a more distant relationship. One cannot point to a single event that fostered this change. As with many other American institutions, the adoption by the press of a less formal style was a legacy of the counterculture movement of the late 1960s and early 1970s. From college campuses to the state Capitol, a new "egalitarian" philosophy redefined relationships that had been in place for decades. A general disdain for authority and business attire by younger reporters was accompanied in 1974 by disillusionment with government following the Watergate scandal and the forced resignation of President Richard Nixon.

The central role of the Washington press corps in toppling a sitting President served to initiate a more adversarial climate between the media and government than had existed previously. In Tennessee, the press—including for the first time aggressive investigative reporting by television—was instrumental in exposing flagrant corruption in Gov. Ray Blanton's administration from 1975 to 1979.[2] Several members of the administration, including the Governor, eventually served time in prison on charges that ranged from the sale of pardons to kickbacks received from the illegal issuance of liquor licenses. The combination of the two historic episodes of federal and state government corruption in the 1970s had a lasting impact on the relationship of the press and state government in Tennessee. While the Tennessee press rarely reflected the degree of antagonism and cynicism often associated with its colleagues in Washington, it was clear that a new, less receptive mindset had taken hold in Nashville among those who described and commented on the activities of state government.

Capitol Hill Press Corps

Assembling an accurate list of the media outlets that collectively make up the Capitol Hill Press Corps depends to some extent on how one defines "coverage" of state government and state politics. The list can be divided generally among those newspapers, wire services, television stations, and radio networks that keep reporters in the Legislative Plaza all year, those who send reporters to Nashville only during the five-month legislative session, and those outlets whose coverage is limited largely to special events at the Capitol. When referring to the Capitol Hill Press Corps, most who work in state government are speaking of reporters who have a presence on Capitol Hill either all year or during the spring legislative session.

Print Media

Following national trends, the 1980s and 1990s witnessed the closure of major daily newspapers in each of Tennessee's four largest cities. In each instance, closure resulted from the financial inability of two papers to operate successfully in a single market. After the closing of the *Memphis Press-Scimitar* in 1983 and the *Knoxville Journal* in 1991, the Capitol Hill print media remained for another seven years a relatively constant group representing nine newspapers, four of which assigned reporters to cover the Hill on a twelve-month basis. The final collapse of two-newspaper towns occurred with the closure in 1998 of the *Nashville Banner* and the *Chattanooga Times* in 1999. The financial demise in the 1980s of United Press International left the Associated Press as the only wire service covering Tennessee state government.

The elimination of competition in the state's four largest cities had an impact—both good and bad—on political reporting. Partisan debates can be positive. If, however, partisanship infringes on reporting, it can motivate papers to increase the volume and tone of their rhetoric, sometimes to the point that objectivity is compromised. In such an atmosphere, a legislator who proposes a legitimate program may be labeled a "liberal big spender." One who opposes such a program may likewise be described as "heartless." Such oversimplification by newspapers often distorts complicated issues and undermines the credibility of legislators who may have done nothing more than engage in reasonable debate. In one-newspaper cities, there is less pressure to "win" such debates and thus less temptation to use rhetoric that is harsh and unnecessary. At times, however, the absence of

Fig. 10.2. Headquarters of the *Memphis Commercial Appeal,* the major daily newspaper in West Tennessee. Photo by William Lyons.

aggressive competition can make a newspaper complacent. If a newspaper can never be called to task for sloppy or indifferent reporting, there is little incentive to take a provocative stance on difficult or controversial issues. A more cautious approach to political reporting can be further reinforced when a paper is owned by an out-of-state corporation whose interest in local issues is incidental. A paper unaccountable to its competition and afraid to offend readers (or advertisers) is too often incapable of generating creative thought. To the extent this attitude has been fostered by the closure of some of the state's leading newspapers, the overall quality of political reporting in Tennessee has suffered.

The quality of reporting by individual newspapers and wire services has varied over the years, reflecting changes in personnel and the degree to which publishers—increasingly from out of state—care about Tennessee politics. With exceptions, the quality of a paper's political coverage depends on the number of reporters assigned to Capitol Hill, their years of experience on the Hill, whether they view their assignment as permanent or as a launching pad to something elsewhere, and whether they have succumbed to burnout, in which case they allow their skills to be corroded by cynicism. More often than some legislators might wish to concede, selected newspapers and the Associated Press on Capitol Hill have enjoyed years when political reporting was comprehensive, objective and provocative. Likewise, over time most of the same papers also experienced periods

Politically Important Tennessee Newspapers

Determining a paper's "ideological barometer" is important for understanding its relationship to issues and individuals in state government. The following is an annotated list of the Capitol Hill print media, arranged alphabetically by city.

- *Chattanooga News–Free Press:* A consistent champion of Republican statewide candidates and perhaps the most partisan of Tennessee's major dailies, the *Free Press* was sold by the McDonald family in 1998 to WEHCO Media, Inc. and then merged with the more Democratic *Chattanooga Times* in 1999. When the *Free Press* could find no policy reason for its decision not to endorse Democrat Ned McWherter for Governor in 1986, an editorial explained its Republican endorsement on the grounds that, six years earlier, McWherter had endorsed Democrat Walter Mondale for President.

- *Jackson Sun:* The largest daily paper between Memphis and Nashville, the *Sun* is owned by the Gannett syndicate and is the most prominent paper in rural West Tennessee. As the paper of choice for many of the legislature's rural Democratic leaders, the *Sun's* influence is often disproportionate to its circulation.

- *Johnson City Press-Chronicle:* Among the smallest papers once represented on Capitol Hill, the *Press-Chronicle* is locally owned. The paper has not been ideologically rigid, often endorsing Republicans in local races and Democrats in statewide campaigns.

- *Kingsport Times-News:* Although its circulation is larger than those of some of its peers on Capitol Hill, this northeastern Tennessee paper located 275 miles from Nashville has been erratic in its interest and coverage of state politics. No longer locally owned, the *Times-News* in the 1990s drifted increasingly toward use of the Associated Press for state political coverage.

- *Knoxville News-Sentinel:* Owned by the Scripps-Howard syndicate, the *News-Sentinel* expanded its political coverage in the mid-1980s with two full-time Capitol Hill reporters. Although its editorial policies tilt decisively toward Republicans, the paper has endorsed a number of Democrats in local and statewide elections.

- *Memphis Commercial-Appeal:* The state's largest newspaper also is owned by Scripps-Howard, resulting in occasional sharing of stories and information with the *Knoxville News-Sentinel.* Frequently criticized for allotting too much space to Arkansas and Mississippi politics at Tennessee's expense, strong commitment to Capitol Hill has made the *Commercial-Appeal* a leader in coverage of Tennessee government.

- *Nashville Tennessean:* Purchased by the Gannett syndicate in 1979, the *Tennessean* played a central role in political reporting during the second half of the twentieth century. Though not as rigidly partisan as in the 1960s and 1970s, the paper remains tilted toward Democratic candidates and committed to reform of Tennessee's tax system.

of drift and mediocrity. What follows is a description of Tennessee's most influential print media, most of which maintain a presence on Capitol Hill.

Associated Press

The Associated Press is a not-for-profit cooperative owned by more than fifteen hundred daily newspaper members. Founded in New York City in 1848, the AP is the country's oldest and largest news organization. The AP plays an important role in political coverage at the state and national level. Dozens of the state's county newspapers as well as many of the smaller dailies use the AP exclusively for political coverage. A decision in the late 1980s to replace aging reporters with younger and more aggressive talent upgraded sharply the quality of the AP's political coverage, although staff time on the Hill was reduced in the late 1990s.

Tennessee Journal

Published weekly, this review of legislative and judicial issues is known for its snappy format and willingness to jab humorously at both Democrats and Republicans. The *Tennessee Journal* is edited by M. Lee Smith, a former advisor to Gov. Winfield Dunn. Read statewide by about twelve hundred political activists and state and local government officials, the *Journal* has access to a broad range of information through its policy of not divulging sources. The *Journal* has been described as "must reading for political junkies and insiders around the state."[3]

Influence of the Print Media

The most influential contingent of the Capitol Hill Press Corps is composed of reporters who write for newspapers, the wire services, and state political journals. For most reporters, assignment to Capitol Hill is recognition of a higher than average caliber of talent. Reporters in the print media have a distinct advantage over their colleagues in television and radio. In the majority of cases, newspapers and journals provide space that enables reporters to pursue issues in far greater depth than possible in a sixty- or ninety-second television news segment. The nature of the print media allows the inclusion of numbers, names and other detailed information that is usually impractical for use in radio and television. While one can review the facts of a newspaper article repeatedly, viewers usually get only one, or at most two, chances to see a television news story. Newspaper articles are frequently clipped and filed by a variety of readers and special interest groups. The time and effort required to tape and file television and radio news make the process so difficult that for most citizens newspapers remain the record of choice.

On occasion, the influence of print political reporters can be disproportionate in relation to the number of persons who actually read their stories. The viewing audience for state and local news at six o'clock and ten o'clock on Nashville's three premier television stations is far larger than those who read political stories in the city's daily newspaper. These figures do not, however, reflect the fact that the newspaper's political news is read regularly by virtually every elected official, business executive, and political activist in the capital city. Given a choice, political candidates seeking votes would prefer their name and image appear on the six o'clock television news. In contrast, those seeking to influence attitudes among the political or financial community generally would prefer positive stories and editorial support in the *Nashville Tennessean*.

Much, but certainly not all, of reporters' influence is measured by the circulation of respective papers and journals.[4] A Governor or Cabinet official likely will be more attuned to a positive or negative article in the *Memphis Commercial-Appeal* (fig. 10.2) than one published in the *Kingsport Times-News*. Again, exceptions to this rule are found in Nashville, where the influence on statewide politics of the *Tennessean* and, prior to its closing in 1998, the *Nashville Banner* was disproportionate to their circulation. Even though its circulation dropped by more than half during the 1980s and 1990s, the *Nashville Banner*, despite its partisan Republican tone, continued to be read regularly by a majority of Democratic and Republican officials when in Nashville. Thus, a Capitol Hill reporter for the *Banner* often found a broader readership among Tennessee's power elite than his colleagues from Memphis or Chattanooga who wrote for papers with much larger circulations.[5]

A political reporter's influence on events and elected officials also can come from a second factor unrelated to the size or location of a reporter's newspaper. From time to time individual reporters have helped shape events as the result of a particularly thorough or embarrassing piece of investigative reporting. An investigative story and subsequent editorials in December 1996 by the *Memphis Commercial-Appeal* led to the resignation of the Deputy Governor after the paper's Capitol Hill reporter uncovered alleged conflicts of interest involving the health-care industry. A lengthy examination of campaign financing and lobbyist influence in 1994 by the *Knoxville News-Sentinel* resulted in modest reforms of laws governing lobbying and legislative campaign contributions. A well-researched exposé in 1995 by the *Chattanooga Times* raised serious questions about state government decisions leading up to and following a fog-related multi-car pileup near a paper mill on Interstate 75 that killed thirteen persons. None of these events would have unfolded as they did without the influence of solid and hard-hitting political reporting.

The Role of Editorial Comment

Journalistic ethics require reporters to present stories objectively, without personal or political bias. The majority of Capitol Hill reporters make a good-faith gesture toward this noble goal, although most would privately concede it is impossible to study an issue or individual and not develop an opinion that, at least in subtle ways, shades the tone of a story. The boundaries of fairness that restrain reporters do not apply to the editorial staffs of newspapers, television stations, and, in many instances, radio stations. Both government and the media understand that the rules of the game place few limits on editorial opinion so long as the public can easily make the distinction between objective reporting and political commentary. Newspapers confine editorials, along with letters to the editor, to one or two clearly identified pages of daily papers or in a special Sunday section. Television and radio editorials customarily are aired at or near the conclusion of a news broadcast.

Among Tennessee's Capitol Hill newspapers, standards vary regarding the proper purpose, style, and taste of editorial commentary. Editorials are by nature designed to advocate a particular opinion. Editorials can be positive or negative, although in a democracy the media's function as a public watchdog results in a majority of editorials that are critical of government actions or inactions. Most newspaper editorials are written in the elevated style of a university debate, so much so in some cases that they exceed the reading level—and the interest—of a majority of the public. Some editorial writers attempt to convey political opinion with humor. Others find it necessary to employ sarcasm to explain their point of view. Not surprisingly, great bitterness resides between the victims of such sarcasm and editorial writers who lay claim to intellectual or moral certainty.

Since the days of George Washington, government officials have complained about the unfairness of editorial commentary. Some complaints are valid. The *Knoxville News-Sentinel* in 1998 crossed the line of good taste when an editorial columnist referred to the Tennessee House Speaker as the Antichrist. Such gross transgressions are rare. Most complaints originate in a basic misunderstanding—at times from both sides—about the media's role in the debate of public issues. Reporters and editorial writers do not exist to be cheerleaders for individuals, agendas, or political parties. Likewise, journalists have an obligation to understand clearly the line separating skepticism and cynicism. Their mission is to provide the public with adequate and accurate information with which to evaluate their elected leaders. In theory, the process assigns a reporter the task of finding out if a river is polluted and who is responsible. The elected official must explain why it is dirty and how the river can be made clean. The editorial writer attributes blame for the pollution and evaluates the cleanup proposal. Assuming they have read or heard all of the information, the public then attempts to sort out the truth from a mix that is roughly one part fact and two parts opinion. The public's failure to hear or understand any part of the story complicates the political process and adds to the tension that is a permanent fixture in the relationship between a government that seeks to tell only what it wants the public to know and a press that literally wants to know everything.

The unending debate about the proper role of editorial commentary often ignores data indicating that fewer than seven percent of the public reads and remembers the contents of the editorial page. Politicians who understand this fact are more likely to take in stride the occasional jabs thrown by their colleagues in the media. Those who cannot resist throwing a counter-punch ignore one of government's oldest maxims: "Never get into an argument with someone who buys ink by the barrel."

Television News

Coverage of political events by sixteen of Tennessee's network-affiliated television stations differs in several important respects from the print media. Most significant is the fact that television reporting requires a vastly greater investment in equipment and personnel. Covering a legislative hearing or a Governor's press conference involves at least two persons, one to operate the camera plus the "talent," or reporter, who directs the coverage and conducts the interviews. A live shot requires a third person located outside in a highly equipped van to coordinate the uplink. The costs involved with television news coverage prohibit stations outside Nashville from covering all but the most important political events. With the exception of the Governor's inauguration, the Governor's annual Budget Message and State of the State Message, and one or two isolated events each year, television coverage by local reporters of activities on Capitol Hill is limited to three of Nashville's network-affiliated stations. For Tennessee's remaining thirteen network stations affiliated with ABC, CBS and NBC, state government news is confined largely to reading copy from the AP wire and local papers accompanied by occasional interviews with area legislators.

Even in Nashville, television political reporters often are forced to compete with a distinct disadvantage. For the great majority of newspaper reporters, a Capitol Hill assignment means spending their time exclusively in the Capitol or the Legislative Plaza, all day, every day. A constant presence among government officials, their staff and other members of the press provides access to valuable information that is simply not available to television reporters who on most days must rush to an event and hurriedly attempt to digest the relevant facts. A television reporter's standard procedure involves arriving at an event shortly before it starts and quickly attempting to understand an issue by reading a bill summary or press release. The format includes shooting some "B-roll," or background footage, a short on-camera introduction of the topic, a seven- to nine-second sound bite with one or two individuals, and a fifteen-second wrap-up. Having spent less than two hours on Capitol Hill, the reporter drives back to the station, where the tape is edited and the narrative fitted to the sixty-second, ninety-second, or two-minute time slot allotted for the story. If coverage of the event occurred in the afternoon, as is often the case, the reporter is under considerable pressure to develop a coherent and entertaining segment for the six o'clock news. Such conditions provide a difficult challenge for television news to analyze political events in a manner that is thorough and thoughtful.

As difficult as the process is for television reporters, they must compete against the print media with still another handicap. On the whole, newspapers do not suffer from frequent turnover in Capitol Hill reporters. Like their Washington colleagues in both the print and electronic media, a number of the print reporters in Tennessee have worked ten years or more on the Hill. In contrast, Nashville television stations experience a far higher rate of turnover among their reporters in a business in which salary limitations encourage the talent always to be in search of an internal promotion or a new job in larger markets such as Chicago or Dallas. In an atmosphere in which it takes even the brightest person at least two years to learn the ropes, a succession of new reporters makes it extremely difficult for television to provide depth or insight to its political coverage.

Despite these inherent disadvantages, television has made some significant contributions to the quality of coverage of Tennessee government. The lack of detail associated with television news reporting at times can be overcome with an emotional impact that can be conveyed only with a powerful visual reference. A series of segments in 1986 that focused on unsanitary and unsafe nursing homes played an important role in reform legislation enacted in 1987.[6] A similar series that illustrated the dilapidated conditions and lack of resources in rural schools provided a stark visual image for legislators who enacted sweeping education reforms in 1992. Perhaps the most memorable moment for television journalism in Tennessee occurred in 1977, when Gov. Ray Blanton gave an intoxicated interview in which he promised to pardon a recently convicted double murderer. The image of a drunken, belligerent Governor shocked Tennesseans. The interview catapulted the reporter to a successful career in Chicago and contributed to the victory in 1978 of "reform" gubernatorial candidate Lamar Alexander.[7]

In summary, television is a powerful but limited medium. Television coverage of Tennessee politics reflects a far greater disparity of quality and influence than found among the state's leading newspapers. Outside of Nashville, television coverage of state government is at best superficial and at worst an obstacle to the thoughtful discussion of important public policy questions. Within Nashville, television will continue to play a secondary role to the print media until reporters are assigned to state government on a full-time basis and news directors make a commitment to reporting government news that may have little entertainment value. In the absence of such a commitment, television's political reporting will retain its dual personality, at times shallow and pointless, yet capable of coverage that on occasion can produce a public response far beyond the reach of the most eloquent newspaper reporter.

Radio News

Reflecting another national trend of growing financial pressure and increasing fragmentation of the market, a substantial number of Tennessee's urban radio stations in the 1980s and 1990s abandoned their news segments in favor of computerized music formats. Despite these changes, radio news retained an important niche in the coverage of state government. Radio shares one handicap with television in that its news segments must be short, often as brief as fifteen seconds and rarely longer than thirty seconds. The lack of a visual image places added pressure on a report that must be clear, concise, and meaningful. These two obstacles are balanced somewhat by distinct advantages radio reporters have over their television colleagues. Radio is cheap to produce, requiring only a reporter and a tape recorder. Unlike television, radio listeners expect brief explanations of stories, thus allowing radio reporters to cover three or four events in a single day. Finally, many radio stations devote more time to news than do television stations. Even the shortest segments, if repeated two or three times an hour for an entire day, can reach a large number of listeners in a manner that enables them to remember what they have heard.

By the close of the twentieth century, no individual radio station had attempted to assign a full-time reporter to Capitol Hill. The broadest and most influential political coverage was provided by the Tennessee Radio Network. Composed of some ninety stations located across the state, the Tennessee Radio Network arguably reaches more citizens than any other media outlet in the state. The network is especially influential in rural counties, where local newspapers do not have reporters in Nashville and political coverage is limited. In such counties, a legislator's ability to get fifteen seconds of radio time is worth far more than a front-page story in one of the state's large daily newspapers. While radio news will never achieve the status of newspaper or television coverage, it will just as certainly remain an important part of political reporting. Statewide officials who ignore the role of radio news do so at their peril.

The Internet

By the end of the century, a new medium for the dissemination of political news offered potential for stemming the decline in readership caused by the closure of daily metropolitan newspapers. The state's major remaining newspapers established web sites from which persons throughout Tennessee could receive up-to-date information on political events.[8] Even more significant, a group of former Capitol Hill reporters organized a political journal dispersed solely on the Internet. The fledgling web site, named simply "Tennessee Politics," had a sassy format and a policy of not divulging sources.[9] Its ability to find a niche in Tennessee political reporting will be tested by time.[10]

The Strange Courtship of Government and the Media

Few relationships are stranger and more volatile than the one existing between the media and government officials. Like jealous lovers, each constantly suspects the other's motives, though neither is capable of breaking off the relationship. They doubt the complete truthfulness of every comment, yet the media find in government an endless source of important stories, often flavored with the controversy and corruption that kindle the public's interest. Although virtually all feel abused by the media for reporting they perceive as inaccurate or unfair, most government officials grudgingly return to the relationship. Some politicians return time and gain because their egos require them to see their names in the newspapers and on television. Most return because in a culture where the market is dominated by image and name recognition, it is impossible to live without the media.

Setting the Standard

More than any single individual, Lamar Alexander transformed the manner in which Tennessee's modern government institutions relate to both the statewide and local media. Alexander's two terms as Governor from 1979 to 1987 redefined the role of the Governor's press office and, indirectly, the press operations of the executive and legislative branches of government. No longer a two-person office limited to handling calls and issuing bland press releases on employment statistics or road projects, the press operation under Alexander became a central component of efforts to shape public opinion and influence the legislative process. Strong difference of opinion existed then and now about the degree to which Alexander's emphasis on public relations intentionally confused image with substance. These arguments aside, even his strongest critics acknowledge the extent of his media skills and their long-term impact on the relationship between government and the media in Tennessee.

Under Alexander, every major activity and decision was evaluated through the filter of its public relations value. After losing his first campaign to a rural candidate of marginal ability, Alexander's second campaign in 1978 used the media to help recast his public image from that of a country club elitist to a folksy reform candidate who represented the best of what Tennesseans wanted in their Governor. From his trademark red-and-black plaid shirt to his ragtime band, every aspect of Alexander's campaign message was tailored by a Washington public relations firm he kept on retainer throughout his administration.[11]

After the inauguration, Alexander's senior staff reflected the role that media relations would play in administration policy. Alexander's Deputy Governor, his Chief of Staff, his Senior Policy Advisor, and three other senior aides all came from a background as newspaper reporters. Their collective impact on the style and image of the Governor's Office was profound.

Alexander's tenure produced a large number of media "firsts" for Tennessee government. Alexander was the first to deliver his annual Budget Message and State of the State Message on live television, often with props such as a satellite picture of Tennessee or the headlight of an automobile. He was the first to use the annual meeting of the Tennessee Press Association as a forum for major policy announcements. An accomplished pianist, Alexander played with local symphonies (see chapter 6). The Governor's Office organized well-publicized "Community Days," at which Alexander would drop by for an hour or so to help paint a church or senior citizens' center. His final year in office was consumed with dozens of "Homecoming" events for Tennessee communities. Throughout his administration, every budget and every major policy initiative was accompanied by a slogan. The Governor's annual budget became the "Bare Bones" or "No Frills" budget. The state's economic development program became "Safe Growth." A child nutrition initiative was labeled "Healthy Children." The list was endless.

Alexander's most significant and—at least in political and public relations terms—most successful initiative was his "Master Teacher" program. With typical flair, Alexander announced his plan during a televised address to the Tennessee Press Association one week after his second inauguration. Alexander had boldly chosen to take on the powerful forty-thousand-member Tennessee Education Association with a proposal to evaluate teachers and award salary supplements to those judged to be outstanding. In town after town, before Rotary Clubs and local chambers of commerce, Alexander began each speech with the same line and the same prop. Holding up a penny, he would declare, "In Tennessee, not one teacher is paid one penny more for doing a good job." The public relations effort for Alexander's Master Teacher proposal reached heights of saturation and sophistication never before witnessed in Tennessee. The "One Penny" statement was on billboards, on radio—even in monthly statements from banks and utilities that Alexander had encouraged to join his effort. The fact that the slogan oversimplified a very complex issue mattered little. For the first time in state history, a majority of Tennesseans had become convinced, through the sheer power of a government-directed media campaign, to support raising their sales taxes a full cent in the name of a creative but untested education experiment.

Alexander's legacy is a case study of the power and influence of the media to separate in the public's mind an issue's image from its substance. Alexander's "Better Schools" initiatives achieved what at best could be called mixed success. Salaries increased for a majority of Tennessee teachers. Sharing about half of the additional sales tax revenues increased the relative position of higher education from near the bottom to above the average for southern states. On the downside, shortly after Alexander left office in 1987, the state was sued successfully by dozens of rural counties on grounds that their local schools systems received inadequate funding. Twelve years after its passage, the reform's career-ladder centerpiece was repealed with the support of a Republican Governor and the Republican leader of the Senate. For Alexander, these setbacks did little to tarnish the reputation his media campaign had created as the nation's "Education Governor." Alexander was named President of the University of Tennessee in 1989. After a brief tenure at UT, Alexander was selected by President George Bush as Secretary of Education in 1991. Alexander's selection coincided with the threat by the Tennessee Supreme Court to take over Tennessee's schools unless the Governor and legislature took immediate steps to provide adequate and equitable funding. Few observers nationwide noticed the irony.

The image Alexander created of himself as a successful education governor accompanied him for years as he attempted to market his image in successive presidential campaigns. Back in Tennessee, the success he enjoyed with the media as Governor had an equally lasting impact on the emphasis that subsequent political leaders placed on public relations. Alexander's success illustrated the lengths to which an aggressive and well-planned media strategy could overcome political opposition, both in the legislature and among the public. Though privately contemptuous of what they disdained as "PR management," Democrat legislators grudgingly conceded that Alexander had redefined the way in which government communicated with the media and, through the media, with the public. In order to compete with Alexander's media operation, House Democrats in the early 1980s upgraded the emphasis and quality of their press operations. Republicans followed suit. Weekly summaries of legislative events were prepared for local papers under the byline of the "Representative Smith Legislative Report." Legislative press offices for the first time prepared radio spots for legislators to send to their hometown stations. Dozens of legislators distributed largely self-serving newsletters that summarized legislative issues. The collective approach of these efforts at times was awkward and the quality often spotty, but the result was a much broader discussion of government issues among the media and the public. In direct response to Alexander's public relations juggernaut, the legislature had been forced to move from virtually no organized strategy to a full-fledged press operation in less than ten years.

Telling the Story

Alexander recognized first what other elected officials in time would understand: Tennessee had become a big state with more than five million citizens. With the exception of inner-city Memphis, political machines had been replaced by the media as the best way to reach and motivate voters. If officials wished to gain public support for a program or idea, Alexander realized they must do two things: reduce the idea to a simple, easily expressed message and use the media in a host of creative ways to place the message—time and again—in the minds of the public.

Many of the techniques Alexander used to promote his message were not original, even in Tennessee. Alexander's contribution to Tennessee's modern political culture lies in the skill with which he developed a long-term media strategy and coordinated every day's activities to reinforce his message. If, for example, a Governor wishes to emphasize a priority of funding rural schools, the message must be repeated in some fashion every week for months. Ideally, the stories are accompanied with pictures of staged events that, in this instance, might have the Governor unloading a new box of textbooks and carting them into a school in front of photographers and television cameras. Since Alexander, governors, legislators, and other public officials in Tennessee have been more conscious of media relations, though each has had individual variations of style and effectiveness. The most successful instinctively know the boundary between an image the public views as "open" and one seen as transparently fake. The media's antennas for such deception, while not perfect, are usually sound. Legislators who grandstand to garner exposure usually end up ridiculed, frozen out, or both, by a media that do not suffer most fools gladly.

The process of telling a political story to the media can be divided into two general groups of techniques. The more conventional involves a variety of public techniques.

- *Press Release:* The most common form of political news, the press release contains a brief summary of the event, along with statistics and artificial quotes. Government officials prefer the press release because it protects them from direct media questions and makes it possible for reporters to develop a story with minimum effort.

- *Press Conference:* Preferred by the media, a press conference allows direct questions on a variety of issues, leaves the media less subject to manipulation, and forces officials to think on their feet. Sound preparation for a press conference is often the most important characteristic of a high-quality press operation. Since Alexander, regular press conferences have become routine for Tennessee governors, who often try to build such events around a theme.
- *Annual Events:* Each year there are events such as the Budget Message and the State of the State Message, along with the annual conventions of important groups such as the Tennessee Farm Bureau, the Tennessee Labor Council, and the Tennessee Business Roundtable, that can provide governors and legislators a supportive forum for policy statements.
- *Ribbon Cuttings and Photo-ops:* Manufactured events that range from bridge openings to photos with a state championship basketball team, they are read and seen by far more persons than are editorial commentaries. Although an intrusion on the schedules of conscientious governors, these events play an important role in maintaining a sense of connection between citizens and their government.

Government and the media also employ two private, less conventional means of communication. If used carefully, each can serve the ends of both parties without compromise. If used inappropriately, they can unfairly damage reputations and do a disservice to the public.

- *"Off the Record" Conversations:* Serving two distinct purposes, these conversations provide important context for the reporter while enabling government officials to tell their side of a story without fear of seeing their comments quoted in the newspaper. The practice is appropriate as a means of assisting reporters in understanding the background or details of an issue so long as both parties agree on the parameters of what may and may not be quoted.
- *"Leaking" Information:* The most controversial form of communication, leaks always are accompanied by a political agenda that the reporter is willing to further in exchange for an exclusive story. When reporters do not confirm such information and file stories based upon "unnamed sources," they unfairly put at risk the credibility of those involved in the story while leaving them unable to confront their accusers.

The extent to which individual governors, legislators, and other government officials use these methods to communicate with the press reflects a combination of attitude and self-esteem. Some have little reluctance to hide their contempt for a press they are convinced is incompetent and biased. Others choose simply to avoid the press whenever possible, never overcoming an apprehension about their inability to deal with a process they view as inherently threatening. The most self-confident and generally most effective group of government officials establishes a more professional relationship with the press. They keep to themselves whatever misgivings they have about the press's collective or individual shortcomings. They offer the press occasional stories or comments without being pushy. When asked for comment, they are straightforward, at worst not disclosing all they may know about the issue in question.

The Media and the Political Process

The individual media outlets in the Capitol Hill Press Corps devote varying amounts of time and resources to five types of activities important to the political process in Tennessee. These activities can be summarized as reporting facts, bringing issues to lawmakers' attention, coverage of campaigns, analysis of issues and programs, and investigative reporting. The relative emphasis on any of these activities continually reshapes the media's impact on political decisions by governors and legislators. Most observers close to the process would agree that the Tennessee press performs two functions well. The quality of the remaining three functions has been less consistent.

Just the Facts

By most standards, the Capitol Hill Press Corps does a good job of reporting the basic facts surrounding state government issues. The majority of stories originate from actions or statements from the Governor, legislators, or Cabinet officials. During the legislative session the pace and volume of issues can result in errors or omissions by reporters spread too thin to avoid mistakes. Observers are usually unaware that some of these mistakes are the responsibility of local newspaper editors, known as "droolers" by their Capitol Hill colleagues. These shortcomings aside, most newspaper reporters are diligent in providing the public an objective general description of issues, who supports and opposes them, and the issues' potential impact. Citizens can acquire a reasonable understanding of state government by reading on a regular basis any of the newspapers represented on Capitol Hill.

Each of the Capitol Hill newspapers also does an adequate job of bringing local issues and needs to the attention of state lawmakers. Whether it be the need for a new road, state park renovations, or a downtown riverfront development, newspapers can be counted upon each year to wedge into a state budget one or two projects that otherwise would have been omitted. One of the most notable examples of such lobbying occurred in 1998, when both Chattanooga newspapers took exception to the Governor's budget exclusion of a building project at the University of Tennessee at Chattanooga. The project was added within two days of front-page stories critical of the decision.

Campaign Coverage

The consistent quality associated with reporting issues and raising awareness of local needs does not extend to media coverage in Tennessee of legislative and gubernatorial campaigns. With only occasional exceptions, the accuracy or soundness of candidates' proposals goes largely unchallenged. Reporting too often is limited to a point-counterpoint format dictated by negative and often irrelevant charges from the candidates. For better or worse, the contemporary campaign coverage of most newspapers appears timid compared to more passionate coverage from the 1950s and 1960s. At least three factors contribute to this perception. When Tennessee's larger cities contained two or more newspapers, competition for readers motivated papers to take sides in local and state races. The Nashville Banner and the Knoxville Journal, both of which have since folded, regularly printed political editorials on the front page and published political cartoons that would be viewed as tasteless in today's climate. Identification with a party or political faction produced an aggressive approach to the reporting of candidates and issues that does not exist in one-newspaper towns. The trend was accelerated in the 1970s and 1980s, when newspapers were purchased by out-of-state chains with little emotional interest in Tennessee politics. Although each sale was accompanied by similar promises "not to meddle in editorial policies," the effect over time at several newspapers was an obvious lessening of the passion that once shaped political coverage.

A final contribution to the receding priority of political campaign coverage is the simple fact that fewer people read newspapers. The emergence of television in the last quarter of the twentieth century supplanted to a great extent the role of newspapers as the public's primary source of news and entertainment. By the late 1970s, candidates used a saturation strategy of television commercials almost exclusively to communicate a sound-bite message with voters. In the space of less than a decade, newspaper endorsements and even newspaper coverage were replaced by television visibility as the priority of statewide campaigns.

Turning Over Rocks

The lack of aggressive reporting in Tennessee political campaigns is linked to another role from which many believe newspapers retreated during the last two decades of the century. High-quality political coverage requires more than a regular summary of quotes and activities by lawmakers. The upper tier of political reporting is reserved for those who provide serious analysis to complicated issues. On occasion Tennessee newspapers have exhibited the highest standard of such reporting. Coverage of the state's banking crisis in 1983 by the *Nashville Tennessean* and the *Knoxville News-Sentinel* was superb. A decade later, the *Tennessean* joined the *Memphis Commercial-Appeal* and the Associated Press in excellent in-depth analysis of Tennessee's replacement of the Medicaid program with TennCare.

Unfortunately, such high standards of analysis do not always accompany proposals for prison privatization, welfare reform, school finance, and other far-reaching policy changes. One simple criteria used to evaluate reporting determines whether proposals are explained with something more than terms defined by their advocates or opponents. A second criteria measures whether the reporter regularly checks the accuracy of claims made by government officials, or, at best, provides a meaningful context in which to evaluate these claims. The media in 1997 left unchallenged the assertion that privatizing Tennessee's prisons would save annually some $100 million, a figure that was later pared to less than $25 million after staff reviewed budget documents. Similarly, pronouncements about industrial investment, child mortality, or the number of persons removed from the welfare rolls have meaning only when compared to similar data in other states. The tendency to avoid detailed evaluation is most glaring in regard to coverage of the state budget. Most reporters limit "analysis" of the multi-billion-dollar document to a list of local projects, totals for major budget programs, and the pay raise for teachers and state employees. When reporters, individually or collectively, engage an issue with thorough research backed by provocative editorial comment, the result tends more often than not to have an impact on decisions by the Governor and the legislature. When the media retreats from this level of participation in the political process, decisions may not reflect the public's interest or wishes.

A final activity associated with the Capitol Hill Press Corps is also one that lapsed in priority during the 1980s and 1990s. Investigative reporting—the collection and piecing together of information not offered voluntarily by government officials—has occupied a special place throughout Tennessee history. Elections have turned and careers have been made and lost on the basis of investigative journalism that uncovered corruption or gross incompetence. Investigative reporting by newspapers in the late 1980s exposed widespread corruption in the office of the Secretary of State, who later committed suicide. Equally aggressive reporting in the 1990s about conditions in the Arlington Mental Health Center played a role in a federal court order to improve staffing and funding for the facility.

One should not confuse well-researched stories with another category that seeks to pass for investigative reporting. How many miles the Governor puts on the state plane or the ten-year cost of a legislator's travel make for dramatic headlines and easy stories. While such stories certainly have a place in political coverage, they are not an adequate substitute for issues that require far more time and thought. From 1992 to 1998, Tennessee increased state spending for K–12 schools some $900 million—the nation's largest percentage increase—with little effort by the media to examine whether local school systems used the money wisely or legally. During the 1980s and 1990s, tens of millions of dollars in federal job training funds flowed to entities called Private Industry Councils, with little oversight by the state and no interest by the media. This does not suggest either program was corrupt or flawed. The issue is whether the media abandoned its responsibility as watchdog over such enormous amounts of taxpayer dollars.

In fairness to the media, investigative reporting is not conducted without risk. Such reporting, even when accurate, can make reporters persona non grata among the sources on whom they depend. If criminal intent is implied, the smallest mistake can result in costly litigation and loss of credibility for the newspaper. Risks aside, investigative reporting that requires weeks or months is an expensive use of limited resources in a period of growing financial pressures for newspapers. At the close of the century, patterns of reporting indicated these risks and costs played a significant role in the media's coverage of the Tennessee political system.

The Media's Search for Identity

In some ways, Tennessee's media experienced broader changes during the last quarter of the twentieth century than the political process they covered. The changes affected—in both a positive and negative way—their coverage of Tennessee government. Political scandals in Washington and Nashville produced a more distant relationship between the Capitol Hill Press Corps and public officials, although the relationship was never as cynical or as negative as that found in Washington or in many other state capitals. The closing of major daily newspapers reduced the diversity and tempered the passion of political reporting. The purchase of several remaining newspapers by out-of-state chains removed traditional alliances between local owners and political parties and factions. Publishers and reporters by and large no longer shared the close familiarity with governors and legislators enjoyed by their predecessors in the 1950s and 1960s. As the importance of personal relationships diminished, the rapid expansion of computer technology increased the quality and timeliness of reporting. Even as the quality of newspaper coverage improved, the emergence of television—particularly the expansion of cable networks—cut drastically into the number of citizens who used newspapers as a source of political news.

Meanwhile, government discovered and perfected new strategies to use the media—television in particular—as a vehicle to further political agendas. Numerous reporters and public officials decried the trend that gave image priority over substance. Despite this indignation, officials who understood best the changing tastes and habits of the public were most effective in communicating with the media and, through the media, influencing the political process. They grasped the fact that only a small percentage of Tennesseans understand or care about the details of state government. In such a climate, context was not important if a media relations firm could get their name and image before the public in a manner that conveyed accessibility and concern.

None of these changes should be interpreted as suggesting that political reporting in Tennessee is in a period of decline, either in quality or in its importance to the process of government. Indeed, in a state that has been transformed from an agrarian backwater into a complex economy with more than five million citizens, the role of the press in providing accurate and comprehensive coverage of state government is more important than ever. In the same way that dramatic changes forced the Governor and the legislature to reexamine their respective roles, the health of the Tennessee political process requires that the press undergo a comparable reexamination. Democracy does not allow for divorce between government and the press. At issue in the future is the level of passion and commitment that binds them in a common purpose.

Part IV

PUBLIC POLICY IN TENNESSEE

11

Education

People attending the elementary school's fall fund-raiser are lined up out the door of the cafeteria by 6:30. They mingle in the hall, decorated with stick-figure drawings from the first and second graders. As small children run around their feet, the sheriff and the local state representative chat with the pastor of the Little Zion Baptist Church, reassuring one another that the University of Tennessee football team will defeat Florida next week. They wait patiently for a five-dollar supper of spaghetti and iced tea served by mothers from the Parent-Teachers Organization. Very little of the conversation among parents and grandparents touches on contemporary education issues. As they have done for years, they are gathered on a warm Saturday evening to show support for their community school.

Since the end of the World War II in 1945, public education has dominated the attention and resources of Tennessee state government far more than any other issue. With some nine hundred thousand students in K–12 schools, education touches every community and the large majority of Tennessee citizens. Education traditionally is the top

Fig. 11.1. A public school teacher. Education is the largest segment of the state budget, with K–12 and higher education together accounting for more than half of state expenditures. *Source:* State of Tennessee Photographic Services.

priority of candidates in legislative races. Even more so than tax policy, education decisions at the state level arguably affect more people, generate more emotion, and have greater long-term political consequences. Although health care emerged in the 1980s and 1990s as an issue of growing concern, health-related issues did not begin to rival the political, economic, and financial importance of education.

Education is the largest segment of the state budget, with K–12 and higher education together accounting for more than half of state expenditures. The 138 public school systems in Tennessee employ more than sixty thousand people and spend almost $4.5 billion per year in state, federal, and local funds.[1] Education is the largest budget item of every city or county government that supports a school system. In contrast to the 1960s and 1970s, when low-skill and low-wage labor was common in most Tennessee factories, the reputation of a local school system is today an important factor in the competition for new industries with higher-paying jobs. To an unprecedented degree, a community's image and economic success are linked to the quality of its schools.

Understanding the politics of education in Tennessee begins with an appreciation for the emotions generated among those associated directly or indirectly with K–12 schools. Citizens who discuss in the abstract issues such as prisons or welfare become passionate when the topic turns to decisions that affect their children's education (fig. 11.1). Such passions intensify in dozens of "one high school communities" across Tennessee, where the local high school is a visible reflection of the personality and priorities of area residents. The auditorium or gymnasium is frequently the largest room in the county and the site where citizens gather to discuss local issues or participate in cultural events. Whether it is football in Kingsport, Oak Ridge, or Gallatin, or girls' basketball in Shelbyville, Livingston, or Carthage, Friday night high school athletic events often are the focal point of civic pride and the only time when all segments of the community gather in a common cause.

State and local policy makers are confronted by another characteristic unique to education. Unlike health care, corrections, or economic development, most voters consider themselves "experts" on education. Virtually every adult in Tennessee attended school for a decade or more and has children or grandchildren in school. While the vast majority of these citizens have few specific opinions about most state government issues, large numbers are not reluctant to express themselves forcefully on a broad range of education topics, from curriculum to school funding. Such democratic participation in local education can be positive or negative, depending largely on the ability of leaders to make parents and other interested parties feel a part of the process. Where successful, strong public participation in the schools can contribute to higher student achievement and increased financial support from city councils and county commissions. Unfortunately, it is just as common to encounter conflict among elected officials, education administrators, parents, and citizens unable to reach consensus about a community's goals and the appropriate level of financial commitment to education. In Tennessee, communities where such conflict exists frequently are among the nation's most underfunded and underachieving school districts.

A final factor influencing education policy at the state level is the natural desire by most governors to leave a lasting monument to their administration. Except for education, the major policy areas of state government—health care, roads, juvenile and adult corrections, state parks, and environment—for the most part do not lend themselves to initiatives that would have a long-term statewide association with a governor. In contrast, many Tennesseans can quickly name the education initiatives of several governors: Frank Clement's free textbooks;

Buford Ellington's establishment of community colleges; Winfield Dunn's creation of statewide kindergarten; Lamar Alexander's Master Teacher program; and Ned McWherter's Basic Education Program, which raised standards and implemented a new "equalized" funding formula to help poorer counties. The desire by Tennessee governors to leave an education legacy is good in so far as it makes education a priority issue. On occasion, however, the compulsion by governors and their staff to initiate education reforms can lead to tinkering with a delicate process that sometimes benefits most from being allowed to function as intended.[2]

A Lot of Cooks in the Kitchen

One factor inhibiting the ability to develop and implement sound education policy is the multilayered system of decision making in Tennessee's primary and secondary schools. Taken separately, each layer of the education bureaucracy represents a legitimate purpose or an initiative justified at the time of its inception by the state legislature. Progressive state legislation in 1925 brought needed structure to education by standardizing graduation requirements and creating local boards of education to formalize school management.[3] Attempts to raise the caliber of teaching resulted in the creation in 1984 of a Career Ladder program for teachers and a new State Board of Education with expanded powers. Sweeping reforms enacted in 1992 strengthened academic standards, instituted a new state school finance formula, and sought to clarify responsibilities among state and local administrators.[4] Still, Tennessee shares with most states an education system in which a variety of parties in the state capital and local communities assert the right to make policy decisions. Rarely do all the parties speak with one voice. The inability to find consensus among competing agendas produces an education policy that often is a process of one step forward and two steps sideways. Seeking to understand this process begins with the major education players.

Commissioner of Education

The most important and most influential voice in Tennessee education policy is the Commissioner of the State Department of Education. Historically, the Commissioner of Education comes from a background as a school superintendent, a principal, or a senior administrator in higher education. Appointed by the Governor, the Commissioner has three primary responsibilities. The first involves articulating the Governor's position on education issues to a variety of groups, including the legislature, the State Board of Education, the Tennessee Education Association, and local education officials. Equally important but not apparent to most outsiders is the Commissioner's key role in the internal jousting for budget priority that takes place among cabinet members in all administrations. Finally, the Commissioner oversees the day-to-day management of 138 local school systems.[5]

State Board of Education

In Tennessee the State Board of Education has, at least on paper, a greater degree of decision-making authority than found in most states. The board's statutory powers to make decisions regarding curriculum, funding distribution, testing, and graduation requirements date to 1984, when Senate Speaker John Wilder reconstituted the board as the price for his support for Gov. Lamar Alexander's proposal to raise the state sales tax and implement a controversial program of performance-based salary supplements for teachers.[6] The board's nine members are nominated by the Governor, subject to approval by the legislature. The board in turn hires an Executive Director to manage the full-time staff and serve as the board's liaison.

From its inception, the board has had difficulty determining the precise boundaries of its responsibilities. While the board can adopt any number of policies, many of these policies cannot be implemented without financial support from the administration and the legislature. The relationship is further complicated if the board and its Executive Director are at odds with the priorities of a new Governor and Education Commissioner. Because such a situation leads to gridlock, since 1985 an unwritten understanding has emerged that the Commissioner of Education, acting on behalf of the Governor, will coordinate most major education initiatives. The board's most important decisions are usually made only after seeking approval from the Commissioner and the education leaders of the House and Senate.

Senate and House Education Committees

The Tennessee General Assembly assigns responsibility for legislative education decisions to the respective education committees of the House and Senate. The state's comprehensive education reforms in 1992 were made possible in part because of a close working relationship among a Democratic Governor, a Republican chair of the Senate Education Committee, and his Democratic counterpart in the House. The bond between the leaders of the two committees endured throughout the 1990s and was an important reason most of the reforms survived attempts by opponents to weaken them. Although the legislature was under considerable pressure to repeal some of the 1992 reforms—particularly the move from elected to appointed school superintendents—the House and Senate abided by decisions of their respective education committees to maintain the reforms.

Tennessee Education Association

Teachers in all but two of the state's 138 school systems are represented by the Tennessee Education Association (TEA), a professional organization affiliated with the National Education Association. Unlike the American Federation of Teachers, TEA does not recognize the right to strike. Representing some forty thousand teachers and principals, TEA is one of the state's most active and influential lobbying organizations, and its endorsement and financial support are coveted by legislative candidates. TEA's legislative success over the years has been mixed. In the late 1970s, the organization won the right—without the threat of strike—for teachers to negotiate salary contracts with local boards of education. TEA lost a bitter fight in 1984 to prevent performance-based pay for teachers. The group in 1992 acquiesced to a "value-added" evaluation plan to measure student learning—and the teacher's impact on that learning—as part of a state commitment to large funding increases for the classroom. In 1998, TEA successfully resisted the Governor's legislative efforts to implement a program of non-public Charter Schools. For the most part, TEA has worked more effectively with Democratic governors, although the organization provides political endorsements to both parties.

Local Boards of Education

From 1925 until 1992, local education boards in Tennessee varied widely in competence, style, and effectiveness. Some boards were appointed by city councils or county commissions. Some were elected from the city or county at large, others by districts of varying size. In many communities, board members were well educated and committed to high standards and strong financial support for schools. Meanwhile, in the adjacent county one might find board members who had not graduated from high school and whose primary concern was patronage authority over the hiring of teachers and staff. The 1992 reforms required that all board members be elected from districts of equal size. The 1992 law also mandated that board members attend annual seminars on education issues such as personnel law and school finance.[7]

The progress brought about by the 1992 reforms left unresolved at the local level the same conflict that existed in Nashville. Although Tennessee's 138 local school systems are far fewer than those found in states such as Georgia or Oklahoma, the presence of multiple systems remains an obstacle to progress in several small counties.[8] More important, local education boards in Tennessee do not possess the authority, as they do in some states, to raise revenues through property taxes. In the absence of this power, a tension will always exist between the goals of the board of education and the city council or county commission that must raise property or sales taxes to finance the board's agenda.

School Superintendents

Much as the Commissioner of Education articulates statewide education policy, the School Superintendent is the leader and spokesperson for schools located in a city, county, or special school district. Until 1992, superintendents were selected by a variety of means, including direct election, appointment by the school board, and appointment by the local governing body. In districts where superintendents were elected, criteria for qualification limited the pool of candidates to the point where elections were frequently bitter contests between an incumbent superintendent and a principal in the same system. The losing faction often was punished through transfers and demotions, sowing the seeds for further recrimination and making it difficult for the community to develop any semblance of consensus for important decisions.

Even if the superintendent was elected without opposition, a second, more fundamental problem existed with a local school board whose members also were elected. When faced with hard decisions such as school construction or the consolidation of small schools into one larger one, both parties claimed to speak with the mandate of the people. In dozens of Tennessee communities, disagreements between elected superintendents and elected school boards produced a stalemate that thwarted progress. The 1992 legislative changes required that all school districts have elected school boards that in turn would hire superintendents for a four-year period. The 1992 law also made it possible for school boards to hire superintendents who were not educators and who did not live in the district. Although these changes generated considerable opposition in several communities, they succeeded in producing a system of local governance that on the whole was less politicized and clearer in the assignment of responsibilities.

The Other Players

If the education bureaucracy was not complicated enough, forging a sound and consistent education policy is made more challenging by the roles of other players in the political process. Mayors and county executives can, based on their interest and influence, be very important parts of education decisions. The authority of city councils and county commissions to pass education budgets and raise revenues at times makes these bodies as important as school boards. Leaders of the business community have a large stake in education quality and are often a presence behind the scenes. And, of course, parents and other interested citizens represent a broad range of philosophies and preferences as to school policies. The ability to find consensus among these discordant voices at the local level can be a daunting task. Multiplied by 138 systems at the state level, the challenge can be overwhelming.

Performance, Funds, and Fairness

With a few notable exceptions, the range of issues confronting K–12 education in Tennessee is much the same as those in a majority of southern states. Because teachers in Tennessee cannot legally strike, the state's schools do not encounter the periodic shutdowns found in many larger urban systems in the nation's northern and western regions. Likewise, at the close of the twentieth century only a handful of Tennessee counties had substantial numbers of Hispanic families, meaning that bilingual education had not yet emerged as a challenge to the legislature and most local school boards. Although federal court-ordered busing in the 1970s led to substantial "white flight" in some communities, black students represented a majority of public school enrollment only in Memphis (fig. 11.2), Jackson, and two or three small rural West Tennessee counties. In Nashville, black and white leaders in 1999 agreed on a $206 million plan to end federal control, reduce busing, and return to neighborhood schools.[9] Perhaps most important in a political sense, the percentage of K–12 students statewide attending private schools remained fewer than one in six, indicating the level of support for public education, while not always deep, was broader than found in several southern states.

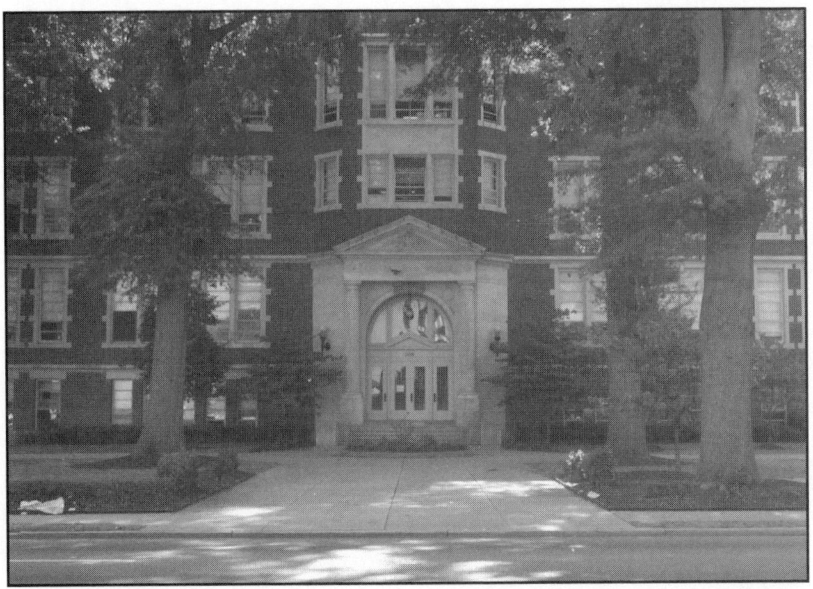

Fig. 11.2. Central High School, Memphis. Photo by William Lyons (class of 1966).

Tennessee schools have been less fortunate in escaping other problems. For discussion purposes, the challenges confronting the state's education system are divided into two general categories. The first category encompasses academic quality and includes the performance of students and teachers. One must keep in mind that every combination of strength and weakness exists among the nearly two thousand K–12 schools in Tennessee. Oases of learning are found among lower-income students in both rural and urban schools. Simultaneously, there are well-funded school districts in which students and teachers perform well below community expectations.

Issues in a second category focus on the adequacy and equity of state and local funding for public schools. Becoming familiar with the distinction between "funding adequacy" and "funding equity" is critical to understanding the forces behind education reform that occurred in Tennessee in the 1980s and 1990s and shaped education policy well into the twenty-first century. "Adequacy" refers to a school system having enough funds to provide a basic level of education resources. "Equity" refers to the amount of education funding a school system has in relation to other systems. For nearly two centuries, Tennessee, like most every other state, had a school finance system that did not incorporate the notion of equity—the idea that it is fundamentally unfair for students in one community to attend schools funded at half the level of the schools in the adjoining county. As they had found in attempting to improve academic performance, policy makers would discover a large gap between appreciating the problem of funding inequity and solving it.

Academic Performance: Halfway Home and a Long Way to Go

Published by the Southern Growth Policies Board in the late 1980s, Halfway Home and a Long Way to Go was the report of a two-year study chaired by Mississippi Governor Ray Mabus on the status of education and economic development in the South. In a number of important ways, the report's title captured the progress and challenges of Tennessee schools as they entered the twenty-first century. To the surprise of many whose impressions remained grounded in the 1950s, a substantial portion of the state's education system was in reasonably sound shape. Two or three dozen Tennessee communities were producing good—in some instances outstanding—public schools. Facilities were modern, teachers received a competitive salary, and students by and large performed at a level competitive with some of the best public school systems in America. Interestingly, a cluster of the state's best-funded school systems was located in the small towns of Northeast Tennessee that benefited from rapid industrialization after the Second World War.

As in many states, the report found that academic performance dropped sharply from the top twenty-five percent of schools to the remainder. Performance in many Tennessee classrooms lagged behind national norms, especially in science and social studies. The majority of Tennessee students scored below their peers on college entrance examinations. (Tennessee's consistently high ranking on the SAT examination is misleading, due to the fact that most students take the ACT examination required by the state's public universities.) A lower percentage of Tennesseans attended and graduated from college. Among those who graduated from high school, about a third had taken a hodgepodge of courses that did not prepare them for either college or a vocation. The percentage of high school students who dropped out was high, and the number who took advanced courses was low. Rural teachers were usually underpaid, and too often—especially in math and science—not certified to teach the courses to which they were assigned.[10]

Although it is not always possible to make a clean separation when discussing academic and financial issues, policy makers at the state and local level can—on occasion—address academic performance without a substantial increase in funding. Beginning in the early 1980s, events within and outside Tennessee laid the groundwork for a gradual but steady move toward higher standards for students and teachers. Many of the initiatives reflected a regional trend supported and promoted by the Southern Regional Education Board, an Atlanta organization that networked southern legislators and governors such as Arkansas' Bill Clinton and Tennessee's Lamar Alexander. While some states figured it out faster than others, all eventually realized that northern and foreign industries wishing to locate in the South viewed good schools as an important criterion in their decisions. As the South's momentum toward higher expectations for teachers and students gained strength, the enthusiasm for more rigorous standards was picked up in Tennessee by governors and senior legislators who largely knew what they wanted to do, if not exactly how to do it.

Education Funding

"If You Don't Have a Wal-Mart, You're Out of Luck." Using his unique West Tennessee way of simplifying a complicated problem, Gov. Ned McWherter used this expression time and again to describe an education challenge even more pressing than inadequate academic standards. In the 1960s and well into the 1970s, Tennessee was a very poor state in which per capita income consistently ranked around forty-eighth or forty-ninth. Not surprisingly, state and local funding for schools reflected the same general rankings. Beginning in the early 1980s, two profound economic changes, one external and one internal, had a dramatic impact on Tennessee schools. Decisions in Detroit and Tokyo to open a new frontier of the automobile industry in the South led to an explosion of new high-wage manufacturing jobs, eventually pushing Tennessee's per capita income ranking to thirty-second, which was among the highest and fastest jumps ever by a state (see chapter 4). Occurring simultaneously with Tennessee's surge in per capita income was an equally historic shift in retail commerce. Acres of shopping malls and discount chains sprang up in the state's large and mid-sized cities. Hundreds of thousands of Tennesseans who previously had shopped on the local courthouse square now drove fifty or more miles to spend larger incomes on groceries, clothing, and durable goods.

The shift in retail buying habits, while greatly expanding the choices available to rural consumers, had a devastating and unanticipated impact back home in their community schools. Funding for schools was shared between the state and local governments, with revenues for the local share derived primarily from property and sales taxes. As residents began in greater numbers to cross county lines to shop, many counties experienced a severe drop in sales tax revenues. Literally, Tennessee communities without a Wal-Mart could not hope to generate the funds needed to provide schools with even the basic tools for a sound education system. For dozens of counties, the issue was no longer whether citizens were prepared to sacrifice in the form of higher taxes for good schools. In one of the great ironies of Tennessee history, the state's period of greatest economic growth produced an ever-widening education system of haves and have-nots. Left unchecked, this fundamental shift in the state's tax base threatened endless funding cuts in schools already burdened with underpaid teachers, substandard buildings, and serious shortages of instructional supplies. These schools could expect no relief from a state funding formula that allocated the same funds per student in all 138 school systems. In relatively normal times, attempts to make even small changes in state education policy face a formidable set of political obstacles. In times of crisis, however, conventional politics are turned upside down, providing the opportunity for reforms previously believed impossible.

Turning the Ocean Liner

"Education reform" is one of the most threadbare terms in American politics. In much the same way that sports broadcasters often refer to routine plays as "incredible," the term "education reform" has come to describe everything from the inconsequential to the truly radical. Some have frequently confused "reform" with what is really only a change of process, preferring to believe that improved learning will accompany the piling on of additional rules governing things like the square footage of classrooms or playgrounds. Others who seek "reforms" to further religious and political agendas can often be found at local school board meetings engaging in discussions about textbooks or evolution. One of the most frustrating voices belongs to believers in the "single bullet theory," the idea that a single simple answer exists to every complicated problem. These usually well-intentioned citizens ignore broader issues while devoting considerable energy to debates such as prayer in school, sex education, tenure, or whether teachers use phonics for reading instruction. This should not suggest that bureaucrats and political activists are solely responsible for watering down the meaning of education reform. Across the country, many college faculty join a variety of public officials in a continuous redefinition of the issue. Terms such as "holistic reform," "systemic reform" and "empowerment" fall in and out of favor as the words become overused and their meaning exhausted.

During a decade that spanned roughly the mid-1980s through the mid-1990s, virtually every state in America underwent politically high-profile efforts to "reform" education. The education reform movement took root when the idea dawned upon a previously apathetic public that a relationship existed between the deterioration of America's world economic denomination and a relative decline in the standards of American schools. President George Bush was so concerned that in 1989 he summoned the nation's governors to an Education Summit at the University of Virginia to encourage state-level reforms. Predictably, the education "reforms" that followed varied greatly in style and substance. In the South, as elsewhere, some "reform" efforts were little more than press releases and task forces. However, a number of southern states, including Florida, South Carolina, Kentucky, Georgia, and Tennessee, put forth good-faith attempts to raise both standards and funding for their schools.

Beginning in 1983, two Tennessee governors, one Republican and one Democrat, undertook to upgrade K–12 education with reforms that were meaningful, expensive, and accompanied by exceptional political risk. Their efforts said much about the political complexity of education reform and why Tennessee succeeded in implementing some reforms that failed in other states. The two governors also found that, like a large ocean liner, turning around something as massive as a state education system requires time, patience, and a steady hand.

"Not One Teacher Is Paid One Penny More for Doing a Good Job"

For nearly eighteen months in 1983–84, Gov. Lamar Alexander repeated this phrase to rally public support for legislation that contained a sincere, if flawed, attempt to change the status quo of the Tennessee education system. More so than the actual contents of the reforms, Alexander's promotion of his program and his successful fight with the educational bureaucracy transformed the education climate in Tennessee. At its most basic level, Alexander's proposal argued persuasively that some teachers were better than others and that, as a means of keeping them in the profession, these "Master Teachers" should be paid significantly higher salaries.[11] His plan inferred that higher salaries would attract good students to the teaching profession and that teachers striving to obtain Master Teacher status would generate improved student performance. Most parents and members of the business community accepted Alexander's premise without giving much thought to its practical applications. Even the governor's staff did not initially grasp the magnitude of the effort required to evaluate forty thousand teachers fairly in an era prior to the introduction of the desktop computer. Even more important, they did not fully account for the extent to which teacher and student performance can be affected by a lack of materials such as textbooks and laboratory equipment or the number of students in the classroom.

Neither of these reservations ultimately proved convincing enough for political opponents to overcome popular support for Alexander's "Better Schools" legislative package and the one-cent increase in the state sales tax to fund it. The battle in the General Assembly was the most bitter of the decade, a struggle that both Alexander and the Tennessee Education Association approached as a fight to the political death. TEA registered thirty-five additional lobbyists to fight the legislation. Also choosing up sides were superintendents, local school boards, and large portions of the state's business community. Unveiled in January 1983, prior to his second inauguration, the centerpiece Master Teacher portion of Alexander's proposal failed three months later by one vote in the Senate Education Committee. Over the next summer and fall the original bill was amended and fashioned into a more palatable piece of legislation. Alexander raised the stakes the following January by convening Tennessee's first Special Session of the legislature in modern times. Alexander renewed his call for the Better Schools program with the most effective media campaign in the state's history (see chapter 10). This time Senate passage was relatively easy. In the House, the education portion of the package passed with votes to spare, while the accompanying sales tax increase squeaked by with a one-vote margin.[12]

Ultimately Alexander's proposal to implement performance-based pay for teachers fell victim to its own expectations. For different reasons, the plan was oversold by both its proponents, some of whom believed it a revolutionary answer to America's schools, and its adversaries, who wished for partisan reasons to set Alexander up for a fall. Even if teachers had bought into the idea of performance-based pay—which they did not—the scheme was doomed by an evaluation plan that was too complicated, too expensive, and implemented without adequate preparation. Hundreds of appeals by teachers who were denied salary supplements choked the system and damaged its credibility. The program's original purpose was further compromised when former opponents added an assortment of principals, assistant principals, and other nonteachers to the evaluation process. The years following Alexander's high-profile legislative victory saw several states enact similar versions of Tennessee's teacher evaluation reforms. In time, however, even Tennessee Republicans lost interest in funding a program that supporters conceded had done little to boost student performance. In 1997, Alexander's experiment effectively died when the legislature cut off salary supplements to future applicants with the support of a Republican governor and the Senate's Republican Leader, an original sponsor of the 1984 legislation.

In fairness to Alexander, his reform movement deserved recognition for the spotlight it cast on education and its willingness to challenge outdated assumptions about the performance of students and teachers. To the degree that Alexander shook Tennesseans from their complacency, he deserves credit, as some suggest, for "getting education off of the back burner" of political discussion. Across the nation, Tennessee's reputation rose a notch or two in the eyes of those who had viewed the state as an educational backwater. Some minor components of the reform package, such as summer academies for gifted students and university Centers of Excellence, were a lasting success.

With this credit, however, Alexander must also assume a share of the blame for ignoring a problem much more serious than teacher evaluations. Only a small portion of funds from the 1984 sales tax increase found its way into dozens of school systems with classrooms lacking for the most basic educational resources. The situation became so desperate that in 1988, one year after Alexander left office, seventy-seven small school systems sued the state of Tennessee.[13] The counties filed suit on grounds that state education funding was neither adequate nor equal, and that the situation had deteriorated to the point their plight was unconstitutional. Even as the Small Schools Lawsuit reached the Tennessee Supreme Court, Alexander used the notoriety from his education reform efforts to become Secretary of Education under President Bush. In yet another irony of Tennessee politics, when the Tennessee Supreme Court heard the case damning Tennessee's education system, the plaintiff for the small schools was Lewis Donelson, Alexander's former state Commissioner of Finance.

The Gathering Storm

The passage of Alexander's Better Schools package in 1984 raised, albeit temporarily, both the public's support and expectations for the state's schools. Perhaps unfairly, increased expectations turned to disillusion as citizens realized it would take much more than performance-based pay for teachers to improve student test scores. The absence of immediate progress made schools an easy target for those eager to accuse lawmakers of "throwing money at the problem." The reaction to Alexander's reforms coincided with an attitude of distrust and cynicism toward government articulated by President Ronald Reagan and taken up in most states by the conservative wing of the Republican Party. As the anti-government and anti-tax rhetoric intensified, efforts to raise revenues for education in local communities came under fierce attack. Sometimes without regard for facts or needs in an individual school system, critics of public education enjoyed great success throughout the state in opposing school bond referendums and property tax proposals. Many school systems found themselves caught in the "death spiral," underfunded to the point the product was so bad much of the community no longer wished to increase funding at all.

In even worse shape were other school systems, in which the problem was more economic than political. Despite the willingness of county governments to raise tax rates, these communities simply did not have the sales or property tax base to generate substantially more money regardless of the tax rate. Property and sales tax rates much higher than the state average did not produce enough money to repair leaking roofs, replace textbooks, or purchase gasoline for school buses. Depending upon one's definition of "basic needs" for schools, by the late 1980s some three to four dozen largely rural school systems did not have enough money to provide basic educational services.

Amid the political exhaustion that followed Alexander's reforms in 1984, it was evident that a decent interval would be required before the public, the General Assembly, or the new Governor would entertain further reform efforts. In 1988, when Tennessee's rural school systems turned to the courts for relief, the effort represented a revolutionary idea in a state where court-ordered busing had soured public attitudes toward the judiciary. The plaintiffs employed a creative strategy, shifting focus from the issue of adequate funding and staking their hopes on grounds the courts would find Tennessee schools were inequitably funded. The Tennessee Constitution is largely silent on the issue of education, requiring only that the "General Assembly shall provide for the maintenance, support and eligibility standards of a system of free public schools."[14] On July 25, 1991, educators and legislators in Tennessee's largest cities were concerned when the Davidson County Chancery Court ruled that the existing system of funding the public schools was unconstitutional. But they were stunned in 1993, when the Tennessee Supreme Court agreed that some systems were funded at unacceptably higher levels than others. In the absence of action by the legislature to relieve the funding imbalance, the court indicated it would employ a "Robin Hood" solution in which education funds from wealthier communities would be taken away and given to poorer school systems.[15]

Panic and anger were distributed in roughly equal amounts among school systems standing to lose millions of dollars in a political climate that made it extremely difficult to replace lost funds through higher taxes. In Texas and New Jersey, fights over funding equalization had threatened to tear apart state legislatures unable to agree on a consensus plan. The challenge in Tennessee put to the supreme test the public's commitment to real education reform and the ability of the legislature to produce a compromise solution out of potential chaos. Into the spotlight moved the most unlikely of education reformers, a sharecropper's son whose formal education had ended at the twelfth grade.

Catching the Right Wave

Ned McWherter had been elected governor in 1986 with a message promising to bring Tennessee's rural counties back into the state's economic mainstream. His four-point plan to disperse economic growth included building roads, expanding primary health care, managing solid and toxic wastes, and strengthening the state's K–12 education program. Having served fourteen years as Speaker of the House, McWherter appreciated more than most the importance of political timing, or, as his younger staff members put it, "catching the right wave" in the legislature. Even had he wanted to do so, McWherter could not have marshaled adequate public and legislative support for more reforms and another tax increase in the years immediately following the battle over Alexander's education package. The legislature was in no mood for a replay of the 1984 reform fight. Much of the public was disillusioned with schools that performed no better than before. Most important, the teachers and administrators in a massive educational system could not be asked to accept more controversial changes without adequate time to absorb the first round of reforms.

McWherter's long experience with state finance quickly led him to the conclusion that the majority of Tennessee schools needed a larger and more equitable distribution of funds. He also recognized that Alexander's reform efforts left him with both an opportunity and a challenge. The opportunity resided in the renewed interest by Tennesseans in the importance of high-quality schools. The challenge was in overcoming the public's cynicism toward calls for more taxes to fund yet another round of education "reforms" that skeptics predicted would be "more of the same." To complicate matters further, McWherter's first term in the late 1980s was conducted against the backdrop of anti-government and anti-tax sentiment echoed daily by Tommy Hopper, the high-profile executive director of the Tennessee Republican Party. National media reports of seven rancorous and unsuccessful special sessions of the Texas Legislature made clear that any simultaneous attempt to raise taxes and reallocate funds among urban and rural communities in Tennessee would be extremely difficult. In a partisan climate dominated by calls for reduced taxes and reduced spending, raising taxes in the absence of far-reaching reforms would be political suicide.

With the aid of his Commissioner of Education and his Senior Policy Advisor, McWherter in 1990 developed a five-part strategy designed to buy time and build public support for education reforms. Externally, he enlisted the State Board of Education, with the input of the state's education constituencies, to determine the basic education needs, or education "tool box," required as a floor below which no school system would be allowed to fall. The Governor also embarked with his Cabinet on a statewide tour that conducted more than five hundred community meetings to solicit public comment on education. Internally, McWherter's aides were quietly at work on far-reaching reforms that would address virtually every aspect of standards, governance, and funding of the state's education system. Unbeknown to all but his closest advisors, McWherter also was preparing to propose along with his education reforms an equally radical overhaul of the state's tax system, including an elimination of the state sales tax on food and the implementation for the first time of a state tax on income. McWherter packaged these initiatives in the context of the Small Schools Lawsuit that threatened a court-ordered transfer of education funds from wealthier school systems to poorer ones. In a state where the federal courts in 1985 had taken over the prison system, McWherter repeatedly raised the specter of the courts also taking over the public schools. This fear played through the state's entire education structure, producing a rare unity in opposition to a judicial takeover and the political opening McWherter sought.[16]

The Deal: More Money for Higher Standards

The collective input from five hundred public meetings convinced McWherter that public education faced two fundamental problems that had to be addressed before gaining support for a tax increase. Foremost, parents and citizens complained they had no meaningful way of knowing how well or poorly their schools were performing. In addition, they felt alienated from an education system perceived as distant and indifferent to public concerns. McWherter responded by offering a deal: more funds and more flexibility in return for higher standards and greater accountability from students and teachers.

The simplicity of the offer disguised its scope. McWherter reversed a forty-year trend by returning a large portion of decision making to local communities. He prevailed upon the State Board of Education to repeal some thirty-seven hundred rules and regulations, allowing individual schools to determine everything from how many minutes to teach reading to the appropriate square footage of classrooms. Even more far-reaching, he proposed allowing school boards to spend new state funds according to local needs so long as the funds stayed in the classroom and were not used for salary increases. Some schools preferred more textbooks and computers. Others wished to provide advanced courses in physics or languages. Site-based management was authorized, but not required, to allow parents and teachers to participate in budget decisions. For the first time in memory, local communities experienced an expansion of meaningful education choices.

The expansion of local decision making was accompanied by higher academic standards. In addition to the existing core curriculum, students would be required to take courses in world history, geography, and government. The "general track" curriculum would be repealed, forcing students to choose a program of applied vocational courses or college preparatory studies. Prior to receiving a high school diploma, students would have to pass a new, more rigorous exit examination that measured knowledge of science and social studies as well as math and verbal skills.

McWherter's most controversial reforms involved a complete realignment of relationships among local administrators and teachers. All superintendents would henceforth be appointed, serving in a new role as CEO at the pleasure of the elected school board. Principals would sign performance contracts with the superintendent. Performance would include the yearly learning gains of students, measured system by system, school by school and classroom by classroom. Called the "value-added" system, results would be published annually in local newspapers. In school systems that repeatedly did not meet state standards, both the superintendent and the school board would be subject to termination. While the scope of McWherter's proposal caught many in the education community by surprise, its impact was sufficient to rekindle public support for a final try at changing the system.[17]

"Some Get the Coffee Mugs and Some Get the Rolltop Desk"

Although viewed as too aggressive and even ill-conceived by some, McWherter's curriculum and governance proposals in fact were only a vehicle on which to carry his recommendation to change dramatically the way by which local schools received state funds. Stripped of its legal formalities, the Tennessee Supreme Court had conveyed a simple message to the Governor and the legislature: "Change the funding system or we will change it for you." From McWherter's perspective, he had been thrown into the briar patch.

The Tennessee Supreme Court had given every indication that Tennessee schools would be made to meet constitutional requirements, not through a mandated tax increase but through the redistribution of funds from wealthier districts to poorer ones. McWherter's response was to propose a substantial increase in total state funds for education, with a disproportionate share going to the poorest communities. Using a complex formula to measure a county's tax base, McWherter's proposed new funding plan for the first time allocated state education funds on the basis of a community's relative wealth instead of solely on the number of students. Under such a plan, the poorest counties would receive up to 85 percent of total education funds from the state, while wealthier communities such as Nashville might realize something closer to 55 percent of their education funds from the state.

The plan's proposed funding increases for education exceeded anything in the state's experience. Using data accepted by the court, state funding in 1992 represented 70 percent of the total needed to provide a minimum funding floor, or Basic Education Plan (BEP), for each of Tennessee's 138 school districts. Under McWherter's plan, full funding was projected after six years and an increase of approximately $1.1 billion in state funds, nearly doubling the 1992 state funding base of $1.2 billion. Salary increases would be in addition to the BEP funding. In practical terms, the proposal by 1998 would increase state funds in the range of 125 to 150 percent for the poorest school systems, a figure beyond the dreams of teachers, administrators, and parents. Estimated funding increases in urban and wealthier systems, while substantially smaller in percentage terms, was enough to prevent a rebellion among urban legislators. When asked by legislators to explain the complicated concept of equalized funding, McWherter replied with a phrase borrowed from his friend, Gov. Ann Richards of Texas. "It's like when they read the will after your grandmother dies. Some get the coffee mugs, and some get the rolltop desk." The legislature rejected the proposal for tax reform but accepted McWherter's education reforms with only minor modifications. Despite the sales tax increase receiving a total of only three votes from Memphis and Nashville legislators in the House, the education and tax bills were passed by a coalition of rural Democrats and Republicans with votes to spare.[18]

Legacy of Education Reform

Each year following the 1992 education initiatives provided an increasingly clear picture of the limits and potential for Tennessee's K–12 schools as the state entered the twenty-first century. The experience also shed light on issues related to the strategies of developing meaningful reforms and moving those reforms through the thicket of the political process.

On the positive side, successive legislatures and a change in the Governor's Office did not impede the full implementation of Tennessee's new education funding formula. From 1992 to full funding of the Basic Education Plan in 1998, the 98 percent funding increase for Tennessee's K–12 schools led the nation. Other indicators suggested a relationship does in fact exist between funding and performance if increased funding is accompanied by higher expectations. The number of Tennessee elementary schools accredited by the Southern Association of Colleges and Schools increased from 39.8 percent in 1992 to 60.3 percent in 1998. The hiring of some ninety-four hundred new teachers reduced by a third the number of class-size waivers and by a fifth the number of teachers conducting courses for which they were not certified. By the close of the century, hundreds of schools had renovated facilities, adequate numbers of textbooks, and computer technology unavailable in 1992. In the classroom, Tennessee students reflected significant gains in math, reading, language arts, and science compared with results from 1992. More students were taking advanced high school courses and fewer required remedial training in college.[19]

The optimism generated by these encouraging trends was tempered by a realization that the reforms had not eliminated a number of obstacles to education progress. In several school systems the enthusiasm that accompanied the 1992 reforms had been replaced by carping about the fairness of "state mandates." Numerous county commissions used the unprecedented increase in state education funds as an excuse to ignore local funding responsibilities. Rather than use achievement tests as a means of identifying problems, many superintendents and school boards assailed the validity of the tests when their systems posted low scores. In a scene reminiscent of the fable of the grasshopper and the ant, some local school boards put off lowering class size in the hope that the 2002 timetable for reduced classes would be repealed by the legislature.

Other limitations of the 1992 reforms became apparent. Improving the quality of superintendents and school boards cannot prevent bickering or ensure a commitment to excellence among county commissions, county executives, mayors, and the business community. Reforms do not eliminate political and religious agendas. Neither can they mitigate the problems of drugs or domestic violence that are fixtures in many Tennessee communities. Reforms can remove some ineffective principals and teachers, but not all of them. Most important, state-initiated reforms simply cannot supplant local attitudes about the importance of education. Where attitudes of indifference exist, no combination of funding, academic standards, or any other policy change will make a great deal of difference.

Tennessee's experience with education reform provides two valuable lessons. First, unlike their counterparts in several southern states, the majority of Tennesseans genuinely want their public schools to do well. If provided a sense of participation and the ability to judge how schools are performing, they will extend enormous latitude to other initiatives. Second, one must have realistic expectations about the potential of any reform effort and what one defines as success. No policy, no matter how well conceived or how well implemented, can overcome cultural and political obstacles in each of the state's 138 school systems. In such a context, significant progress in only two-thirds or even one-half of the state's two thousand schools might be considered a victory.

As the new century unfolded, Tennessee's K–12 educational system, at least at the state level, focused upon issues that were more philosophical in nature. In a move interpreted by some as a lack of confidence in public education, Governor Sundquist and the conservative wing of the Republican Party pushed unsuccessfully for state-funded Charter Schools, formed and administered apart from local school boards. Black legislators from Memphis advocated wearing school uniforms as a means of instilling more discipline among students. Families who home-schooled their children increasingly included middle-class families with educational rather than religious motivation, a fact that forced the legislature to address home-schooling issues in a different context. As important as these issues were to those directly involved, they were insignificant compared to the educational battles that characterized the eight-year period from 1984 to 1992 and shaped the future of Tennessee's K–12 system.

The scope of education reforms in 1984 and 1992 made it unlikely that similar efforts would take place for some time in Tennessee. The road map was set and the distance known: halfway home and a long way to go.

Higher Education

The collection of institutions that includes four-year universities, two-year community colleges, and some two-dozen technology centers comprises Tennessee's public system of higher education. Apart from the intense loyalty that many Tennesseans share with the University of Tennessee's athletic teams, it would be accurate to say that most citizens do not have an emotional attachment to higher education similar to that associated with their local K–12 schools. Because higher education is not managed by a local board, and because the majority of Tennesseans do not have a direct association with higher education, the issues and needs of higher education often are not a priority with much of the public, and, as a consequence, with their elected representatives. This detachment brings both good and bad results. Higher education by and large can conduct its business insulated from many of the political issues that complicate the management of K–12 schools. At the same time, the public's lack of clear understanding about the value of higher education to the state's economic vitality sometimes makes it difficult to achieve the level of funding needed to provide high-quality faculty and programs. The state's higher education program is divided into two systems: the University of Tennessee and the Board of Regents system.

The University of Tennessee

The University of Tennessee, founded in 1794 as Blount College two years before statehood, contains undergraduate campuses in Knoxville (fig. 11.3), Chattanooga, and Martin. The UT Memphis campus houses

Fig. 11.3. Ayres Hall, University of Tennessee, Knoxville. The University of Tennessee is the flagship of the state's system of higher education. Photo by John M. Scheb II.

the university's professional programs in medicine, dentistry, pharmacy, and nursing. The UT Space Institute in Tullahoma is a graduate campus focused on programs in physics, computer science, engineering, and mathematics. Tennessee's flagship institution of higher education is the University of Tennessee's Knoxville campus, the state's federal land grant university and its only public Carnegie I research institution. In 1999, the University of Tennessee joined with the Battelle Memorial Institute in a successful bid to manage the Oak Ridge National Laboratory. Assuming joint management of the laboratory was a major milestone in UT's goal of becoming a leader among the nation's academic research institutions.

State Board of Regents

Tennessee's remaining public higher education institutions are managed by the State Board of Regents. Created in 1972 and headquartered in Nashville, the Board of Regents has a much larger collective enrollment than the University of Tennessee. The Regents have six four-year undergraduate universities: East Tennessee State University in Johnson City, Tennessee Tech in Cookeville, Middle Tennessee State University in Murfreesboro, Tennessee State University in Nashville, Austin Peay State University in Clarksville, and the University of Memphis. Comprehensive Technical Community Colleges are located in Blountville, Knoxville, Chattanooga, Nashville, and Memphis. The Regents also operate nine community colleges and twenty-six technology centers that focus on providing students occupational and technical training.

Tennessee Higher Education Commission

In an effort to avoid the problem of having each institution lobbying the legislature for annual appropriations, the General Assembly in 1967 created the Tennessee Higher Education Commission (THEC). The entity was given the mission of providing a rational and equitable policy of recommending what academic programs an institution should offer and how much state funds each institution should receive. Each fall THEC receives budget requests from the University of Tennessee and the Board of Regents for operational funds and capital funds for new facilities. THEC in turn prioritizes these requests and submits a single funding request for public higher education to the Governor's Commissioner of Finance and Administration.

In theory, THEC's funding requests would be transferred by the Governor to the General Assembly in the administration's proposed state budget. In practice, however, it is common for governors to rearrange spending priorities for higher education based on a variety of educational and political needs. The need, for example, to have all areas of the state feel they have been treated fairly may motivate the Governor to make sure that each of the state's four major cities receives a new facility for its institution, regardless of whether the proposal was recommended by THEC. Over the years THEC board members have also been know to rearrange staff funding priorities by swapping votes for projects in their home communities. These actions, while not unusual in the democratic process, have compromised the credibility and effectiveness of the Higher Education Commission as an oversight board for Tennessee's institutions.

Can Tennessee Higher Education Be Better Managed?

Every few years the Governor and the General Assembly address the issue of how Tennessee's system of higher education is managed.

More specifically, they question whether having three separate higher education boards—two governing boards and a coordinating board—represents the best use of resources and produces the best quality of education. The most recent such study occurred in the late 1990s when Gov. Don Sundquist openly criticized higher education's level of administrative spending. For a variety of reasons, the issue has never been resolved to the satisfaction of all parties.

No real pattern of higher education governance exists in America. One finds all combinations of single governing boards, multiple governing boards, and coordinating boards. Equally important, one finds higher education products of varying quality scattered among the diverse structures of governance. Although Texas has multiple systems, Virginia has two, and North Carolina has only one, all have what most consider high-quality institutions. Across the country, each state's system is a product of largely unique factors that include history, geography, and the influence of individuals whose leadership shaped higher education for decades. In Tennessee, the University of Tennessee system evolved over two centuries from a single campus in Knoxville. This history, when combined with a highly visible athletics program, gives UT, more so than its Regents counterpart, a greater sense of identity and political cohesiveness. The Regents system, while larger than UT, has not yet developed a comparable identity among most Tennesseans.

While the 1998 study of Tennessee's higher education system was critical of its quality and management structure, the study failed to convince a majority of legislators that rearranging the governance chairs would address adequately the basic issues of access, competitive faculty salaries, externally funded research, and academic standards that affect the reputation of Tennessee's higher education system. The debate over governance, like the K–12 debate over prayer in schools, was viewed by some as an effort to find a simple answer to a complicated problem. Until Tennessee's institutions were able to compete for the best faculty and the best students, discussions about governing boards would have little relevance to the future of the state's system of higher education.

Higher Education Issues

Tennessee's higher education system confronts, aside from governance, two fundamental issues that shape a variety of decisions by the legislature and the various institutions. These issues have played a part in the state's higher education system for nearly four decades.

Institutional Mission

The term "institutional mission" is a fancy way of expressing the skills and programs an institution is supposed to provide to the public. As a land grant institution, the University of Tennessee has a broad and generally accepted mission of teaching, research, and public service. UT's mission includes agricultural assistance to farmers, providing technical expertise to cities and counties, and a broad array of research to aid the state's industrial community. UT also provides graduate professional programs in most fields.

Beyond agreeing on the basic mission for UT's Knoxville campus, legislators, governing boards, and much of the public have never produced a mutually accepted sense of what the state's other institutions should do. Each institution, supported by its community, naturally seeks to provide the broadest possible range of academic programs without regard to the collective cost, or need, of these programs in a state with limited resources. Despite its noble intent, the Tennessee Higher Education Commission has been unable to limit the presence of multiple programs such as agriculture and engineering that generate high costs for a limited number of students. The reasons for this failure are found in the inability to overcome political opposition to closing programs once they are started. Thus, while most agree that Tennessee's schools have an oversupply of some programs, few legislators are prepared to begin the reduction process knowing that programs in their district will likely make the list.

Even more expensive than the presence of low-producing academic programs has been the proliferation of branch campuses throughout the state. In a climate of intense competition for new industry, every community sought the advantage of having some kind of higher education facility available to train potential workers. Most communities were willing to pay for most or all of the cost of a building to house the programs if they could be associated with a two-year or four-year institution. The project would become a rallying point for the community and one that area legislators used as a bargaining chip with the Governor. Over a period of about twenty years from the early 1980s until the close of the century, branch campuses sprang up like clover in dozens of small towns across Tennessee. Once established, the system was unable to restrict their growth and mission. By the time Governor Sundquist sought to curtail its growth, the number of branch campuses had become a fiscal spigot that could not be turned off.

Desegregation

Like most southern states, Tennessee has a legacy of segregated higher education. Until the 1960s, black students were not allowed to attend the University of Tennessee and other state institutions. Most attended Nashville's Tennessee State University, a federal land grant institution that enjoyed a national reputation for its athletic teams. As increasing numbers of black students began enrolling at formerly all-white schools, including the University of Tennessee at Nashville, Tennessee State attracted very few white students. The result was the presence in Nashville of two state universities, one integrated and one essentially segregated.

When UT Nashville opened a new downtown campus in 1968, Rita Geier sued the state on behalf of Tennessee State, arguing it was unconstitutional to provide what amounted to a dual system of higher education. After nine years in the courts, the University of Tennessee was forced to close its Nashville campus and merge its faculty and facilities with Tennessee State University. The ruling unleashed a range of emotions from both parties. The goal of the ruling was a single institution in Nashville with a student body that reflected the city's racial mix—about 80 percent white and 20 percent black. Twenty-five years after the merger, Tennessee State's white student enrollment was less than 20 percent, with the number of resident white students almost nonexistent.

The *Geier* ruling had statewide significance. The court embarked on an ambitious and complicated course that established racial "goals" for every institution in Tennessee, sometimes without regard to a host of factors that influence student enrollments. UT Knoxville, for example, was given a goal of tripling its black enrollment to 11 percent, despite the fact that half of the state's black high school graduates came from Shelby County, more than four hundred miles away. Taken together, the court's racial goals for Tennessee's institutions totaled more black students that existed in the entire state. In fairness, the process brought about by the *Geier* litigation did produce needed improvements in the number of black faculty, administrators, and students than might have otherwise occurred at most institutions. What the court could not change, however, is the basic fact that students ultimately will enroll where they choose. One cannot entice enough students or threaten enough institutions to overcome forces that are deeply embedded in the culture of groups and communities across the state.

Assessing the Politics of Education

Education remains in many ways the most politicized issue confronting the Governor and the General Assembly. Education's presence in every community and its position as the largest item in the state budget ensures that debates over adequate funding and academic standards will continue to dominate political campaigns and legislative agendas. Despite significant strides since 1985 in funding and quality for Tennessee's K-12 schools, the debates likely will continue to form along traditional patterns. Rural counties will seek greater funding support from the state at the expense of urban counties. Some communities will encourage more sophisticated testing instruments to measure student performance while in other communities teachers and administrators will resist efforts to link such testing to sanctions or financial rewards. The multitude of education stakeholders will pit school boards against county commissions and school superintendents against local elected officials.

Other trends in Tennessee education are less predictable. Most communities still retain substantial support for public education, making it hard to determine if the growth of private schools in states such as South Carolina and Mississippi will be repeated in Tennessee. This issue will be influenced by the fact that adequate funding in the future for public education is tied directly to the ability of Tennessee's tax structure to generate sufficient revenues. At the close of the century, no one could predict with certainty if and how the emotional issue of tax reform would be resolved. Finally, it is unclear to what extent the federal government will pursue efforts to develop and implement national standards for students and teachers. Although none of these issues is within the ability of state or local education officials to control, each could have a lasting impact on the quality and public support of Tennessee's schools.

The future of higher education is equally unclear. The broad public support enjoyed by the University of Tennessee in the late 1990s did not translate into the level of political support and state funding needed to keep pace with its peers. Other state institutions, despite steady enrollment growth, did not experience the funding increases enjoyed by colleges in almost every state during the decade's economic boom. Funding pressures were made worse by the ad-hoc growth of two-year branch colleges in Tennessee's smaller communities. Faced with flat funding levels for much of the decade, higher education was forced to implement historic tuition increases to pay for salary increases and technology investments. As with Tennessee's K-12 schools, higher education's future was linked directly to whether the political system could modernize the state's tax structure.

Despite these challenges, Tennessee's education program has reason for optimism. The dramatic increases in state funding in the 1990s, particularly in the state's poorest communities, closed much of the historic gap that had existed between rural and urban schools. The appointment of school superintendents, while controversial in some communities, brought more professionalism to local administration and more accountability to parents and local school boards. As a result of reforms, the number of accredited school systems rose sharply, as did graduation rates and the number of Tennessee students who took advanced placement courses. Course options in many schools were broader, and the average class size was smaller. When cast against conditions in the early 1980s, one could argue that Tennessee schools, on the whole, had made considerable gains.

Ironically, these gains sometimes prove to be an obstacle to continued progress. Many communities, taking justifiable pride in the gains of the 1980s and 1990s, do not realize that their schools still fall short of the standards needed for Tennessee to compete successfully in the future for new investments and jobs. Increasingly complex technologies and an information-based economy demand that schools continue the pressure to upgrade standards and expectations. Simply having local support for community schools will not be enough to ensure success. Only those education systems that embrace the idea of a "continuing revolution" will be positioned to compete and win. Whether Tennessee is up to this challenge will depend ultimately on the vision and leadership of future governors and legislators.

12

Health, Welfare, and the Environment

The forty-year-old woman had worked hard all of her life, for the last fifteen years as a waitress in Dyersburg. Although she knew that one day she would collect Social Security, she struggled. Her husband of twenty years was killed in an industrial accident, leaving her with two teenage children, no pension, and no life insurance. She felt an increasing sense of vulnerability. What if she became ill and had to be hospitalized? The little restaurant did not provide health insurance to its five employees. For the past five years, she and her children had been covered by TennCare, Tennessee's bold makeover of Medicaid, designed to help the working uninsured. But now TennCare seemed to be in financial crisis. As she cleaned the table of its glasses and dishes, she wondered whether TennCare would be there when they needed it.

Many people in Tennessee, as in all other states, suffer economic hardship. While this deprivation may fall short of the abject poverty experienced in some areas of the world, it is poverty nonetheless. Prior to the 1930s, people in need looked to their families or their churches for assistance. Today citizens across the country, including those in Tennessee, expect government to provide assistance when individuals are unable to care for themselves, their parents, or their children. Many refer to this as government's obligation to provide a "safety net" of basic services.

One of the most basic services is health care. The federal and state governments share responsibility for providing this service to indigent persons. Another basic service is "welfare," or, as it has been called more recently, "human services." Here, too, federal and state governments work cooperatively to help the poor acquire food, housing, and care for children.

As in other states, protecting the health of five million Tennesseans includes efforts by state government to regulate a number of serious environmental issues. The state's environment is threatened by a wide range of economic activities, including mining, agriculture, manufacturing, and power generation. A variety of other items, including automobile emissions, leaking underground storage tanks, and outdated sewage systems, also threaten the state's air and water. Growing cities and increased consumption create enormous pressures to manage waste safely. Sprawling residential and commercial development threatens environmentally sensitive forests and wetlands and intensifies the danger that threatened animal species will become extinct.

Under what is termed "cooperative federalism," Tennessee shares responsibility with the federal government in three major program areas—health, welfare, and the environment. This cooperation has not always been present. As with other programs, the federal government's role has ebbed and flowed in response to the political philosophy of those in power.[1]

Welfare Policy

In contrast to many European countries, the United States traditionally has been reluctant to involve government in providing public assistance to the needy. Such assistance traditionally was viewed as the responsibility of the family or the church. Prior to the Great Depression in 1929, government assistance was minimal, and that little was provided mainly by local governments. As the United States became increasingly urbanized and children lived farther from their parents, family ties weakened. This trend coincided with the arrival of millions of European immigrants between 1890 and 1920, many of whom brought with them the notion that government should provide aid for citizens in economic distress.

State governments, however, were ill-equipped to accept these responsibilities, because they did not possess the economic resources and because often they were dominated by business and agricultural interests who were not particularly sympathetic to the plight of the poor.

The human tragedy of the Great Depression that began in 1929 and lasted through most of the 1930s wrought a historic shift in American attitudes about government aid and about which government should provide that aid. The crumbling economy pushed millions into unemployment for the first time in their lives. To the extent that they existed at all, state and local government welfare programs were grossly inadequate to meet the unprecedented need for assistance. As the economic depression worsened in 1932, many Americans looked with desperation toward a future marked by poverty and suffering. Beginning in 1933, under the mantle of what he called a "New Deal," newly elected President Franklin Roosevelt greatly expanded the role of the federal government in providing what came to be known as a "safety net" for poor Americans.

One of Roosevelt's major policy initiatives was the Old Age, Survivors, and Disability Insurance Act of 1935, known today as Social Security. Based on a German model, it requires workers to pay part of their wages into the Social Security system through a payroll tax. When they retire, each worker receives an income based on the amount paid into the fund before retirement. The program is not "welfare" in the classic sense, because benefits are not limited to the needy.

The Social Security Act of 1935 also created a program entitled Aid to Families with Dependent Children (AFDC), which would become a mainstay of federal welfare policy. Unlike Social Security, AFDC provided benefits only to categories of persons deemed "needy." The definition of who is and is not "needy" has changed over time and remains a topic of intense political debate. AFDC benefits were funded out of general revenues rather than a special trust fund—a fact that would have serious budgetary and political implications as the years went by.

The creation of Social Security and AFDC during the New Deal represented an important step in the creation of America's policy for social welfare. For the first time, the federal government was establishing a safety net, a guaranteed level of support beneath which individuals would not be allowed to fall. The bitter disagreements between Democrats and Republicans that surrounded these programs continue to the present day.

Roughly thirty years after Roosevelt's New Deal, President Lyndon Johnson declared a "War on Poverty" to address the needs of millions of poor Americans. Seeking to build what he termed the "Great Society," Johnson during the mid-1960s convinced Congress to expand the AFDC program and create the Food Stamp program, an attempt to address hunger by providing needy persons with stamps they could redeem for food items at grocery stores. Even more significant in a financial sense were Johnson's attempts to provide health care to the poor by creating Medicare and Medicaid. Medicare pays for health care for citizens over age sixty-five. Like Social Security, Medicare is funded through a payroll tax and provides health care benefits to seniors, regardless of financial need. Medicaid, on the other hand, was established to provide medical care only for the poor, usually defined as those eligible for AFDC benefits. Partly because of the tremendous expenditures required to conduct the war in Vietnam, Johnson's dream of an American "Great Society" was never realized. Nevertheless, by the end of his administration in 1968, America had in place five major programs—Social Security, AFDC, Food Stamps, Medicare, and Medicaid. These became the foundation of the nation's—and Tennessee's—welfare system.

By design, the states play virtually no role in Social Security and Medicare. They do play a major role in the administration of AFDC, Food Stamps, and Medicaid, however. Although the bulk of the funding comes from the federal budget, the states administer the programs and have some discretion in deciding the eligibility rules governing who receives benefits. This arrangement came to be known as "cooperative federalism."

During the 1980s and 1990s, many critics expressed growing concern over AFDC, which provided checks each month to women and children when there was no man in the home. Critics asserted that AFDC, by giving funds only to single mothers, was fostering an increase in the number of unwed mothers and a decline in the traditional two-parent family. From the 1960s through the 1990s, statistics regarding welfare dependency seemed to support this criticism. The number of families with no male head of household had increased markedly throughout society, but the increase had been most dramatic among the poor. Women who went on AFDC to support their children found it very difficult later to go to work and stop depending on welfare. Children who grew up in families dependent on welfare often failed to acquire job skills and in turn became dependent on welfare as adults.

The Republican takeover of both houses of Congress in 1994 led to the enactment of federal welfare reform designed to address this cycle of welfare dependency. In 1996, AFDC was replaced by Temporary Assistance for Needy Families, in which federal welfare funds are provided to the states in the form of block grants, allowing the states considerable flexibility in determining who is eligible for welfare assistance.[2] The result in many states, including Tennessee, was significant changes in the benefits and expectations of traditional welfare programs.

Welfare Reform

When Don Sundquist ran for Governor of Tennessee in 1994, he emphasized welfare reform as one of his major goals. Upon his election, Sundquist appointed special assistant Leonard Bradley to devise a welfare reform initiative. By November 1995, the Governor announced the Families First program. When the General Assembly convened in 1996, legislators enacted sweeping reforms by overwhelming margins in the House (93–2) and the Senate (29–1). The margins were significant because they reflected a belief even among legislators with large welfare constituencies that the system needed to be changed. Because Tennessee's new program replaced AFDC, approval from the federal Department of Health and Human Services was required. On July 25, 1996, U.S. Vice President Al Gore, formerly Tennessee's U.S. Senator, delivered the news to Governor Sundquist that Families First had been approved. Families First became law on September 1, 1996.[3]

The stated goals of Families First were to reduce the number of persons on welfare, to strengthen families, and to improve the quality of Tennessee's workforce. Contrary to the popular expectation that reducing the number of welfare recipients would save the state money, Families First actually cost considerably more than the program it replaced. Governor Sundquist described the program in the following terms: "Instead of an open-ended entitlement for anyone who qualifies, we are creating a program of time-limited assistance for people who want to work. Instead of signing people up to get checks, we're going to be offering them a contract—a Personal Responsibility Contract with the State of Tennessee. It is a contract that says, we will help you make the transition to self-sufficiency, but you have to work; everybody else does."[4]

Families First differed from AFDC in several ways. Key to the program, and standing in sharp contrast to AFDC, were strict time limits on receiving benefits. Cash benefits were limited to eighteen months and total lifetime benefits to five years. Moreover, benefits did not increase as beneficiaries had additional children.

To receive cash, each person had to file an individual Personal Responsibility Plan (PRP). The plan placed the recipient in an educational or training program geared to finding employment. The PRP also required that parents play an active role in taking responsibility for their children, through such activities as required immunizations and school attendance. All recipients were given childcare assistance, TennCare coverage for health services, transportation, food stamps, and a rent freeze in public housing. Funding these new programs was responsible for a substantial net increase in the cost of Tennessee's welfare system.

The Families First program revolutionized both the philosophy and the administration of Tennessee's welfare system. The number of Tennesseans receiving welfare assistance was reduced substantially during the program's initial year. As anticipated, many were purged from the welfare roles because they refused to sign the personal responsibility agreement. Thirty percent of those who participated gained employment, while large numbers enrolled in job training or education programs. The program placed the state within the national movement to eliminate welfare dependency.

Between October 1997 and September 1998, 62 percent of unemployed welfare recipients obtained employment, according to figures released by the Governor's office. In December 1999, the state received a $6.4 million "bonus" grant from the federal government for its success in moving people off the welfare rolls and into productive employment.

It is difficult to make an objective assessment of the results of Families First. Reductions in Tennessee's welfare population differed little from changes in dozens of other states during the period of explosive economic growth of the 1990s. In addition, how one views the program's value depends in part on one's expectations. Those who wanted to reduce the growing cost of welfare were disappointed. These facts aside, most Tennesseans are more comfortable with a program of welfare benefits that places time limits on benefits and some measure of responsibility on the recipient.

Public Health and the Delivery of Health Care Services

Protecting the public's health is a major responsibility of modern state government. Since the 1960s, the cost of Tennessee government's role in health care has grown from a small part of the state budget to one of the largest and most controversial of state expenditures. At the state level, public health policy involves a wide range of issues, including sanitation, communicable diseases, and the provision of vital health services to all citizens, regardless of their ability to pay. Perhaps more than any other state service, health care programs reflect a growing belief on the part of the public that government has an obligation to serve a wide range of health needs. At the end of the twentieth century, what services to provide and how to pay for them were two of the most serious questions facing Tennessee state government.

Tennessee Department of Health

Following epidemics of cholera and yellow fever that struck the state's large cities in the 1800s, there was a growing belief that the state needed a Cabinet-level department to coordinate the state's public health programs. In 1923, the General Assembly created the Department of Public Health, which in 1983 was expanded and renamed the Department of Health and Environment. In 1991, the enormous scope of the department's responsibilities prompted the General Assembly to break off environmental responsibilities and assign them to a new department—Environment and Conservation. That change left the renamed Department of Health to focus exclusively on matters of public health.

The Tennessee Department of Health has a mission to insure that health services are available to all Tennesseans and to promote the health of the general public. The department works with the federal Centers for Disease Control in monitoring potential epidemics. Department staff also collect data on the Tennessee population that are relevant to health concerns. Among the major public health tasks performed by the department is making immunizations available to all Tennesseans. While this program provides obvious benefits to individuals and families, it also contributes to the health of the community at large. The department supports community health standards by facilitating prenatal care for pregnant women, recruiting physicians for underserved areas, and setting standards for public drinking water. Among the department's more visible tasks is sanitation inspections of restaurants and public posting of their grades. The department also acts as an oversight body regulating the standards and performance of a wide variety of health care entities, such as doctors, dentists, and nursing homes.

From Medicaid to TennCare

Some find it curious that the Department of Health does not manage Tennessee's largest health care responsibility: providing health care services to the more than one million Tennesseans who lack the ability to pay. In most states, this service is provided by the Medicaid program under a cooperative arrangement between the states and the federal government.

In Tennessee, Medicaid is funded by roughly two-thirds federal and one-third state dollars under rules made by the Health Care Finance Administration (HCFA) in the U.S. Department of Health and Human Services. Under this arrangement, the federal government provides matching funding, but states have considerable discretion in deciding who is eligible for Medicaid benefits. One finds very liberal definitions of eligibility in such states as Minnesota and New York, and much more restrictive standards in most southern states. Since its inception in the late 1960s, Medicaid costs have soared in response to the expansion of eligibility and rapid increases in the cost of medical services. In Tennessee as elsewhere, payments for health care services for the poor have grown faster than any other part of the state budget, including corrections.

An additional problem is that hundreds of thousands of working citizens do not have health insurance. Many employers do not provide health insurance, especially for part-time workers. Although some people who lack coverage actively have chosen not to purchase health insurance, many cannot afford the high cost of individual policies. Prior to 1993, most of these uninsured Tennesseans went to hospital emergency rooms when they needed medical attention, producing large medical bills that were never paid.

Tennessee provided its indigent health care services through Medicaid until 1993, when Gov. Ned McWherter and Finance Commissioner David Manning developed the innovative TennCare program. McWherter acted under mounting pressure on the state budget. In a period of about ten years, health care costs had exploded, rising from roughly 10 percent of the state budget to approximately 25 percent of all state expenditures. The election of McWherter's friend, Gov. Bill Clinton of Arkansas, as President of the United States in 1992 provided an opening for Tennessee to seek a waiver from federal Medicaid policies. At McWherter's urging, the Clinton administration pressured the U.S. Department of Health and Human Services to allow states to propose new ways of providing health care traditionally managed through the Medicaid program. Under this process, states petitioned HCFA to experiment with alternative programs that would provide comparable services at lower costs. Governor McWherter's proposal to replace Medicaid was called TennCare. The plan promised to continue fulfilling the mission of Medicaid, while expanding the program to include persons (particularly the working poor) who previously had been uninsured or uninsurable. Amid much skepticism, McWherter claimed that Tennessee could add some four hundred thousand uninsured Tennesseans to the existing eight hundred thousand Medicaid recipients and still save the state a billion dollars over the first five years of the program.

TennCare was an ambitious plan in several respects. One of TennCare's goals was to stop Medicaid's practice of cutting off health care benefits for those who showed employment initiative by getting a job. For these "working poor," TennCare premiums were established on a sliding scale for incomes above the federal poverty level.

Projected cost savings under TennCare were based on the concept of "managed care," which was the centerpiece of the Clinton administration's health care reform initiative. Managed care involves the use of managed care organizations. An MCO is a private company that utilizes networks of doctors, hospitals, clinics, and other health care providers to provide health care services for clients enrolled with that MCO. The MCOs would bid against each other to provide services at the lowest rate. Under TennCare, the state was divided into twelve geographical areas called Community Health Agencies (CHAs), with several MCOs operating in each CHA. TennCare recipients could select any MCO operating within their area. If they did not select an MCO, one was selected for them. Initially, total TennCare enrollment was capped at 1.4 million. By the end of the first year, enrollment was 1.27 million, which included 850,000 former Medicaid recipients and 419,000 formerly uninsured. Thus, nearly 25 percent of the state's population was enrolled in TennCare. The aggressive approach to enrollment reduced the proportion of uninsured in Tennessee to 6 percent by the end of 1994.[5] In less than a year, TennCare had produced in Tennessee the lowest number of uninsured citizens among the fifty states.

TennCare added a number of players who radically changed the politics of health care policy. Foremost among these were the MCOs, each of which received money from the state based on the number of people enrolled with it, whether by choice or assignment. MCOs negotiated with the state for an across-the-board fee per "covered life," including people in very expensive treatment categories. The MCOs in turn reimbursed physicians in its network for services rendered to those covered. The MCO had an incentive to pay as little as possible to those providing the treatment, since the MCO's profit, in effect, was the difference between what it received from the state and what it paid to physicians. Each MCO had to insure that enough general practitioners and specialists were available to provide services to its subscribers.

The revolutionary policy change under TennCare was the idea of paying a fixed amount to MCOs for each individual Tennessean served. Under the old "fee for service" policy, Medicaid had paid any cost charged by any doctor or hospital, with no questions asked.

For the most part, those who participated in the new TennCare program gave it high marks. After a brief adjustment period, people on the program compared it favorably to Medicaid (see table 12.1). Given the fact that TennCare limited a patient's choice of physicians and hospitals, these results were quite encouraging.

TABLE 12.1

SATISFACTION WITH MEDICAID AND TENNCARE, 1993–1998

1993	*1994*	*1995*	*1996*	*1997*	*1998*
Medicaid	*TennCare*	*TennCare*	*TennCare*	*TennCare*	*TennCare*
82	61	75	82	81	83

SOURCE: Statewide telephone survey of TennCare enrollees, conducted by Social Science Research Institute, University of Tennessee, Knoxville, November 1998.

From the point of view of the average recipient, TennCare could have been declared a success. TennCare also appeared to benefit many small businesses that took advantage of TennCare to cut back on company-paid health care benefits, steering their employees to TennCare. This use of the system led the proportion of TennCare enrollees who were of lower income (that is, Medicaid-eligible) to decline from 70 percent to 60 percent between 1996 and 1998.[6]

TennCare was a very innovative approach to a growing problem, and it received attention nationwide. It resulted in savings of billions of dollars over what would have been budgeted under the old Medicaid program. However, TennCare was conceived and implemented rapidly, and confusion among providers and patients, as well as abuse of the program's benefits, threatened TennCare's survival. Because estimates of enrollees and premiums were about 1 percent off target, TennCare finished its first year with a $99 million deficit. The need to control future costs forced TennCare administrators to halt enrollment of uninsured citizens with incomes over Medicaid eligibility limits as of January 1, 1995, and to delay coverage for the chronically mentally ill.[7]

During a period when the need for management was at its greatest, TennCare suffered from a high turnover rate in administrators during the Sundquist administration. By the 1999 legislative session, TennCare's costs showed signs of spinning out of control. TennCare covered almost one in four Tennesseans, or 1.3 million people, and projections were that it would grow to 1.5 million by the end of the year. For a variety of reasons, from MCO mismanagement to insurance companies' practice of "dumping" their sickest patients on TennCare, many MCOs and hospitals were losing money. One of the state's largest health care providers, Vanderbilt University Hospital, lost more than $20 million dollars on TennCare patients in 1998.[8] One MCO, Xantus, which covered 150,000 enrollees, was on the verge of bankruptcy after allegations of mismanagement. By the end of 1999, Blue Cross, Tennessee's largest provider of health insurance, was threatening to pull out of TennCare due to financial losses.

In many ways, TennCare had become a victim of its own success. It created new incentives for both individuals and businesses. Much of the problem stemmed from the decision to extend the previous Medicaid program to the uninsured. Many Tennesseans who otherwise could afford private insurance found that TennCare benefits were cheaper and more generous than those obtained through private insurance. TennCare also increasingly became responsible for the care for very expensive persons, including those with AIDS.

In December 1999, Governor Sundquist proposed a series of adjustments to the TennCare program, including closing enrollment to adults ineligible for Medicaid and limiting prescriptions, home health visits, and other services. The proposed changes, which had to be approved by the federal Health Care Financing Administration, caused advocacy groups and service recipients to worry that the state was about to implement serious reductions in the quality of health care services.

By the end of 1999, the jury was still out on TennCare. Clearly, the program had put Tennessee in the forefront among states experimenting with creative solutions to the problems of health care delivery and financing. Tens of thousands of working Tennesseans who previously had lacked health care coverage now could obtain services for their families. An antiquated Medicaid system that had paid six times more for delivering a baby in Nashville than in Johnson City had been completely revamped. Tennessee's government had injected the health care industry with a serious dose of free-market competition. At the same time, TennCare had been forced to rely upon companies that had little experience in managing programs of such size and complexity. Many doctors and hospitals resented the cost restrictions imposed by TennCare; despite their otherwise conservative politics, they preferred the former program of government-funded fee-for-service health care. Some companies abused the system, and in many cases those in

Nashville who were responsible for monitoring abuses of TennCare were asleep at the wheel.

In summary, TennCare was at once the most liberal and most conservative of initiatives. At the end of the twentieth century, whether TennCare would live up to its considerable promise was a question still unanswered.

Protecting the Environment

Across the state line in North Carolina, Ned Ray McWherter quietly slipped into the canoe between one of his aides and an agent for the Tennessee Wildlife Resources Agency. The river above the Champion Paper mill was perfectly clear, and the Governor could see the rocks on the bottom. About one thousand yards downstream, the party drifted closer to the paper mill, belching smoke on their right. Directly across from the mill, they passed through a bubbling pool the color and thickness of motor oil. From this point on, the river was dark as Coca-Cola. As the canoe approached the shore about a mile downstream, the party was met by the county's sheriff. The sheriff informed the Governor's aide that the party was guilty of unlawful trespassing. Asked for an explanation, the sheriff's answer captured the essence of a controversy that had raged for fifty years: "You're trespassing on Champion's river."

Since the first Earth Day was celebrated in 1973, Americans have become increasingly concerned about the quality of the country's natural environment. The federal government has played a leading role in environmental protection, with the creation of the Environmental Protection Agency in 1970 and the enactment of a number of important environmental statutes, including the Clean Water Act and the Clean Air Act.[9] Increasingly, the states also have become more active in protecting their natural resources. Environmental policy today is a complex web of regulations and enforcement activities at both state and federal levels.[10]

The state's earliest concern with the environment had more to do with public health issues than with preservation of natural resources. Under the Department of Health's division of sanitary engineering, which began keeping track of water pollution by 1930, the focus was on sanitation. In 1937, the General Assembly began to take action to protect fish and game in the state by creating the Department of Conservation. The department administered laws passed by the General Assembly to limit and regulate hunting and fishing. Two years later, the department took over the management of state parks. Later, in 1949, the Tennessee Wildlife Resources Agency assumed charge of programs dealing with hunting and fishing. Until the 1970s, these agencies represented the bulk of Tennessee's environmental efforts.

Tennessee Wildlife Resources Agency

The Tennessee Wildlife Resources Agency (TWRA) was established in 1949 as the Game and Fish Commission. TWRA was reorganized under its present name in 1974 and charged with preserving, conserving, and enhancing Tennessee's fish and wildlife. Governed by a thirteen-member commission, TWRA is funded primarily through income from its sale of hunting and fishing licenses and permits. TWRA operates through four regional offices.

TWRA touches the lives of Tennesseans involved in a variety of sporting activities. Many in this group are intensely interested in state policy and enforcement. Not surprisingly, the TWRA is perhaps the most overtly politicized of state agencies dealing with the environment. Tennesseans who hunt and fish often become emotional about TWRA policies that raise fees or restrict the length of hunting and fishing seasons or the amount of fish and game that can be caught. Persons in many regions of Tennessee who care little about health care or education policy sometimes become politically active in response to TWRA decisions. Appointment to the TWRA board is one of the most coveted and competitive rewards in Tennessee's political system.

Department of Environment and Conservation

By the late 1960s, public concern about deterioration of the environment for the first time placed the issue near the top of the national policy agenda. Prior to the passage of federal legislation mandating stricter regulation of air and water, most states did little to monitor or sanction industries and municipalities that fouled the environment. The same pattern existed in Tennessee, where serious efforts to regulate industrial discharges into rivers and streams, disposal of garbage and toxic wastes, and release of gases into the atmosphere did not begin until the 1970s. Originally housed in the Department of Health and Environment, the state's environmental enforcement programs were split off in the 1990s and, along with the state parks, placed within a new Department of Environment and Conservation.

The Tennessee Department of Environment and Conservation's mission is "to enhance the quality of life of all Tennesseans and to be stewards of our natural environment." The department's responsibilities are broad in scope, including not only the monitoring of air and water quality and enforcement of related regulations, but also provision of recreational services through the state parks system.

The department's Division of Environment is responsible for the politically sensitive task of monitoring air and water pollution in the state. The division's Air Pollution Control staff investigates possible violations of airborne emissions standards set by the Air Pollution Control Board, established in 1967 to determine what levels of pollutants an industry is allowed to put into the air. The division investigates complaints and estimates the impact that new industries would have on air quality.

The Division of Environment also has responsibility for protecting Tennessee's water resources, including protecting groundwater from septic tank contamination and industrial discharge. The Water Pollution Control staff monitors discharges into the state's rivers and streams, investigates complaints, and issues permits to industries that would discharge pollutants into streams. Finally, the Division of Environment inspects municipal and district water supplies to make sure they meet standards set by the state and federal governments.

Most outsiders do not recognize the intensely political nature of many policies and actions that originate in the Division of Environment. The Commissioner of Environment and Conservation, and by extension the Governor, is faced with a serious problem when deciding whether to approve a new industry that will bring five hundred new jobs into the state but also contribute to an already polluted atmosphere. Likewise, political careers of mayors and county executives have been destroyed when the department denied landfill permits, leaving local communities without adequate means of garbage disposal. In Tennessee as in most states, environmental regulations sometimes have been bent or outright ignored in favor of broader political and economic considerations.

Hazardous Waste Regulation

As part of his plan for spreading economic development throughout each region of the state, Gov. Ned McWherter emphasized the need for a comprehensive policy for disposing the chemical wastes generated by the state's large and small businesses. Until the late 1980s, each industry was left largely on its own in determining how and where it could ship and dispose of industrial wastes. With few options and lax regulation, many industries dumped wastes into nearby rivers or stored them in barrels out of sight and out of mind. The result was widespread toxic pollution that threatened the health of thousands of Tennesseans.

In 1989, after extensive negotiations, McWherter signed a historic agreement with Kentucky, Alabama, and South Carolina. As part of the twenty-year agreement, Alabama and South Carolina would bury a portion of the toxic wastes in regulated sites, Kentucky would incinerate another portion, and Tennessee would recycle the remainder. For the first time, Tennessee industries had the ability to make long-term plans for their wastes, and communities could recruit new industries by offering the plan as an incentive.

In addition to industrial wastes, another large-scale environmental issue has dominated the attention of state government in Tennessee. The state is home to massive U.S. Department of Energy (DOE) facilities at Oak Ridge, about thirty miles from Knoxville. Since World War II, these facilities—the Oak Ridge National Laboratory, the Y–12 weapons plant, and the K–25 plant that produced enriched uranium—have been the site of nuclear weapons research and construction, as well as advanced scientific research in a number of areas. Prior to modern understanding of environmental risks, activities at Oak Ridge resulted in contamination of land and water over broad areas of the region. While DOE sought to organize the cleanup, the state played a prominent role in monitoring the process through a local oversight committee that reported to the Tennessee Department of Environment and Conservation.

For many years, groups like Save Our Cumberland Mountains and the Oak Ridge Peace Alliance had been alleging environmental and public health problems resulting from DOE's Oak Ridge operations. The issue gained greater visibility in 1997, when the *Nashville Tennessean* ran a widely read series on health problems in the area. The stories led to hearings in the General Assembly and the appointment of a special investigatory panel by the Governor. Although no scientific consensus emerged linking DOE facilities to widespread health problems, the controversy was a source of distrust between government regulators and citizens who felt threatened by the region's environmental legacies.

Pigeon River

The complexity of environmental policy is evident in the ongoing controversy over pollution of the Pigeon River, which runs out of Haywood County, North Carolina, into Cocke County, Tennessee. In 1908, the

Champion Paper Company opened a paper mill on the banks of the Pigeon River in Canton, North Carolina. The mill provided thousands of jobs for the people in western North Carolina and contributed significantly to the economic development of the region. However, the mill dumped its waste products directly into the river, transforming a pristine stream into a foul-smelling, brown-colored nuisance for people living downstream in Cocke County, Tennessee.[11]

Over the years, Tennessee residents living downstream complained about the river's color and smell. Some even suggested that dioxins released from the plant might be causing increased cancer rates in small communities along the river. For the most part, the complaints fell upon deaf ears. North Carolina officials were predictably concerned about the mill's economic benefits to their state. For several decades, there was little the State of Tennessee could do, even if officials in Nashville had been inclined to take action. In the 1970s, however, a regulatory mechanism was put in place to address problems like the pollution of the Pigeon River. The Federal Water Pollution Control Act Amendments of 1972,[12] better known as the Clean Water Act (CWA), created the National Pollutant Discharge Elimination System (NPDES). Federal law required any industry that discharged a pollutant into the waters of the United States to obtain an NPDES permit. The permits are issued by the U.S. Environmental Protection Agency (EPA) or by appropriate state agencies under authority delegated by EPA. Of course, EPA retains the authority to veto a state-issued permit and can withdraw a state's NPDES permitting authority for failure to enforce CWA standards.

Although the Champion plant failed to meet water quality standards mandated by CWA, the North Carolina Division of Environmental Management granted Champion a new permit in 1981. Granting of the permit prompted the formation in Tennessee of the Dead Pigeon River Council, created to call public attention to the river's pollution and bring pressure to bear on Champion, the EPA, and state officials in Tennessee and North Carolina. Although Champion in 1985 unveiled plans to modernize the plant, the plant's proposed discharge into the water still fell far short of CWA standards.

In 1985, the State of North Carolina issued another water quality permit to Champion, but this time EPA vetoed the state permit and assumed permitting authority for the Champion plant. Champion brought suit in federal court, challenging EPA's action, but lost.[13] The focus then turned to Tennessee, which could grant a water quality variance that would allow Champion to continue production at water quality standards higher than before but much lower than those demanded by affected Tennessee residents. Governor McWherter agonized over the decision, sympathetic to those who would lose their jobs in North Carolina and fearful that Champion might prevail in court if Tennessee denied the water quality variance. His deliberations included a personal trip by canoe down the river and secret discussions with Champion's chief executives. Finally, on Christmas Eve of 1989, McWherter informed North Carolina's Gov. James Martin that Tennessee would deny Champion's water quality variance. The news exploded on both sides of the state line. North Carolina for a period threatened retaliation in the form of economic boycotts, but these never materialized. In the face of negative national publicity, Champion announced a $350 million investment to upgrade its mill at Canton and meet water quality standards. In May 1999, Champion sold the mill to its 1,300 employees. Representatives of the renamed Blue Ridge Paper Company vowed to work to continue reducing pollution of the Pigeon River.

Assessing Heath, Welfare, and Environmental Policy

Health care, social welfare, and environmental policy are three areas in which the roles and responsibilities of state government expanded enormously during the last half of the twentieth century. The proliferation of these programs brought with it large increases in government spending and controversial debates about the proper role of government in providing services. These debates continue.

In Tennessee, the TennCare program has left unresolved several key questions: which citizens should be provided health care services, how these services should be provided, and who should pay for them. Most Tennesseans agree that the old welfare system was a disaster, but many are unsure whether Families First is an effective and affordable solution. Perhaps the most progress has been made in the area of cleaning up Tennessee's air and water. Although much remains to be done, most acknowledge that the state's rivers and streams are much cleaner today than three decades ago.

As the new century unfolds, one suspects that these issues will continue to hold center stage. Tennesseans and their representatives are not finished debating how much the state should pay to provide its citizens with high-quality health care, safe air and water, and a financial safety net below which no Tennessean will be allowed to fall.

13

Corrections

I chose to spend more time on people who obeyed the law than on people who broke the law.
Gov. Lamar Alexander

The Issue Nobody Wants

No area of state government is more challenging than corrections. Large numbers of Tennesseans care deeply about the quality of their schools and the accessibility of health care. Most are content to pay high gas taxes for good roads. They lobby their elected officials for clean air and clean water. They will, up to a point, support various programs of social welfare to assist the poor. Tennesseans on the whole are a good and compassionate people who turn absolutely cold on the issue of prisons.

Out of Sight and Out of Mind

Throughout the years, Tennessee governors and their administrations have received little public recognition or political gain from sound prison management. So long as prison overcrowding does not produce unacceptable backlogs of convicted felons in local jails or a court-ordered mass release of state inmates, most Tennesseans are indifferent to the issues of violence, overcrowding, idleness, and cost associated with prison management. Public indifference to prison conditions results in a predictable lack of enthusiasm on the part of governors and their staffs to address corrections policy. Most governors rarely visit prisons and would admit they seldom dedicate adequate time to an issue that is unpleasant and distasteful. Taking a cue from their boss, senior members of the Governor's staff do not elbow for the opportunity to take the lead on prison policy as opposed to more popular areas such as education or economic development. Likewise, few young men and women wishing to pursue a career in public administration seek to work in a department in which the consequences of a mistake can be the death of guards or inmates. The realities of the job make it hard to blame them. Careers are seldom made but easily lost in the quicksand of corrections policy.

The combination of these factors over time takes its toll on the system. If governors and their staffs assign corrections a low priority, if few talented young persons view it as an attractive profession, and if hard work and creative effort produce little reward, it should come as no surprise that—with only a few notable exceptions—prison policy in Tennessee has suffered greatly from a shortage of talent and attention. The record of the last half of the twentieth century suggests that most governors and legislators have preferred a prison system out sight and out of mind.

Conflicting Public Attitudes

Effective corrections policy is further complicated by another challenge. Like citizens in virtually all of the fifty states, many Tennesseans have inconsistent and conflicting views of prisons and corrections policy. To the extent they think about correctional policy at all, most Tennesseans simply want criminals locked up for a long time. Few citizens bother to consider if and how prison sentences should be tailored to match a broad variety of crimes and circumstances. The basic notion of "lock 'em up and throw away the key" also comes without regard to cost or the implications of such cost to other state programs. Many advocates of this policy either do not understand, or do not care, that a direct relationship exists between the high cost of longer prison sentences and the resources available for other state programs. This group sometimes has difficulty preventing its deep dislike of convicted felons from extending to a general contempt for all aspects of the prison system. Citizens and legislators with such a mindset rarely take into consideration that several thousand low-paid state employees—including a surprising number of women—work in the prisons as guards and support staff. They are indifferent to the educational or psychological needs of the roughly half of all prisoners who will be released within ten years. They likewise tend to dismiss the investments of people and equipment necessary for prisons to reduce the idleness and violence among some of the most dangerous persons in society. In short, most Tennesseans do not care a great deal about humane prisons or safe prisons, and they do not give a lot of thought about how to pay for new prisons or where to put them.[1] Like a majority of Americans, they simply want state government to get criminals off the street and keep them locked up for a long time.

The desire for longer prison sentences is among the few corrections issues that find their way into political campaigns. Unfortunately, the discussion rarely includes all sides of the issue. Candidates, especially challengers, have little to lose by promising "my first day in Nashville" to lengthen sentences for whatever crime has recently been in the local newspapers. Each year witnesses bills filed in the General Assembly to increase prison sentences for drunk driving, child abuse, domestic violence, sexual assault, or other offenses. Although the legislative process in Tennessee is slowed by rules requiring a cost analysis of sentencing proposals, legislators with the temerity to vote against any of these sentencing bills can expect to see a direct-mail piece in the next election calling for their heads on grounds of being "soft on crime." In such an emotional atmosphere, it is difficult for those under attack to explain that many of these critics are the same persons who oppose higher taxes needed to build new prisons.

Of course the Tennessee General Assembly contains members who are knowledgeable of corrections issues and conscientious in their efforts to encourage sound management policies. Since 1985, when the federal district court assumed control of the state's prison system, the legislature has developed a small core of House and Senate members on the Corrections Oversight Committee who spend considerable time reviewing and commenting on various administrative proposals in the corrections system. When working in tandem with governors on prison policy, the Corrections Oversight Committee has contributed to significant progress in the construction and management of prison facilities, most notably the release of the state's prisons from federal control in 1993. In the absence of such cooperation, the result has been frequent disagreement between the legislature and the administration about a variety of correction initiatives. A political process in which few players on either side know or care much about the details of corrections policy finds itself adrift when its few knowledgeable leaders disagree. In a prison system that must respond rapidly to ever-increasing population pressures, the inability to forge a consensus on corrections policy leads to serious problems that have immediate consequences for the management of state prisons and local jails.

The circumstances of overcrowding and neglect that produced the 1980s prison crisis in Tennessee were repeated in much the same fashion in some three dozen states, where federal courts intervened to take over all or part of the corrections system. How Tennessee responded to this crisis—what officials learned and did not learn—provides insight into the philosophy of the state's leaders and the ability of the political system to accommodate lasting changes in a major program of state government.

A World of Its Own

He looked to be in his mid-thirties. Like all inmates, he wore a denim shirt and dark jeans with a white stripe down the sides. He had cut the sleeves from his shirt, revealing enormous arms produced by years of working out with weights. By all accounts, he had been a model inmate during his twelve years in prison. Sitting across a linoleum-topped table in the dim dining hall of Brushy Mountain Prison, he told the Governor his story of how he got drunk in a bar in Cocke County on Christmas Eve and killed a man. Looking up with pained blue eyes, he said his remaining sentence was sixty-six years.

At least one characteristic distinguishes Tennessee's prison system. Historically, Tennessee has had fewer prison inmates per population than most other southern states. Despite doubling the size of its prison system from 1987 to 1994, Tennessee's percentage of incarcerated adults remained significantly smaller than the percentage in Georgia, South Carolina, Florida, Alabama, Mississippi, and Louisiana.[2] Indeed, as late as 1978, Tennessee's prison population was quite small, with some thirty-five hundred inmates housed in one female and six male institutions. With the exception of the Main Prison in Nashville, Tennessee's prisons were often one-half to one-fourth the size of their counterparts in other states. While the infamous Angola Prison in

Louisiana and the Parchman Prison in Mississippi each housed more than three thousand inmates, until the late 1980s only Tennessee's Main Prison regularly housed more than about seven hundred inmates. A 150-year history of small prisons and a relatively small prison system ended when Tennessee's Department of Correction underwent a period of enormous change beginning in the mid-1980s. In a host of ways, these changes catapulted the state's corrections system from the nineteenth century to the twenty-first century in the span of less than a decade.

The history of Tennessee's adult prison system can be divided into three rather distinct periods. The early period lasted from construction of the first state prison in 1831 until roughly 1970. The second period lasted only fifteen years, a tumultuous time of transition for a prison system overwhelmed by enormous growth and challenged in federal courts to defend an outdated style of management. The final period continues to the present and represents Tennessee's struggle to operate a prison system that is both constitutional and affordable.

A Different Time and Place

The evolution of Tennessee's prison system, unlike most other areas of state government, was not a process of slow but steady growth. A single facility housed all male prisoners until the 1890s, when two prisons were constructed in Nashville and at Brushy Mountain. The prison population was so stable that additional beds were not required until the construction of Ft. Pillow Prison in 1936 and DeBerry Prison in 1957 for inmates with severe psychological problems. For most of the twentieth century, the prisons suggested the image and style of a bygone day. All but DeBerry were constructed of stone, designed with guard towers on the corners and double-tiered rows of cellblocks with iron bars in the main housing units. Only administrative offices enjoyed air conditioning. Prior to the 1980s, the great majority of prison guards were white males. Throughout this period wardens often were selected on the basis of political connections. Wardens exercised great discretion in the hiring of guards and the assignment and punishment of inmates. A host of items related to operation of the prison, such as building materials and inmate food, regularly found their way out the back door and into the pickup trucks of wardens and their friends. No doubt many wardens over the years were honest and competent civil servants. One can be confident that others were not. The nature of a prison as a violent and autocratic enclave produced a closed society that at times resembled medieval serfdom. Even today, one cannot fully understand the culture of Tennessee's prison system without some knowledge of the legacy of these four institutions, two of which still house state inmates. Collectively, their descriptions offer a glimpse of what prison life was like during the first century and a half of Tennessee's correction system.

Brushy Mountain Prison

No prison in Tennessee evokes a stronger image and reputation than Brushy Mountain. Located an hour north of Knoxville in Morgan County, "Brushy" was constructed in the 1890s as a maximum-security facility to house some of the state's most notorious criminals (fig. 13.1). The prison is situated in mountain terrain so rough that no wall is needed in the back corner of the facility. Any inmate trying to escape through the opening would plunge to his death in the dense laurel thicket. Brushy's most famous escape attempt occurred in the 1970s, when James Earl Ray, convicted killer of Martin Luther King Jr., remained at large for two days before being captured in a nearby mountain ravine. In a region with little industry, the prison has been the county's leading employer for more than a century. Even today Brushy's staff is comprised largely of white males, some of

Fig. 13.1. Brushy Mountain Prison in Morgan County was constructed in the 1890s as a maximum-security facility to house some of the state's most notorious criminals. *Source:* Tennessee State Library and Archives.

whom represent the third generation of their family to work in the prison. Over the years Brushy has developed a culture among guards and wardens that makes it difficult for the Department of Correction to impose modern management techniques. The facility was renovated in the late 1980s and transformed into a reception center for inmates entering the state prison system.

Cold Creek Prison

Located within sight of the Mississippi River four hundred miles west of Brushy Mountain and fifty miles north of Memphis, Cold Creek is still referred to by many Tennesseans as Fort Pillow, the facility's name from 1936 until 1993. The name was changed in response to concerns that the facility was too closely associated with the Civil War massacre of blacks and Union troops that occurred at the hands of Confederate soldiers at Fort Pillow.[3] Cold Creek contains a one-thousand-acre plantation on which hundreds of inmates raise food and cattle for the prison system. The heat and humidity of the region are oppressive, made worse for inmates and staff by the absence of air-conditioning in the prison cellblocks. In earlier times the prison was run by wardens whose authority was supreme. Stories handed down claim inmates who crossed the wardens routinely "disappeared" and are buried in unmarked graves on the prison farm. To this day, no inmate in the Tennessee prison system volunteers to be sent to Cold Creek.

DeBerry Prison

Perhaps the least known of Tennessee's older prisons, DeBerry for decades was commonly referred to as the "prison for the criminally insane." The inmate profile ranged from psychotic killers to sexual deviants. The original facility was located near the Nashville airport, where DeBerry's mission actually included inmates with a variety of medical as well as psychiatric needs. The prison was a textbook case of how not to design a facility to accommodate the factors of security, medical care and efficient operation. The prison was dangerous, had high maintenance and staff costs, and posed serious challenges to inmates with ambulatory problems. Low pay ensured a high turnover among staff physicians, many of whom were of foreign origin. In such an environment, one could expect most inmates sent to DeBerry with psychiatric problems to become worse instead of better. In 1988 the state sold the prison to the City of Nashville and used the proceeds to help finance a new Special Needs prison across town. Also known as

DeBerry, the new prison is a model facility for inmates with long-term medical and psychiatric needs.

Tennessee State Prison

For nearly a century since its construction in the 1890s, the "Main Prison" was the largest and best-known facility in the correctional system. Intended to house around nine hundred inmates, the prison was designed with long double-tiered cellblocks from which inmates regularly hurled objects, including human feces, on guards below who shielded themselves with chicken wire. Despite forty-square-foot cells narrow enough for an inmate to touch both walls at once, the cells often housed two persons when the prison's population exploded to more than two thousand. The prison compound in some respects resembled a walled English village, with a furniture factory, a mattress factory, a school, a clinic, a gymnasium, and a chapel. Separate from the main cellblocks was Death Row, where in the 1980s some sixty inmates resided in the most rigidly controlled society in Tennessee. Each year hundreds of school kids passed through Death Row to gape at the state's electric chair. Nicknamed "Old Sparky," the chair's legs were blackened from decades of charred skin. Increasingly overcrowded and violent in the early 1980s, the Main Prison became the symbol of all that was outdated and unconstitutional in the state's correctional system. The federal court ordered the prison closed after assuming control of the state's correctional system in 1985. In the years since its closure, the facility has been the location of several motion pictures depicting prison themes.

Spinning Out of Control: 1970-1985

One can point to a number of factors, both internal and external, that led to a rapid deterioration of Tennessee's prison system in the 1970s and early 1980s. The growth of the state's urban centers brought the same exponential rise in crime found in cities throughout the country. The state's justice system had no experience to prepare it for the rapid increase in property and violent crime. Frightened and angry, the public called for "law and order." The General Assembly responded by increasing sentences for a number of violent crimes such as rape and armed robbery.[4] Judges and juries did not hesitate to issue longer sentences for convicted felons. A prison system designed for a different era was gradually overwhelmed.

A Failure of Leadership

At the very time when events called for strong leadership, a series of administrative blunders worsened problems for the Department of Correction. The state's newest prison, Turney Center, was an architectural nightmare that produced a rash of inmate violence. Hailed at its opening in 1969 as the "new generation" of prisons, the facility's housing units had multiple blind corners and, incredibly, were built on stilts that afforded endless hiding places for inmates and their contraband. The Turney fiasco was followed by Gov. Winfield Dunn's attempt in 1973 to locate a new prison in Morristown. Dunn badly misjudged local opposition and pushed construction forward until citizens chopped down power lines and lay in front of bulldozers. Amid horrendous publicity, the project was abandoned, leaving steel girders as a rusting monument to a corrections disaster. Most important, during a period when the state needed to locate new prisons quickly, the Morristown episode served to make future governors hesitant rather than decisive.

Events went from bad to worse. Dunn was succeeded as Governor in 1975 by Ray Blanton, a rural congressman who at times appeared to view his tenure as little more than an opportunity to make money by betraying the public trust. Working through his chief legal counsel and other senior aides, Blanton engaged in the repeated sale of pardons to convicted criminals. A firestorm of criticism erupted among citizens and the media when Blanton promised during a live television interview to pardon a recently convicted double murderer (see chapter 10). With the Department of Correction in turmoil and the Governor vowing to pardon fifty more serious criminals, the FBI seized and padlocked the Governor's Office during the final days of Blanton's administration. In a hastily called ceremony, Lamar Alexander was sworn in as Governor three days early in January 1979 to prevent Blanton from issuing further pardons. In time, Blanton himself was convicted of selling liquor licenses and sentenced to prison.

With Blanton's troubles as a backdrop, Lamar Alexander made crime a centerpiece of his campaign for Governor in 1978. His first legislative package was highlighted by a proposal for mandatory prison sentences for offenses Alexander termed "Class X" crimes.[5] For the second time in less than a decade, the legislature increased sentences for armed robbery, rape, murder, and the sale of more serious drugs such as LSD and heroin.[6] Then, as now, increased prison sentences raised a fundamental issue about the impact of these longer sentences on the operation of the corrections system. Because the financial and operational impact of longer sentences occurs several years after their implementation, many legislators and much of the public do not clearly comprehend the consequences. Stated differently, if society wishes to keep inmates incarcerated longer by increasing sentences, it is crucial to expand the corrections system simultaneously rather than wait until existing prisons are overflowing. In part because prisons are expensive and because he remembered the debacle experienced by his Republican predecessor at Morristown, Alexander deferred efforts to keep up with the accelerating growth in prison inmates. Although early in his first term he opened new prisons funded and built by Governor Blanton, Alexander from 1979 until late 1985 did not ask the legislature to fund a new prison facility. The decision was one for which the Department of Correction would pay dearly.

The pressure building in the prison system was like a water hose bent double with the valve open. Each month saw between one and two hundred more inmates sent into the system than released by the Parole Board. Cells built for one inmate were converted to house two. Inmates were double- and triple-bunked in corridors and prison gymnasiums, where the blare from dozens of radios and stereos was deafening. Support functions such as medical and food services were strained beyond the breaking point. Prison industry could not provide even make-work jobs for the thousands of new inmates. Worsening conditions led to increased turnover among prison guards and staff in urban areas. Rising levels of overcrowding and idleness combined to produce a predictable increase in stabbings and assaults among inmates. A prison system that had functioned reasonably well for 150 years was coming apart at the seams.

Despite the severity of the situation, conditions in Tennessee's prisons remained largely out of sight and out of mind to most legislators and a majority of the public. Few took notice of litigation filed by Legal Services of Middle Tennessee on behalf of inmates that challenged the constitutionality of prison conditions.[7] The chief plaintiff's attorney was Gordon Bonnyman, a capable and conscientious advocate who knew the law and understood well conditions in Tennessee prisons. Bonnyman built a convincing case that several of the state's prisons had levels of overcrowding, idleness, and violence that failed to meet federal constitutional standards. The initial response to Bonnyman's lawsuit from the administration and most legislators was one of contempt. At one hearing after another, the state Attorney General and the Commissioner of Correction promised to do better, buying time in hopes of a miracle. The miracle never came. Sporadic violence among inmates increased. Events exploded in late summer of 1985, when inmates took over a portion of the compound at Turney Prison. Two buildings were burned before authorities regained control of the prison. The Governor, the Attorney General, and legislative leaders were forced to acknowledge a situation that had been obvious for months. Overcrowding had reached the point that Tennessee was losing control of its prisons. In October 1982 the federal court declared prison conditions unconstitutional and assumed effective control of the Department of Correction.[8]

The Court Takes Over

The court appointed a Special Master, a former corrections commissioner from Minnesota, to oversee a lengthy list of some fifteen hundred policy changes that would need to be addressed in various prisons. The change items ranged from the mundane, such as the proper procedure for the use of cell keys, to orders as far-reaching as the closure of the Main Prison. Most significant in immediate terms was an order that the inmate population of some ninety-five hundred be reduced to about seven thousand, notwithstanding the growing backlog of state inmates in local jails. The court stipulated further that the population cap not be exceeded until new prisons were constructed—a process that under the best of circumstances would take more than two years.

Unnoticed by most observers was the fact that many of the stipulations ordered by the court contained items not related directly to constitutional standards. Specifically, no state or federal constitutional precedent prohibited double-celling of inmates so long as the prison provided adequate square footage and appropriate levels of activity and security. In ordering that Tennessee's prison inmates be single-celled, the court was moving into uncharted legal territory in a manner that raised profound questions about federal authority to dictate state correctional policy. The decision by the Governor and the Attorney General not to challenge the constitutionality of these important sections of the court order had serious ramifications. Left unchallenged, the state in effect would be forced to release thousands of inmates, reduce statutory sentences for violent crimes, and essentially double the existing prison system just to maintain the current number of beds. The unwillingness to take on this important legal challenge said much about the state's defeatist attitude by the late fall of 1985.

In November Governor Alexander called the legislature into Special Session to address the prison crisis. After ample finger pointing and venting about the encroachment of federal authority on state government, the General Assembly enacted a legislative package purported to relieve overcrowding and develop a more rational sentencing structure that included alternatives to incarceration.[9] The legislature authorized bonds to finance two new five-hundred-bed maximum-security prisons. (The fact that the Governor and the legislature did not grasp the need to build larger prisons reflected the extent to which corrections policy still had not caught up with events.) The legislature also established a new program to expand the role of local jails by paying counties a fixed per diem cost to house felons with sentences of six years or less. Again, the haste with which the local jails program was drafted prevented legislators from fully appreciating the program's enormous potential for cost increases. Knowing the true costs to house inmates, sheriffs successfully lobbied for a higher reimbursement rate that guaranteed the state-financed program would be a cash cow for many local jails. The Special Session's final act was the creation of the Tennessee Sentencing Commission. Although few legislators at the time fully understood the consequences, they gave the commission a mandate to review the hodgepodge of sentencing statutes and recommend criminal sentences that more closely reflected the seriousness of the crimes and the capacity of the prison system.

The 1985 Special Session adjourned without the usual self-congratulatory comments from the Governor and legislators. Governor Alexander's legislative package had been adopted hurriedly without adequate discussion of whether the various proposals were practical or affordable. While it is impossible to know, one can speculate that most of those involved sensed the Special Session had served only to provide a tourniquet to a serious wound. Those who shared this fear would be proved more perceptive than they realized.

Trying to Grab Hold

Trying to manage the prisons is like courtin' a fat woman. You never quite know where to grab hold.

Gov. Ned McWherter

The twelve months following the 1985 Special Session were largely a wasted year for Tennessee's prison system. Governor Alexander devoted the last year of his administration to "Homecoming '86," an upbeat celebration that had no place for the negative tone of corrections issues. House Speaker Ned McWherter was increasingly focused on his race for Governor and took little part in oversight of the state's response to the federal court. Without strong support from these two leaders, the Attorney General and the Commissioner of Correction were resigned to meetings with the Special Master and prison consultants appointed by the Special Master to provide direction on issues such as security, education, health care and prison construction. The Special Master and his consultants, all from outside Tennessee, operated without a sense of urgency to build facilities quickly or cost efficiently. Meetings were scheduled months apart. Decisions were made, unmade, and deferred. Unfamiliar with the process, intimidated by the court, and unsure of their political support in the last months of the Alexander administration, Tennessee corrections officials could do little but attempt to placate the Special Master. By the time of McWherter's inauguration as Governor in January 1987, designs for the two new prisons, instead of being ready for construction, were literally a blank sheet of paper.

Back on Its Feet

McWherter had used the crisis in Tennessee's prisons to his advantage during the 1986 governor's race. His corrections platform had been expressed in the most general terms, promising only that McWherter would manage the system personally, "help those inmates who want to help themselves, and get tough with the tough." Though totally void of specifics, his message resonated well with voters frustrated with prison problems.[10]

More than any other issue he confronted as Governor, McWherter viewed improved management of the prison system as a personal challenge. McWherter's success in a number of business ventures gave him the confidence—some said the arrogance—to believe he could, in his words, "get his arms around the prison problem."

Most accounts of McWherter's corrections initiatives focus on the historic expansion of the prison system that took place from 1987 to 1994. While it is true that McWherter presided over the construction of more prison beds than all previous Tennessee governors combined, this fact obscures a number of more significant changes he introduced to the philosophy and management of the state's corrections system.

One could argue that McWherter's most important contribution was his basic decision to place corrections on the top tier of state policy issues. He assigned a senior aide to coordinate corrections policy, including the expedited construction of new prisons. McWherter visited every prison, taking time during each visit to meet separately with inmates and staff. The Governor personally reviewed the corrections budget in detail, poring over items such as the staffing in guard towers and the daily food costs at each prison. His micro-management extended even to resolving disputes between architects and contractors of the new prisons. The importance of these actions had less to do with McWherter's expertise than with the impact of his presence on the process. Knowing that a decision would immediately generate positive or negative feedback from the Governor made an extraordinary difference in the attitudes and work habits of persons accustomed to a process "out of sight and out of mind." Design and programming decisions for new prisons that previously had taken weeks were compressed into days. Corrections Department staff took greater initiative with the confidence the Governor would not abandon them if challenged by the court. Like a weary prizefighter, the department was bruised but back on its feet.

Challenging the Court

McWherter's efforts to "grab hold" of corrections involved challenging a number of assumptions that had guided Tennessee corrections policy for a hundred years. The first required changing a management philosophy grounded in the nineteenth century. McWherter believed, correctly, that no one had ever made a serious attempt to control prison costs, largely because the vast majority of corrections commissioners had been former wardens more concerned with security issues than saving money. He raised eyebrows by appointing as Corrections Commissioner Jeff Reynolds, a talented career state employee from the Comptroller's Office. Reynolds was succeeded by Christine Bradley, another long-term state employee who became the nation's only female Corrections Commissioner. Both Reynolds and Bradley understood budgets and spread sheets. Each was willing to change the status quo in a manner that annoyed many wardens and senior prison staff. Labor-intensive guard towers were abandoned in favor of electronic fence detection. Staffing costs were further reduced by requiring guards to perform multiple tasks, such as routine paperwork and serving food in the cellblocks. McWherter sought to soften resistance to these changes by raising the pay of correctional officers.

These and other similar changes were part of a coordinated attempt by McWherter to move away from some of the more far-reaching 1985 court stipulations. After more than a year of meekly following the lead of the court consultants, Tennessee staff became increasingly bold in their efforts to develop a prototype prison whose design could be used like a cookie-cutter to reproduce future facilities more quickly and more cheaply. The implications of this move went far beyond a rebuke of the court consultants. McWherter had no intention of accepting a plan that would spend $300 million, require releasing thousands of convicted felons, and bind the state's prisons to a net reduction in capacity. Even more important, his decision gave evidence McWherter was prepared to challenge the court's ability to claim constitutional authority over management policies of the Tennessee prisons.

McWherter's actions produced an anticipated clash with the Special Master and the court. Prior to a Christmas party at the Governor's residence in 1987, McWherter and the Attorney General were summoned to a chambers meeting with the federal judge, a meeting McWherter likened to "going to the principal's office." For six years, the relationship between the Governor's Office and the court was strained. Rather than challenge the entirety of the 1985 court stipulation at one time, McWherter chose to isolate sections of the order and attack each separately. He assigned the task to Attorney General Charles Burson, a Harvard-educated litigator unafraid, in his words, to "tee it up with the court." In 1987 the stipulation was modified to allow the two new prisons to be enlarged before construction began. In 1988 the state prevailed in its contention that inmates could be double-celled provided total square footage was adequate. These victories emboldened the state to accelerate its strategy of shifting the legal burden of proof from the state to the court. In other words, instead of the state having to prove its policies were constitutional, the court would be challenged to prove individual state policies violated constitutional standards. Without the support of legal precedent, McWherter correctly predicted the court would retreat issue by issue.

The process was an endless series of proposals, counterproposals, threats, and bluffs on the part of both sides. Throughout the period from 1987 to 1993, the Governor and the legislature reshaped Tennessee's prison system in a manner that more closely reflected the philosophy of Tennesseans than the suggestions of the Special Master. Six new prisons were constructed, two in Davidson County and one each in Johnson, Wayne, Lake, and Lauderdale Counties. Expansions and renovations were completed at Fort Pillow, Brushy Mountain, Turney, Shelby County, Davidson County, Bledsoe County, and Morgan County Prisons. A boot camp for youthful offenders was constructed in Wayne County. Operation of the new medium security prison in Wayne County was contracted with a private company under a three-year plan to compare cost and quality with two identical state-run prisons in Johnson and Lake Counties. State payments to local jails for housing state prisoners were modified to reflect more accurately actual costs instead of arbitrary rates.

Among the most significant changes during this period was a comprehensive rewriting of Tennessee's sentencing laws. A product of the 1985 Sentencing Commission, the proposal sought to bring a measure of order and consistency to outdated laws that provided sentences of one year for stealing a five-hundred-dollar stereo and twenty years for stealing a five-hundred-dollar horse. By establishing a sentencing structure with narrow and specific ranges, the new law increased the likelihood that different criminals convicted of similar crimes in Memphis and Byrdstown would receive the same prison sentence. Although amended before its passage and again by subsequent legislatures, the sentencing reforms were a substantial leap forward in efforts to modernize Tennessee's criminal justice system.[11]

By 1991, Tennessee officials felt confident enough to petition the court to release the Department of Correction from federal control. Initially opposed by the Special Master, the petition was finally approved by the federal judge in the summer of 1993. In his ruling, the judge characterized as "remarkable" the progress of Tennessee's prisons since 1985.[12] Violence had been dramatically reduced. Thousands of jobs, including data processing on Death Row, had been created to lessen inmate idleness. A prison system which in 1985 had only one facility accredited by the American Correctional Association had become in seven years the nation's only fully accredited system. The most tumultuous and disruptive period in the history of Tennessee's prisons had come to an end.

No End in Sight

The question, Governor, is not whether you need to build a third new prison. You will need to build a fourth and fifth. The question is whether you can ever build yourself out of the problem.

Don Stoughton, corrections consultant to Gov. Ned McWherter, 1988

Despite the tremendous strides Tennessee had made in the management of its prisons, the state still struggled to keep pace with a growth in the inmate population that showed no signs of slowing. By the 1990s, the impact of increased sentences enacted during the Alexander and McWherter administrations was fulfilling earlier predictions of a prison system that could not build beds fast enough to meet demand. Surprisingly, the chaos of the mid-1980s and the resulting court takeover of the state's prisons had done little to help most Tennesseans understand the relationship between longer sentences and the problems such sentences bring to the management and funding of state government. Large majorities of Tennesseans continued to believe that convicted felons should not be paroled before serving their entire sentence. Faced with this level of public interest, it was only natural that governors and legislators remained responsive to efforts to enact a variety of "crime" packages. Gov. Don Sundquist joined the trend in 1995 with a high-profile crime initiative during his first legislative session.[13]

Giving each governor the benefit of the doubt, the likelihood remains that from 1978 until the end of the twentieth century, none of Tennessee's three governors had a clear sense of the long-term impact their respective sentencing proposals would have on the size and cost of the state's corrections system. Governor Alexander did not propose funds for a new prison until forced by the court at the end of his term. While popular, Governor McWherter's "three strikes" proposal (in a bizarre twist of public relations rhetoric, the proposal was actually a "two strikes" plan that was pitched as "three strikes") to deny parole to felons convicted of two violent crimes generated sharply varying estimates of its eventual cost. Likewise, the legislature's Fiscal Review Committee reported that the cost of Governor Sundquist's 1995 crime bill would be at least twice the amount claimed by the administration. Details aside, one fact was beyond dispute. To avoid the overcrowding that occurred in the 1980s, Tennessee would have to open a new twelve-hundred-bed prison every twenty-four months for as far as one could see into the future.[14]

"Chasing the Curve"

As the twentieth century drew to a close, the pressures of "chasing the curve"—a phrase describing the scramble to find enough prison beds to meet the demand—were taking a toll on the Department of Correction. In the fall of 1995, the department provided the legislature with estimates that the prison population would increase from seventeen thousand to twenty-two thousand inmates by the year 2000. The department quickly double-celled all facilities, dismissing the fact that most had been programmed when built to be half double-celled in order to reduce violence and provide adequate numbers of inmate jobs. Because the department had, in effect, used its last resort first, officials were under great pressure to develop a plan to house thousands of additional inmates that would stream into state prisons over the next decade. Competing philosophies and strategies within the administration impeded the effort. Some suggested sending hundreds of inmates to available facilities in Texas, an idea the legislature rejected as impractical. Others advocated leasing the entire prison system to Nashville-based Corrections Corporation of America, a proposal that failed in 1998 under pressure from the State Employees Association. An effort to build a new prison in Hancock County was withdrawn after community opposition. Overcoming reservations from the State Comptroller, the administration was successful in contracting with a county-owned facility in Hardeman County for the housing of some twelve hundred state inmates.

A series of false starts and changing strategies forced the Department of Correction once again to confront the specter of falling further behind with demands for more beds. By 1999, the growing backlog of convicted state felons forced local jails in Memphis, Knoxville, and Chattanooga to operate with inmate populations 30 to 40 percent in excess of recommended capacity. Meanwhile, efforts to build new prisons were delayed by problems finding communities willing to house corrections facilities. With only a couple of exceptions, both McWherter and Sundquist had sidestepped this issue by building new prisons in counties where older prisons were already located. As the labor market in these counties became exhausted, the administration increasingly found it necessary to delay construction while spending considerable time trying to identify suitable locations. The task became even more difficult after inmates successfully executed a Christmas escape from the Riverbend Maximum Security facility in December 1998. Despite pedaling harder and harder, the state continued to lose ground.

Are There Any Options?

From the early 1970s until the present, state officials addressing the corrections problem have been consumed with the task of building and acquiring more beds. From time to time throughout this period of rapid prison construction, voices inside and outside state government have urged lawmakers to consider a variety of alternatives to placing inmates in expensive prisons for extended periods. As one might expect, those advocating alternative sentencing programs gained the largest audience in the mid-1980s, when the federal court placed a cap on the population of the state prison system. For a period of some ten to twelve years, the state expanded a number of programs designed to keep convicted felons out of state prisons.

Tennessee houses a larger than usual number of convicted felons in local jails. Until the 1980s, the great majority of state felons in local jails were limited to recently convicted inmates awaiting transfer to a prison facility. As noted, a new trend emerged in the early 1980s, when, in an attempt to acquire beds quickly "on the cheap," the state sought to encourage counties to house more felons by paying a higher per diem rate to keep inmates who could be expected to serve less than two years prior to parole. Many sheriffs, particularly in smaller counties, used the state program as a way of generating extra funds for their jails. What began as a gradual increase in the number of state felons housed in local jails exploded in 1985, when the court put in place a population cap and effectively shut off the intake valve into the state prison system. Within eighteen months, jails in the state's largest counties were operating at 125 to 150 percent capacity. Just as officials recovered from the shock of losing a lawsuit filed against the state prison system, the state was sued by county inmates in Knoxville and county officials in Chattanooga on grounds that the large numbers of state inmates produced unacceptable levels of overcrowding and violence. In a span of less than five years, local jails had been removed as a practical option for easing the overcrowding in state prisons.

Extraordinary circumstances led legislators and administration officials to be more receptive to sentencing alternatives for growing numbers of inmates. Under the label of "Community Corrections," hundreds of convicted felons were allowed to remain in their communities under court order to perform work and report regularly to a probation officer. Following the lead of Georgia, Tennessee constructed a marine-style boot camp in Wayne County with the hope that an intense regimen of work and drill would save younger felons from a life of crime. A concept called "Contract Sentencing" enabled inmates to acquire sentence credits and shorten prison time by fulfilling specified commitments for education and good behavior. Technological advances made it possible to provide felons with electronic bracelets as a means of keeping up with their whereabouts outside of prison. By the mid-1990s, roughly two of three felons under state supervision were on probation, on parole, or in some form of alternative sentencing.

Tennessee also has flirted with the idea of contracting some portion of the prison system to private companies, particularly Nashville-based Corrections Corporation of America. Lamar Alexander unsuccessfully proposed privatizing the entire system in 1985. Don Sundquist also proposed, with the support of Senate and House leaders, to privatize several prison facilities in 1998. Such far-reaching proposals have never been able to overcome a deep anxiety among legislators about surrendering such a large and important state responsibility.

The combination of alternative sentencing programs provided only a temporary pause in the pressure on the population of the state prison system. Even a sharp increase in the number of inmates released monthly by the Board of Pardons and Paroles did not produce any breathing room for state officials. Indeed, while there is a lack of data to prove the theory, many are convinced that the state system will always be full, no matter how many prisons are built and how many sentencing alternatives are utilized. The theory is based on the belief that most judges and district attorneys will reject alternative programs and seek to impose the maximum prison sentences so long as beds are available in state facilities. Stated differently, as soon as beds become free, the system will move quickly to fill them.

Regardless of the cause, the presence of this phenomenon has motivated discussion of whether governors, legislators, and the public should consider fundamental changes in Tennessee's criminal statutes. Some contend it would be more practical for felons convicted of property crimes to repay their victims than spend several years in prison at substantial taxpayers' expense. Given that nearly a third of state felons are incarcerated for theft or burglary, such a change would have a dramatic impact on the size and cost of the prison system. The state legislature is not likely to enact such radical changes absent a dramatic shift in public opinion. Since such a shift did not occur amid events in the 1980s and 1990s, one finds it difficult to imagine the circumstances under which Tennessee might enjoy a respite from the pressure to continuing building prisons. Until that day arrives, the state will have no choice but to continue chasing the curve.

Lost among the Numbers

The history of the Tennessee prison system since 1970 is most often told in the context of two simple problems: how to provide more beds and how to pay for them. Virtually every other debate, from the desirability of alternative sentencing programs to the proper boundaries of federal oversight, has its origin in the basic struggle of supply versus demand. The demand is produced by a criminal justice system that in just two decades generated a sixfold increase in inmates for the prisons without regard or responsibility for providing a comparable supply of beds from limited state resources. In a political system in which judges and district attorneys are elected, the pressure to pursue longer sentences will usually prevail over voices urging greater balance among the growing portion of the budget spent for prisons and the needs of education, health care, and other equally worthy state services. At an intellectual level most policy makers understand and appreciate this dilemma. They must function, however, in a culture in which public emotions of fear and retribution are real, making it politically impossible for governors and legislators to get off the merry-go-round of longer sentences and more prisons. Their failure to stop the ride is not a sign of cowardice or moral weakness. So long as they represent the public will, lawmakers will continue down a road with no guideposts or destination.

Perhaps the most disturbing aspect of the corrections system in Tennessee, as in most states, is how the obsession with numbers has largely eliminated the human factor from the policy dialogue. One can speculate that whether in the Governor's Office or in the Legislative Plaza, virtually every corrections-related discussion quickly gravitates to the issue of numbers: What is the number of state inmates in local jails? What is the number of inmates released last month by the Parole Board? What is the number of new beds that can be funded during the next legislative session? If true, a discussion so dominated by numbers makes it extremely difficult to remember that the prison system is not an abstraction like the Department of Transportation but a place inhabited by thousands of human beings. In such an atmosphere, many are quick to generalize about corrections issues as diverse and complicated as any in state government. After all, it is easier to dismiss the notion of rehabilitation than identify and help those inmates who might become productive members of society. Policy decisions are less troublesome if one ignores the hundreds of inmates who undergo sincere religious conversions while in prison, or those who succeed in acquiring educational and vocational skills that increase the chances for a productive life. Tennessee's prisons contain thousands of inmates who committed serious offenses at an early age but who for more than two decades have been model prisoners within a society more violent than most citizens could ever imagine. Despite these and other mitigating factors, Tennesseans by and large have not taken them into account when discussing issues such as sentence credits, early release, or mandatory sentencing. In the minds of most, more than twenty thousand inmates are lumped together in a faceless mass. They are merely numbers, to be added by state government like mileage on the interstate highway system.

Barring unforeseen circumstances, Tennessee's corrections system will be driven by the numbers for years to come. Until one experiences the August heat of Cold Creek Prison, or looks into the eyes of an inmate in a maximum security housing unit of Riverbend, or witnesses a visitation by wives and children at Brushy Mountain, it is impossible to appreciate fully the multitude of sights, sounds, and emotions that make up a prison system. After such experiences does one contemplate, if only briefly, the human dimensions of a prison system that most Tennesseans still prefer to keep out of sight and out of mind.

14

Financing Tennessee Government

The biggest problem Tennessee has in reforming its tax system is the fact that it's been so well managed.

Former Finance Commissioner Lewis Donelson, Senate Finance Committee, 1999

At the beginning of the twenty-first century, the State of Tennessee had an annual budget of more than $16 billion. While this figure may strike the average citizen as an extremely large amount of money, the state's responsibilities easily consumed these resources. As Tennessee experienced significant growth in population and personal income, the pressure for state expenditures, especially in the areas of education, health care, and corrections, increased at a similar pace.

Compared with other states, Tennessee maintains a low per capita tax burden and low per capita expenditures for state services. The low level of taxation is a source of great pride to some Tennesseans but a cause for concern to others. As in all states, many in Tennessee prefer a bare minimum of state services in exchange for very low state taxes. Others, however, believe that Tennessee's low level of government funding reduces the quality of state services to a point that the state's future is endangered. Still others want good schools, clean water, and adequate numbers of prison beds for convicted felons, but they are not convinced that these expectations require additional tax revenues. Together, these three perspectives shape the political discussion about how much state government should spend and the tax policy used to gather the revenues needed to fund state services. At one level, the debate is quite simple—a choice between a small government and something larger. At another, it is among the most complicated issues in the political process. At all levels, the question of how state government pays its bills is the most important and most controversial issue in the political dialogue.

The amount of taxes raised and the manner in which they are raised reflect a state's values and political culture. Fiscal policy, while boring to many, is the point where "the rubber meets the road" in any political system. More than any country in the world, the American states serve as public policy laboratories, varying remarkably in levels of taxation and spending, methods of taxation, and variety and quality of state services. Although many of these variations are the product of economic forces beyond the control of individual states, most differences in financial policy are the product of conscious decisions made over the years by generations of Governors and legislators. As a result of such decisions made more than a century ago, Tennessee has fewer fiscal options than many states. The Tennessee Constitution prohibits the use of a state lottery and, at least in the minds of many income tax opponents, prohibits the enactment of a state tax on personal income. Moreover, the Tennessee Constitution is among the most difficult charters to amend (see chapter 2).

The Tennessee Constitution, as amended in 1978, requires that "expenditures for any fiscal year shall not exceed the state's revenues and reserves, including the proceeds of any debt obligation for that year."[1] The 1978 amendment was followed in the 1980s by legislative efforts to prohibit Tennessee's state budget from growing faster than the state's personal income. Tennessee, unlike the federal government, cannot engage in deficit spending. Not only must the General Assembly approve a balanced budget each year, but also the Governor must reduce spending during the budget year if revenues are less than expected. The combination of these two constraints on state spending proved effective in holding down the growth of state spending during the last two decades of the twentieth century.

The state's fiscal discipline was strengthened further by the establishment of a system of checks and balances between the Governor and the General Assembly. The Tennessee Constitution created two offices to manage the collection of taxes and its distribution to state programs (see chapter 5). The Treasurer and Comptroller of the Treasury are elected by a majority vote of both houses of the General Assembly to serve two-year terms. The General Assembly has placed financial responsibilities in both offices. The Treasurer is the investor of state funds and is responsible for overseeing the proper distribution of state funds by the Department of Finance and Administration. The Comptroller is responsible for the audit function, among others, to make sure that the executive branch spends funds in accord with the legislature's intent.

As one examines Tennessee's financial system and the political issues that accompany tax policy, it is important to keep in mind a significant characteristic of the state's financial management. By and large, since the 1950s Tennessee has had a well-managed state government. Despite being a state where taxes were very low, Tennessee squeezed out education, health care, and road programs that, if not among the nation's best, were at least competitive among states with comparable levels of wealth. One can argue that a major reason for this quality of management was the unusually long tenure of several individuals and their protégés, who made careers in the offices of the Treasurer and Comptroller (see chapter 3).

Ironically, the fact that Tennessee's finances were well managed for four decades made it more difficult in the 1990s to convince the public of the need to reform a tax system that was no longer viable. It was against this backdrop in the 1990s that two Governors and the state legislature struggled with a political issue that threatened both the financial and the political stability of Tennessee.

Reliance on Federal Funds

Throughout most of American history, federal and state governments operated almost totally independent of one another. Each had its own well-defined sphere of responsibilities and was responsible for raising its own revenue. The federal government was responsible for foreign policy and national defense, major internal improvements such as canals and harbors, security needs associated with westward expansion, and maintaining tax and tariff policies to stimulate a capitalist economy. Federal duties included regulating weights and measures, coining money, and providing uniform rules for interstate trade. State and local governments alone were responsible for public education and for building and maintaining the public infrastructure, primarily roads and bridges. The first major departure from this notion of "dual federalism" was the Morrill Land Grant Act of 1862, which transferred federal lands to the states to establish state colleges, such as the University of Tennessee, that were oriented toward agriculture and engineering.[2] The Morrill Act, however, did not represent a fundamental shift in the federal-state relationship.

The nature of the federal-state relationship began to change significantly in the 1930s, with the onset of the Great Depression and the willingness of the President and Congress to take dramatic steps to create employment (see chapter 4). The Emergency Relief and Reconstruction Act of 1933 provided low-interest loans to states for highway construction programs. The federal government's first efforts to fund road construction foreshadowed massive federal grants to the states, beginning in the 1950s, to construct and maintain the interstate highway system.

By 1937, during the most aggressive period of President Franklin D. Roosevelt's New Deal, federal grants to the states rose dramatically to nearly $300 million per year.[3] Much of the increase was due to a new federal role in providing for social welfare and creating job programs for millions of unemployed Americans. During the 1930s, the local share of welfare spending decreased from more than 90 percent to 11 percent. The state share increased from 9 percent to 23 percent, but the federal government's share, nonexistent prior to the Depression, reached 67 percent.[4] The trend was not reversed for nearly seventy years.

After the welfare programs in the 1930s and the interstate highway construction program in the 1950s, the third and most dramatic increase in federal aid to the states accompanied President Lyndon Johnson's War on Poverty in the mid-1960s. The amount of federal money flowing to the states doubled between 1960 and 1966. By 1970, the total doubled a second time and by 1975 doubled yet again.[5] Most of these increases were due to the greatly expanded federal role in providing for social welfare, through such programs as Aid to Families with Dependent Children (AFDC) and Medicaid, the program of health care for the poor. Today, more than four hundred federal programs provide grants to the states in such programmatic areas as welfare, education, the environment, housing, transportation, disability services, and unemployment insurance. The portions of these programs paid for by federal and state funds vary according to the relative wealth of each state. Even so, most of the programs represent major policy commitments from which states would find it very difficult to extricate themselves without considerable outcry from those who favor or benefit from the services. In other words, all but the most conservative citizens would find it difficult today to support eliminating federal funds that build interstate highways, support local hospitals, or provide food for poor school children. In Fiscal Year 1998, federal funds appropriated to the states totaled approximately $253 billion. Tennessee's share of these funds was in excess of $5 billion.[6] In fiscal year 2000, 35 percent of Tennessee's total budget came from Washington (see table 14.1).

TABLE 14.1

TENNESSEE REVENUE SOURCES, FISCAL YEAR 2000

Total State Budget	$16.7 billion
From State Funds	$8.3 billion
From Federal Funds	$5.9 billion
Other Sources	$2.4 billion
From Bonds	$138.0 million

SOURCE: Tennessee General Assembly, Senate and House Finance, Ways and Means Committees, Budget Fact Book 1999–2000.

Money, more than any single factor, influences public policy at all levels of government. Despite rhetorical speeches in Congress from time to time about the need to "cut federal red tape" and "get the federal government off the backs of the states," the fact remains that federal funds rarely are given to the states without extensive guidelines directing how the money can be spent. If one listens carefully, most political speeches do not advocate reducing the amount of federal money given to the states, but rather these federal regulations that dictate how the money can be spent. Employing what are known as categorical grants, Congress often uses federal dollars to "encourage" states to implement policies that may or may not be in tune with a state's priorities or political values. That tendency was particularly pronounced during the 1960s and 1970s, when, in response to a wave of urban riots, the national government became much more active in addressing a wide variety of social problems, especially in the larger cities. The busing of schoolchildren, ordered by federal courts and occurring nationwide, formed an emotional backdrop for implementation of the new social programs.

In part because many state governments were viewed as incompetent, corrupt, or resistant to the intent of the new laws, Congress wanted to make certain that states used federal dollars according to strict programmatic guidelines. In truth, in the late 1960s, some states—perhaps including Tennessee—were opposed to many of the federal initiatives and were not equipped to handle such a large increase in administrative responsibilities. The result was a growing hostility between federal and state governments that lasted for two decades. The animosity abated somewhat in 1992, with the election of President Bill Clinton, a former Governor of Arkansas and former chair of the National Governors Association. Clinton encouraged Governors to take an aggressive stance in calling on Congress and federal agencies to allow states to experiment with more creative ways to deliver services funded with federal grants. In particular, states sought to make changes in the administration of welfare and Medicaid, two federal programs universally acknowledged to be bloated and poorly managed. The Governors argued that giving their states flexibility to make decisions about eligibility and benefits would reduce costs, improve the quality of services, and generate new ideas that might work elsewhere. The Clinton administration and the Republican-controlled Congress responded favorably to a number of these initiatives. Among them were Tennessee's 1993 proposal to place the state's $4 billion Medicaid program under a managed care structure called TennCare, and a 1996 welfare reform plan called Families First. In a few significant areas, Congress moved away from the use of categorical grants and toward the use of block grants that gave states more leeway in using federal money. Several federal agencies took a similar approach, loosening their rules governing the use of federal grant money.

TennCare and Families First: Breaking with Tradition

In 1993, Tennessee's Gov. Ned McWherter negotiated with President Bill Clinton and Secretary of Health and Human Services Donna Shalala to allow Tennessee to become one of the first states to withdraw completely from a major federal program while retaining the program's funding. TennCare was a creative attempt, first, to provide health insurance to Tennessee's uninsured workers for the first time; and, second, to bring financial stability to a Medicaid program whose share of the state budget had grown from 10 percent to 26 percent in a little over a decade. The proposal involved 800,000 indigent Tennesseans on Medicaid, plus another 400,000 working uninsured. Instead of the traditional "fee-for-service" Medicaid plan, TennCare proposed, in effect, to privatize Medicaid by letting companies bid for the right to provide health care. A unique blend of conservative and liberal philosophy, TennCare was approved by Secretary Shalala in November 1993, just in time to implement the program in January 1994 (see chapter 12).

By the late 1990s, a combination of factors produced serious problems that threatened TennCare's viability. Among these were a high rate of turnover in state TennCare administrators, a health care industry resistant to competition, and managed care companies poorly equipped for the scale and speed of TennCare's changes. The state was forced to make major modifications in TennCare when Blue Cross, the state's largest insurer of TennCare patients, in 1999 threatened to withdraw from the program.

Despite TennCare's problems, those familiar with the financing of health care and state government realized that the new program had achieved enormous savings—so large that it would be practically impossible to return to the old Medicaid system. At the end of the twentieth century, TennCare occupied about the same proportion of the state budget as in 1993—an important fact, since health care's share of the budget had grown by 150 percent in the previous fifteen years. Thus, while TennCare became a favorite target for legislators seeking explanations for the state's budget shortfalls, Republican Gov. Don Sundquist was steadfast in insisting that TennCare—a Democratic proposal—must be retained as a cornerstone of the state's financial strategy.

Tennessee's second major departure from a federal program was Families First, an effort to reform a welfare program that had little real support in either the Democratic or Republican parties in Tennessee. Like TennCare, Families First represented a radical departure from its predecessor, the federal Aid for Families with Dependent Children program. Families First initially was characterized as a program that would generate net savings by taking long-term recipients off welfare and relieving the government of support payments. At the program's inception in 1996, however, state government actually increased welfare spending by some $60 million for items, such as daycare and transportation, that were needed to assist welfare recipients in working or in job training. While the number of Tennessee's welfare recipients declined significantly, similar declines occurred in virtually every state, making it impossible to determine how much of the change was due to Families First and how much could be traced to the historic growth of the nation's economy in the 1990s. Despite the inability to evaluate fully the program's contribution to the state's financial obligations, Families First remained popular with most legislators and much of the public.

For all their shortcomings, Families First and TennCare represented two of the nation's most ambitious and creative efforts to reverse the intrusion of the federal government into state affairs and to deliver services more efficiently.

Sources of State Revenue

Roughly one-third of Tennessee's annual budget is funded by federal grants, leaving the state to raise the remaining two-thirds of the revenues required to finance state programs. Like all states, Tennessee raises money in a variety of ways. Unlike all but seven states, Tennessee does not have a broad-based tax on personal income. A few states have unique circumstances that make it possible to generate substantial state revenues. Alaska receives a portion of revenues from the sale of oil from its North Slope oil fields. Nevada's economy and state budget are based upon gambling revenues. Florida has sales tax revenues from tourism that dwarf those in other states. In Tennessee, which lacks a special revenue source such as oil or gambling, about 55 percent of state revenues come from the sales tax. The remaining revenues represent an assortment of specialized taxes and fees on business profits, gasoline, alcohol and a wide array of other items (see fig. 14.1).

Largely due to the absence of a state tax on property and personal income, Tennessee traditionally has been a low-tax state, with per capita rates of state taxation among the one or two lowest in the nation. While good in the sense that citizens give less money to the government, low taxes also mean less money available to support state services. Despite one of the nation's most robust state economies, Tennessee's per capita revenue collections were the lowest in the South in 1994 and remained so through the remainder of the 1990s.[7] While low taxes have been a source of pride to many citizens and legislators, the tradition has had a profound effect on the state's ability to fund high-quality services, especially education.

Not only is Tennessee's revenue base relatively small, but also it suffers further from what economists refer to as "inelasticity." A tax system is considered inelastic if growth in tax revenue does not keep pace with growth in the economy. The cost of providing services tends to increase as the economy grows. Like those in all other occupations, teachers and state employees expect periodic salary raises. The cost of textbooks

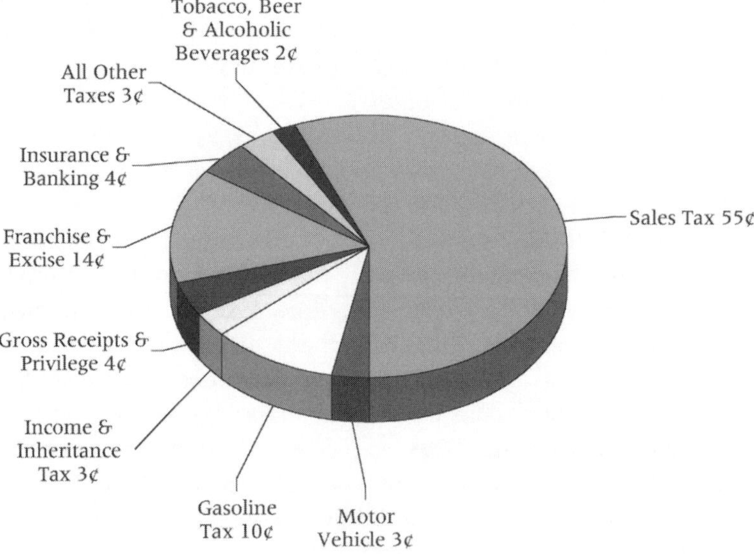

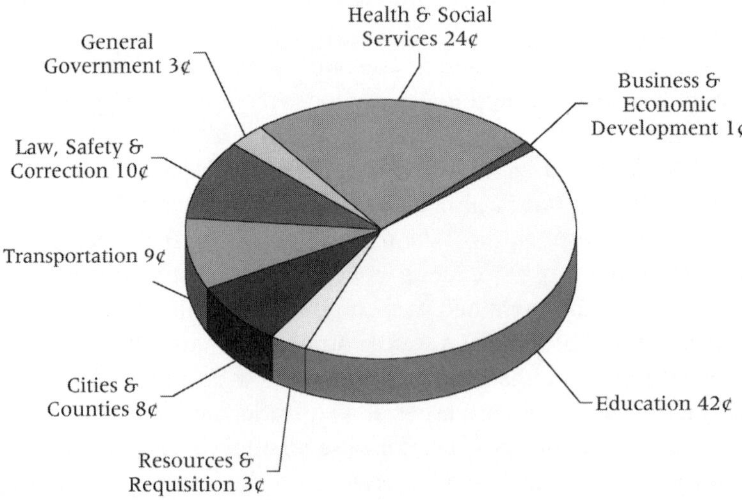

Fig. 14.1. Where Tennessee Tax Dollars Come From and Where They Go (Fiscal Year 2000). ***Source:*** **Tennessee Department of Revenue.**

increases. Health insurance premiums rise. Population increases generate a need for more schools, prisons, roads, and other state services. While most Tennessee Governors and legislators do not wish to expand the size or cost of government, many want to improve the quality of programs such as K–12 schools and higher education. When Tennessee's per capita income ranked forty-eighth, it followed that most state services would be funded at a comparable level. In the 1980s and early 1990s, Tennessee's remarkable economic growth moved its ranking among the states in per capita income upward toward the low thirties. Many Tennesseans believed that the prosperity should be reflected in a better quality of state services, especially in education. Ironically, as Tennessee's increase in personal income made it possible to provide better services, revenue was growing at rates much slower than the economy, due to the state's antiquated tax structure. In other words, at the very time most Tennesseans were able to pay for better services, the state's revenue shortfall resulted in these services being cut rather than improved. Compounding the problem, Tennessee's revenue shortfalls in the late 1990s occurred while most other states were experiencing historic levels of revenue surpluses.

The principal reason for the inelasticity of the tax system and the state's revenue shortfalls is Tennessee's heavy reliance on the sales tax. A sales tax is structured to derive revenues from the income people spend and not the income they earn. The difference is dramatic, both in terms of the implications for financial management and the philosophical statement the tax system makes about who should carry the burden of funding state government. Philosophically, the sales tax stands at the opposite pole from the income tax, which targets the money individuals earn, whether in their jobs or through savings and investments. Personal income is a much more accurate indicator of the state's wealth and economic growth than sales tax receipts. Whether taxing income is a fairer or more desirable vehicle for funding government is an entirely different question—one that has generated the most emotional political debates in the state's recent history.

Sales Tax

The sales tax is the foundation of Tennessee's tax structure for supporting state government. The state collects 6 percent on the sale of tangible goods and certain services. Local governments have the option of adding on up to 2.75 percent, making the maximum sales tax rate in Tennessee 8.75 percent, which is among the highest in the nation.

The sales tax is collected by the merchant at the point of sale and forwarded to the state Department of Revenue, which sends a portion of the revenues to the state Treasury and redirects a smaller portion to city and county governments where the sale occurred. This policy of "state shared taxes" has generated serious financial problems for many local governments since the development of regional shopping malls that attract sales taxes from thousands of persons who live in other counties (see chapter 11). The sales tax is applied to items that are bought in Tennessee or, in some cases such as construction items, purchased outside the state but "used" in Tennessee. The sales tax is paid by the person who makes the purchase rather than by the business selling the product. Businesses pay sales tax on the raw materials they purchase while creating their final products.

The sales tax has several practical advantages. The process is administratively convenient for the state. The burden to collect and forward taxes rests with the merchant, thus keeping to a minimum the state's need for a bureaucracy to administer tax collections. Because the sales tax is collected in relatively small amounts, it is less subject to taxpayer default. The sales tax is difficult for people to avoid (at least without leaving the state), as everyone buys goods in stores. Even those whose incomes are derived from unlawful activities pay the sales tax every time they purchase commodities in Tennessee.

From the perspective of managing state government, the principal disadvantage of the sales tax is the fact that it captures an ever-decreasing portion of the state's economic growth. The problem occurs largely for three reasons. Over the years, the General Assembly has exempted a large number of items and services from the sales tax. These exemptions became more important as Tennessee's economy, like all state economies in the 1970s and 1980s, began to shift sharply away from an emphasis on manufacturing toward an emphasis on services. Because many of these services—including medical, financial, and legal services—were not taxed and were protected by strong lobbying groups, their relative increase within the economy produced a corresponding decrease in the portion of the economy subject to taxation. Finally, the emergence of Internet commerce in the late 1990s further slowed the rate of growth in Tennessee's sales tax revenues. Tennesseans who buy luggage or clothing on the Internet do not pay sales tax in Tennessee. Beginning in the mid-1990s, the combination of exemptions, the growing importance of untaxed services, and Internet commerce gradually produced worsening revenue shortfalls for state government. These shortfalls occurred in a state government that for two decades had been viewed by Wall Street and others as one of the best managed (at least in financial terms) among the fifty states.

As frustrating as the sales tax became from a management perspective, large numbers of Tennesseans were concerned more with the philosophical implications of placing such a large tax on consumption items. The sales tax generally is regarded as *regressive.* This term means that the lower a person's income, the greater the share of it taken by the sales tax. Every person pays a percentage of his or her income for sales taxes on necessities: food, gasoline, clothes, and similar items. If a single mother makes $30,000, for example, the percentage she pays for necessities is two or three times larger than the percentage paid by someone earning more than $100,000. Many states have eliminated the sales tax on food and medicines, which makes the sales tax less regressive, because lower-income people spend a higher proportion of their income on food and medicine. Tennessee has no such exemptions, making its sales tax highly regressive.

Depending upon rates and exemptions, an income tax is less regressive. Under a flat income tax, all taxpayers would pay the same proportion of their income to the government. Under a progressive plan, such as the current federal income tax, higher-income taxpayers pay higher rates of taxation.

Not all Tennesseans, it must be emphasized, have philosophical problems with the sales tax. Indeed, a large number believe that the sales tax is the fairest revenue source, since all persons who buy certain goods pay the tax. For others, their lack of enthusiasm for the sales tax is outweighed by their distrust of government and their fear and loathing of a tax on income, so that the sales tax becomes the lesser of two evils.

Hall Income Tax

Although Tennessee does not have a broad-based tax on salaries and wages, it does have a tax of 6 percent on income derived from dividends and interest on investments. This tax, known as the Hall Income Tax, has a significant exemption level and accounts for only about 1.5 percent of the state's revenues. Nevertheless, the tax is controversial, especially among wealthier Tennesseans who have significant investment income. The Hall Income Tax also has a disproportionate impact on retired persons, many of whom receive substantial income from investments. Moreover, the Hall Income Tax is an issue of particular concern to small, wealthy communities such as the

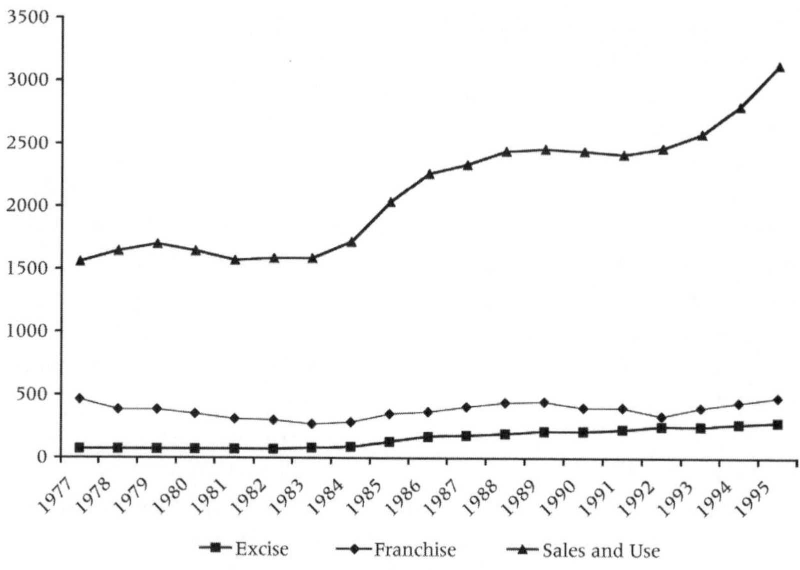

Fig. 14.2. Revenue from Excise, Franchise, and Sales and Use Taxes, 1977–1995. ***Source:*** **Tennessee Department of Revenue.**

Nashville suburb of Belle Meade that do not have a sales tax and fund their limited services with revenues collected in their jurisdiction from the Hall Income Tax.

Figure 14.2 illustrates how sales tax revenues rise and fall without relation to economic expansion in the economy as a whole. Following sales tax rate increases in 1977 and 1984, revenues from the sales tax grew faster than the economy. Within about three years, the growth flattened out and eventually fell behind the rate of economic expansion. Historic economic growth in the 1990s kept sales tax revenues growing at a healthy pace longer than usual and helped Gov. Don Sundquist avoid major financial problems until the late 1990s. Eventually, however, even Sundquist, a long-time opponent of the income tax, changed his position in response to the inability of the sales tax to provide adequate funds for Tennessee's budgeted expenses.

Corporate Excise and Franchise Tax

When corporations conduct business in Tennessee, they are charged a 6 percent excise tax on profits derived from doing business in the state.

These same corporations pay a .25 percent franchise tax on the value of the property they own in Tennessee or their corporate stock, whichever is greater. First enacted in 1923, this tax is not assessed on the proceeds of sole proprietors and partnerships, including many who deliver professional services. During the mid-1990s, Tennessee witnessed the creation of thousands of such partnerships, a blatant attempt by individuals with large incomes to avoid taxes through use of a classic tax "loophole." In 1999, the legislature amended the law to apply the tax to limited liability corporations (LLCs), a favorite tax-free harbor of many corporations.[8] Figure 14.2 shows that corporate franchise and excise tax revenues remained relatively flat as sales tax revenues increased, reflecting a conscious effort by many companies to avoid taxes and explaining why the legislature modified the corporate excise and franchise tax to include LLCs.

The example of the LLCs illustrates another facet of tax policy and the financial management of an entity as vast as state government. On any given day, dozens of highly skilled accountants and tax lawyers are at work with the primary goal of helping their companies and clients avoid state taxes. By taking advantage of an extraordinarily complex combination of tax laws enacted by the fifty states and the federal government, they often seek to structure their companies' operations in a manner that makes it difficult, if not impossible, to collect taxes without investing large amounts of time and energy. A Tennessee company located in Memphis, for example, for tax reasons may file documents to have the company legally housed in Delaware or South Dakota. Knowing that the State of Tennessee has a relatively small staff in the Department of Revenue to combat these kinds of tax-avoidance strategies, many companies have no qualms about doing everything possible within the law to avoid paying taxes.

Other Taxes

Tennessee levies special taxes on a number of items at the time of sale, including tobacco, alcohol, and motor fuels. These taxes have been imposed because of the special nature of the product taxed. Tobacco and alcohol taxes often are referred to as "sin taxes." In the case of alcohol, the laws regarding its sale and taxation represent an evolution of intense efforts during the late nineteenth and early twentieth centuries to outlaw, and then make legal again on a limited basis, the consumption of liquor and beer. Until the mid-1980s, only four Tennessee counties allowed the sale of liquor by the drink. Thus most

Tennesseans were required to purchase alcohol at liquor stores, where inflated prices were made even higher with high taxes. Tennessee took the opposite approach with tobacco, imposing relatively low state taxes on a product important to farmers in about three dozen counties. The tax on gasoline and diesel fuel is unique, in that all the proceeds are allocated to the State Transportation Fund and are used exclusively for the construction and maintenance of roads and bridges. Tennessee's motor fuel tax is relatively high compared to that in other states, causing many truck stops to locate just across the state line from border cities such as Memphis, Chattanooga, and Bristol. The high motor fuel tax is justified on the grounds that paying for road projects on a cash basis saves the state money by avoiding the need to float bonds and pay the resulting interest.

Tobacco Settlement

In the fall of 1998, a consortium of states, originally led by Florida and Mississippi, reached a $250 billion settlement with the tobacco industry after seeking damages for costs incurred by the states as a result of citizens who got sick from smoking. While Tennessee was not a party to the original suit, it did benefit from the settlement, under which states agreed not to seek further damages in exchange for a massive cash settlement. The settlement was the largest in American history. Tennessee's portion of the settlement, based on soft assumptions about future tobacco sales, was an estimated $4.7 billion over a twenty-year period. The financial windfall predictably generated disagreement between the Governor and members of the General Assembly, most of whom had specific ideas about how to spend the money. Some wished to earmark the funds to help tobacco farmers who were switching to other crops. There was also pressure to spend the money to strengthen the TennCare program. Ultimately, the Governor and the legislative leadership chose to save the money and allow it to earn interest. Coming in the midst of a revenue shortfall, the decision said a great deal about the conservative philosophy that guides the financial management of Tennessee state government.

"Tax Reform"

Since the 1940s, Tennessee has relied on the sales tax to fund well over half of state government. The sales tax at times is referred to accurately as both stable and unstable, a fact that can confuse those trying to understand Tennessee's system of state finance. The sales tax can be called stable because, during periods of economic downturn, its revenues do not decline as sharply as revenues from taxes on income or corporate profits. As measured over a longer period of time, however, the annual growth rate of sales tax revenues tends to decline gradually, making it an unstable—or less predictable—means of providing reliable funding for state programs. The pattern has been consistent since the 1960s. Immediately after an increase in the sales tax, state government is awash with revenues for about two years. By about the fifth year, the decline in growth of sales tax revenues produces revenue shortfalls. The Governor and legislature cut the budget for a year or two, then enact another sales tax increase of one or one-half cent, usually in the name of education. Every Governor and virtually every Finance Commissioner since 1970, whether Republican and Democrat, has reached the same conclusion. From the perspective of sound financial management, it is impractical for Tennessee to continue funding a multi-billion-dollar government with an antiquated tax structure based disproportionately on the revenues from a sales tax that does not provide a stable and predictable source of revenues.

McWherter's Proposal

All the arguments about revenue shortfalls, budget instability, and the regressive nature of the sales tax are just another case of inside political baseball to most Tennesseans, who know little and care less about the details of state finance. Given that a large majority of the public did not believe the state had a structural fiscal problem, most Governors were afraid openly to call for broad tax reform. In the mid-1970s, Gov. Ray Blanton consistently advocated a proposal to reduce the sales tax and substitute a tax on income. Any chance he may have had was ruined by the scandals that plagued his administration. Gov. Lamar Alexander, after passing the largest tax increase in Tennessee history, pledged to make tax reform a "front burner" issue; but he left office with no proposal and no effort to design one.

Tennessee's first serious effort at tax reform came during the first year of Gov. Ned McWherter's second term in 1991. The essence of McWherter's proposal was elimination of the sales tax on food, reduction of the remaining sales tax from 6.5 percent to 4 percent, and a 4 percent tax on income, with exemptions for dependents and low-income families. McWherter tied the tax reform proposal to broad-based reforms in K–12 education.

McWherter's tax reform effort never got off the ground. The proposal was killed by a combination of legislators who opposed taxing income and those who supported an income tax but were terrified by the reaction it generated among the voters. Although a supporter of tax reform, the Democratic Majority Leader of the Senate refused to sponsor the Governor's bill. No other member of the Senate's Democratic leadership stepped forward. Although privately they supported tax reform, some Democrats believed, with justification, that if the public identified them as responsible for enacting an income tax, Republicans would take control of the General Assembly for the next generation. If chances ever existed for passage, they evaporated when senators on the fence witnessed the defection of the leadership of the Governor's party. The tax reform proposal, ultimately sponsored in the Senate by a Republican, never came to a vote in committee. Education reform was deferred, and the state budget, including funding for schools, was cut dramatically.

The following January 1992, McWherter called the legislature into special session for another attempt at tax reform, this time with a modified proposal that pleased neither supporters nor opponents of reforming the existing system. With little legislative support, McWherter's efforts to promote the income tax were half-hearted. The special session adjourned without action on the tax proposal, although it was evident that McWherter's education reforms had substantial support. The legislature reconvened in regular session, quickly enacted the education plan, and funded it with yet another increase of half a percent in the sales tax rate.

Sundquist's Proposals

In January 1999, some eight weeks after his November reelection, Gov. Don Sundquist surprised Tennesseans by announcing that state government was projecting a $600 million shortfall in revenues in the next fiscal year. The announcement was particularly jarring to many observers because, during his first term and throughout his 1998 campaign, Sundquist never had mentioned an impending fiscal crisis. The timing of the sudden reversal left many skeptical about the Governor's claims. Sundquist's response to the looming revenue shortfall was a proposal to revamp the Tennessee tax system.

The Governor's plan would have eliminated the sales tax on groceries, saving the average family of four almost five hundred dollars a year. To raise the needed revenues, the Governor proposed replacing the franchise and excise taxes with a 2.5 percent tax on the amount that

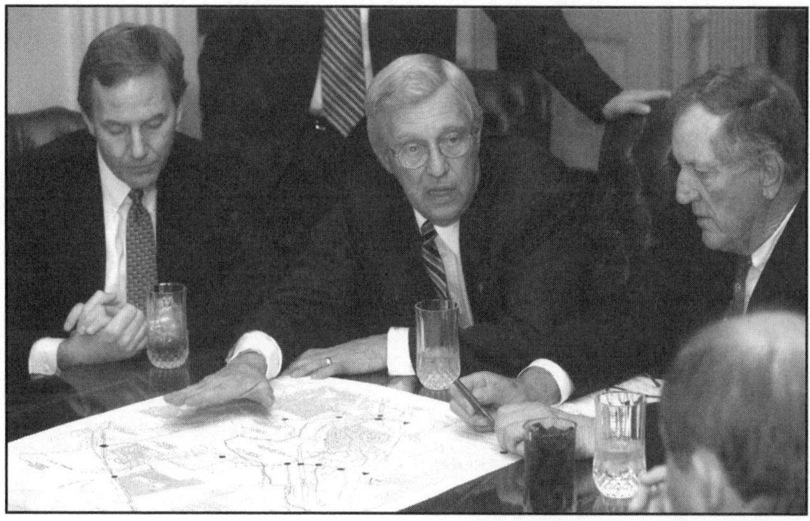

Fig. 14.3. During his second term as governor (1999–2002), Don Sundquist proposed a state income tax to deal with what he termed a "fiscal crisis." ***Source:*** **State of Tennessee Photographic Services.**

a company paid its employees, beyond a fifty-thousand-dollar exemption (fig. 14.3). Although the administration went to great lengths to emphasize that the proposal was not an income tax, most Tennesseans eventually figured out the proposal's purpose. In an attempt to provide a stable revenue stream, the Governor was attempting to capture more of Tennessee's economic growth, only with this proposal the tax would be paid by employers rather than individuals.

Reaction to the Governor's proposal was mixed, although many were surprised that it came from a Republican Governor with a history of professed antipathy to taxation. The reform proposal came at a time of emerging consensus within the General Assembly that the present tax system was incapable of producing enough revenue to fund even a modest level of state services. Despite this consensus, there was no agreement regarding which groups should provide the additional revenues. A tax proposal based on a company's wages did not fully take into consideration whether the business made a large or small profit. Indeed, many businesses with relatively small payrolls generated large profits, while some large industries might experience little or no profit in a given year. The greatest opposition came from small business owners, physicians, and attorneys who would be hit hard by the proposed tax on profits and payrolls. Much of Tennessee's business community, which had strongly supported Sundquist's election, turned on the Governor. Following the lead of their financial contributors, legislative Republicans withheld support. Repeating the experience with McWherter's tax reform legislation, Sundquist's proposal to change business taxes died without a formal vote.

Before the special session ended, however, a sudden swell of legislative support for a tax on income emerged, brought on by the growing realization that no other practical alternative existed; the outdated sales tax was inadequate. In whispered conversations in the legislative halls and at cocktail receptions, one sensed that the unthinkable actually might happen—a coalition of Republicans and Democrats, supported by a Republican Governor, would find seventeen votes in the Senate and fifty in the House to enact an income tax. We will never know how close they came, although some close to the leaders contend that, for about twenty-four hours in April 1999, the votes were identified in both House and Senate. Whatever the true commitments were, the fragile coalition fell apart when the state Republican Party chairman issued a press release threatening all who supported the income tax.

Sundquist reacted to the defeat of his proposal and the spontaneous efforts to enact an income tax by doing something that stunned many of his supporters and opponents. The Governor called the legislature into special session again in November 1999 to consider a 3 percent tax on personal incomes and elimination of the sales tax on groceries. The proposal sent shock waves through the state's political system, particularly the Republican Party. As a candidate and a first-term governor, Sundquist always had expressed unqualified opposition to an income tax. Many Republican candidates for the General Assembly likewise had expressed very strong opposition to an income tax. These Republicans felt betrayed when their titular leader suddenly did an about-face on this fundamental question. As measured in financial management terms, Sundquist's proposal was a great improvement over the existing tax system. Even so, by late fall of 1999, the Governor was confronting open rebellion in the Republican Party. Ironically, Sundquist had considerable Democratic support, but the Democrats were not about to crawl out on the income tax limb unless a substantial number of Republicans went with them.

Sundquist's income tax proposal never received a recommendation for passage from the Senate Finance, Ways and Means Committee. An alternative plan, authored by Sen. Bob Rochelle (D-Lebanon), called for a graduated income tax without eliminating the sales tax on groceries. This plan was recommended to the floor of the Senate by the Finance Committee, by a single vote. Opponents of an income tax became nervous. Many observers believed that sufficient support existed to pass the measure in the House of Representatives, where Speaker Jimmy Naifeh and the rest of the House leadership were advocates of tax reform. The situation reflected a strange, almost surreal shift of political forces, as a Republican Governor became aligned with the Democratic leadership and opposed by most Republican legislators. The day before the Senate was scheduled to vote on the income tax, the House Republican Caucus held a press conference to announce that its members would not support their Governor. Key Republican state senators also voiced intense opposition. Ultimately, the Senate adjourned the special session without voting on the bill, leaving "on the record" regarding the income tax only the eleven senators who had voted in the Finance Committee.

In contrast to McWherter, Sundquist did not give up on his fight for tax reform. He traveled the state, making the case on college campuses and at civic clubs. Despite the bruising legislative defeats he experienced in 1999, Sundquist returned in the 2000 legislative session with yet another proposal for a state tax on income. The proposal generated modest legislative support and a great deal of public opposition. During the late spring, however, another compromise proposal emerged that, for a fleeting moment, appeared to have majority support among legislators. The proposal would have implemented a 5 percent tax on incomes of more than $100,000 ($200,000 for married couples), which would have affected fewer than 2 percent of the state's taxpayers. The outburst of public opposition to the proposal indicated just how intensely a majority of Tennesseans objected to any tax of any kind on personal income. Like the others before it, the compromise proposal to tax Tennessee's highest incomes died without a formal vote.

Sundquist's income tax proposal died in the General Assembly simply because a majority of Tennesseans opposed it. As noted in chapter 8, public opposition to the income tax solidified in the late 1990s. To some extent, the increased opposition was due to the strong anti-tax rhetoric that many politicians, beginning with Ronald Reagan and including Don Sundquist, had used over the preceding two decades. A sizable number of Republican and Democratic legislators, including some who acknowledged the state's financial dilemma, had campaigned on the promise that they never would support an income tax. Within the Republican Party, a growing faction was increasingly hostile to the idea of increasing revenues of any kind at any time, not bothering or caring to determine how to pay for new prisons, teachers' salaries, or other state obligations.

Given this background, it should not have come as a surprise when, in the fall of 1999, Governor Sundquist's income tax proposal was greeted with deeply emotional opposition. In a repeat of the reception accorded McWherter's proposal in 1991, the General Assembly and the Governor's office were deluged by phone calls and e-mails opposing the income tax. Talk radio hosts across the state fanned the flames of protest, often with erroneous information. On the day in 1999 when the Senate adjourned a special session, hundreds of cars honking their horns to protest the income tax encircled the state capitol. A few supporters of tax reform, including representatives of higher education who believed that tax reform was essential to the state's future, came to Nashville to speak in favor of the Governor's plan. Their voices, however, were drowned out by populist anti-tax furor.

Financial Paralysis

As Tennessee entered the new century, the state faced its worst financial dilemma since the economic collapse of the 1930s. Tennessee's revenue shortfalls in the 1990s, unlike those of the Great Depression, came during the period of strongest economic growth in the state's history, a fact that produced enormous frustration among groups affected by state spending. The impact of the shortfalls on the financial management of state government was predictable. Teachers and state employees received no salary increases. Vacant state jobs went unfilled, to the point that many programs could not fulfill their responsibilities and remaining employees repeatedly were forced to work double shifts. State parks became shabby. College campuses such as the University of Tennessee at Knoxville went year after year without an increase in state appropriations. Despite a very real deterioration in quality of state services, however, most Tennesseans did not notice. When cuts are made little by little, the difference from one year to the next rarely is discernible by most of the public. Only after several consecutive years of cuts can one fully appreciate the negative impact of the state's tax system on the quality of Tennessee's programs and services.

The frustration of continued fiscal crisis was compounded by the inability of the political system to respond with a long-term solution. In the past, the Governor and General Assembly, working together, had demonstrated a remarkable ability to address serious problems in education, prisons, and health care. This ability to address problems cooperatively was severely strained by the state's fiscal crisis and the bad feelings created by the Sundquist administration's response to it.

The fiscal and political crisis that occurred in the 1990s revealed a great deal about the forces that would shape state government early in the twenty-first century. While large numbers of legislators certainly were personally opposed to a tax on income, a majority of legislators, Republican and Democrat, privately acknowledged that some type of tax on income was the only solution to Tennessee's financial problems. Why did this majority not translate into a solution? The answer to that question depends upon one's view of legislative responsibility. Many legislators who opposed tax reform could say honestly that they were reflecting the majority view in their districts. This argument must be weighed against the obligation of legislators to make decisions they know are justified, even though their constituents might not understand or agree. To put it more bluntly, should elected officials be expected to sacrifice their careers in order to do what they believe is right? Many viewed Tennessee's continued inability to address a growing financial problem to be a disturbing answer to that question.

Assessing the Politics of Tax Policy

Tennessee's fiscal paralysis at the beginning of the twenty-first century spotlighted a question that has plagued political institutions throughout history. In Tennessee, the debate was not about whether the state should have a large and expensive government—most citizens and legislators preferred to maintain a modest level of services. The question that could not be resolved was how to pay for a level of education, health care, and other services that most Tennesseans wanted. Even as Tennessee's bond rating was downgraded by Wall Street in the summer of 2000, years of sound fiscal management, combined with a strong economy, made it very difficult to convince the public that a crisis existed. The fact that Governor Sundquist made no mention of the need for tax reform during his 1998 reelection campaign made it more difficult for the public to rally around his income tax proposals in 1999 and 2000. Republicans in the General Assembly were placed in an untenable position—to support their Governor, they would have had to repudiate their own campaign promises. On the other side of the aisle, Democrats were not prepared to commit political suicide, even for a cause in which most deeply believed. The inevitable product of these forces was acrimony, distrust, and a serious threat to the unique political culture that had defined Tennessee state government for several decades.

Part V

LOCAL GOVERNMENT AND POLITICS IN TENNESSEE

15

The Politics of Local Government

Much of what happens in Tennessee government takes place among the elected representatives of cities and counties. City councils, county commissions, and school boards across the state each week make numerous decisions that directly affect the lives of Tennesseans. An important aspect of Tennessee's political culture has been the General Assembly's decision to grant extensive decision-making authority to local governments. Tennessee does not, for example, have a state property tax. The state extends to cities and counties exclusive authority to collect property taxes and determine the tax rate. The state also authorizes cities and counties to control land use through zoning regulations that categorize property as residential, commercial, agricultural, or industrial. Counties are required by state law to provide public safety, transportation, and educational services, although local budget decisions have a great deal to do with the quality of these services. Cities and towns decide what services, if any, they will provide beyond what is offered by their respective counties.

Local governments are diverse, perhaps to a fault. Many Tennesseans probably are confused by the complexity of the governments closest to them. Ironically, despite the fact that they are

Fig. 15.1. Memphis City Hall. Photo by William Lyons.

closer to our daily lives than state or national government, local governments often are the victims of public apathy. Voter turnout for city and county elections regularly lags far behind that for statewide and national elections. This trend is at least partially attributable to the confusing nature of local government. Citizens often face a maze of overlapping local government structures, including counties, cities, towns, school districts, and special districts. Complicating matters further, these structures often differ greatly in different communities.

Tennessee and the other forty-nine states are integral parts of the federal system. The states are sovereign entities that cannot be eliminated or combined by federal action. While states are "protected" within the federal system, cities and counties are creatures of the state and can be created or eliminated by state legislatures in accord with the provisions of state constitutions. Once established, cities and counties seldom go out of existence, although the twenty-first century may witness increasing consolidation of cities and counties. Moreover, Memphis (fig. 15.1), Nashville, and Knoxville are examples of how local governments often reflect important differences in local political culture within the state's larger political entity. One cannot fully understand state politics in Tennessee without an appreciation of the history of local government and issues pertaining to it.

Units of Local Government: Counties, Cities, and Towns

In the United States, the county is the primary unit of local government, a tradition this country inherited from Britain. Counties were established primarily as administrative subdivisions of states, so that services such as law enforcement, transportation, and education could be delivered by a government in reasonable proximity to citizens. Today, a large majority of Tennessee counties, at varying levels of scope and quality, provide such services as parks, libraries, health and welfare programs, economic development, and cultural activities that go well beyond the responsibilities mandated by state law.

Counties also serve as the basic organizing unit for the political process. Counties are the basic units upon which political parties are organized. Typically, each county has a chairperson and executive committee for the Democratic and Republican parties. These party leaders sometimes play an important role in the recruitment of political leaders at both the local and the state level. Local, state, and federal elections are conducted and supervised by county election commissions. County election commissions are responsible for voter registration, qualification of candidates, conducting the elections, and tallying votes.[1] Counties thus are responsible for much of the procedure, if not the policy, of the political process.

Tennessee's Ninety-five Counties

In 1777, the North Carolina legislature created Washington County, which included all of present-day Tennessee. By 1879, Washington County had been subdivided into ninety-five counties. Aside from a few boundary modifications, that structure remains intact today. Tennessee has about three times as many counties as Pennsylvania and about half as many as Georgia. Tennessee's relatively large number of counties is a product of the state's geography, its early statehood, and its prior history as part of North Carolina.

Counties, as the basic mechanism for delivering services, had to be sized appropriately so that services could be delivered to citizens living within their boundaries. The nineteenth-century General Assembly determined that "reasonable access" meant the ability to travel by horse or wagon to and from the county courthouse in a day. Until the expansion of the state and county road system, from the 1930s until roughly the 1960s, many of Tennessee's communities were not easily reached. If the state were being organized into counties today, in an age of telephones and rapid transportation, certainly many fewer counties would be created—maybe even two-thirds fewer. The forces of tradition, community jealousy, and simple inertia make it unlikely that, short of financial collapse, existing counties will change. So long as most Tennesseans are comfortable with the current structure of counties, little prospect exists for consolidation of counties.

Cities and Towns

Cities and towns are municipal corporations established by the state upon petition by a number of citizens. The establishment of cities and towns is a result of Tennessee's evolution from an agricultural economy into an industrial and service economy that requires more densely populated communities. Cities and towns are established for a variety of reasons, some of which may be conflicting. The majority of residents in a community may make a collective decision to have more services, such as fire protection and garbage collection. Other communities may desire zoning regulations, to make it possible to regulate the size and nature of residential and commercial growth. On occasion, communities will attempt to incorporate for precisely the opposite reason—to avoid zoning regulations or required sewers and roads. Often people living close together in a prosperous community wish for more or better schools than the county is willing to provide. As Tennessee developed as a state and more people lived in closer proximity, these issues created a need for governments to provide services not offered by existing counties.

The line separating the duties of cities and counties never has been a clear one. This vagueness has combined with the emotional issue of land use to create tension between cities wishing to expand their boundaries and suburban residents who want to avoid annexation. This tension defined much of the debate among local governments as Tennessee entered the twenty-first century.

As in most states, the politics of Tennessee's cities and towns are incredibly diverse. The issues often revolve around local personalities, taxation, the location of schools, and disputes over land use. In communities with large African American populations, race often forms an undercurrent in political decisions. In some counties with a dominant central city, support of or hostility to that city among county residents often defines relationships between the city and county governments. In communities experiencing demographic change, conflicts can emerge about the types and quality of services provided by the community. Occasionally, all of these factors are at play in a single county.

Memphis Politics

Edward H. Crump, better known as "Boss Crump," dominated Memphis politics in the first half of the twentieth century. Crump's political machine exerted control statewide. His ability to deliver large numbers of votes to a preferred candidate for statewide office often meant the difference between victory and defeat.

Crump made a major contribution to the development of African American political strength in the city. In return for minor political favors, Crump saw to it that blacks were registered and turned out as a reliable voting bloc. This political activity grew into activism centered around churches in the minority community.

Race emerged gradually as a factor in Memphis politics until the assassination of Dr. Martin Luther King there in 1968. After the riots that followed Dr. King's murder, race became an undercurrent in every major political issue in Memphis and Shelby County. While the tension at that time centered on the rights of sanitation workers to bargain collectively with the city, it soon focused on the city's political structure. The city's growing black minority had been systematically underrepresented. White residents tended to vote as a bloc to frustrate the candidacy of blacks seeking citywide political office. Angered by court-ordered busing of public school students, thousands of other whites left the city and moved to suburbs in Shelby County.

By the mid-1970s, blacks represented a majority of residents in Memphis. Their growing numbers translated into political strength that eventually led to the election of Harold Ford to Congress in 1974. Ford retained the seat for over twenty years, until being succeeded by his son in 1996. In one of the great ironies of southern politics, the heir to Boss Crump's white political machine in Memphis was the Ford family, which for the last quarter of the twentieth century was a major force in both state and local politics.

Like Crump, the Ford family was not invincible. After several contentious elections characterized by increasing polarization, a former Superintendent of Schools, Dr. Willie Herenton (pictured right), was elected in 1991 as the city's first black mayor. He was reelected in 1995 and 1999. In 1999, Herenton defeated, among others, Joe Ford, the brother of Harold Ford.

Fig. 15.2. Dr. Willie Herenton.

Representation of Urban Interests in the General Assembly

Since both cities and counties are creatures of the state, the boundaries of their authority and their political representation in Nashville are defined in large measure by the General Assembly. Prior to the U.S. Supreme Court's landmark decision in *Baker v. Carr* (1962),[2] the Tennessee General Assembly had an overwhelmingly rural perspective. Because legislative district lines had not been redrawn in decades, cities such as Memphis and Chattanooga, which had grown in population, had not experienced a comparable increase in number of state legislators. Cities had a profound interest in challenging the political status quo.

Urban advocates believed that redistricting the General Assembly according to the principle of "one person, one vote" would lead to much stronger representation of city interests. This was a simplistic expectation, for suburban areas outside of central cities were among the areas receiving the greatest increases in representation. These areas often had interests diametrically opposed to those of the cities they bordered. The redistricting reforms mandated by the U.S. Supreme Court brought about enormous changes in state and local governments, but not always the ones anticipated or desired by cities and counties. The balance of political power in the legislature shifted, as the traditional contest between urban and rural interests gave way to a new triangular combination that included the unique priorities of suburban communities. Cities received more legislative representation; in many instances, however, the new representatives were black Democratic legislators who parted ways with their hometown Republican colleagues. Despite the implementation of "one person, one vote" in the early 1960s, with a single two-year exception, rural legislators retained leadership of the Tennessee Senate and House from the 1960s through the close of the century.

County Government

Prior to 1978, Tennessee counties were governed by a patchwork system grafted onto a hopelessly outmoded structure known as the County Court of Quarterly Sessions. Comprised of justices of the peace, the old county court served as the main institution of county government until it was eliminated by a constitutional amendment in 1978. Until these changes, no clear lines separated legislative, executive, and judicial powers. The Tennessee Constitutional Convention of 1977 recommended changing the state constitution in major ways relating to the governing of counties. The voters approved these changes in 1978. The modifications gave counties a government structure that could raise revenues and manage large budgets, undertake construction projects such as schools and sewers, and generally function in the manner required by a community with tens or even hundreds of thousands of residents. The changes to Article VII of the Tennessee Constitution gave the state's counties a more modern form of governance.

The changes approved by the voters in 1978 changed the face of county government and altered the state's role in county affairs. To a large degree, the changes shifted power from the state to the hands of local voters. Prior to the 1978 changes, counties had been required to seek private acts of the General Assembly for any legislative initiatives not provided for under the state's code or constitution. While private acts still are required for special situations, Tennessee counties today have far more discretion than they had in the state's first 175 years.

The state allows deviation from the basic form of the county through the consolidation of city and county governments. Otherwise, the county may vary from the conventional form of local government by means of a charter, the equivalent of a local constitution. A charter cannot be altered by the General Assembly without the approval of the county's voters in a referendum.

The Tennessee Constitution's 1977 governance reforms for counties provided for the election of a county executive and a lawmaking body. The lawmaking body, usually referred to as the county commission, cannot exceed twenty-five members. To guard against the exclusion of minority groups, commissioners must be elected from districts of roughly equal population.

Counties have some discretion with county home rule, a feature that allows counties with special needs, such as the larger urban counties, to develop more complex structures to handle those needs. Tennessee counties can opt for home rule by submitting a charter to their voters. This charter cannot be at odds with the Tennessee Constitution. The charter option allows counties to have some control over their structures and to create offices they find useful. For instance, Shelby County and Nashville-Davidson both have mayors with unique powers. Most counties have a county executive, who has less budgetary and executive authority. Changes to the charter must be approved by county voters.

Adopting a County Charter

If a county wishes to depart from the standard form of government prescribed by the Tennessee Constitution, a charter commission must be created to set forth recommended changes. A charter commission can be established in various ways. The commission must prepare a charter for public vote within nine months of being established. While the charter commission can propose a variety of governance changes, including consolidation with another government, the proposed charter cannot alter the election of the constitutionally mandated county officers.

Counties can pass ordinances for such things as parking or trash disposal and can provide for fines for violation. Counties may not, however, extend their authority over taxation beyond that allowed by the state. As of the end of the twentieth century, only Knox and Shelby counties had availed themselves of the county charter option. Each has unique elements. Knox County, for example, elects its own law director every eight years. Because the law director is a creature of the Knox County Charter rather than the Tennessee Constitution, Knox County voters can change their charter to limit the law director's terms. They cannot, however, vote to limit the terms of the constitutional officers.

County Executive

In Tennessee, a county executive is elected to serve as the chief executive officer of the county. The county executive prepares and administers a budget, hires employees, and represents the county in a multitude of areas, from economic development to relationships with other counties and cities. The basic charter grants the county executive veto power over actions of the county commission, but this veto can be overridden by a majority of the commission. The county executive has authority to appoint a number of board and commission members, as well as the heads of the various county departments. The county executive must be at least twenty-five years old and must have resided in the county for one year prior to filing the nominating petition prior to the election.

Compared with other states, the actual power of a county executive in Tennessee is limited. Much of the county executive's effectiveness lies in an ability to work cooperatively with other units of government, including cities and towns within the county, as well as state and even federal officials. Unlike mayors, however, the county executive must work with other elected officials who head departments in the county government. These relationships can create great difficulty in a host of areas, from preparing the county budget to the assignment of accountability for county programs. The fact that the trustee, property assessor, register of deeds, and various clerks of court are independently elected heads of their own departments limits the county executive's ability to hold personnel and policies in the respective county departments accountable for their actions and the operation of their programs. The problem is compounded if these elected officials make decisions that have a budgetary impact on other county functions. The collection of fees and the surpluses they generate are a constant source of friction between county executives and the county officials with whom they are obligated to work.

The county executive's relationship with independently elected officials has encountered particular difficulty in the areas of law enforcement and education. The sheriff is a high-profile official in almost all counties and, except in Davidson County, is responsible for law enforcement within the county. The sheriff usually is in a position to employ a large number of deputies and jail personnel. Moreover, the buildings, automobiles, and other items needed to perform law enforcement tasks create substantial demands on the county budget.

The sheriff submits the department budget to the county executive for inclusion in the overall county budget. Unique features of the sheriff's duties, combined with notions of independence that derive from the sheriff's election and historical ability to influence other county elections, can lead to difficulties in integrating the sheriff's budgetary priorities with the county's overall plans for personnel, purchasing, and general operation of county government. The situation is made more sensitive by the fact that the sheriff's political clout often leaves other elected members of the county commission unwilling to risk a confrontation by holding the sheriff to the same policies and expectations as exist for other departments.

The funding and operation of schools are annual challenges for a county executive and the county commission. The commission is charged with setting the budget and tax rate for all county spending categories, including K–12 education. In Tennessee, however, elected school boards set policy for the public schools. This division of responsibility creates a situation in which commissions are voting to spend dollars without control over how those dollars are spent. School boards likewise must make policies without the ability to raise revenues to fund those policies, depending instead upon the support of a county commission that may or may not share the school board's priorities.

The presence of a county executive, sheriff, school board, and other constitutional officers—all separately elected—contributes to the complexity of governing Tennessee's counties. While challenging, these difficulties are not insurmountable and often may be overcome by skillful strategy and interpersonal communication.

Sheriff

As in most states, the sheriff is the chief law enforcement official in each of Tennessee's counties (except Nashville–Davidson County, where there is a metro police force). While the sheriff is a constitutional officer and must be elected in each county, a sheriff's duties are not enumerated in the state constitution. The General Assembly has specified duties for sheriffs in the Tennessee Code.[3] The duties pertain to enforcement of laws and court orders and administration of county jails. These seemingly legalistic duties disguise the fact that, in most counties, the sheriff is a major player in county politics.

Like the other constitutional county officers, the sheriff is elected by the voters of the county, including those who may live in cities, and serves for a term of four years, with no term limit. Sheriffs must be twenty-one years old, qualified to vote in the county, and have no felony convictions. Sheriffs also must have graduated from high school and be certified by a qualified psychological professional as being free from mental disorders. These latter requirements were added in the 1980s, after a number of Tennessee sheriffs were convicted of serious crimes, mostly related to the sale and distribution of illegal drugs.[4]

Sheriffs in many southern states traditionally financed their offices and, to a large degree, their salaries, with fines collected for speeding and other offenses. The system was an invitation to corruption. Tennessee sheriffs today can collect fines and fees, but the revenues must be turned over to the county's general fund. Perhaps the most significant and controversial source of such revenues is the sale of boats, cars, and other items seized from drug dealers. The large revenues derived from such confiscated property pose a tremendous temptation to sheriffs and are an endless source of frustration to state and local entities attempting to keep track of the money. An example of such frustration occurred in 1997, when Knox County Sheriff Tim Hutchinson built a firing range for the Sheriff's Department without prior knowledge of, or budgetary approval by, the Knox County Commission.

The office of sheriff, especially in a small county, is a highly desirable job and one that is highly politicized. The sheriff often is the most politically powerful individual in a county. A major employer, the sheriff hires personnel for law enforcement, the county jail, and related services. Although often not thought of by the public in the same category as county executives or state legislators, one can safely assume that none of these elected officials crosses the sheriff except by accident.

Fee Offices

Every four years, the voters of each county choose a number of county constitutional officers at the same time they choose the county executive and sheriff. These offices are known as "fee offices" because they are funded primarily though the collection of fees for services performed for the public. The offices generate substantial revenues and employ a significant number of people, usually as political patronage. They sometimes exist as personal fiefdoms within county government, where they can become sources of conflict with the county executive and county commission.

County Clerk

The most important of the fee officers is the county clerk. The clerk is the official keeper of the county's records, including financial records. The clerk collects various county taxes, including hotel and motel taxes and any tax on automobiles. The office also dispenses state license plates and is the location where citizens can transfer automobile titles. The clerk also can perform marriages and issue marriage licenses.

Register of Deeds

Tennessee voters also elect a register of deeds in county elections. The register's office is the official repository of public records having to do with transfer or sale of personal property and real estate in the county. The office generates a lot of traffic from attorneys and real estate professionals involved in buying and selling property. The register collects taxes on mortgages and property transfers, a portion of which the state uses to purchase buffer property around state parks and recreational areas.

Trustee

Each county also elects a county trustee. The trustee collects all property taxes on behalf of the county and may collect property taxes on behalf of any cities and towns in the county. The trustee also is charged with investing any temporary surplus funds, a significant source of revenue in larger counties. The trustee distributes sales tax revenues to the appropriate county government entities.

Clerk of Court

The clerk of court is also elected at the county level in Tennessee. The clerk keeps up with all paperwork necessary for the functioning of the court system. The clerk is responsible for seeing that oaths are administered, minutes are kept, and, most important, that the records of all judgments rendered by the courts are in proper order. The clerk is usually, but not always, the clerk for chancery, sessions, and criminal courts. The General Assembly has passed private acts to establish separate clerks of chancery courts in some counties.

Property Assessor

The Tennessee Constitution requires that each county elect a property assessor to set a value on each parcel of land (including buildings on that land) in the county. The assessor also must determine the value of business "tangible personal property" owned by each of the county's businesses. These judgments, when combined with a county's tax rate, determine the amount of property taxes that individuals and businesses must pay. Citizens have the right to appeal their assessments.

County Election Cycle

The county, as the state's primary unit of local government, forms the basis for election of other local officials. All counties elect county clerks of court, property assessor, trustee, and register of deeds, along with the sheriff, trustee, county executive, school board, and county commissioners. Electing so many offices leads to a splintering of the county political process and produces fatigue and confusion among voters. Campaigns for these offices can be partisan in nature and involve both local primaries and general elections. Because dozens, if not hundreds, of courthouse jobs are at stake, the campaigns are spirited, even desperate at times, with countless yard signs cluttering roads and vacant lots. Despite the fact that not one person in twenty can name most of the county officials, election of most county officers is required by the state constitution. Thus it is highly unlikely that voters ever will provide the support needed to make the positions appointed.

School Boards

As a result of Tennessee's 1992 education reforms, all of the state's counties and municipalities entrust the management of local schools to elected school boards. Ninety percent of Tennessee's school districts are "dependent"—that is, they lack legal authority to raise their own funds.

School boards set policy for their respective school systems and submit their budgets to county commissions for approval. The exceptions are fourteen independent, or "special," school districts created by special acts of the Tennessee General Assembly. These districts, which are not managed or funded by county or city governments, receive funding directly from the citizens living within their boundaries, in accord with tax rates set by private acts of the Tennessee General Assembly.[5]

School board responsibilities run the gamut from hiring and salary policies for teachers to dress codes and standards for expulsion for students. The day-to-day operation of the school system is the responsibility of a Director of Schools, still called "the superintendent" in most communities. Until the 1990s, the majority of Tennessee's 139 school superintendents were elected, although a majority of Tennessee students resided in districts with appointed superintendents. One of the most significant changes in education governance occurred when the 1992 reforms required election of all school boards, each of which in turn would appoint a superintendent under the terms of a fixed contract.

Eliminating any elected official typically elicits criticism that the public is being denied the right to elect the official of its collective choosing. Highly controversial, this far-reaching legislation fundamentally altered circumstances in which the school system, particularly in small counties, often was torn apart by elections among superintendents, principals, and school board members who had no intention of working together after a bitter campaign. Those systems with elected superintendents were required to change to school board appointment by the year 2000. In contrast to the old system, in which both the elected superintendent and elected school board claimed a mandate from the voters, under the new law the superintendent worked for the school board and had clear duties and responsibilities. The superintendent had authority over personnel and management policies but was accountable to the school board for the performance of the schools.

The mandated appointment of superintendents by elected school boards was part of a comprehensive package of education reforms passed with the hope that K–12 education would benefit from greater professionalism and less overt politics. Appointing the school superintendent fit well within this package. Previously, elected superintendents had to raise substantial funds and make decisions with an eye toward the electorate. Now, an appointed superintendent need satisfy only a majority of the school board—hopefully, by providing a good education to students in the district.

Governing Cities and Towns

Cities are corporations formed for the particular purpose of providing additional services to those who live in a defined area of a county. Cities are formed according to the provisions of state laws and must expand according to state law as well.

In Tennessee, any discussion of urban areas must include the "Big Four" cities of Nashville, Memphis, Knoxville, and Chattanooga. While very different in many respects, these cities long have shared the interests, problems, and opportunities characteristic of America's medium-sized cities. The General Assembly often legislates separately for these cities as a class and sometimes passes "local bills" with the assent of the delegation from the county where the city is located.

While one may think of the four large cities when one thinks of Tennessee's municipalities, the state has hundreds of cities and towns under 100,000 in population. These smaller municipalities deliver a mixture of urban services to their citizens. The menu of services provided by these small cities varies, but the politics involved in selecting, funding, and managing these services often are as contentious as those found in Memphis, Nashville, Chattanooga, or Knoxville.

Cities can do only what the State of Tennessee lets them do.[6] Even those cities with home rule charters, allowable after the Constitutional Convention of 1953, cannot do anything that is inconsistent with state law. The state limits the type and amount of local taxes that can be imposed. For instance, while a community may opt to impose a local option on their sales tax, the increase may not be greater than is allowed by the General Assembly.

Services

Cities are permitted but not compelled to provide a variety of services. All Tennessee towns and cities receive a portion of the sales taxes collected in their jurisdictions, as well as other state taxes earmarked for cities.

These taxes include specific taxes levied on alcohol, gasoline, diesel fuel, and portions of the Hall Income Tax on interest and dividends.

Tennessee law enables a city to be formed with no intention of levying taxes or providing services. A city can consist of little more than a geographically defined area with a minimal government. On occasion, cities are established primarily to avoid annexation, to implement zoning standards, and to manage other lifestyle issues, without any immediate intention of providing services other than those provided by the county. In 1980, when residents of western Knox County voted to incorporate, forming the town of Farragut, they did not institute a property tax or provide basic fire, police, or education services. Rather, one of Tennessee's wealthiest communities focuses its activities on providing parks and recreational programs, while maintaining zoning regulations to protect the property values of expensive subdivisions.

At the other end of the spectrum, some Tennessee cities are quite ambitious in providing an array of services consistent with the expectations and lifestyle of the community. The City of Oak Ridge, for example, long has relied on a property tax to fund an excellent school system with teachers compensated well above the state average.

Most Tennessee cities and towns, especially those with populations greater than ten thousand, opt to provide a fairly broad array of services. One of the most obvious urban services is fire protection. While volunteer fire departments may be adequate for rural areas and subscription services often provide suitable services for suburban areas, the high density of larger cities demands a full-time, professional fire department. Likewise, most cities opt for a police force to supplement the work of the county sheriff.

A substantial number of Tennessee cities choose to operate their own school systems, a decision that has created serious funding problems for county school systems denied the larger city tax base. Many municipal school systems were established because residents were dissatisfied with the funding and quality of the county school system. Indeed, the top tier of Tennessee schools, as measured by per-pupil spending, consists almost entirely of municipal systems. Most but not all of Tennessee's medium-sized and large cities operate their own school systems. Most smaller communities have opted to leave education to their respective counties, although there are many exceptions to this trend. Lenoir City, with fewer than ten thousand residents, operates its own system rather than have its students educated in the

Loudon County schools. Germantown, a large and wealthy suburb of Memphis, while offering many municipal services, does not operate its own school system.

Due in large part to financial factors, the trend may be toward consolidation of city and county school systems. Nashville has had a unified school system since the early 1960s. Knoxville operated a city school system until 1991, when a majority of its voters approved a local initiative to cease operating the system. The education of all Knox County children, including those in the city of Knoxville, became the responsibility of Knox County. Chattanooga and Hamilton County residents consolidated their school systems in 1997.

An important aspect of the consolidation issue is the fact that a county government does not have the option of getting out of the school business. This is one of the major differences between cities and counties. Counties exist to provide a minimum level of services mandated by the state. Cities are formed when citizens want more services or, in a handful of instances, when they wish to avoid annexation by a neighboring city. A city can choose to stop performing any service and can even give up its charter completely. A county, however, is established by the General Assembly and cannot be eliminated by its citizens.

Incorporation and Annexation

Two of the most contentious issues in local politics are incorporation and annexation. Incorporation is the process by which a community becomes a city or town. Annexation is the process by which a municipality extends its boundaries to take in additional land, residents, and businesses. A city often wishes to annex industrial or residential areas in order to control growth along its perimeters, but a more common reason is to expand its tax base. Residents living outside city limits often oppose annexation because they do not wish to pay the higher property taxes required to support benefits that accompany city residency. Others do not want to send their children to city schools or conform to city zoning regulations. Incorporation sometimes is viewed as a strategy by which suburban communities can avoid annexation by a nearby city.

Becoming a City or Town: Incorporation

In Tennessee as in most other states, a group of citizens can petition to have an election among people living in a defined area to determine whether the voters wish to incorporate as a municipality. In Tennessee, any community that wishes to become incorporated must have a minimum population of five hundred and must lie five miles from an existing incorporated area of population greater than one hundred thousand, or within three miles of an existing city or town with a population under one hundred thousand.[7] These limitations are important and are the product of past conflicts.

The state has an interest in insuring the orderly growth of its cities. If a small group of people were allowed to form its own community too close to an existing one, this would hamper the existing community's ability to expand sewers, roads, industrial parks, and other items in an orderly fashion. A proliferation of nearby incorporated towns eventually would lead to governmental fragmentation and place the city's future growth in jeopardy. The minimum size requirement insures that towns are not created carelessly, without the size needed for a meaningful political unit.

The state allows a community to incorporate or to change its form by means of a special charter established by an act of the General Assembly. However, most new municipalities come into existence after voters approve one of the state's basic charters that incorporation proponents put on the ballot.

Tennessee provides what many call a cafeteria approach to municipal incorporation. Those seeking to become a town or city can choose a governance option that best fits the characteristics and values of those who live in the proposed municipality. These options include the following:

- *Mayor-alderman.* This is a "weak mayor" form, in which the mayor is a member of a five- to seven-member city council and is not in charge of the day-to-day administrative process.
- *City manager.* In Tennessee, this form was used first in Kingsport in 1917 and then in Alcoa in 1919. In a city manager form, the council hires a city manager to be responsible for the day-to-day running of the city. The mayor is a member of the council and sometimes is chosen by council.
- *Home rule cities.* Home rule cities can amend their charters by majority vote of their citizens, without corresponding to a charter spelled out in state legislation. Home rule was made possible after voters approved changes recommended by the 1953 Constitutional Convention. Tennessee cities long had sought home rule, which has the benefit of allowing cities to draft charters tailored to their individual circumstances. All of Tennessee's largest cities have home rule charters.

"Tiny Towns" Fiasco

In 1998, the General Assembly enacted what became known as the "Tiny Towns" Act,[8] a law that made it much easier for small communities to incorporate. Passage of the legislation produced an explosive reaction by the state's cities and a landmark court resolution of the conflict. The law drastically reduced (to 225) the number of residents necessary to form a town and greatly shortened the distance required between the new town and its neighbors. Such an incorporation would override a larger community's annexation, even if the annexation procedures already had started.

The legislation's original intent was to allow the Fayette County community of Hickory Withe to incorporate. Senate Speaker John Wilder represented the community, adding to the intensity of the issue. Although different versions of the story exist, the details of the legislation somehow escaped the scrutiny of the Tennessee Municipal League (TML), the state's major representative of urban interests. The state's largest cities, especially Memphis, were put in a difficult—some said impossible—position by the new law. Immediately after the passage of the law, four small communities surrounding Memphis initiated efforts to incorporate. Fortunately for TML and for existing communities, the Tennessee Supreme Court ruled that the legislation violated a constitutional technicality and declared the new law invalid.

The entire "Tiny Towns" episode did little to enhance public confidence in the legislative process. The General Assembly's reputation suffered, as many lawmakers admitted they had voted to pass the legislation without careful reading. Speaker Wilder did not enhance his reputation, except possibly as one whose legislation could pass with minimal scrutiny. Even Governor Sundquist admitted he had signed the legislation without subjecting it to close examination.

The biggest loser in the fiasco was probably the Tennessee Municipal League. Mayors of the major cities blasted TML for being asleep at the wheel when the bill was passed. Following the incident, much of the staff resigned or retired, and the four larger cities formed an independent organization to represent their interests. They did not, however, withdraw from TML. Criticism eventually resulted in the restructuring of the organization and a lessening of its influence in the General Assembly.

Annexation

As areas around cities have become more densely populated, cities historically have sought to expand their boundaries to include them.

City leaders tend to believe that their cities need to grow to remain viable. However, residents outside the city do not necessarily share this view. Often they do not wish to pay higher taxes for city services, such as increased police and fire protection, street lighting, sewers, and garbage pickup. However, many suburban residents living just outside cities like Knoxville and Chattanooga work, shop, and regularly attend events inside the city limits. They use city streets and contribute to congestion and pollution. Their suburban communities owe their very existence to the cities they surround. City leaders often point to these factors in justifying annexation of suburban areas.

Under state legislation effective prior to 1998, any city or town attempting annexation had the burden of demonstrating that the proposed annexation was "reasonable." Residents in the area to be annexed had the right to a jury trial, with the jury drawn from the entire county and not just the city. The city had the difficult task of convincing an often skeptical jury that people who did not wish to be annexed should be brought into the city against their will. The old law allowed one person in a proposed annexation area to bring such a trial.

Frustrated by opposition to residential annexation, some cities resorted to "strip annexation" or "finger annexation," in which they annexed businesses and other areas along highways and roads reaching out from the city. In many cases, a business desires to come into a city so that it may receive city fire and police protection, sidewalks, zoning standards, and, for some restaurants, a license to sell liquor. Some corporations, such as Goody's retail stores, headquartered in Knoxville, have requested annexation to insure the necessary services before agreeing to establish a corporate headquarters.

Cities benefited from such finger annexations, because they recovered a portion of the sales tax proceeds generated by annexed businesses. In contrast, county governments chafed at finger annexations, because they lost sales tax revenues. Because annexations must be contiguous, the annexed area often included a roadway reaching to the targeted business, which made for highly irregular city boundaries. By 1998, finger annexation had become an issue that required attention by the General Assembly.

Annexation Legislation of 1998

In 1998, the General Assembly enacted far-reaching legislation designed to bring about a more rational process of annexation and growth in urban areas.[9] The act placed a moratorium on incorporation near city boundaries and ended the practice of finger annexation. The legislation also required each incorporated city or town and each county government to form a committee to participate in formulating a policy to govern the county's future growth. The committees were directed to assign all areas in the respective county to one of three categories.

The first designated category, known as the Urban Growth Boundary, included neighborhoods within city or town boundaries, as well as areas clearly urban in nature. Often there was great disagreement concerning what is clearly "urban" in nature. Under the new law, the appropriate city or town could annex any areas currently outside their borders and urban in nature, without a vote of those living in these areas. Moreover, anyone living in the area subject to annexation would have the burden of demonstrating that annexation was unreasonable. This represented a sharp departure from the prior situation.

Most important, anyone challenging the annexation would present arguments not before a jury, but in a chancery or circuit court before a judge. Under the new law, any property owner challenging an annexation would have a difficult time making the case that the annexation was "unreasonable" unless able to prove that the annexing city did not have an adequate plan for funding and delivering new services.

The importance of changing from a jury trial to a bench trial is difficult to overstate. Historically, the jury pool for such cases always included substantial representation of those living outside a city's boundaries. These residents usually identified with the argument that individual property owners should not be brought into a city against their will. When issues are framed in this manner, a city has a hard time making the case that its need to grow should override an individual's freedom to resist annexation and higher taxes. In fact, most cities had given up attempting to annex when such a trial could be expected. A judge, however, is much more likely to uphold the reasonableness of annexation, especially if the proposal is grounded in a rational process. In a dramatic shift of circumstances, anyone owning property in an Urban Growth Boundary zone could expect to have little legal recourse to avoid annexation.

The second designation elaborated in the 1998 legislation was the Planned Growth Area. This category represented all areas in the county outside municipal boundaries where growth could be expected to occur. A city was not allowed to annex places in the planned growth area, so property owners here were protected from annexation.

The third category was Rural Areas, where high-density development, such as apartments or shopping malls, were prohibited for twenty years. The Rural Areas category raised serious issues regarding economic development. In many urban counties, the only large tracts of undeveloped land lie in what likely would be classified a rural agricultural zone. The new law would run afoul of large companies or industries that might be eyeing land far outside cities and towns for some potential large-scale development. While classification of the area as a rural zone indeed might create difficulties, these difficulties seemed surmountable.

Perhaps the most intriguing aspect of the new law was the decision-making process by which areas were assigned to the three categories. The probability was not high that cities, towns, and the county committees would agree on the boundaries of the various zones. In such cases, the final decision would rest with a panel of administrative law judges in Nashville. While the possibility of an imposed decision about boundaries could be expected to stimulate cooperation, the likelihood remained that some property owners outside cities and towns could find themselves in the urban growth zone and so face subsequent annexation, due to the decisions of a judicial panel in Nashville. In such instances, the chances were great that conflicts between local governments or even violence on the part of angry individuals could challenge the effectiveness of the law.

In 1999, the process mandated by the new law got under way, but not without conflict. In Chattanooga and Knoxville, city and county officials could not agree on the boundaries for the Urban Growth Zone. The Knox County Commission refused to designate any of the area outside the City of Knoxville for urban growth, leaving the final decision to be made in Nashville. That pattern likely would be replicated statewide between cities wanting to grow and county residents resistant to new taxes.

Metropolitan Government

The 1998 annexation legislation was designed to deal with some of the problems that often arise between municipal governments and the government of the counties in which they are located. Increasingly common when several governments coexist in a single metropolitan area, these problems make it very difficult to plan and coordinate such services as roads, schools, and sanitation. Wealthier suburban communities on the fringes of several Tennessee cities threaten to close off the growth of their metropolitan neighbors, leaving them with costly problems and the prospect of a diminishing tax base. Some Tennesseans believe that a solution to these problems is the consolidation of existing municipal governments into a single government for the entire county.

Not all Tennesseans view the presence of multiple governments within a county as a bad thing. Some contend that having a variety of governments provides an opportunity for residents to seek the type of community that they prefer.[10] While many would opt to pay extra taxes for better schools, garbage collection, or sewers, others might be content with only the barest minimum of services. Some might welcome strict zoning ordinances; others would oppose them. Germantown, for example, has strict zoning and signage requirements that might not be accepted by the majority of citizens in Memphis. Most residents of Halls have no desire to be part of Knoxville. Some observers believe that anxiety about urban schools often underlies county residents' opposition to annexation. This concern has been addressed in Nashville, Knoxville, and Chattanooga, where city and county school systems have merged.

Nashville was the first city in Tennessee (and among the first in the nation) to create a single metropolitan government in a county. Tennessee's Constitutional Convention of 1953 made possible such a consolidation of city and county governments. The resulting constitutional amendment allowed smaller governments in an area to retain their autonomy if they wanted to provide services above and beyond those provided by the new metropolitan government. The constitutional provision, along with the later actions by the General Assembly, provides a framework for consolidation. First, a charter commission is appointed to write a charter spelling out the structure and powers of the proposed government. The proposed charter then is submitted to the voters. The charter provides details concerning the new government, including the size of the representative body, the scope of services, and a process for delivering different services at varying tax rates to the county's urban and rural areas.

The charter commission is designed to give all existing governments in a region proposed for consolidation seats at the table when the blueprint for a proposed new government is drawn. The county government, the central city, and each other incorporated city or town are represented. This charter commission is granted discretion to propose anything that does not violate either the state constitution or existing state statute.

Of all the provisions of the Tennessee Constitution, one inevitably gives rise to disputes in discussions of consolidation. The county sheriff is a "constitutional officer," meaning that each county must elect a sheriff. Historically, the sheriff has performed two major functions. As the county's chief law enforcement officer, the sheriff is in charge of those who enforce state and local statutes. The sheriff's second function has been as "chief jailer." This latter role has grown in importance, especially in larger urban areas, as the number of prisoners has increased and the county's role in housing these prisoners has expanded accordingly. Most sheriffs would rank their law enforcement responsibilities as more rewarding than managing the county jail.

In larger metropolitan areas, the sheriff shares law enforcement responsibility with the central city's police chief. City police departments ostensibly were established because the more densely populated urban areas demand a higher level of police presence. While cities require more law enforcement personnel, it is sometimes difficult to see why it is any more efficient for taxpayers to fund two law enforcement agencies than two school systems. Questions of efficiency aside, any city and county charter commission must confront the "sheriff issue." Should the sheriff, who must continue to be elected, be the new government's chief law enforcement officer? Or should the sheriff serve only as chief jailer, while the city's police chief serves as the chief law enforcement officer for the combined governments?

As an elected official, the sheriff differs in key ways from city police chiefs, who almost always are appointed by a mayor or city manager. City law enforcement, as one among several departments, operates within the context of overall policies and priorities established by the city's governing structure. Advocates of appointment also cite the likelihood that a chief will be better educated, more professional, and less political than an elected sheriff, who must raise enough money to run for election every four years.

Sheriffs always can be expected to oppose a reduction in their duties and, by definition, in their political influence. Among their most persuasive arguments is a long-held American principle that persons with the power of incarceration periodically must be held accountable to the voters. While advocates of "good government" and efficient administration tend to support appointment, alienating the sheriff can deal a death blow to chances for any charter referendum.

Many observers believe that the debate over law enforcement had a major impact on the defeat of the Knoxville–Knox County charter proposal in 1998.[11]

Nashville–Davidson County

After the Constitutional Convention of 1953, Nashville and Davidson County were the most likely candidates for consolidating city and county governments in Tennessee. Nashville would be the first to attempt the change, largely because the city had a visionary mayor who saw the long-term benefits of overcoming the petty disputes among multiple governments.

Davidson County had been governed by the old "Quarterly Court" system that had been in place in Tennessee counties for more than a century. The system was presided over by the county judge, who served a quasi-executive function. Fifty-five elected and independent magistrates served in the court's legislative body. The court met only four times a year unless a special meeting was called. Meanwhile, a thirty-member[12] council constituted the legislative body for the City of Nashville, whose executive duties were carried out by a strong elected mayor.

The unification effort proved difficult. Even though consolidation advocates viewed the old structures as hopelessly inadequate, entrenched political forces complicated Nashville's move toward unification. In the 1950s, the "metropolitan solution" was an untried gamble, making voters vulnerable to fears and misinformation spread by opponents.

The first attempt to consolidate Nashville and Davidson County was defeated by the voters in 1958. The defeat followed a campaign in which the city and county power structure overwhelmingly favored the metro charter. The list included the city's leading newspapers, the *Tennessean* and the *Nashville Banner,* Mayor Ben West of Nashville, and County Judge Beverly Briley. The charter passed in the city of Nashville but failed outside the city. It fell short of gaining the necessary majorities both inside and outside the city. Voters outside the city responded to the opposition's argument that their taxes would increase.

The defeat and subsequent victory of the consolidation forces in Nashville serve as lessons in how to pass—or not pass—a charter outside as well as inside the central city. After the initial metro charter rejection, Mayor Ben West began a very aggressive campaign of annexation. Taken to its extreme, annexation could deliver what the vote on consolidated government had not. The areas of proposed annexation would have to pay full city taxes upon being brought into the city, despite the absence of any clear plan for providing them the full range of city services. The city also charged those who lived outside the city, but worked in the city, a fee for using the city streets.

Anger and confusion generated by the annexation effort led to another consolidation charter. The second charter created an urban services district and a general services district. Those living in the latter would receive a lower level of urban services and pay lower taxes. This second charter campaign created much more interest, with discussions centering not so much on abstract principles as on politics and personalities. Ben West opposed the second charter, and many who were angry at Mayor West for his aggressive annexation perceived a vote for the charter as a means of expressing their anger at the mayor.

In 1962, Nashville and Davidson County voters approved the charter by a solid, if not overwhelming, majority (56 percent). A year later, Nashville–Davidson County became a national model for structural reform of metropolitan areas. While Nashville's government has its shortcomings, especially a large and often unwieldy legislative body, few Nashvillians seriously have suggested going back. As Knoxville and Memphis continue to struggle with the cumbersome decision-making apparatus of dual governments, Nashville has emerged as one of the South's leading cities.

Other Attempts at Consolidation

Nashville's successful consolidation of city and county governments has not been easily copied by other cities. Memphis and Shelby County failed in an attempt to unify in 1962. Further efforts are unlikely, given the tension between black majorities in the city and white majorities outside the city. Many white suburban residents enjoy not being in the City of Memphis, while many African American city residents do not wish to sacrifice power and patronage to become a minority in a countywide structure.

Knoxville and Knox County have returned time and again to the issue of consolidated government, always ending in failure. The first of four attempts was made in 1959. The latest failure occurred in 1996. Each time, the initiative passed in the city and failed in the area outside the city.[13] The reasons for failure have been clear; the factors at work in the first failure in Nashville continue to operate. Residents outside the city simply do not believe that promised benefits outweigh the reality of higher taxes.[14]

Assessing Local Politics

Among Tennessee's most interesting and most contentious politics are those that take place in the state's cities, towns, and counties. These squabbles, sometimes petty and sometimes profound in their consequences, are rooted in an archaic governance structure that for decades has survived half-hearted reform efforts by the General Assembly.

Mayors, county executives, and county commissions fight endlessly over real or perceived efforts to raid their tax bases. Sheriffs do not get along with chiefs of police. The long ballot and seemingly endless campaign calendar for county offices seem to confuse voters. Accountability is clouded further by education issues. In this arena, county commissions control the purse strings, school boards make policy, and superintendents try to play an unwinnable hand.

Tennessee cities have had reasonable opportunities to structure their governments without excessive interference from the General Assembly. Nashville-Davidson's consolidation demonstrates that a community can utilize a structure designed to overcome the limitations of outdated city and county divisions. Most observers would rate Nashville's experiment with areawide government as a success. Certainly few, if any, advocate returning to the old structure.

Despite Nashville's record of success, only tiny Moore County, with fewer than seven thousand persons, has followed Nashville's example by consolidating its government with the county seat of Lynchburg. As the state entered a new century, the most pressing issue facing local governments was whether they could fashion a rational process to guide future growth in areas lying between cities and nearby towns. To many familiar with the state's economic forces, prosperity awaited those communities capable of freeing themselves of pointless jealousy. For these communities, cooperation—not endless competition—would define their futures.

Appendix

Constitution of the State of Tennessee Adopted in Convention at Nashville, February 23, 1870.

Proclaimed and in Effect, May 5, 1870, as Amended.

Preamble and Declaration of Rights

Whereas, The people of the territory of the United States south of the river Ohio, having the right of admission into the General Government as a member State thereof, consistent with the Constitution of the United States, and the act of Cession of the State of North Carolina, recognizing the ordinance for the government of the territory of the United States north west of the Ohio River, by their Delegates and Representatives in Convention assembled, did on the sixth day of February, in the year of our Lord one thousand seven hundred and ninety-six, ordain and establish a Constitution, or form of government, and mutually agreed with each other to form themselves into a free and independent State by the name of the State of Tennessee, and,

Whereas, The General Assembly of the said State of Tennessee (pursuant to the third section of the tenth article of the Constitution,) by an act passed on the Twenty-seventh day of November, in the year of our Lord one thousand eight hundred and thirty-three, entitled "An Act" to provide for the calling of a Convention, passed in obedience to the declared will of the voters of the State, as expressed at the general election of August, in the year of our Lord one thousand eight hundred and thirty-three, did authorize and provide for the election by the people of delegates and representatives, to meet at Nashville, in

Davidson County, on the third Monday in May, in the year of our Lord one thousand eight hundred and thirty-four, for the purpose of revising and amending, or changing, the Constitution, and said Convention did accordingly meet and form a Constitution, which was submitted to the people, and was ratified by them, on the first Friday in March, in the year of our Lord one thousand eight hundred and thirty-five, and,

Whereas, The General Assembly of said State of Tennessee, under and in virtue of the first section of the first article of the Declaration of Rights, contained in and forming a part of the existing Constitution of the State, by an act passed on the fifteenth day of November, in the year of our Lord one thousand eight hundred and sixty-nine, did provide for the calling of a Convention by the people of the State, to meet at Nashville, on the second Monday in January, in the year of our Lord one thousand eight hundred and seventy, and for the election of delegates for the purpose of amending or revising the present Constitution, or forming and making a new Constitution; and,

Whereas, The people of the State, in the mode provided by said Act, have called said Convention, and elected Delegates to Represent them therein; Now, therefore, We, the Delegates and Representatives of the people of the State of Tennessee, duly elected, and in Convention assembled, in pursuance of said Act of Assembly, have ordained and established the following Constitution and form of government for this State, which we recommend to the people of Tennessee for their ratification: That is to say—

Article I

Declaration of Right

SEC. 1. ALL POWER INHERENT IN THE PEOPLE— GOVERNMENT UNDER THEIR CONTROL.

That all power is inherent in the people, and all free governments are founded on their authority, and instituted for their peace, safety, and happiness; for the advancement of those ends they have at all times, an unalienable and indefeasible right to alter, reform, or abolish the government in such manner as they may think proper.

SEC. 2. DOCTRINE OF NONRESISTANCE CONDEMNED.

That government being instituted for the common benefit, the doctrine of nonresistance against arbitrary power and oppression is absurd, slavish, and destructive of the good and happiness of mankind.

SEC. 3. FREEDOM OF WORSHIP.

That all men have a natural and indefeasible right to worship Almighty God according to the dictates of their own conscience; that no man can of right be compelled to attend, erect, or support any place of worship, or to maintain any minister against his consent; that no human authority can, in any case whatever, control or interfere with the rights of conscience; and that no preference shall ever be given, by law, to any religious establishment or mode of worship.

SEC. 4. NO RELIGIOUS OR POLITICAL TEST.

That no political or religious test, other than an oath to support the Constitution of the United States and of this State, shall ever be required as a qualification to any office or public trust under this State.

SEC. 5. ELECTIONS TO BE FREE AND EQUAL—RIGHT OF SUFFRAGE.

The elections shall be free and equal, and the right of suffrage, as hereinafter declared, shall never be denied to any person entitled thereto, except upon conviction by a jury of some infamous crime, previously ascertained and declared by law, and judgment thereon by a court of competent jurisdiction.

SEC. 6. TRIAL BY JURY—QUALIFICATIONS OF JURORS.

That the right of trial by jury shall remain inviolate, and no religious or political test shall ever be required as a qualification for jurors.

SEC. 7. UNREASONABLE SEARCHES AND SEIZURES—GENERAL WARRANTS.

That the people shall be secure in their persons, houses, papers and possessions, from unreasonable searches and seizures; and that general warrants, whereby an officer may be commanded to search suspected places, without evidence of the fact committed, or to seize any person or persons not named, whose offences are not particularly described and supported by evidence, are dangerous to liberty and ought not to be granted.

SEC. 8. NO MAN TO BE DISTURBED BUT BY LAW.

That no man shall be taken or imprisoned, or disseized of his freehold, liberties or privileges, or outlawed, or exiled, or in any manner destroyed or deprived of his life, liberty or property, but by the judgment of his peers or the law of the land.

SEC. 9. RIGHT OF THE ACCUSED IN CRIMINAL PROSECUTIONS.

That in all criminal prosecutions, the accused hath the right to be heard by himself and his counsel; to demand the nature and cause of the accusation against him, and to have a copy thereof, to meet the witnesses face to face, to have compulsory process for obtaining witnesses in his favor, and in prosecutions by indictment or presentment, a speedy public trial, by an impartial jury of the County in which the crime shall have been committed, and shall not be compelled to give evidence against himself.

SEC. 10. DOUBLE JEOPARDY PROHIBITED.

That no person shall, for the same offence, be twice put in jeopardy of life or limb.

SEC. 11. NO EX POST FACTO LAWS.

That laws made for the punishment of acts committed previous to the existence of such laws, and by them only declared criminal, are contrary to the principles of a free Government; wherefore no ex post facto law shall be made.

SEC. 12. NO CORRUPTION OF BLOOD OR FORFEITURE OF ESTATES.

That no conviction shall work corruption of blood or forfeiture of estate. The estate of such persons as shall destroy their own lives shall descend or vest as in case of natural death. If any person be killed by casualty, there shall be no forfeiture in consequence thereof.

Sec. 13. Treatment after arrest.

That no person arrested and confined in jail shall be treated with unnecessary rigor.

Sec. 14. Prerequisites to criminal charge.

That no person shall be put to answer any criminal charge but by presentment, indictment or impeachment.

Sec. 15. Bailable offenses—Habeas corpus.

That all prisoners shall be bailable by sufficient sureties, unless for capital offences, when the proof is evident, or the presumption great. And the privilege of the writ of Habeas Corpus shall not be suspended, unless when in case of rebellion or invasion, the General Assembly shall declare the public safety requires it.

Sec. 16. Restrictions on bail, fines and punishment.

That excessive bail shall not be required, nor excessive fines imposed, nor cruel and unusual punishments inflicted.

Sec. 17. Open courts—Redress of injuries—Suits against the State.

That all courts shall be open; and every man, for an injury done him in his lands, goods, person or reputation, shall have remedy by due course of law, and right and justice administered without sale, denial, or delay. Suits may be brought against the State in such manner and in such courts as the Legislature may by law direct.

Sec. 18. No imprisonment for debt.

The Legislature shall pass no law authorizing imprisonment for debt in civil cases.

Sec. 19. Freedom of speech and press.

That the printing presses shall be free to every person to examine the proceedings of the Legislature; or of any branch or officer of the government, and no law shall ever be made to restrain the right thereof. The free communication of thoughts and opinions, is one of the invaluable rights of man, and every citizen may freely speak, write, and print on any subject, being responsible for the abuse of that liberty. But in prosecutions for the publication of papers investigating the official conduct of officers, or men in public capacity, the truth thereof may be given in evidence; and in all indictments for libel, the jury shall have a right to determine the law and the facts, under the direction of the court, as in other criminal cases.

Sec. 20. No retrospective laws.

That no retrospective law, or law impairing the obligations of contracts, shall be made.

Sec. 21. No man's services or property taken without consent or compensation.

That no man's particular services shall be demanded, or property taken, or applied to public use, without the consent of his representatives, or without just compensation being made therefor.

Sec. 22. No perpetuities or monopolies.

That perpetuities and monopolies are contrary to the genius of a free State, and shall not be allowed.

Sec. 23. Right of assembly.

That the citizens have a right, in a peaceable manner, to assemble together for their common good, to instruct their representatives, and to apply to those invested with the powers of government for redress of grievances, or other proper purposes, by address or remonstrance.

Sec. 24. Militia—Civil authority.

That the sure and certain defense of a free people, is a well regulated militia; and, as standing armies in time of peace are dangerous to freedom, they ought to be avoided as far as the circumstances and safety of the community will admit; and that in all cases the military shall be kept in strict subordination to the civil authority.

SEC. 25. MARTIAL LAW—PUNISHMENT.

That no citizen of this State, except such as are employed in the army of the United States, or militia in actual service, shall be subjected to punishment under the martial or military law. That martial law, in the sense of the unrestricted power of military officers, or others, to dispose of the persons, liberties or property of the citizen, is inconsistent with the principles of free government, and is not confided to any department of the government of this State.

SEC. 26. RIGHT TO BEAR ARMS—REGULATIONS.

That the citizens of this State have a right to keep and to bear arms for their common defense; but the Legislature shall have power, by law, to regulate the wearing of arms with a view to prevent crime.

SEC. 27. QUARTERING SOLDIERS.

That no soldier shall, in time of peace, be quartered in any house without the consent of the owner; nor in time of war, but in a manner prescribed by law.

SEC. 28. NO ONE COMPELLED TO BEAR ARMS.

That no citizen of this State shall be compelled to bear arms, provided he will pay an equivalent, to be ascertained by law.

SEC. 29. NAVIGATION OF THE MISSISSIPPI.

That an equal participation in the free navigation of the Mississippi, is one of the inherent rights of the citizens of this State; it cannot, therefore, be conceded to any prince, potentate, power, person or persons whatever.

SEC. 30. NO HEREDITARY HONORS.

That no hereditary emoluments, privileges, or honors, shall ever be granted or conferred in this State.

SEC. 31. BOUNDARIES OF THE STATE.

That the limits and boundaries of this State be ascertained, it is declared they are as hereafter mentioned, that is to say: Beginning on the extreme height of the Stone mountain, at the place where the line of Virginia intersects it, in latitude thirty-six degrees and thirty minutes north; running thence along the extreme height of the said mountain, to the place where Watauga river breaks through it; thence a direct course to the top of the Yellow Mountain, where Bright's road crosses the same; thence along the ridge of said mountain, between the waters of Doe river and the waters of Rock creek, to the place where the road crosses the Iron Mountain; from thence along the extreme height of said mountain, to the place where Nolichucky river runs through the same; thence to the top of the Bald Mountain; thence along the extreme height of said mountain to the Painted Rock, on French Broad river; thence along the highest ridge of said mountain, to the place where it is called the Great Iron or Smoky Mountain; thence along the extreme height of said mountain to the place where it is called Unicoi or Unaka Mountain, between the Indian towns of Cowee and Old Chota; thence along the main ridge of the said mountain to the southern boundary of this State, as described in the act of cession of North Carolina to the United States of America; and that all the territory, lands and waters lying west of said line, as before mentioned, and contained within the chartered limits of the State of North Carolina, are within the boundaries and limits of this State, over which the people have the right of exercising sovereignty, and the right of soil, so far as is consistent with the Constitution of the United States, recognizing the Articles of Confederation, the Bill of Rights and Constitution of North Carolina, the cession act of the said State, and the ordinance of Congress for the government of the territory northwest of the Ohio; Provided, nothing herein contained shall extend to affect the claim or claims of individuals to any part of the soil which is recognized to them by the aforesaid cession act; And provided also, That the limits and jurisdiction of this State shall extend to any other land and territory now acquired, or that may hereafter be acquired, by compact or agreement with other States, or otherwise, although such land and territory are not included within the boundaries herein before designated.

SEC. 32. PRISONS AND PRISONERS.

That the erection of safe and comfortable prisons, the inspection of prisons, and the humane treatment of prisoners, shall be provided for.

SEC. 33. SLAVERY PROHIBITED.

That slavery and involuntary servitude, except as a punishment for crime, whereof the party shall have been duly convicted, are forever prohibited in this State.

SEC. 34. RIGHT OF PROPERTY IN MAN.

The General Assembly shall make no law recognizing the right of property in man.

Article II

Distribution of Powers

SEC. 1. DIVISION OF POWERS.

The powers of the Government shall be divided into three distinct departments: the Legislative, Executive, and Judicial.

SEC. 2. LIMITATION OF POWERS.

No person or persons belonging to one of these departments shall exercise any of the powers properly belonging to either of the others, except in the cases herein directed or permitted.

Legislative Department

SEC. 3. LEGISLATIVE AUTHORITY—TERM OF OFFICE.

The Legislative authority of this State shall be vested in a General Assembly, which shall consist of a Senate and House of Representatives, both dependent on the people. Representatives shall hold office for two years and Senators for four years from the day of the general election, except that the Speaker of the Senate and the Speaker of the House of Representatives, each shall hold his office as Speaker for two years or until his successor is elected and qualified, provided however, that in the first general election after adoption of this amendment Senators elected in districts designated by even numbers shall be elected for four years and those elected in districts designated by odd numbers shall be elected for two years. In a county having more than one senatorial district, the districts shall be numbered consecutively. [As amended: Adopted in Convention, December 9, 1965; approved at election, November 8, 1966; Proclaimed by Governor, December 2, 1966.]

SEC. 4. APPORTIONMENT OF SENATORS AND REPRESENTATIVES.

The apportionment of Senators and Representatives shall be substantially according to population. After each decennial census made by the Bureau of Census of the United States is available[,] the General Assembly shall establish senatorial and representative districts. Nothing in this Section nor in this Article II shall deny to the General Assembly the right at any time to apportion one House of the General Assembly using geography, political subdivisions, substantially equal population and other criteria as factors; provided such apportionment when effective shall comply with the Constitution of the United States as then amended or authoritatively interpreted. If the Constitution of the United States shall require that Legislative apportionment not based entirely on population be approved by vote of the electorate, the General Assembly shall provide for such vote in the apportionment act. [As amended; Adopted in Convention, December 9, 1965; approved at election, November 8, 1966; Proclaimed by Governor, December 2, 1966.]

SEC. 5. NUMBER OF REPRESENTATIVES—APPORTIONMENT.

The number of Representatives shall be ninety-nine and shall be apportioned by the General Assembly among the several counties or districts as shall be provided by law. Counties having two or more Representatives shall be divided into separate districts. In a district composed of two or more counties, each county shall adjoin at least one other county of such district; and no county shall be divided in forming such a district. [As amended; Adopted in Convention, December 9, 1965; approved at election, November 8, 1966; Proclaimed by Governor, December 2, 1966.]

SEC. 5A. REPRESENTATION BY QUALIFIED VOTER.

Each district shall be represented by a qualified voter of that district. [As added; Adopted in Convention, December 10, 1965; approved at election, November 8, 1966; Proclaimed by Governor, December 2, 1966.]

Sec. 6. Number of senators—Apportionment.

The number of Senators shall be apportioned by the General Assembly among the several counties or districts substantially according to population, and shall not exceed one-third the number of Representatives. Counties having two or more Senators shall be divided into separate districts. In a district composed of two or more counties, each county shall adjoin at least one other county of such district; and no county shall be divided in forming such a district. [As amended; Adopted in Convention, December 9, 1965; approved at election, November 8, 1966; Proclaimed by Governor, December 2, 1966.]

Sec. 6a. Representation by qualified voter.

Each district shall be represented by a qualified voter of that district. [As added; Adopted in Convention, December 10, 1965; approved at election, November 8, 1966; Proclaimed by Governor, December 2, 1966.]

Sec. 7. Time of elections.

The first election for Senators and Representatives shall be held on the second Tuesday in November, one thousand eight hundred and seventy; and forever thereafter, elections for members of the General Assembly shall be held once in two years, on the first Tuesday after the first Monday in November. Said elections shall terminate the same day.

Sec. 8. Legislative sessions—Governor's inauguration.

The General Assembly shall meet in organizational session on the second Tuesday in January next succeeding the election of the members of the House of Representatives, at which session, if in order, the Governor shall be inaugurated. The General Assembly shall remain in session for organizational purposes not longer than fifteen consecutive calendar days, during which session no legislation shall be passed on third and final consideration. Thereafter, the General Assembly shall meet on the first Tuesday next following the conclusion of the organizational session unless the General Assembly by joint resolution of both houses sets an earlier date.

The General Assembly may by joint resolution recess or adjourn until such time or times as it shall determine. It shall be convened at other times by the Governor as provided in Article III, Section 9, or by the presiding officers of both Houses at the written request of two-thirds of the members of each House. [As amended; Adopted in Convention, December 10, 1965; approved at election, November 8, 1966; Proclaimed by Governor, December 2, 1966; As amended, Adopted in Convention, December 20, 1977; approved at election, March 7, 1978; Proclaimed by Governor, March 31, 1978.]

Sec. 9. Qualifications of representatives.

No person shall be a Representative unless he shall be a citizen of the United States, of the age of twenty-one years, and shall have been a citizen of this State for three years, and a resident in the county he represents one year, immediately preceding the election.

Sec. 10. Senators—Qualifications.

No person shall be a Senator unless he shall be a citizen of the United States, of the age of thirty years, and shall have resided three years in this State, and one year in the county or district, immediately preceding the election. No Senator or Representative shall, during the time for which he was elected, be eligible to any office or place of trust, the appointment to which is vested in the Executive or the General Assembly, except to the office of trustee of a literary institution.

Sec. 11. Election of officers—Quorum—Adjournments.

The senate and house of representatives, when assembled, shall each choose a speaker and its other officers; be judges of the qualifications and election of its members, and sit upon its own adjournments from day to day. Not less than two-thirds of all the members to which each house shall be entitled shall constitute a quorum to do business; but a smaller number may adjourn from day to day, and may be authorized, by law, to compel the attendance of absent members.

Sec. 12. Each house to make its own rules.

Each House may determine the rules of its proceedings, punish its members for disorderly behavior, and, with the concurrence of two-thirds, expel a member, but not a second time for the same offence;

and shall have all other powers necessary for a branch of the Legislature of a free State.

Sec. 13. Privilege of members.

Senators and Representatives shall, in all cases, except treason, felony, or breach of the peace, be privileged from arrest during the session of the General Assembly, and in going to and returning from the same; and for any speech or debate in either House, they shall not be questioned in any other place.

Sec. 14. Power to punish other than members.

Each House may punish by imprisonment, during its session, any person not a member, who shall be guilty of disrespect to the House, by any disorderly or any contemptuous behavior in its presence.

Sec. 15. Vacancies.

When the seat of any member of either House becomes vacant, the vacancy shall be filled as follows:

(a) When twelve months or more remain prior to the next general election for legislators, a successor shall be elected by the qualified voters of the district represented, and such successor shall serve the remainder of the original term. The election shall be held within such time as provided by law. The legislative body of the replaced legislator's county of residence at the time of his or her election may elect an interim successor to serve until the election.

(b) When less than twelve months remain prior to the next general election for legislators, a successor shall be elected by the legislative body of the replaced legislator's county of residence at the time of his or her election. The term of any Senator so elected shall expire at the next general election for legislators, at which election a successor shall be elected.

(c) Only a qualified voter of the district represented shall be eligible to succeed to the vacant seat. [As amended; Adopted in Convention, December 10, 1965; approved at election, November 8, 1966; Proclaimed by Governor, December 2, 1966; As amended; Adopted in

Convention, October 24, 1977; approved at election, March 7, 1978; Proclaimed by Governor, March 31, 1978.]

Sec. 16. Limitation upon power of adjournment.

Neither House shall, during its session, adjourn without the consent of the other for more than three days, nor to any other place than that in which the two Houses shall be sitting.

Sec. 17. Origin and frame of bills.

Bills may originate in either House; but may be amended, altered or rejected by the other. No bill shall become a law which embraces more than one subject, that subject to be expressed in the title. All acts which repeal, revive or amend former laws, shall recite in their caption, or otherwise, the title or substance of the law repealed, revived or amended.

Statutes expressly purporting to repeal, revive, or amend former laws must recite in their caption, preamble, or body the title, substance, or subject of the law sought to be repealed, revived, or amended. But the requirement of the constitution as to the recitation of the title or substance of former laws sought to be repealed, revived, or amended applies only to statutes which expressly purport to repeal, revive, or amend former laws, and not to statutes operating, by necessary implication from their positive provisions, to repeal, revive, or amend former laws.

Sec. 18. Passage of bills.

A bill shall become law when it has been considered and passed on three different days in each House and on third and final consideration has received the assent of a majority of all the members to which each House is entitled under this Constitution, when the respective speakers have signed the bill with the date of such signing appearing in the journal, and when the bill has been approved by the Governor or otherwise passed under the provisions of this Constitution. [As amended; Adopted in Convention, September 29, 1977; approved at election, March 7, 1978; Proclaimed by Governor, March 31, 1978.]

Sec. 19. Rejection of bill.

After a bill has been rejected, no bill containing the same substance shall be passed into a law during the same session.

Sec. 20. Style of laws—Effective date.

The style of the laws of this state shall be, "Be it enacted by the General Assembly of the State of Tennessee." No law of a general nature shall take effect until forty days after its passage unless the same or the caption thereof shall state that the public welfare requires that it should take effect sooner.

Sec. 21. Journal of proceedings.

Each House shall keep a journal of its proceedings, and publish it, except such parts as the welfare of the State may require to be kept secret; the ayes and noes shall be taken in each House upon the final passage of every bill of a general character, and bills making appropriations of public moneys; and the ayes and noes of the members on any question, shall, at the request of any five of them, be entered on the journal.

Sec. 22. Open sessions and meetings—Exception.

The doors of each House and of committees of the whole shall be kept open, unless when the business shall be such as ought to be kept secret.

Sec. 23. Compensation of members of General Assembly.

Each member of the General Assembly shall receive an annual salary of $1,800.00 per year[,] payable in equal monthly installments from the date of his election, and in addition, such other allowances for expenses in attending sessions or committee meetings as may be provided by law. The Senators, when sitting as a Court of Impeachment, shall receive the same allowances for expenses as have been provided by law for the members of the General Assembly. The compensation and expenses of the members of the General Assembly may from time to time be reduced or increased by laws enacted by the General Assembly; however, no increase or decrease in the amount thereof shall take effect until the next general election for Representatives to the General Assembly. Provided, further, that the first General Assembly meeting after adoption of this amendment shall be allowed to set its own expenses. However, no member shall be paid expenses, nor travel allowances for more than ninety Legislative days of a regular session, excluding the organizational session, nor for more than thirty Legislative days of any extraordinary session.

This amendment shall take effect immediately upon adoption so that any member of the General Assembly elected at a general election wherein this amendment is approved shall be entitled to the compensation set herein. [As amended; Adopted in Convention, May 12, 1953; approved at election, November 3, 1953; Proclaimed by Governor, November 19, 1953; As amended; Adopted in Convention, December 10, 1965; approved at election, November 8, 1966; Proclaimed by Governor, December 2, 1966.]

Sec. 24. Appropriation of public moneys.

No public money shall be expended except pursuant to appropriations made by law. Expenditures for any fiscal year shall not exceed the state's revenues and reserves, including the proceeds of any debt obligation, for that year. No debt obligation, except as shall be repaid within the fiscal year of issuance, shall be authorized for the current operation of any state service or program, nor shall the proceeds of any debt obligation be expended for a purpose other than that for which it was authorized.

In no year shall the rate of growth of appropriations from state tax revenues exceed the estimated rate of growth of the state's economy as determined by law. No appropriation in excess of this limitation shall be made unless the General Assembly shall, by law containing no other subject matter, set forth the dollar amount and the rate by which the limit will be exceeded.

Any law requiring the expenditure of state funds shall be null and void unless, during the session in which the act receives final passage, an appropriation is made for the estimated first year's funding.

No law of general application shall impose increased expenditure requirements on cities or counties unless the General Assembly shall provide that the state share in the cost.

An accurate financial statement of the state's fiscal condition shall be published annually. [As amended; Adopted in Convention, November 30, 1977; approved at election, March 7, 1978; Proclaimed by Governor, March 31, 1978.]

Sec. 25. Defaulters ineligible.

No person who heretofore hath been, or may hereafter be, a collector or holder of Public Moneys, shall have a seat in either House of the

General Assembly, or hold any other office under the State Government, until such person shall have accounted for, and paid into the Treasury, all sums for which he may be accountable or liable.

Sec. 26. Ineligibility—Lucrative offices.

No Judge of any Court of law or equity, Secretary of State, Attorney General, Register, Clerk of any court of Record, or person holding any office under the authority of the United States, shall have a seat in the General Assembly; nor shall any person in this State hold more than one lucrative office at the same time; provided, that no appointment in the Militia, or to the office of Justice of the Peace, shall be considered a lucrative office, or operative as a disqualification to a seat in either House of the General Assembly.

Sec. 27. Right of protest.

Any member of either House of the General Assembly shall have liberty to dissent from and protest against, any act or resolve which he may think injurious to the Public or to any individual, and to have the reasons for his dissent entered on the journals.

Sec. 28. Taxable property—Valuation—Rates.

In accordance with the following provisions, all property real, personal or mixed shall be subject to taxation, but the Legislature may except such as may be held by the State, by Counties, Cities or Towns, and used exclusively for public or corporation purposes, and such as may be held and used for purposes purely religious, charitable, scientific, literary or educational, and shall except the direct product of the soil in the hands of the producer, and his immediate vendee, and the entire amount of money deposited in an individual's personal or family checking or savings accounts. For purposes of taxation, property shall be classified into three classes, to wit: Real Property, Tangible Personal Property and Intangible Personal Property.

Real Property shall be classified into four (4) subclassifications and assessed as follows:

(a) Public Utility Property, to be assessed at fifty-five (55%) percent of its value;

(b) Industrial and Commercial Property, to be assessed at forty (40%) percent of its value;

(c) Residential Property, to be assessed at twenty-five (25%) percent of its value, provided that residential property containing two (2) or more rental units is hereby defined as industrial and commercial property; and

(d) Farm Property, to be assessed at twenty-five (25%) percent of its value.

House trailers, mobile homes, and all other similar movable structures used for commercial, industrial, or residential purposes shall be assessed as Real Property as an improvement to the land where located.

The Legislature shall provide, in such manner as it deems appropriate, tax relief to elderly low-income taxpayers through payments by the State to reimburse all or part of the taxes paid by such persons on owner-occupied residential property, but such reimbursement shall not be an obligation imposed, directly or indirectly, upon Counties, Cities, or Towns.

The Legislature may provide tax relief to home owners totally and permanently disabled, irrespective of age, as provided herein for the elderly.

Tangible Personal Property shall be classified into three (3) subclassifications and assessed as follows:

(a) Public Utility Property, to be assessed at fifty-five (55%) percent of its value;

(b) Industrial and Commercial Property, to be assessed at thirty (30%) percent of its value; and

(c) All other Tangible Personal Property, to be assessed at five (5%) percent of its value; provided, however, that the Legislature shall exempt Seven Thousand Five Hundred ($7,500) Dollars worth of such Tangible Personal Property which shall cover personal household goods and furnishings, wearing apparel and other such tangible property in the hands of a taxpayer.

The Legislature shall have power to classify Intangible Personal Property into subclassifications and to establish a ratio of assessment to value in each class or subclass, and shall provide fair and equitable methods of apportionment of the value of same to this State for purposes of taxation. Banks, Insurance Companies, Loan and Investment

Companies, Savings and Loan Associations, and all similar financial institutions, shall be assessed and taxed in such manner as the Legislature shall direct; provided that for the year 1973, or until such time as the Legislature may provide otherwise, the ratio of assessment to value of property presently taxed shall remain the same as provided by law for the year 1972; provided further that the taxes imposed upon such financial institutions, and paid by them, shall be in lieu of all taxes on the redeemable or cash value of all of their outstanding shares of capital stock, policies of insurance, customer savings and checking accounts, certificates of deposit, and certificates of investment, by whatever name called, including other intangible corporate property of such financial institutions.

The ratio of assessment to value of property in each class or subclass shall be equal and uniform throughout the State, the value and definition of property in each class or subclass to be ascertained in such manner as the Legislature shall direct. Each respective taxing authority shall apply the same tax rate to all property within its jurisdiction.

The Legislature shall have power to tax merchants, peddlers, and privileges, in such manner as they may from time to time direct, and the Legislature may levy a gross receipts tax on merchants and businesses in lieu of ad valorem taxes on the inventories of merchandise held by such merchants and businesses for sale or exchange. The portion of a Merchant's Capital used in the purpose of merchandise sold by him to non-residents and sent beyond the State, shall not be taxed at a rate higher than the ad valorem tax on property. The Legislature shall have power to levy a tax upon incomes derived from stocks and bonds that are not taxed ad valorem.

This amendment shall take effect on the first day of January, 1973. [As Amended; Adopted in Convention, September 14, 1971; Approved at election, August 3, 1972; Amendment approved at election, November 2, 1982.]

Sec. 29. Counties and towns—Power to tax—Credit.

The General Assembly shall have power to authorize the several counties and incorporated towns in this State, to impose taxes for County and Corporation purposes respectively, in such manner as shall be prescribed by law; and all property shall be taxed according to its value, upon the principles established in regard to State taxation. But the credit of no County, City or Town shall be given or loaned to or in aid of any person, company, association or corporation, except upon an election to be first held by the qualified voters of such county, city or town, and the assent of three-fourths of the votes cast at said election. Nor shall any county, city or town become a stockholder with others in any company, association or corporation except upon a like election, and the assent of a like majority. But the counties of Grainger, Hawkins, Hancock, Union, Campbell, Scott, Morgan, Grundy, Sumner, Smith, Fentress, Van Buren, and the new County herein authorized to be established out of fractions of Sumner, Macon and Smith counties, White, Putnam, Overton, Jackson, Cumberland, Anderson, Henderson, Wayne, Cocke, Coffee, Macon, Marshall, and Roane shall be excepted out of the provisions of this Section so far that the assent of a majority of the qualified voters of either of said counties voting on the question shall be sufficient when the credit of such county is given or loaned to any person, association or corporation; Provided, that the exception of the counties above named shall not be in force beyond the year one thousand eight hundred and eighty; and after that period they shall be subject to the three-fourths majority applicable to the other counties of the State.

Sec. 30. Articles not taxable—Inspection fees.

No article, manufactured of the produce of this State shall be taxed otherwise than to pay inspection fees.

Sec. 31. Acts forbidden the State.

The credit of this State shall not be hereafter loaned or given to or in aid of any person, association, company, corporation or municipality; nor shall the State become the owner in whole or in part of any bank or a stockholder with others in any association, company, corporation or municipality.

Sec. 32. Amendments to Constitution of United States.

No Convention or General Assembly of this State shall act upon any amendment of the Constitution of the United States proposed by Congress to the several States; unless such Convention or General Assembly shall have been elected after such amendment is submitted.

SEC. 33. NO STATE BONDS TO DEFAULTING RAILROADS.

No bonds of the State shall be issued to any Rail Road Company which at the time of its application for the same shall be in default in paying the interest upon State bonds previously loaned to it or that shall hereafter and before such application sell or absolutely dispose of any State bonds loaned to it for less than par.

Article III

Executive Department

SEC. 1. GOVERNOR'S EXECUTIVE POWER.

The Supreme Executive power of this State shall be vested in a Governor.

SEC. 2. ELECTION OF GOVERNOR.

The Governor shall be chosen by the electors of the members of the General Assembly, at the time and places where they shall respectively vote for the members thereof. The returns of every election for Governor shall be sealed up, and transmitted to the seat of Government, by the returning officers, directed to the Speaker of the Senate, who shall open and publish them in the presence of a majority of the members of each House of the General Assembly. The person having the highest number of votes shall be Governor; but if two or more shall be equal and highest in votes, one of them shall be chosen Governor by joint vote of both Houses of the General Assembly. Contested elections for Governor shall be determined by both Houses of the General Assembly, in such manner as shall be prescribed by law.

SEC. 3. GOVERNOR'S QUALIFICATIONS.

He shall be at least thirty years of age, shall be a citizen of the United States, and shall have been a citizen of this State seven years next before his election.

Sec. 4. Governor's term of office.

The Governor shall be elected to hold office for four years and until a successor is elected and qualified. A person may be eligible to succeed in office for additional four-year terms, provided that no person presently serving or elected hereafter shall be eligible for election to more than two terms consecutively, including an election to a partial term.

One succeeding to the office vacated during the first eighteen calendar months of the term shall hold office until a successor is elected for the remainder of the term at the next election of members of the General Assembly and qualified pursuant to this Constitution. One succeeding to the office vacated after the first eighteen calendar months of the term shall continue to hold office for the remainder of the full term. [As amended; Adopted in Convention, May 19, 1953; approved at election, November 3, 1953; Proclaimed by Governor, November 19, 1953; As amended; Adopted in Convention, October 10, 1977; approved at election, March 7, 1978; Proclaimed by Governor, March 31, 1978.]

Sec. 5. Governor as commander-in-chief—Calling out militia.

He shall be commander-in-chief of the Army and Navy of this State, and of the Militia, except when they shall be called into the service of the United States; But the Militia shall not be called into service except in case of rebellion or invasion, and then only when the General Assembly shall declare, by law, that the public safety requires it.

Sec. 6. Pardons and reprieves.

He shall have power to grant reprieves and pardons, after conviction, except in cases of impeachment.

Sec. 7. Governor's compensation.

He shall, at stated times, receive a compensation for his services, which shall not be increased or diminished during the period for which he shall have been elected.

Sec. 8. Governor may require information.

He may require information in writing, from the officers in the executive department, upon any subject relating to the duties of their respective offices.

Sec. 9. Governor may convene the legislature.

He may, on extraordinary occasions, convene the General Assembly by proclamation, in which he shall state specifically the purposes for which they are to convene; but they shall enter on no legislative business except that for which they were specifically called together.

Sec. 10. Governor to execute laws.

He shall take care that the laws be faithfully executed.

Sec. 11. Governor to give information to the legislature.

He shall, from time to time, give to the General Assembly information of the state of the government, and recommend for their consideration such measures as he shall judge expedient.

Sec. 12. Vacancy in office of governor.

In case of the removal of the Governor from office, or of his death, or resignation, the powers and duties of the office shall devolve on the Speaker of the Senate; and in case of the death, removal from office, or resignation of the Speaker of the Senate, the powers and duties of the office shall devolve on the Speaker of the House of Representatives.

Sec. 13. Ineligibility for governorship.

No member of Congress, or person holding any office under the United States, or this State, shall execute the office of Governor.

Sec. 14. Governor to make temporary appointments.

When any officer, the right of whose appointment is by this Constitution vested in the General Assembly, shall, during the recess, die, or the office, by the expiration of the term, or by other means, become vacant, the Governor shall have the power to fill such vacancy by granting a temporary commission, which shall expire at the end of the next session of the Legislature.

Sec. 15. Seal of State.

There shall be a Seal of this State, which shall be kept by the Governor, and used by him officially, and shall be called the Great Seal of the State of Tennessee.

Sec. 16. Grants and commissions to be sealed and signed by the Governor.

All grants and commissions shall be in the name and by the authority of the State of Tennessee, be sealed with the State Seal, and signed by the Governor.

Sec. 17. Secretary of state.

A Secretary of State shall be appointed by joint vote of the General Assembly and commissioned during the term of four years; he shall keep a fair register of all the official acts and proceedings of the Governor; and shall, when required lay the same, and all papers, minutes and vouchers relative thereto, before the General Assembly; and shall perform such other duties as shall be enjoined by law.

Sec. 18. Bills to be approved by the governor—Governor's veto—Bills passed over governor's veto.

Every Bill which may pass both Houses of the General Assembly shall, before it becomes a law, be presented to the Governor for his signature. If he approve, he shall sign it, and the same shall become a law; but if he refuse to sign it, he shall return it with his objections thereto, in writing, to the house in which it originated; and said House shall cause said objections to be entered at large upon its journal, and proceed to reconsider the Bill. If after such reconsideration, a majority of all the members elected to that House shall agree to pass the Bill, notwithstanding the objections of the Executive, it shall be sent, with said objections, to the other House, by which it shall be likewise reconsidered. If approved by a majority of the whole number elected to that House, it shall become a law. The votes of both Houses shall be determined by yeas and nays, and the names of all the members voting for or against the Bill shall be entered upon the journals of their respective Houses.

If the Governor shall fail to return any bill with his objections in writing within ten calendar days (Sundays excepted) after it shall have been presented to him, the same shall become a law without his signature. If the General Assembly by its adjournment prevents the return of any bill within said ten-day period, the bill shall become a law, unless disapproved by the Governor and filed by him with his objections in writing in the office of the Secretary of State within said ten-day period.

Every joint resolution or order (except on question of adjournment and proposals of specific amendments to the Constitution) shall likewise be presented to the Governor for his signature, and on being disapproved by him shall in like manner, be returned with his objections; and the same before it shall take effect shall be repassed by a majority of all the members elected to both houses in the manner and according to the rules prescribed in case of a bill.

The Governor may reduce or disapprove the sum of money appropriated by any one or more items or parts of items in any bill appropriating money, while approving other portions of the bill. The portions so approved shall become law, and the items or parts of items disapproved or reduced shall be void to the extent that they have been disapproved or reduced unless repassed as hereinafter provided. The Governor, within ten calendar days (Sundays excepted) after the bill shall have been presented to him, shall report the items or parts of items disapproved or reduced with his objections in writing to the House in which the bill originated, or if the General Assembly shall have adjourned, to the office of the Secretary of State. Any such items or parts of items so disapproved or reduced shall be restored to the bill in the original amount and become law if repassed by the General Assembly according to the rules and limitations prescribed for the passage of other bills over the executive veto. [As amended; Adopted in Convention, May 20, 1953; approved at election, November 3, 1953; Proclaimed by Governor, November 19, 1953; As amended; Adopted in Convention, October 18, 1977; approved at election, March 7, 1978; Proclaimed by Governor, March 31, 1978.]

Article IV

Elections

Sec. 1. Right to vote—Election precincts—Military duty.

Every person, being eighteen years of age, being a citizen of the United States, being a resident of the State for a period of time as prescribed by the General Assembly, and being duly registered in the county of residence for a period of time prior to the day of any election as prescribed by the General Assembly, shall be entitled to vote in all federal, state, and local elections held in the county or district in which such person resides. All such requirements shall be equal and uniform across the state, and there shall be no other qualification attached to the right of suffrage.

The General Assembly shall have power to enact laws requiring voters to vote in the election precincts in which they may reside, and laws to secure the freedom of elections and the purity of the ballot box.

All male citizens of this State shall be subject to the performance of military duty, as may be prescribed by law. [As amended; Adopted in Convention, May 25, 1953; Approved at election, November 3, 1953; Proclaimed by Governor, November 19, 1953; As amended; Adopted in Convention, October 20, 1977; approved at election, March 7, 1978; Proclaimed by Governor, March 31, 1978.]

SEC. 2. RIGHT OF SUFFRAGE MAY BE EXCLUDED FOR CRIME.

Laws may be passed excluding from the right of suffrage persons who may be convicted of infamous crimes.

SEC. 3. PRIVILEGES OF VOTERS.

Electors shall, in all cases, except treason, felony, or breach of the peace, be privileged from arrest or summons, during their attendance at elections, and in going to and returning from them.

SEC. 4. MODE OF VOTING.

In all elections to be made by the General Assembly, the members thereof shall vote viva voce, and their votes shall be entered on the journal. All other elections shall be by ballot.

Article V

Impeachments

SEC. 1. IMPEACHMENT.

The House of Representatives shall have the sole power of impeachment.

SEC. 2. TRIAL OF IMPEACHMENTS.

All impeachments shall be tried by the Senate. When sitting for that purpose the Senators shall be upon oath or affirmation, and the Chief Justice of the Supreme Court, or if he be on trial, the Senior Associate Judge, shall preside over them. No person shall be convicted without the concurrence of two-thirds of the Senators sworn to try the officer impeached.

Sec. 3. How prosecuted.

The House of Representatives shall elect from their own body three members, whose duty it shall be to prosecute impeachments. No impeachment shall be tried until the Legislature shall have adjourned sine die, when the Senate shall proceed to try such impeachment.

Sec. 4. Who may be impeached.

The Governor, Judges of the Supreme Court, Judges of Inferior Courts, Chancellors, Attorneys for the State, Treasurer, Comptroller and Secretary of State, shall be liable to impeachment, whenever they may, in the opinion of the House of Representatives, commit any crime in their official capacity which may require disqualification; but judgment shall only extend to removal from office, and disqualification to fill any office thereafter. The party shall, nevertheless, be liable to indictment, trial, judgment and punishment according to law. The Legislature now has, and shall continue to have, power to relieve from the penalties imposed, any person disqualified from holding office by the judgment of a Court of Impeachment.

Sec. 5. Officers liable to indictment and removal from office.

Justices of the Peace, and other civil officers, not hereinbefore mentioned, for crimes or misdemeanors in office, shall be liable to indictment in such courts as the Legislature may direct; and upon conviction, shall be removed from office by said court, as if found guilty on impeachment; and shall be subject to such other punishment as may be prescribed by law.

Article VI

Judicial Department

Sec. 1. Judicial power.

The judicial power of this State shall be vested in one Supreme Court and in such Circuit, Chancery and other inferior Courts as the Legislature shall from time to time, ordain and establish; in the Judges thereof, and in Justices of the Peace. The Legislature may also vest such jurisdiction in Corporation Courts as may be deemed necessary. Courts to be holden by Justices of the Peace may also be established.

SEC. 2. SUPREME COURT.

The Supreme Court shall consist of five Judges, of whom not more than two shall reside in any one of the grand divisions of the State. The Judges shall designate one of their own number who shall preside as Chief Justice. The concurrence of three of the Judges shall in every case be necessary to a decision. The jurisdiction of this Court shall be appellate only, under such restrictions and regulations as may from time to time be prescribed by law; but it may possess such other jurisdiction as is now conferred by law on the present Supreme Court. Said Court shall be held at Knoxville, Nashville and Jackson.

SEC. 3. SUPREME COURT JUDGES.

The Judges of the Supreme Court shall be elected by the qualified voters of the State. The Legislature shall have power to prescribe such rules as may be necessary to carry out the provisions of section two of this article. Every Judge of the Supreme Court shall be thirty-five years of age, and shall before his election have been a resident of the State for five years. His term of service shall be eight years.

SEC. 4. JUDGES OF INFERIOR COURTS.

The Judges of the Circuit and Chancery Courts, and of other inferior Courts, shall be elected by the qualified voters of the district or circuit to which they are to be assigned. Every Judge of such Courts shall be thirty years of age, and shall before his election, have been a resident of the State for five years and of the circuit or district one year. His term of service shall be eight years.

SEC. 5. ATTORNEY GENERAL AND REPORTER.

An Attorney General and Reporter for the State, shall be appointed by the Judges of the Supreme Court and shall hold his office for a term of eight years. An Attorney for the State for any circuit or district, for which a Judge having criminal jurisdiction shall be provided by law, shall be elected by the qualified voters of such circuit or district, and shall hold his office for a term of eight years, and shall have been a resident of the State five years, and of the circuit or district one year. In all cases where the Attorney for any district fails or refuses to attend and prosecute according to law, the Court shall have power to appoint an Attorney pro tempore.

Sec. 6. Removal of judges and attorneys.

Judges and Attorneys for the State may be removed from office by a concurrent vote of both Houses of the General Assembly, each House voting separately; but two-thirds of the members to which each House may be entitled must concur in such vote. The vote shall be determined by ayes and noes, and the names of the members voting for or against the Judge or Attorney for the State together with the cause or causes of removal, shall be entered on the Journals of each House respectively. The Judge or Attorney for the State, against whom the Legislature may be about to proceed, shall receive notice thereof accompanied with a copy of the causes alleged for his removal, at least ten days before the day on which either House of the General Assembly shall act thereupon.

Sec. 7. Compensation of judges.

The Judges of the Supreme or Inferior Courts, shall, at stated times, receive a compensation for their services, to be ascertained by law, which shall not be increased or diminished during the time for which they are elected. They shall not be allowed any fees or perquisites of office nor hold any other office of trust or profit under this State or the United States.

Sec. 8. Jurisdiction of inferior courts.

The jurisdiction of the Circuit, Chancery and other Inferior Courts, shall be as now established by law, until changed by the Legislature.

Sec. 9. Judge's charge.

The Judges shall not charge juries with respect to matters of fact, but may state the testimony and declare the law.

Sec. 10. Certiorari.

The Judges or Justices of the Inferior Courts of Law and Equity, shall have power in all civil cases, to issue writs of certiorari to remove any cause or the transcript of the record thereof, from any inferior jurisdiction, into such court of law, on sufficient cause, supported by oath or affirmation.

Sec. 11. Incompetency of judges—Special judges.

No Judge of the Supreme or Inferior Courts shall preside on the trial of any cause in the event of which he may be interested, or where either of the parties shall be connected with him by affinity or consanguinity, within such degrees as may be prescribed by law, or in which he may have been of counsel, or in which he may have presided in any inferior Court, except by consent of all the parties. In case all or any of the Judges of the Supreme Court shall thus be disqualified from presiding on the trial of any cause or causes, the Court, or the Judges thereof, shall certify the same to the Governor of the State, and he shall forthwith specially commission the requisite number of men, of law knowledge, for the trial and determination thereof. The Legislature may by general laws make provision that special Judges may be appointed, to hold any Courts the Judge of which shall be unable or fail to attend or sit; or to hear any cause in which the Judge may be incompetent.

Sec. 12. Requisites of writs and process.

All writs and other process shall run in the name of the State of Tennessee and bear test and be signed by the respective clerks. Indictments shall conclude, "against the peace and dignity of the State."

Sec. 13. Clerks of courts.

Judges of the Supreme Court shall appoint their clerks who shall hold their offices for six years. Chancellors shall appoint their clerks and masters, who shall hold their offices for six years. Clerks of the Inferior Courts holden in the respective Counties or Districts, shall be elected by the qualified voters thereof for the term of four years. Any Clerk may be removed from office for malfeasance, incompetency or neglect of duty, in such manner as may be prescribed by law.

SEC. 14. FINES EXCEEDING FIFTY DOLLARS TO BE ASSESSED BY JURY.

No fine shall be laid on any citizen of this State that shall exceed fifty dollars, unless it shall be assessed by a jury of his peers, who shall assess the fine at the time they find the fact, if they think the fine should be more than fifty dollars.

SEC. 15. DISTRICTS IN COUNTIES—JUSTICES AND CONSTABLES. [REPEALED.]

Article VII

State and County Officers

SEC. 1. COUNTY GOVERNMENT—ELECTED OFFICERS—LEGISLATIVE BODY—ALTERNATE FORMS OF GOVERNMENT.

The qualified voters of each county shall elect for terms of four years a legislative body, a county executive, a Sheriff, a Trustee, a Register, a County Clerk and an Assessor of Property. Their qualifications and duties shall be prescribed by the General Assembly. Any officer shall be removed for malfeasance or neglect of duty as prescribed by the General Assembly.

The legislative body shall be composed of representatives from districts in the county as drawn by the county legislative body pursuant to statutes enacted by the General Assembly. Districts shall be reapportioned at least every ten years based upon the most recent federal census. The legislative body shall not exceed twenty-five members, and no more than three representatives shall be elected from a district. Any county organized under the consolidated government provisions of Article XI, Section 9, of this Constitution shall be exempt from having a county executive and a county legislative body as described in this paragraph.

The General Assembly may provide alternate forms of county government[,] including the right to charter and the manner by which a referendum may be called. The new form of government shall replace the existing form if approved by a majority of the voters in the referendum.

No officeholder's current term shall be diminished by the ratification of this article. [As amended; Adopted in Convention, July 24, 1959; approved at election, November 8, 1960; Proclaimed by Governor, December 1, 1960; As amended; Adopted in Convention, December 6, 1977; approved at election, March 7, 1978; Proclaimed by Governor, March 31, 1978.]

Sec. 2. Vacancies.

Vacancies in county offices shall be filled by the county legislative body, and any person so appointed shall serve until a successor is elected at the next election occurring after the vacancy and is qualified. [As amended; Adopted in Convention, December 6, 1977; approved at election, March 7, 1978; Proclaimed by Governor, March 31, 1978.]

Sec. 3. Treasurer and comptroller.

There shall be a Treasurer or Treasurers and a Comptroller of the Treasury appointed for the State, by the joint vote of both houses of the General Assembly, who shall hold their offices for two years.

Sec. 4. Other elections and vacancies.

The election of all officers, and the filling of all vacancies not otherwise directed or provided by this Constitution, shall be made in such manner as the Legislature shall direct.

Sec. 5. Civil officers—Election—Vacancies.

Elections for Judicial and other civil officers shall be held on the first Thursday in August, one thousand eight hundred and seventy, and forever thereafter on the first Thursday in August next preceding the expiration of their respective terms of service. The term of each officer so elected shall be computed from the first day of September next succeeding his election. The term of office of the Governor and of other executive officers shall be computed from the fifteenth of January next after the election of the Governor. No appointment or election to fill a vacancy shall be made for a period extending beyond the unexpired term. Every officer shall hold his office until his successor is elected or appointed, and qualified. No special election shall be held to fill a vacancy in the office of Judge or District Attorney, but at the time herein fixed for the biennial election of civil officers; and such vacancy shall be filled at the next Biennial election recurring more than thirty days after the vacancy occurs.

Article VIII

Militia

SEC. 1. MILITIA OFFICERS TO BE ELECTED.

All militia officers shall be elected by persons subject to military duty, within the bounds of their several companies, battalions, regiments, brigades and divisions, under such rules and regulations as the Legislature may from time to time direct and establish.

SEC. 2. STAFF OFFICERS TO BE APPOINTED.

The Governor shall appoint the Adjutant-General and his other staff officers; the Major-Generals, Brigadier-Generals, and commanding officers of regiments, shall respectively appoint their staff officers.

SEC. 3. EXEMPTIONS FROM ATTENDING MUSTERS.

The Legislature shall pass laws exempting citizens belonging to any sect or denomination of religion, the tenets of which are known to be opposed to the bearing of arms, from attending private and general musters.

Article IX

Disqualifications

SEC. 1. INELIGIBILITY OF MINISTERS AND PRIESTS TO SEATS IN LEGISLATURE.

Whereas Ministers of the Gospel are by their profession, dedicated to God and the care of souls, and ought not to be diverted from the great duties of their functions; therefore, no Minister of the Gospel, or priest of any denomination whatever, shall be eligible to a seat in either House of the Legislature.

SEC. 2. NO ATHEIST SHALL HOLD A CIVIL OFFICE.

No person who denies the being of God, or a future state of rewards and punishments, shall hold any office in the civil department of this State.

SEC. 3. DUELISTS SHALL HOLD NO OFFICE.

Any person who shall, after the adoption of this Constitution, fight a duel, or knowingly be the bearer of a challenge to fight a duel, or send or accept a challenge for that purpose, or be an aider or abettor in fighting a duel, shall be deprived of the right to hold any office of honor or profit in this State, and shall be punished otherwise, in such manner as the Legislature may prescribe.

Article X

Oaths, Bribery of Electors, New Counties

SEC. 1. OATH OF OFFICE.

Every person who shall be chosen or appointed to any office of trust or profit under this Constitution, or any law made in pursuance thereof, shall, before entering on the duties thereof, take an oath to support the Constitution of this State, and of the United States, and an oath of office.

SEC. 2. OATH OF MEMBERS OF THE GENERAL ASSEMBLY.

Each member of the Senate and House of Representatives, shall before they proceed to business take an oath or affirmation to support the Constitution of this State, and of the United States and also the following oath: I . . . . do solemnly swear (or affirm) that as a member of this General Assembly, I will, in all appointments, vote without favor, affection, partiality, or prejudice; and that I will not propose or assent to any bill, vote or resolution, which shall appear to me injurious to the people, or consent to any act or thing, whatever, that shall have a tendency to lessen or abridge their rights and privileges, as declared by the Constitution of this State.

Sec. 3. Punishment of electors and candidates for bribery.

Any elector who shall receive any gift or reward for his vote, in meat, drink, money or otherwise, shall suffer such punishment as the law shall direct. And any person who shall directly or indirectly give, promise or bestow any such reward to be elected, shall thereby be rendered incapable, for six years, to serve in the office for which he was elected, and be subject to such further punishment as the Legislature shall direct.

Sec. 4. New counties—Approach of county lines to court-house—Limit to reduction of counties—Exceptions—Vote necessary to detach fractions for formation of new counties or to remove a county seat—Liability for existing debt.

New Counties may be established by the Legislature to consist of not less than two hundred and seventy-five square miles, and which shall contain a population of seven hundred qualified voters; no line of such County shall approach the Court House of any old County from which it may be taken nearer than eleven miles, nor shall such old County be reduced to less than five hundred square miles. But the following exceptions are made to the foregoing provisions viz.: New Counties may be established by the present or any succeeding Legislature out of the following Territory to wit: Out of that portion of Obion County which lies west of low water mark of Reel Foot Lake: Out of fractions of Sumner, Macon and Smith Counties; but no line of such new County shall approach the Court House of Sumner or of Smith Counties nearer than ten miles, nor include any part of Macon County lying within nine and a half miles of the Court House of said County nor shall more than twenty square miles of Macon County nor any part of Sumner County lying due west of the western boundary of Macon County, be taken in the formation of said new County: Out of fractions of Grainger and Jefferson Counties but no line of such new County shall include any part of Grainger County north of the Holston River; nor shall any line thereof approach the Court House of Jefferson County nearer than eleven miles. Such new County may include any other Territory which is not excluded by any general provision of this Constitution: Out of fractions of Jackson and Overton Counties but no line of such new County shall approach the Court House of Jackson or Overton Counties nearer than ten miles, nor shall such County contain less than four hundred qualified voters, nor shall the area of either of the old Counties be reduced below four hundred and fifty square miles: Out of fractions of Roane, Monroe, and Blount Counties, around the town of Loudon; but no line of such new County shall ever approach the towns of Maryville, Kingston, or Madisonville, nearer than eleven miles, except that on the south side of the Tennessee River, said lines may approach as near as ten miles to the Court House of Roane County.

The Counties of Lewis, Cheatham, and Sequatchie, as now established by Legislative enactments[,] are hereby declared to be Constitutional Counties. No part of Bledsoe County shall be taken to form a new County or a part thereof or be attached to any adjoining County. That portion of Marion County included within the following boundaries, beginning on the Grundy and Marion County line at the Nickajack trace and running about six hundred yards west of Ben Poseys, to where the Tennessee Coal Rail Road crosses the line, running thence southeast through the Pocket near William Summars crossing the Battle Creek Gulf at the corner of Thomas Wootons field, thence running across the Little Gizzard Gulf at Raven Point, thence in a direct line to the Bridge crossing the Big Fiery Gizzard, thence in a direct line to the mouth of Holy Water Creek, thence up said Creek to the Grundy County line, and thence with said line to the beginning; is hereby detached from Marion County, and attached to the County of Grundy. No part of a County shall be taken off to form a new County or a part thereof without the consent of two-thirds of the qualified voters in such part taken off; and where an old County is reduced for the purpose of forming a new one, the Seat of Justice in said old County shall not be removed without the concurrence of two-thirds of both branches of the Legislature, nor shall the Seat of Justice of any County be removed without the concurrence of two-thirds of the qualified voters of the County. But the foregoing provision requiring a two-thirds majority of the voters of a County to remove its County seat shall not apply to the Counties of Obion and Cocke. The fractions taken from old Counties to form new Counties or taken from one County and added to another shall continue liable for their pro rata of all debts contracted by their respective Counties prior to the separation, and be entitled to their proportion of any stocks or credits belonging to such old Counties.

SEC. 5. TO VOTE WITH OLD COUNTY.

The citizens who may be included in any new County shall vote with the County or Counties from which they may have been stricken off, for members of Congress, for Governor and for members of the General Assembly until the next apportionment of members to the General Assembly after the establishment of such new County.

Article XI

Miscellaneous Provisions

SEC. 1. EXISTING LAWS NOT AFFECTED BY THIS CONSTITUTION.

All laws and ordinances now in force and use in this State, not inconsistent with this Constitution, shall continue in force and use until they shall expire, be altered or repealed by the Legislature; but ordinances contained in any former Constitution or schedule thereto are hereby abrogated.

SEC. 2. NO IMPAIRMENT OF RIGHTS.

Nothing contained in this Constitution shall impair the validity of any debts or contracts, or affect any rights of property or any suits, actions, rights of action or other proceedings in Courts of Justice.

SEC. 3. AMENDMENTS TO CONSTITUTION.

Any amendment or amendments to this Constitution may be proposed in the Senate or House of Representatives, and if the same shall be agreed to by a majority of all the members elected to each of the two houses, such proposed amendment or amendments shall be entered on their journals with the yeas and nays thereon, and referred to the general assembly then next to be chosen; and shall be published six months previous to the time of making such choice; and if in the general assembly then next chosen as aforesaid, such proposed amendment or amendments shall be agreed to by two-thirds of all the members elected to each house, then it shall be the duty of the general assembly to submit such proposed amendment or amendments to the people at the next general election in which a Governor is to be chosen. And if the people shall approve and ratify such amendment or amendments by a majority of all the citizens of the State voting for Governor, voting in their favor, such amendment or amendments shall become a part of this Constitution. When any amendment or amendments to the Constitution shall be proposed in pursuance of the foregoing provisions the same shall at each of said sessions be read three times on three several days in each house.

The Legislature shall have the right by law to submit to the people, at any general election, the question of calling a convention to alter, reform, or abolish this Constitution, or to alter, reform or abolish any specified part or parts of it; and when, upon such submission, a majority of all the voters voting upon the proposal submitted shall approve the proposal to call a convention, the delegates to such convention shall be chosen at the next general election and the convention shall assemble for the consideration of such proposals as shall have received a favorable vote in said election, in such mode and manner as shall be prescribed. No change in, or amendment to, this Constitution proposed by such convention shall become effective, unless within the limitations of the call of the convention, and unless approved and ratified by a majority of the qualified voters voting separately on such change or amendment at an election to be held in such manner and on such date as may be fixed by the convention. No such convention shall be held oftener than once in six years. [As amended: Adopted in Convention, May 27, 1953; Approved at election, November 3, 1953; Proclaimed by Governor, November 19, 1953.]

Sec. 4. Power to grant divorces.

The Legislature shall have no power to grant divorces; but may authorize the Courts of Justice to grant them for such causes as may be specified by law; but such laws shall be general and uniform in their operation throughout the State.

Sec. 5. Lotteries.

The Legislature shall have no power to authorize lotteries for any purpose, and shall pass laws to prohibit the sale of lottery tickets in this State.

Sec. 6. Changing names—Adoption—Legitimation.

The legislature shall have no power to change the names of persons, or to pass acts adopting or legitimatizing persons; but shall, by general laws, confer this power on the Courts.

Sec. 7. Interest.

The General Assembly shall define and regulate interest, and set maximum effective rates thereof. If no applicable statute is hereafter enacted, the effective rate of interest collected shall not exceed ten percent (10%) per annum.

All provisions of existing statutes regulating rates of interest and other charges on loans shall remain in full force and effect until July 1, 1980, unless earlier amended or repealed. [As amended; Adopted in Convention, December 1, 1977; approved at election, March 7, 1978; Proclaimed by Governor, March 31, 1978.]

Sec. 8. General laws only to be passed.

The Legislature shall have no power to suspend any general law for the benefit of any particular individual, nor to pass any law for the benefit of individuals inconsistent with the general laws of the land; nor to pass any law granting to any individual or individuals, rights, privileges, immunitie [immunities], or exemptions other than such as may be, by the same law[,] extended to any member of the community, who may be able to bring himself within the provisions of such law. No corporation shall be created or its powers increased or diminished by special laws but the General Assembly shall provide by general laws for the organization of all corporations, hereafter created, which laws may, at any time, be altered or repealed and no such alteration or repeal shall interfere with or divest rights which have become vested.

Sec. 9. Power over local affairs—Home rule for cities and counties—Consolidation of functions.

The Legislature shall have the right to vest such powers in the Courts of Justice, with regard to private and local affairs, as may be expedient.

The General Assembly shall have no power to pass a special, local or private act having the effect of removing the incumbent from any municipal or county office or abridging the term or altering the salary prior to the end of the term for which such public officer was selected, and any act of the General Assembly private or local in form or effect applicable to a particular county or municipality either in its governmental or its proprietary capacity shall be void and of no effect unless the act by its terms either requires the approval by a two-thirds vote of the local legislative body of the municipality or county, or requires approval in an election by a majority of those voting in said election in the municipality or county affected.

Any municipality may by ordinance submit to its qualified voters in a general or special election the question: "Shall this municipality adopt home rule?"

In the event of an affirmative vote by a majority of the qualified voters voting thereon, and until the repeal thereof by the same procedure, such municipality shall be a home rule municipality, and the General Assembly shall act with respect to such home rule municipality only by laws which are general in terms and effect.

Any municipality after adopting home rule may continue to operate under its existing charter, or amend the same, or adopt and thereafter amend a new charter to provide for its governmental and proprietary powers, duties and functions, and for the form, structure, personnel and organization of its government, provided that no charter provision except with respect to compensation of municipal personnel shall be effective if inconsistent with any general act of the General Assembly and provided further that the power of taxation of such municipality shall not be enlarged or increased except by general act of the General Assembly. The General Assembly shall by general law provide the exclusive methods by which municipalities may be created, merged, consolidated and dissolved and by which municipal boundaries may be altered.

A charter or amendment may be proposed by ordinance of any home rule municipality, by a charter commission provided for by act of the General Assembly and elected by the qualified voters of a home rule municipality voting thereon[,] or, in the absence of such act of the General Assembly, by a charter commission of seven (7) members, chosen at large not more often than once in two (2) years, in a municipal election pursuant to petition for such election signed by qualified voters of a home rule municipality not less in number than ten (10%) percent of those voting in the then most recent general municipal election.

It shall be the duty of the legislative body of such municipality to publish any proposal so made and to submit the same to its qualified voters at the first general state election which shall be held at least sixty (60) days after such publication and such proposal shall become effective sixty (60) days after approval by a majority of the qualified voters voting thereon.

The General Assembly shall not authorize any municipality to tax incomes, estates, or inheritances, or to impose any other tax not authorized by Sections 28 or 29 of Article II of this Constitution. Nothing herein shall be construed as invalidating the provisions of any municipal charter in existence at the time of the adoption of this amendment.

The General Assembly may provide for the consolidation of any or all of the governmental and corporate functions now or hereafter vested in municipal corporations with the governmental and corporate functions now or hereafter vested in the counties in which such municipal corporations are located; provided, such consolidations shall not become effective until submitted to the qualified voters residing within the municipal corporation and in the county outside thereof, and approved by a majority of those voting within the municipal corporation and by a majority of those voting in the county outside the municipal corporation. [As amended: Adopted in Convention, June 4, 1953; Approved at election, November 3, 1953; Proclaimed by Governor, November 19, 1953.]

Sec. 10. Internal improvements to be encouraged.

A well regulated system of internal improvement is calculated to develop the resources of the State, and promote the happiness and prosperity of her citizens; therefore it ought to be encouraged by the General Assembly.

Sec. 11. Homestead and personal property exemptions.

There shall be a homestead exemption from execution in an amount of five thousand dollars or such greater amount as the General Assembly may establish. The General Assembly shall also establish personal property exemptions. The definition and application of the homestead and personal property exemptions and the manner in which they may be waived shall be as prescribed by law. [As amended; Adopted in Convention, October 7, 1977; Approved at election, March 7, 1978; Proclaimed by Governor, March 31, 1978.]

Sec. 12. Education's inherent value—Public schools—Support of higher education.

The State of Tennessee recognizes the inherent value of education and encourages its support. The General Assembly shall provide for the maintenance, support and eligibility standards of a system of free public schools. The General Assembly may establish and support such postsecondary educational institutions, including public institutions of higher learning, as it determines. [As amended; Adopted in Convention, October 11, 1977; approved at election, March 7, 1978; Proclaimed by Governor, March 31, 1978.]

Sec. 13. Game and fish.

The General Assembly shall have power to enact laws for the protection and preservation of Game and Fish, within the State, and such laws may be enacted for and applied and enforced in particular Counties or geographical districts, designated by the General Assembly.

Sec. 14. Racial intermarriage.

[Repealed.]

Sec. 15. Religious holidays.

No person shall in time of peace be required to perform any service to the public on any day set apart by his religion as a day of rest.

Sec. 16. Bill of rights to remain inviolate.

The declaration of rights hereto prefixed is declared to be a part of the Constitution of this State, and shall never be violated on any pretence whatever. And to guard against transgression of the high powers we have delegated, we declare that everything in the bill of rights contained, is excepted out of the General powers of government, and shall forever remain inviolate.

Sec. 17. County offices.

No County office created by the Legislature shall be filled otherwise than by the people or the County Court.

Schedule

SEC. 1. TERMS OF PUBLIC OFFICERS—APPOINTMENTS—EXCEPTIONS.

That no inconvenience may arise from a change of the Constitution, it is declared that the Governor of the State, the members of the General Assembly and all officers elected at or after the general election of March one thousand eight hundred and seventy, shall hold their offices for the terms prescribed in this Constitution.

Officers appointed by the courts shall be filled by appointment, to be made and to take effect during the first term of the court held by Judges elected under this Constitution.

All other officers shall vacate their places thirty days after the day fixed for the election of their successors under this Constitution.

The Secretary of State, Comptroller and Treasurer shall hold their offices until the first session of the present General Assembly occurring after the ratification of this Constitution and until their successors are elected and qualified.

The officers then elected shall hold their offices until the fifteenth day of January one thousand eight hundred and seventy-three.

SEC. 2. SUPREME COURT JUDGES—VACANCIES—ATTORNEY GENERAL AND REPORTER.

At the first election of Judges under this Constitution there shall be elected six Judges of the Supreme Court, two from each grand division of the State who shall hold their offices for the term herein prescribed.

In the event any vacancy shall occur in the office of either of said Judges at any time after the first day of January one thousand eight hundred and seventy-three it shall remain unfilled and the Court shall from that time be constituted of five Judges. While the Court shall consist of six Judges they may sit in two sections, and may hear and determine causes in each at the same time, but not in different grand divisions at the same time.

When so sitting, the concurrence of two Judges shall be necessary to a decision.

The Attorney General and Reporter for the State shall be appointed after the election and qualification of the Judges of the Supreme Court herein provided for.

Sec. 3. Oath of office mandatory.

Every Judge and every officer of the executive department of this State and every Sheriff holding office under this Constitution, shall, within twenty days after the ratification of this Constitution is proclaimed, take an oath to support the same, and the failure of any officer to take such oath shall vacate his office.

Sec. 4. Statutes of limitations.

The time which has elapsed from the sixth day of May one thousand eight hundred and sixty one until the first day of January one thousand eight hundred and sixty seven shall not be computed, in any case affected by the statutes of limitation, nor shall any writ of error be affected by such lapse of time.

Notes

Chapter 1

1. Wilma Dykeman, *Tennessee: A Bicentennial History* (New York: Norton, 1975), 22–29.
2. See, e.g., Stanley J. Folmsbee, Robert E. Corlew, and Enoch L. Mitchell, *Tennessee: A Short History* (Knoxville: Univ. of Tennessee Press, 1969), 72.
3. See also Ben Allen and Dennis T. Lawson, "The Wataugans and the 'Dangerous Example,'" *Tennessee Historical Quarterly* 26 (1967): 136–47.
4. Theodore Roosevelt, *Winning of the West* (New York, 1904), 1:213.
5. See also Archibald Henderson, "Richard Henderson: The Authorship of the Cumberland Compact and the Founding of Nashville," *Tennessee Historical Magazine* 2 (1916): 155–74.
6. Dykeman, *Tennessee,* 60–61.
7. See Samuel Cole Williams, *History of the Lost State of Franklin* (Johnson City, Tenn.: Watauga Press, 1924); rev. ed. (New York: Press of the Pioneers, 1933).
8. Dykeman, *Tennessee,* 67–69.
9. Despite the implication of the name, this territory did not include the area that later would become the state of Kentucky.
10. Lee Seifert Greene, David Grubbs, and Victor Hobday, *Government in Tennessee,* 4th ed. (Knoxville: Univ. of Tennessee Press, 1982), 10.
11. Jonathan M. Atkins, *Parties, Politics, and Sectional Conflict in Tennessee: 1832–1861* (Knoxville: Univ. of Tennessee Press, 1997), 23.
12. Ibid., 14.
13. The Tennessee Supreme Court's decision came in a case in which a Cherokee man, James Foreman, had been accused of murder. The question was whether Tennessee courts had jurisdiction over the case. See Folmsbee, Corlew, and Mitchell, *Tennessee: Short History,* 154.
14. Dykeman, *Tennessee,* 75.
15. Atkins, *Parties,* 19.
16. Ibid.
17. For an excellent summary and analysis of the case, see Richard C. Cortner, *The Apportionment Cases* (Knoxville: Univ. of Tennessee Press, 1970).
18. Colegrove v. Green, 328 U.S. 549 (1946).

19. *Baker v. Carr,* 369 U.S. 186, 237 (1962).
20. *Reynolds v. Sims,* 377 U.S. 533 (1964).
21. William Lyons, John M. Scheb II, and Lilliard Richardson, *American Government: Politics and Political Culture* (St. Paul, Minn.: West Publishing Co., 1995), 4–7.
22. For the classic discussion of variations in American political culture, see Daniel Elazar, *American Federalism: A View from the States* (New York: Thomas Crowell, 1966), 85–86.
23. Dykeman, *Tennessee,* 11.
24. Atkins, *Parties.*
25. Ibid., 3.

Chapter 2

1. Tennessee Constitution, Art. IX, Sec. 1.
2. *McDaniel v. Paty,* 435 U.S. 618 (1978).
3. Ann Bowman and Richard Kearney, *State and Local Government,* 3rd ed. (Boston: Houghton Mifflin, 1996), 58–59.
4. Lewis Laska, *The Tennessee State Constitution: A Reference Guide* (New York: Greenwood Press, 1990), 2–7.
5. Laska, *Tennessee State Constitution,* 3.
6. Atkins, *Parties,* 3.
7. Poll taxes were not required for voting until 1870; they were the first of many efforts after the Civil War to deny suffrage to free slaves.
8. Tennessee Constitution of 1796, Art. 5, Sec. 1.
9. "Private acts," referred to as "special acts" in some quarters, are legislative acts aimed at particular parties or objects, as distinct from "statutes," which are laws of general applicability.
10. Robert White, "Remarks Made to the Constitutional Convention of 1953," in *Journal and Debates of the Constitutional Convention, 1953* (Nashville: Limited Constitutional Convention, 1953, State of Tennessee, 1953), 519.
11. Laska, *Tennessee State Constitution,* 4–5.
12. *Tennessee Small Schools v. McWherter,* 851 S.W. 2d 139, 150 (Tenn. 1993).
13. Greene, Grubbs, and Hobday, *Government in Tennessee,* 4th ed., 4–7.
14. The Tennessee Constitution permits the General Assembly to determine whether delegates are elected from House or Senate districts and other details of the election of delegates.
15. *Baker v. Carr,* 369 U.S. 186 (1962).
16. *Reynolds v. Sims,* 377 U.S. 533 (1964).
17. Lee Seifert Greene, David H. Grubbs, and Victor C. Hobday, *Government in Tennessee,* 3rd ed. (Knoxville: Univ. of Tennessee Press, 1975), 31.

18. See *Brown v. Board of Education,* 347 U.S. 483 (1954); *Loving v. Virginia,* 388 U.S. 1 (1967).
19. Laska, *Tennessee State Constitution,* 156.
20. Sec. 31 refers to the boundaries of the state.
21. Laska, *Tennessee State Constitution,* 53.
22. Tennessee Constitution, Art. I, Sec. 3.
23. Laska, *Tennessee State Constitution,* 33.
24. Tenn. Code Ann. §39-17-101.
25. *State ex rel. Swann v. Pack,* 527 S.W. 2d 99, 117 (Tenn. 1975).
26. See *Reynolds v. United States,* 98 U.S. 145 (1878); *Employment Division v. Smith,* 494 U.S. 872 (1990).
27. Otis H. Stephens Jr. and John M. Scheb II, *American Constitutional Law,* 2d ed. (Belmont, Calif.: West/Wadsworth, 1999), 350.
28. See Tenn. Code Ann. §§39-17-1301 et seq.
29. *Oliver v. United States,* 466 U.S. 170 (1984).
30. *State v. Lakin,* 588 S.W. 2d 593 (Tenn. 1979); *State v. Doelman,* 620 S.W. 2d 96 (Tenn. 1981).
31. *Illinois v. Gates,* 462 U.S. 213 (1983).
32. *State v. Jacumin,* 778 S.W. 430 (Tenn. 1989); *State v. Valentine,* 911 S.W. 2d 328 (Tenn. 1995).
33. *Robinson v. California,* 370 U.S. 660 (1962).
34. *Wallace v. State,* 245 S.W. 2d 192 (Tenn. 1952).
35. *State ex rel. Hemby v. O'Steen,* 559 S.W. 2d 340 (Tenn. 1977).
36. *State v. Austin,* 618 S.W. 2d 738 (Tenn. 1981).
37. *Pearson v. State,* 521 S.W. 2d 225 (Tenn. 1975).
38. Sen. Curtis Person (R-Memphis), quoted in *Senate Republican News,* May 8, 1997.
39. *Morris v. Gross,* 572 S.W. 2d 902, 907 (Tenn. 1978).
40. See, e.g., *Ford Motor Co. v. Moulton,* 511 S.W. 2d 690, 695–97 (Tenn. 1974); *Saylors v. Riggsbee,* 544 S.W. 2d 609 (Tenn. 1976).
41. Tennessee Constitution, Art. I, Sec. 8.
42. See Tenn. Code Ann. §§9-8-301 et seq.
43. *Greenhill v. Carpenter,* 718 S.W. 2d 268 (Tenn. App. 1986).
44. Laska, *Tennessee State Constitution,* 39–40.
45. *Tennessee Small Schools v. McWherter,* 851 S.W. 2d 139 (Tenn. 1993).
46. *Griswold v. Connecticut,* 381 U.S. 479 (1965).
47. *Davis v. Davis,* 842 S.W. 2d 588, 599 (1992).
48. *Campbell v. Sundquist,* 926 S.W. 2d 250 (Tenn. Ct. App. 1996).
49. *Bowers v. Hardwick,* 478 U.S. 186 (1986).
50. *Campbell v. Sundquist,* 926 S.W. 2d 250, 265 (Tenn. Ct. App. 1996).
51. *Hawk v. Hawk,* 855 S.W. 2d 573, 579 (Tenn. 1993).

52. *Doe v. Sundquist,* 2 S.W. 3d 919 (Tenn. 1999).
53. *Tennessee Municipal League v. Thompson,* 958 S.W. 2d 333 (1997).
54. *Evans v. McCabe,* 52 S.W. 2d 159 (1932).
55. Tenn. Att. Gen. Op. 67 (Mar. 3, 1976).
56. Tenn. Code Ann. §40-20-112.
57. See Cortez A. M. Ewing, "Early Tennessee Impeachments," *Tennessee Historical Quarterly* 16, no. 4 (Dec. 1957): 291–334; Robert H. White, "Impeachment Procedure in Tennessee," unpub. paper located in the Tennessee State Library and Archives.
58. Greene, Grubbs, and Hobday, *Government in Tennessee,* 86.
59. In Tennessee, the Circuit Court is a trial court of general jurisdiction, having the authority to hear both civil and criminal cases. The Chancery Court was constituted as a "court of equity," as distinct from a "court of law," but that distinction has lost much of its meaning. However, the Chancery Court remains a court of exclusively civil jurisdiction.
60. Tenn. Att. Gen. Op. 69 (Mar. 1982).
61. *Torasco v. Watkins,* 367 U.S. 488 (1961).
62. Tennessee Constitution, Art. XI, Sec. 4.
63. Tennessee Constitution, Art. XI, Sec. 6.
64. There have been four failed attempts to consolidate Knoxville and Knox County: 1959, 1978, 1983, and 1996.
65. *Tennessee Small Schools v. McWherter,* 851 S.W. 2d 139, 156 (Tenn. 1993).

Chapter 3

1. See *Medians* (New York: Moody's Investors Service. Each year, Moody's Public Finance Department publishes rankings that assess a state's financial posture. These rankings include pension systems, per capita state debt, and per capita state debt as a percentage of personal income. Taken together, these indicators show Tennessee's management of state finances to have been extremely conservative.
2. Although the State Budget, published by the Tennessee Department of Finance and Administration, is a useful and well-organized tool for examining state expenditures, precise budget figures for each state program are located in the Appropriations Bills enacted each legislative session. The full text of each Appropriations Bill is found in *Public Acts and Resolutions of the State of Tennessee,* published annually by the General Assembly.
3. Tennessee Constitution, Art. II, Sec. 6.
4. Tennessee Constitution, Art. II, Secs. 5a and 6a.
5. Tennessee General Assembly, *Legislative Record,* 1995–96.

6. Tennessee Constitution, Art. II, Sec. 17, attempts to limit the scope of individual bills by stating, "No bill may become a law which embraces more than one subject, that subject to be expressed in the title." In recent years, some legislators have sought to circumvent the intent of the Constitution by filing bills with extremely "broad" captions that cover large sections of the Tennessee Code Annotated. The intent of these broad captions can be twofold. One purpose can be to disguise the actual intent of legislation from lobbyists or legislative opponents until the sponsor is ready to move the bill in committee. A second purpose can be to have a blank bill ready and filed in case unexpected events make such a bill needed after the deadline for filing bills has passed. The confusion generated by the increasing number of "caption bills" forced the House and Senate in 1999 to adopt rules attempting to limit, or at least control, their use.
7. *Permanent Rules of Order,* Senate, State of Tennessee, Rule 83; *Permanent Rules of Order,* House of Representatives, State of Tennessee, Rule 8.
8. McWherter's election as House Speaker in 1973 was one of the most famous and significant in state history. McWherter defeated the incumbent, Jim McKinney of Nashville, by one vote in the House Democratic Caucus to become the Democratic candidate for Speaker. With the Democrats holding a precarious 50–49 margin in the House, Republican Gov. Winfield Dunn, during a midnight meeting at the Executive Residence, attempted to persuade Nashville Democrat Charles Pruitt to vote for the Republican candidate for Speaker. Pruitt did not switch, and the next day McWherter was elected Speaker by one vote. On the basis of a single vote, McWherter went on to become one of Tennessee's most powerful speakers and a two-term Governor. The coalition of rural West Tennessee legislators that elected McWherter in 1973 remained the power base of the House for the remainder of the twentieth century.
9. An excellent example of the long-term impact of subcommittees on state policy involves laws governing the sale of alcohol. For decades, the state's liquor wholesalers have successfully sought to restrain competition in an effort to avoid pressure to lower prices. Compared to many states, Tennessee has restrictive limitations on the number of wholesale and retail businesses allowed to sell liquor and wine. Numerous attempts to increase the small number of liquor wholesalers or to allow wine sales in grocery stores have been defeated in subcommittees. In one of the odd relationships found in the legislature, some of the legislators associated with the Christian Coalition often support the liquor industry in efforts to restrict competition.
10. National Conference of State Legislatures, "Size of State Legislative Staff: 1979, 1988 and 1996," Feb. 5, 1997.

11. Charles Mathesian, "The Sick Legislature and How to Avoid It," *Governing,* Feb. 1997, 16–20.
12. Tennessee Registry of Elections, *Annual Report,* 1998.

Chapter 4

1. Tennessee Constitution, Art. III, Sec. 4. The 1954 election was the first that elected a Governor to a four-year term. The 1978 election was the first in which a Governor could run for a second consecutive four-year term.
2. *Public Acts and Resolutions of the State of Tennessee* (1923), chap. 7.
3. *Public Acts and Resolutions of the State of Tennessee* (1925), chap. 115.
4. William H. Combs and William E. Cole, *Tennessee: A Political Study* (Knoxville: Univ. of Tennessee Press, 1940), 74.
5. *Knoxville News-Sentinel,* Dec. 24, 1988, p. 1.
6. The Interstate Hazardous Waste Compact was one of the most complicated and significant multistate agreements signed during the 1980s. The compact was an effort to help each state avoid some of the politically volatile aspects of managing industrial wastes. Under the agreement, Alabama and South Carolina accepts wastes from each state in highly regulated landfills, Kentucky accepts wastes for incineration, and Tennessee accepts wastes for recycling. By producing and organizing the data on waste production, Tennessee was the leader in developing the agreement.
7. *Nashville Banner,* Feb. 4, 1981, p. 1.
8. One way to demonstrate the Governor's influence is to compare spending requests in the State Budget document presented by the Governor at the beginning of each legislative session with funding totals for the same requests in the Appropriations Bill enacted at the session's conclusion. In Tennessee, unless the proposed State Budget is predicated upon a tax increase that is not approved by the legislature, the great majority of spending recommendations in the Budget are enacted in identical fashion in the Appropriations Bill. In Congress as in many other states, the administration's proposed budget differs greatly from the budget ultimately enacted by the legislative body.
9. A representative example of the many organizations that dispense funds through the Governor's Office is the Appalachian Regional Commission (ARC). Created by Congress during the 1960s to promote economic development in Appalachian communities, ARC has broadened its definition of "economic development," in response to the wishes of the state governors who make up the ARC board. With the support of Gov. Ned

McWherter (then ARC Chair), Gov. Carroll Campbell of South Carolina used ARC funds as part of an incentive package for BMW to locate a new plant in Spartanburg. ARC grants are used by Tennessee Governors for a wide variety of projects in East Tennessee.

10. Information provided by William Fox, Center for Business and Economic Research, Univ. of Tennessee at Knoxville.

Chapter 5

1. Tennessee Constitution, Art. VII, Sec. 3.
2. Tenn. Code Ann. §9-9-101.
3. Tenn. Code Ann. §§4-31-104 to 117.
4. Tenn. Code Ann. §4-3-5101.
5. Tennessee Constitution, Art. VII, Sec. 3.
6. Tennessee State Treasurer, *Annual Report,* 1998.
7. Tennessee Constitution, Art. III, Sec. 17.
8. The *Tennessee Blue Book,* published biennially by the Secretary of State, contains informative sections on the legislative, executive, and judicial branches of state government, as well as election returns, historical information on the state, and a wealth of state, county, and municipal data.
9. Tenn. Code Ann. §§4-15-101 to 107.
10. Tennessee Constitution, Art. VI, Sec. 5.
11. On Tennessee boards and commissions, see *Tennessee Blue Book* and Tenn. Code Ann., Sec. 4-3-101, "Administration Departments and Divisions."
12. Tenn. Code Ann., §§4-29-112 and 4-29-218. The Department of Children's Services was created in 1998 in a consolidation of various services from the state departments of Education, Human Services, Mental Health, and Youth Development.
13. Tenn. Code Ann. §§4-3-1601 to 1603.
14. E. S. Browning and Helen Cooper, *Wall Street Journal,* Nov. 24, 1993, p. A-1.
15. Tennessee's many boards and commissions are authorized by statutory provisions scattered throughout the Tennessee Code.
16. Tenn. Code Ann. §68-11-104.
17. Tenn. Code Ann. §3-1408.
18. The *State Budget* document published by the Department of Finance and Administration contains personnel totals for most state agencies. An examination of budget documents from the mid-1980s until 2000 reveals that, during this period, the Department of Correction was the only executive branch agency with a substantial growth in personnel.

Chapter 6

1. As of 1990, 22 states used some form of judicial merit selection and retention. See Sara Mathias, *Electing Justice: A Handbook of Judicial Selection Reforms* (Chicago: American Judicature Society, 1990), 142.
2. *State v. Odom,* 928 S.W. 2d 18 (1996).
3. See Traciel V. Reid, "The Politicization of Retention Elections: Lessons from the Defeat of Justices Lanphier and White," *Judicature* 83, no. 2 (Sept.–Oct. 1999): 68–77
4. Alexander Hamilton, *The Federalist,* no. 78.
5. *Miller v. Conlee,* 37 Tenn. 432 (1858); *Arrington Trustee v. Cotton,* 60 Tenn. 317 (1872).
6. See, e.g., Institute of Judicial Administration, *Preliminary Report on the Judicial System of Tennessee* (New York: Lalso Institute of Judicial Administration, 1971).
7. John M. Scheb II and Stephen J. Rechichar, *The Politics of Judicial Modernization: The Case of the Tennessee Court System* (Knoxville: Bureau of Public Administration, Univ. of Tennessee, 1986); Thomas R. Van Dervort, "The Changing Court System," in *Tennessee Government and Politics: Democracy in the Volunteer State,* ed. John R. Vile and Mark Byrnes (Nashville, Tenn.: Vanderbilt Univ. Press, 1998), 55–57.
8. See Brian J. Ostrom et al., *State Court Caseload Statistics: Annual Report 1992* (Williamsburg, Va.: National Center for State Courts, 1994), 165–66.
9. In Tennessee, small claims are those civil cases in which the amount at issue is less than $10,000. However, in counties with populations greater than 70,000, the limit of sessions court jurisdiction is $15,000.
10. Greene, Grubbs, and Hobday, *Government in Tennessee,* 3rd ed., 159.
11. David B. Rottman, Carol R. Flango, and R. Shedine Lockley, *State Court Organization, 1993* (Washington, D.C.: USGPO, 1995; published for the Bureau of Justice Statistics, U.S. Department of Justice), 391.
12. City of Knoxville Charter, Art. V, Sec. 501.
13. Tenn. Code Ann. §21-1-103.
14. This is a constitutional question upon which opinions differ. The Supreme Court's decision in *State ex rel. Coleman v. Campbell,* 3 Shannon's Cases 355 (1875), suggests that the state constitution mandates separate circuit and chancery courts. However, the Tennessee Attorney General has opined otherwise; see Tenn. Att. Gen. Op. 576 (Nov. 3, 1981).
15. Frederic S. Le Clercq, "The Tennessee Court System," *Memphis State Univ. Law Review* 8, no. 2 (Special Issue, 1978): 219.
16. *Public Acts and Resolutions of the State of Tennessee* (1925), chap. 100, §1.
17. *Public Acts and Resolutions of the State of Tennessee* (1967), chap. 226, §1.

18. The other such state is Alabama. Two states, Texas and Oklahoma, have specialized appellate courts for criminal cases, but these are courts of last resort, not intermediate appellate courts. See Rottman, Flango, and Lockley, *State Court Organization, 1993.*
19. On the jurisdiction of the Court of Appeals, see Tenn. Code Ann. §16-4-108.
20. Tenn. Code Ann. §16-5-108.
21. Of course, any state supreme court decision on a matter of federal law can be reviewed by the U.S. Supreme Court on a writ of certiorari.
22. Tenn. Code Ann. §16-3-201(d)(2).
23. Tenn. Code Ann. §16-3-501.
24. Tenn. Code Ann. §§16-3-401 et seq.
25. See *Campbell v. Sundquist,* 926 S.W. 2d 250 (Tenn. Ct. App. 1996).
26. Tennessee Code Annotated, vol. 7, 1997 Replacement (Charlottesville, Va.: Michie Co., 1997). See Code Commission Notes on §39-13-510, pp. 274–75.
27. *Kidd v. McCanless,* 292 S.W. 2d 40, 43 (1956).
28. *Baker v. Carr,* 369 U.S. 186 (1962).
29. *Tennessee Small Schools v. McWherter*, 894 S.W. 2d 734, 734 (1995).
30. *Tennessee Municipal League v. Thompson,* 958 S.W. 2d 338 (1997).
31. *Public Acts and Resolutions of the State of Tennessee* (1997), chap. 98.
32. Tenn. Code Ann. §16-3-201(d).
33. *Tennessee Municipal League v. Thompson,* 958 S.W. 2d 333, 338 (1997).
34. Tennessee Constitution, Art. VI, Secs. 3 and 4.
35. Combs and Cole, *Tennessee: A Political Study,* 167.
36. *Public Acts and Resolutions of the State of Tennessee* (1971), chap. 198, §1.
37. See Robert Keele, "The Politics of Appellate Court Selection in Tennessee," in *The Volunteer State: Readings in Tennessee Politics,* ed. Dorothy F. Olshfski and T. McN. Simpson III, 231–58 (n.p.: Tennessee Political Science Association, 1985).
38. See Tenn. Code Ann. §17-4-102.
39. Tennessee Constitution, Art. V, Sec. 2.
40. Tennessee Constitution, Art. V, Sec. 4.
41. See Van Dervort, "Changing Court System," 58.
42. *In re Murphy,* 726 S.W. 2d 509 (Tenn. 1987).
43. For an in-depth account of the David Lanier scandal, see Darcy O'Brien, *Power to Hurt* (New York: Harper-Collins, 1996).
44. *Gideon v. Wainwright,* 372 U.S. 335 (1963).
45. *Argersinger v. Hamlin,* 407 U.S. 25 (1972).
46. See Tenn. Code Ann. §§8-14-201 et seq.
47. Tennessee Constitution, Art. I, Sec. 14.
48. Van Dervort, "Changing Court System," 74.

Chapter 7

1. John Crittenden, *Parties and Elections in the United States* (London: Prentice-Hall, 1982), 3.
2. Exceptions, of course, are judicial merit retention elections, as well as certain municipal elections, which are nonpartisan in character.
3. Harold D. Lasswell, *Politics: Who Gets What, When and How* (New York: McGraw-Hill, 1938).
4. Atkins, *Parties,* 54–55.
5. Tenn. Code Ann. §2-1-114.
6. *Tennessee Municipal League v. Thompson,* 958 S.W. 2d 338 (1997).
7. Tom Humphrey, "Income Tax Issue Bound to Return; Legislators Expect Hostile Public," *Knoxville News Sentinel,* Nov. 21, 1999, p. A-1.
8. Rules of the Tennessee Registry of Election Finance (chap. 0530-1-1).
9. Tenn. Code Ann. §3-6-102.
10. The limit in 1999 was $50.
11. Tom Humphrey, "When Is a Lobbyist Not Really a Lobbyist?" *Knoxville News Sentinel,* Oct. 14, 1999.

Chapter 8

1. See, e.g., William Lyons and John M. Scheb II, "Ideology and Candidate Evaluation in the 1984 and 1988 Presidential Elections," *Journal of Politics* 54 (May 1992): 573–84.
2. The first Tennessee Poll was taken in April 1989; we are using surveys conducted through October 1998. In every instance, respondents were interviewed by telephone and selected by random-digit dialing. Sample sizes varied slightly, but except for the 1994 survey (n=694) and the Fall 1996 survey (n=665), sample sizes exceeded 800 respondents. In all editions of the Tennessee Poll, the demographics were such that we can be confident that samples are representative of the adult population of the state. The margin of error for each edition of the Tennessee Poll is no more than four percentage points at the 95% confidence level.
3. In most years, the Social Science Research Institute (SSRI) conducted more than one Tennessee Poll. To simplify the presentation as well as to smooth out variations stemming from sampling error, averages have been computed for each year.
4. V. O. Key Jr., *Southern Politics in State and Nation* (New York: Vintage Books, 1949), 78.
5. Robert H. Swansborough, "The Tennessee Voter," in *The Volunteer State: Readings in Tennessee Politics,* ed. Dorothy F. Olshfski and T. McN. Simpson III (n.p.: Tennessee Political Science Association, 1985), 43. Based on a

1981 statewide survey, Swansborough estimated the distribution of party identification as approximately 42% Democrat, 33% Independent, and 25% Republican. Using the 1980 National Election Study, Swansborough estimated the level of Republican identification throughout the South at approximately 17%.

6. For the sake of simplicity, we have collapsed the Tennessee Poll's seven-point party identification measure for question wording) into a trichotomy, in which the categories are "Democrat," "Independent," and "Republican."
7. The same question was included in the Spring and Fall 1996 editions of the Tennessee Poll, with similar results.
8. Greene, Grubbs, and Hobday, *Government in Tennessee,* 3rd ed., 66.
9. Ibid.

Chapter 9

1. In Tennessee, localities have the option of opting out of the primary process for judicial elections. This became a matter of some concern in Shelby County in 1998.
2. Some counties elect additional officials in accord with their county charters.
3. See William Lyons, "Reform and Response in American Cities," *Social Science Quarterly* 59 (June 1978): 118–32.
4. *Reynolds v. Sims,* 377 U.S. 533 (1964).
5. Section 2 of the Voting Rights Act, as amended in 1982, prohibits any "standard, practice, or procedure . . . which results in a denial or abridgement of the right of any citizen of the United States to vote on account of race." This provision has been used extensively to challenge apportionment schemes. See, e.g., *Thornburg v. Gingles,* 478 U.S. 30 (1986).
6. *Rural W. Tenn. African-American Affairs Council v. McWherter,* 836 F. Supp. 453 (W.D. Tenn. 1993), vacated, 512 U.S. 1248 (1994).
7. *Johnson v. DeGrandy,* 512 U.S. 997 (1994).
8. *Rural West Tennessee African-American Affairs Council, Inc. v. McWherter,* 877 F. Supp. 1096 (W.D. Tenn. 1995).
9. U.S. Constitution, Art. I, Sec. 4.
10. The applicable provisions of the U.S. Constitution are the Equal Protection Clause of the 14th Amendment and the 15th Amendment, which prohibits racial discrimination in voting. The applicable federal statute is the Voting Rights Act of 1965, as amended.
11. Tenn. Code Ann. §2-11-201.
12. See William Lyons and John M. Scheb II, "Early Voting and the Timing of the Vote: Unanticipated Consequences of Electoral Reform," *State and Local Government Review* 31, no. 2 (Spring 1999): 147–52.

13. See Steven Rechichar, Michael Fitzgerald, William Lyons, and Floydette Cory, *Electoral Triumph and Administrative Trials: Gubernatorial Elections in Tennessee, 1970–1982* (Knoxville: Bureau of Public Administration, Univ. of Tennessee, 1986).
14. See John Bibby, *Politics, Parties, and Elections in America* (Chicago: Nelson-Hall, 1987).
15. See Larry Sabato, *Feeding Frenzy: How Attack Journalism Has Transformed American Politics* (New York: Free Press, 1991).

Chapter 10

1. A good general treatment of the role of media in American politics is Doris A. Graber, *Mass Media and American Politics*, 5th ed. (Washington, D.C.: Congressional Quarterly Press, 1996).
2. During 1977 and 1978, media coverage of Gov. Ray Blanton, particularly his alleged sale of pardons to state prisoners, was the most widely covered and controversial political story in Tennessee during the last half of the century. For the first time, television news, especially in Nashville, rivaled newspapers in coverage of a political scandal. The story broke when Lee Smith, a former assistant to Gov. Winfield Dunn and editor of the *Tennessee Journal*, recognized a recently convicted double-murderer working as a state photographer in the Legislative Plaza. The ensuing firestorm of editorial criticism produced what was probably the low point in relations between the media and a Tennessee governor.
3. Quote attributed to the MacNeil/Lehrer News Hour by the *Tennessee Journal* web site, located at www.mleesmith.com/tenn/tnj.html.
4. Tennessee Press Association pamphlet.
5. A similar pattern applies to the *Tennessee Journal*, a weekly update of Tennessee politics published statewide by Lee Smith, a former policy advisor to Gov. Winfield Dunn.
6. Newspaper clips, 1986 nursing homes.
7. Carol Marin of Nashville's NBC affiliate produced what may have been Tennessee's most notable television interview with a government official. Returning from a trip in 1977, Governor Blanton got off the plane drunk and became increasingly belligerent with Marin during the interview. When Marin asked Blanton if political connections were related to providing work-release status to a recently convicted double-murderer, the Governor defiantly stated that he would soon grant a full pardon to the inmate. Blanton later refused to back down from his promise in the face of criticism from virtually every media outlet in Tennessee. An FBI inves-

tigation ensued, resulting in agents padlocking Blanton's capitol offices and seizing his files just prior to the end of his term in January 1979. In an extraordinary event, Governor-elect Lamar Alexander was sworn into office three days early to avoid anticipated pardons for dozens of inmates before Blanton's term officially expired. Marin's pursuit of the scandal led to a successful career at the NBC affiliate in Chicago.

8. For example, the *Knoxville News Sentinel* is on-line at www.knoxnews.com; the *Tennessean* is found at www.tennessean.com, and the *Memphis Commercial Appeal* is at www.gomemphis.com.
9. The site is located at www.tennpolitics.com.
10. It should be noted that the State of Tennessee also has a presence on the Web at www.state.tn.us. The site contains a lot of useful information about the state legislature, courts and government agencies. It also provides a vehicle for "public education" on such matters as tax reform.
11. Alexander's primary media advisor was Doug Bailey, partner in the Washington public relations firm of Bailey & Deardorf. Bailey was responsible for Alexander's trademark red and black shirt, his 1978 walk across Tennessee, and many of the slogans that accompanied Alexander's initiatives. Bailey was the first, but not the last, public relations professional to be on retainer to a Tennessee Governor.

Chapter 11

1. *Tennessee Blue Book, 1999–2000* (Nashville: Tennessee Secretary of State, 1999), 158.
2. Policy debates most frequently center on curriculum, student testing, and teacher evaluation. The McWherter administration, early in its first term, sought to amend the teacher Career Ladder evaluation process implemented by Alexander. The Sundquist administration in turn tried to alter the "value-added" evaluations of teachers and students put in place by McWherter. The State Board of Education, comprised of appointees from the previous Governor, frequently is caught in the middle of such disputes.
3. *Public Acts and Resolutions of the State of Tennessee* (1925), chap. 115.
4. *Public Acts and Resolutions of the State of Tennessee* (1992), chap. 535.
5. The text alternately uses 138 and 139 as the number of school systems in Tennessee. The number was reduced from 139 to 138 when the Chattanooga and Hamilton County school systems merged in the mid-1990s.
6. *Public Acts and Resolutions of the State of Tennessee* (1st Extraordinary Session, 1984), chap. 6, secs. 3 and 29.
7. *Public Acts and Resolutions of the State of Tennessee* (1992), chap. 535, sec. 33.

8. Only a handful of Tennessee counties have more than two school systems. Two notable exceptions are Carroll and Gibson counties, both in rural West Tennessee. The two small counties together have nine school systems, one of which consists of a single school with grades 1–12.
9. *Nashville Tennessean,* Jan. 24, 1999, p. 1.
10. Tennessee Department of Education, *Annual Statistical Report,* 1990.
11. *Public Acts and Resolutions of the State of Tennessee* (1st Extraordinary Session, 1984), chap. 7, sec. 6.
12. The Alexander administration approached the final House vote on the one-cent sales tax increase with 52 votes, needing 50 for passage. On the day of the vote, one legislator was absent due to illness. To the Governor's consternation, a second legislator absent was Republican Dale Kelley of Huntingdon, a basketball referee who, on the day of the biggest vote in years, was committed to work an NCAA game out of state. As the House convened on Wednesday afternoon, Alexander's legislative lieutenants debated whether to delay the vote and risk losing their thin majority. Despite last-minute attempts by the opposition to convert nervous legislators, the tax bill passed with the bare minimum of 50 votes.
13. *Tennessee Small Schools Systems v. McWherter,* filed in Davidson County Chancery Court, July 7, 1988.
14. Tennessee Constitution, Art. XI, Sec. 12.
15. *Tennessee Small Schools Systems v. McWherter,* 851 S.W. 2d 139 (Tenn. 1993).
16. Tennessee's experience with federal oversight of the state prison system after 1985 was a more important factor than many realized in the strategy of education reform in 1991–92. The federal court's order to release inmates and spend millions on prison facilities was the backdrop for fears that the courts would take control of Tennessee's schools in a similar fashion. Governor McWherter did not go out of his way to clarify that the *Small Schools* litigation was in the state Supreme Court and not federal court. Whether the justices, all of whom were friends of McWherter, understood the political climate and consciously assisted the realization of McWherter's goal may never be clear. What is clear is that, without the threat that the court might take over the schools, McWherter might never have succeeded in putting together a coalition of legislators broad enough to raise taxes and simultaneously restructure the state's school finance formula.
17. *Public Acts and Resolutions of the State of Tennessee* (1992), chap. 535.
18. The new school finance formula gave a highly disproportionate part of new revenues from the tax increase to rural school systems. Thus it is not surprising that the measure did not receive support in the House from Memphis and Nashville legislators. To those responsible for gathering the

votes, the most significant development was the lack of vocal opposition from urban legislators. Urban opposition had stymied similar finance reform proposals in Texas and New Jersey in the years preceding Tennessee's efforts. In other words, although Tennessee's urban legislators could not bring themselves to vote for a plan that gave most of the new revenues to rural districts, the fear of a court takeover of the schools motivated many to keep quiet about their opposition.

19. *21st Century Schools Report Card* (Nashville: Tennessee Department of Education, 1999).

Chapter 12

1. See Ann Bowman and Richard Kearney, *State and Local Government* (3rd ed. Boston: Houghton-Mifflin, 1996).
2. See 42 USCA §§301 et seq.
3. See Tenn. Code Ann. §§71-3-151 et seq.
4. Remarks of Gov. Don Sundquist, Nov. 7, 1995.
5. William Lyons and John M. Scheb II, "Managed Care and Medicaid Reform in Tennessee: The Impact of TennCare on Access and Health-Seeking Behavior," *Journal of Health Care for the Poor and Underserved* 10 (Aug. 1999).
6. "TennCare Enrollment Shows Disturbing Trends," *Nashville Tennessean,* Feb. 11, 1999.
7. D. M. Mirvis, C. F. Chang, C. J. Hall, G. T. Zaar, and W. B. Applegate, "TennCare: Health Care Reform for Tennessee," *Tennessee's Business* 6 (1995): 11–22.
8. "Sundquist's TennCare Proposals Get Support," *Nashville Tennessean,* Feb. 11, 1999.
9. Some of the more important statutes are the Clean Air Act of 1970, 42 USCA §§7401–7642; the Federal Water Pollution Control Act of 1972 (Clean Water Act), 33 USCA §§1251–1387; the Resource Conservation and Recovery Act of 1976 (RCRA), 42 USCA §§6901–6992; the Toxic Substances Control Act of 1976 (TSCA), 15 USCA §§2601–2671; and the Comprehensive Environmental Response, Compensation and Liability Act of 1980 (CERCLA), 42 USCA §§9601–9675.
10. See Bowman and Kearney, *State and Local Government,* 3rd ed., chap. 18.
11. See Richard A. Bartlett, *Troubled Waters: Champion International and the Pigeon River Controversy* (Knoxville: Univ. of Tennessee Press, 1995).
12. See 33 USC §§1251 et seq.
13. See *Champion v. EPA,* 648 F. Supp. 1390 (WDNC 1987); *Champion v. EPA,* 850 F. 2d 182 (4th Cir. 1988).

Chapter 13

1. Tennessee Poll, May 1997, conducted by the Social Science Research Institute, Univ. of Tennessee, Knoxville. This random telephone survey of 600 adults had a margin of error of +/-4 percentage points at the 95% confidence level.
2. U.S. Department of Justice, Bureau of Justice Statistics, *Sourcebook of Criminal Justice Statistics* (Washington, D.C.: USGPO).
3. Demands to change the name of Fort Pillow Prison to Cold Creek Prison reflected a growing sensitivity of white legislators to the concerns of black voters in their districts. While blacks remained a minority of registered voters in most legislative districts, they represented a majority of Democratic votes for many white Democratic legislators in the West Tennessee Caucus.
4. Unlike the crime packages of Alexander, McWherter, and Sundquist, the sentencing changes in the early 1970s often came one at a time as initiatives from various legislators. This ad hoc approach to criminal sentencing laws resulted in a hodgepodge of sentences that provided wide differences in prison time served for similar crimes.
5. *Public Acts and Resolutions of the State of Tennessee* (1979), chap. 318.
6. Class X sentencing was done away with when the legislature enacted the Criminal Sentencing Reform Act of 1989; see Tenn. Code Ann. §§40-35-101 et seq.
7. *Grubbs et al. v. Blanton,* U.S. District Court for the Middle District of Tennessee, 1978.
8. Contrary to the opinion of most political leaders, the court had been reasonably patient with the state's reluctance to improve prison conditions. The original suit was filed in 1978. Hearings were conducted in 1981. The court found the prison system unconstitutional in 1982, appointed a Special Master in 1983, and ordered further improvements made in 1984. None of these events served to jolt either the Governor or the legislature into action. Perhaps the inattention was due to the bitter fight over education reforms taking place during 1983–84.
9. *Public Acts and Resolutions of the State of Tennessee* (1st Extraordinary Session, 1985), chs. 3–7.
10. McWherter sensed correctly that many Tennesseans were frustrated with the violence and rising costs of the state prison system. While McWherter understood that solutions to the corrections problems would be complicated, he also knew that it would be impossible to explain detailed solutions to the public during a political campaign. Voters concerned with prison issues appeared to respond more to the force of McWherter's personality than to any specific plan or idea.

11. *Public Acts and Resolutions of the State of Tennessee* (1990), chap. 980.
12. *Grubbs et al. v. McWherter,* U.S. District Court for the Middle District of Tennessee, 1993. (The defendant named in the litigation changed with each new Commissioner of Correction.)
13. *Public Acts and Resolutions of the State of Tennessee* (1996), chap. 928.
14. *Felony Projection Populations,* Tennessee Department of Correction, July 1997.

Chapter 14

1. Tennessee Constitution, Art. II, Sec. 24.
2. The University of Tennessee is the state's land grant institution.
3. Morton Grodzins, *The American System* (Chicago: Rand-McNally, 1966), 49–50.
4. Herbert Jacob and Kenneth Vines, *Politics in the American States* (Boston: Little, Brown, 1971), 440–41.
5. James Q. Wilson, *American Government,* 5th ed. (Lexington, Mass.: D. C. Heath, 1992), 55.
6. U.S. Census Bureau, *Federal Aid to the States for Fiscal Year 1998.*
7. Kelly Edmiston and Matthew Murray, "Finances of Tennessee State Government," in *Tennessee Government and Politics: Democracy in the Volunteer State,* ed. John R. Vile and Mark Byrnes (Nashville, Tenn.: Vanderbilt Univ. Press, 1998), 187.
8. Tenn. Code Ann. §67-4-2008.

Chapter 15

1. Tenn. Code Ann. §§2-12-101 et seq.
2. *Baker v. Carr,* 369 U.S. 186 (1962).
3. Tenn. Code Ann. §8-8-201.
4. The qualifications of the sheriff are set forth in Tenn. Code Ann. §8-8-102.
5. David Kanervo, "Local Government and Politics," in *Tennessee Government and Politics: Democracy in the Volunteer State,* ed. John Vile and Mark Byrnes (Nashville, Tenn.: Vanderbilt Univ. Press, 1998), 76–91.
6. This principle is known as Dillon's Rule.
7. Tenn. Code Ann. §6-18-103(b).
8. "An act to amend Tennessee Code Annotated Title 6, Ch. 1, Part 2; Title 6, Ch. 18, Part 1 and Title 6, Ch. 30, Part 1, relative to the distribution of situs-based tax collections after new municipal incorporations and the timing of elections to incorporate new municipalities."
9. Tenn. Code Ann. §6-58-111.

10. See Vincent Ostrum, Charles M. Tiebout, and Robert Warren, "The Organization of Government in Metropolitan Areas: A Theoretical Inquiry," *American Political Science Review* 55 (1961): 831–42.
11. See William Lyons and John M. Scheb II, "Saying 'No' One More Time: The Rejection of Consolidated Government in Knox County, Tennessee." *State and Local Government Review* 30 (1998): 92–105.
12. The council had 21 members until the 1960 annexation under Mayor Ben West.
13. In 1996, a problem in separating city and county "early voting" ballots made it impossible to know whether the initiative passed inside the city.
14. See Lyons and Scheb, "Saying 'No' One More Time."

Bibliography

Atkins, Jonathan M. *Parties, Politics, and Sectional Conflict in Tennessee: 1832–1861.* Knoxville: Univ. of Tennessee Press, 1997.

Combs, William H., and William E. Cole. *Tennessee: A Political Study.* Knoxville: Univ. of Tennessee Press, 1940.

Cortner, Richard C. *The Apportionment Cases.* Knoxville: Univ. of Tennessee Press, 1970.

Dykeman, Wilma. *Tennessee: A Bicentennial History.* New York: Norton, 1975.

Fitzgerald, Michael R., and William Lyons. "The Promise and Performance of Privatization: The Knoxville Experience." *Policy Studies Review* 5, no. 3 (Feb. 1986): 606–13.

Folmsbee, Stanley J.; Robert E. Corlew; and Enoch L. Mitchell. *Tennessee: A Short History.* Knoxville: Univ. of Tennessee Press, 1969.

Folz, David H.; Linda Gaddis; William Lyons; and John M. Scheb II. "Saturn Comes to Tennessee: Citizen Perceptions of Public Impacts." *Social Science Quarterly* (Mar. 1994): 793–803.

Folz, David H., and John M. Scheb II. "Prisons, Politics and Profits: The Tennessee Privatization Experiment." *Judicature* 73, no. 2 (Aug.–Sept. 1989): 98–102.

Greene, Lee Seifert; David Grubbs; and Victor Hobday. *Government in Tennessee.* 3rd ed., 1975; 4th ed. Knoxville: Univ. of Tennessee Press, 1982.

Hopkins, Anne, and William Lyons. "Toward a Classification of State Electoral Change: A Note on Tennessee." *Journal of Politics* (Feb. 1980): 209–226.

Hopkins, Anne; William Lyons; and Steve Metcalf. "The Presidential Election in Tennessee." In *The 1984 Presidential Election in the South,* ed. Robert P. Steed, Lawrence W. Morland, and Tod A. Baker. New York: Praeger, 1986. 208–28.

Key, V. O., Jr. *Southern Politics in State and Nation.* New York: Knopf, 1949.

Lambert, Walter N. *Governments in Knox County.* Knoxville: Bureau of Public Administration, Univ. of Tennessee, 1965.

Laska, Lewis L. *The Tennessee State Constitution: A Reference Guide.* New York: Greenwood Press, 1990.

Lyons, William, and John M. Scheb II. "Early Voting and the Timing of the Vote: Unanticipated Consequences of Electoral Reform." *State and Local Government Review* 31, no. 2 (Spring 1999): 147–52.

———. "Managed Care and Medicaid Reform: The Impact of TennCare on Access and Health-Seeking Behavior." *Journal of Health Care for the Poor and Underserved* 10 (Aug. 1999): 328–37.

———. "Saying 'No' One More Time: The Rejection of Consolidated Government in Knox County, Tennessee." *State and Local Government Review* 30 (1998): 92–105.

Olshfski, Dorothy F., and T. McN. Simpson III, eds. *The Volunteer State: Readings in Tennessee Politics.* N.p.: Tennessee Political Science Association, 1985.

Scheb, John M., II. "Six Tennesseans Who Served on the United States Supreme Court." In *Tennessee's Role in U.S. Constitutional Development.* N.p.: Tennessee Political Science Association, 1987.

Scheb, John M., II, and Stephen J. Rechichar. *The Politics of Judicial Modernization: The Case of the Tennessee Court System.* Knoxville: Bureau of Public Administration, Univ. of Tennessee, May 1986.

Scheb, John M., II, and Thomas D. Ungs. "Competing Orientations to the Judicial Role: The Case of Tennessee Judges." *Tennessee Law Review* 54, no. 3 (Fall 1986): 391–411.

Vile, John, and Mark Byrnes, eds. *Tennessee Government and Politics: Democracy in the Volunteer State.* Nashville: Vanderbilt Univ. Press, 1998.

Index

Government and Politics in Tennessee was designed and typeset on a Macintosh computer system using Quark software. The text is set in Meridien and the chapter openings are set in Washington. This book was designed by Bill Adams, typeset by Kimberly Scarbrough, and manufactured by Thomson-Shore, Inc. The paper used in this book is designed for an effective life of at least three hundred years.